Endorsement

This interesting and thorough book explaining "God's Purpose for the Ages" viewed through the prophetic passages of the Bible, can be an invaluable key to understanding those passages which refer to things we cannot relate to from our earthly perspective and to realize the larger context of God's ultimate plan. The book does not require an understanding of Bible prophecy or the end times in order to read and comprehend its meaning. Mike Brown is a layman and so writes to lay people, both inside and outside the church. The book is written in language anyone can understand and uses examples anyone can relate to. While the book is somewhat lengthy, it can be read in small segments which are presented in a logical sequence so that the reader can move at his or her own pace.

As you read this book, be ready for many familiar yet not completely clear passages to be given a new or more enhanced meaning to you. I found myself saying things like "Oh, now I see" or "I always wondered what that meant." I remember the feeling I had when wearing glasses for the first time. I could see the blades of grass and the leaves on the trees. I was in awe. I got the same feeling from reading Mike's book. Let's admit it; we can all use a little help understanding Scripture, just like some of us need a little help with our eyesight. Mike is kind enough to help us learn to view the Bible through the lens of prophecy to increase our understanding, fulfillment and joy when reading it. As any good teacher, he helps us to learn to discern for ourselves. Books like Ezekiel, Daniel and Revelation suddenly begin to "fit in" with the other books and "God's Purpose for the Ages" is brought within our reach.

Steve Perryman

CELEBRATING GOD'S PURPOSE FOR THE AGES

DRAWING NEARER TO THE GOD OF ORIGIN AND ETERNAL DESTINY THROUGH BIBLE PROPHECY

Mike Brown

Written by Mike Brown

Published by OneHope Publishing
Printed by Kindle Direct Publisning, an Amazon.com Company
Available from Amazon.com, and other retail outlets

Inexpressible thanks are given to Cheryl Brown, Leanne Phelps, Steve Perryman and Larry Toering who assisted significantly with proofreading and editing, and to Nathan Phelps for his great technical assistance.

Copyright © 1st Edition 2005 - Mike Brown

Copyright © 2nd Edition 2016 - Mike Brown

All rights reserved under International Copyright Law. Permission is granted to copy exerts from this book for non-profit usage, so long as such copy does not violate scripture copyrights.

ISBN: 978-0-9976300-0-8

On the Cover:
As the scripture on the back cover speaks figuratively of a prophetic day dawning, the front cover shows the dawning of a new day in Israel as the sun rises over the Sea of Galilee, symbolizing that anticipated new day in the redemptive agenda. The view was photographed by the author in 2008 from the seaside city of Tiberias, viewed with wife Cheryl and dear friends and traveling companions Don and Velma Siemens.

A number of scripture translations have been quoted herein. References indicate translation version using the following abbreviations:

ESV	English Standard Version
KJV	King James Version
NASB	New American Standard Bible (1995 update)
NCV	New Century Version
NIV2011	New International Version (2011 update)
NKJV	New King James Version
RSV	Revised Standard Version

Note that different translations employ different conventions for text formatting. For example, capitalization varies, and for different reasons. In compliance with copyright permissions requirements, I have not altered these varying conventions within this book, which creates an inconsistent style between the various texts.

Scripture Copyright Permissions:
Scripture quotations marked (ESV) are taken from the ESV® Bible (The Holy Bible, English Standard Version®), copyright © 2001 by Crossway, a publishing ministry of Good News Publishers. Used by permission. All rights reserved."

Scripture quotations marked (NASB) are taken from the New American Standard Bible®, Copyright © 1960, 1962, 1963, 1968, 1971, 1972, 1973, 1975, 1977, 1995 by The Lockman Foundation. Used by permission.

Scripture quotations marked (NCV) are taken from the New Century Version®. Copyright © 2005 by Thomas Nelson. Used by permission. All rights reserved.

Scripture quotations marked (NIV2011) are taken from the Holy Bible, New International Version®, NIV®. Copyright © 1973, 1978, 1984, 2011 by Biblica, Inc.™ Used by permission of Zondervan. All rights reserved worldwide.

Scripture quotations marked (NKJV) are taken from the New King James Version®. Copyright © 1982 by Thomas Nelson. Used by permission. All rights reserved.

Scripture quotations marked (RSV) are taken from the Revised Standard Version of the Bible, copyright © 1946, 1952, and 1971 the Division of Christian Education of the National Council of the Churches of Christ in the United States of America. Used by permission. All rights reserved.

Scripture Quotations marked (KJV) are taken from the King James Version of the Bible. Used by permission.

Old Testament dates and time intervals taken from Thompson Chain Reference Bible, New International Version, Copyright © 1983 by The B. B. Kirkbride Bible Company, Inc. and The Zondervan Corporation

Other Books by this Author:

- The Mysterious Magi of Christmas
  Renewing the Christmas Mystique by Distinguishing the Biblical from the Traditional (2016 paperback 40 pages, available on Amazon. ISBN- 978-0-9976300-1-5)

- The Vision of the Patriarchs
  Messages to Us from Revealed Insights of the Hebrew Pioneers (2016 paperback 85 pages, available on Amazon. ISBN-978-0-9976300-2-2)

- Something to Boast About
  Uncovering and Meeting Every Person's Greatest Need of the Heart (2018 paperback 55 pages, available on Amazon. ISBN-978-0-9976300-3-9)

- When God Answers
  Like Memorial Stones, Answered Prayers Testify that God is listening (2019 paperback 90 pages, available on Amazon. ISBN-978-0-9976300-0-8)

TABLE OF CONTENTS

	Page
Preface	2
Scripture Convention	7

PART 1: EMBRACING BIBLE PROPHECY
1. A Passion for His Return — 9
2. Preparing for His Coming — 28
3. Understanding Prophecy — 42
4. The Interpretation of Prophecy — 58

PART 2: PROPHETIC UNVEILING OF HIS GLORY
5. A First Portrait of Christ Exalted — 73
6. A Second Portrait of Christ Exalted — 94

PART 3: REDEMPTION PROPHISIED
7. Atonement Prophesied — 109
8. Resurrection — 133
9. A Hidden Mystery Revealed — 153

PART 4: THE DAY OF THE LORD
10. There Is an Enemy — 176
11. Satan's Earthly Kingdom — 189
12. The Antichrist — 201
13. The Tribulation — 215
14. Rise of an Evil World Empire — 234
15. God's Wrath Against the Empire — 247
16. The First Resurrection and Rapture — 258
17. Mystery Babylon the Great — 289
18. The Return of Christ — 299
19. Armageddon: Christ Victorious — 325
20. The Imminence of His Coming — 338
21. What About Israel? — 344
22. The Conversion of Israel — 360
23. Israel in the Tribulation — 372

PART 5: FULFILLMENT
24. The Millennium — 388
25. Judgment — 394
26. Glory — 411
27. Prophecy, the Final Evangel — 437

Bibliography — 453

PREFACE

If I were asked to identify the greatest need in western Christianity at this time, I would say without hesitation that I believe it is to restore a sufficiently high and glorious view of God, and of Jesus, the Christ. We have neglected his written message to us. Over the last century our Christian passions have shifted from being God-focused to being mission-focused. Self-centeredness has crept in. We have crafted our worship to be excellent, relevant, and appealing. In other words--to suit us. Our relationship with him is casual. We have not denied God outright. We have simply pushed Him to the sidelines; we have failed to ascribe to Him the glory of which He is worthy. We invite Him to be Lord over our comfort zone, but dare not approach him too closely. Consequently the world does not see us as being passionately in love with God.

Vocationally I am a biblical layman. I worked my whole career as a professional engineer in the oil and gas production industry, functioning as product engineer, project engineer, and in research and development. Given that, I suppose I bring a somewhat analytical approach to studying scripture. I have taught Sunday school for forty years, mostly to adults. During that time I have developed a romance with the Bible. More importantly, through His word and prayer, I am getting to know God Himself insofar as He has revealed Himself to us. In becoming more and more aware of Him, I regularly ask, "Lord, make my overwhelming passion be to know and understand and love You."

Several years ago, at the urging of my Sunday School class, we embarked on a study through the book of Revelation that spanned about a year and a half. I had studied and taught from Bible prophecy before, but not to the degree of this study. This study began a leap of understanding for me. It overwhelmed me with the greatness of God. It astonished me at the consistency of his purpose. As the teacher, I was in all ways a fellow student of the topic. I remain a Bible and prophecy 'student.'

That Sunday School series was finished, yet I could not lay my interest in it aside. As I moved on to other topics of teaching and personal study, I continued to revert back to it, and to revel in the way prophecy presents God from a different perspective. Viewing God through the lens of prophecy elevates our perception of Him. This view is a very encouraging, purpose-filled panorama. It is not just about events and times. Rather, it's about knowing the God who has revealed Himself in a different way than many believers ever embrace. It is about beholding the God of creation and eternal destiny, of simultaneous love and consuming righteousness, of gentle mercy against the backdrop of frightening glory. Prophecy makes God and His purposes expand in our psyche. To know God! To know Jesus! Is the God of creation really knowable, this One who is profound beyond our wildest imaginations? Jesus said the greatest commandment is to love God with all of our heart, mind, soul and strength. This is the purpose and the passion from which I have written. If you love God in this way, or desire to love Him in this way--this is the reason I now invite you to read this book, and share in that passion.

In that light, this book is not limited to so-called "end-time" prophecy, but looks at prophecy from beginning to end. We are trying to grasp the big picture of God's purposes. Biblical prophecy runs throughout scripture. Much of it has been fulfilled and revealed already. Much is yet to be fulfilled. We will look at both.

Does the Bible seem to you like a collection of somewhat disconnected stories, different styles of literature, and different authors? Have you wondered if there is a unifying message that connects Genesis and Nehemiah and Matthew and Colossians? The answer is 'yes!' There is a unifying theme. There is a singular purpose running through scripture. That singular Bible message is the story—God's story—of **redemption**. It is possible to understand redemption from only a personal perspective. In that focus, the main thrust is answering the question, 'How do I get to heaven?' But how many of us have asked, 'Why did God redeem us? What is His ultimate purpose for us?' A study of biblical prophecy is a great approach to uncovering God's self-revelation and purpose for a lost and wandering mankind. Through prophecy, we will seek to not only put events in order, but to discover something of the ultimate purpose for them all.

This book is written from a layman's perspective. It is not written to the intelligentsia of Christian doctrine, but to the man or woman who has, perhaps, never before become immersed in biblical prophecy. It is written to those who have had doubts or even apprehension about studying biblical prophecy. My envisioned audience is a reader who is, however, familiar with basic biblical teachings, certainly the teachings surrounding Jesus' death and resurrection. It is not within the scope of this book to develop these foundational doctrines.

Also, I have assumed at least a cursory familiarity of biblical structure by the reader. Understanding basic Old and New Testament construction will be most beneficial. About 50% of this book is scriptural text. A familiarity with the book names of both testaments will be helpful so that the reader can understand when the scripture-writer's perspective is looking forward or backward toward the cross of Christ. We will parallel prophetic passages with 'non-prophetic' passages, showing the unified consistency of prophecy and doctrine.

My objective in writing this book has been to focus on the God behind the prophesied historical plans. While I have tried to put together the technical aspects of biblical prophecy in an orderly way, my desire has been to present the major topics from a theological perspective. It is not the events that should capture our intrigue, but the One whose purpose and strategy is seen in them. It should not be the timeline that entices us to turn another page, but the author of eternity Himself. I am awed by the theology found in prophecy. God's self-revelation does not come to us as a philosophy. It is not an imaginative reality. No! God has worked within His created world in real, historical context. He has entered our realm of reference and made His purposes known to us, not only in the historical setting, but for eternity. The key to that knowledge of His purposes is found only in the Bible.

I am not suggesting that the purposes and redemptive principles contained in prophetic literature are different from those found in other parts of scripture. They are not; they are consistent with them. But prophecy soars far beyond what we know of God from other portions of the Bible. If we were to ignore prophecy in its broad sense, we would lose much in our understanding of God and His purposes. Prophecy is so prevalent and so intertwined within all of scripture, that it is doubtful we could extract it at all, even if we were so inclined.

The teacher in me is never fully satisfied only with learning, but longs to share what was learned. In that light, this writing is an overflow from my own zealous pursuit of the knowledge of God. For me, writing this was a worship experience, and I desire to share it. My desire is that the reader might become infected with the same enthusiastic hunger that has captured me, a hunger for knowing with intimacy the God of prophecy. That is why I have written this book.

Jesus himself had much to say about our attitude toward the subject of his coming again, and end-time prophecy. Some may approach it with curiosity. Some with apprehension; or doubts. Prophecy is part of God's word. It deserves our diligent devotion, just like other portions of scripture. It should not be avoided because of apparent difficulties. Even if we are incorrect about some interpretations, still the majesty and continuity of God's grand purposes can overshadow our errors. So it is my hope that this study will cause you to desire the *mind of Christ* concerning biblical prophecy, as you do with other scriptures.

One of the more difficult obstacles to understanding prophecy is its large volume of material, and the fact of its being so widely scattered throughout the Bible. It is not arranged chronologically. It is not all contained in the biblical literature formally designated 'prophecy.' This problem is the basis for the structure of this book. In an effort to gather these scattered scriptures into a more easily comprehensible framework, I have taken a topical approach in writing it.

This is not an in-depth commentary of the many passages quoted. It is primarily a gathering of them from all of scripture and arranging them into a topical framework for logical, progressive understanding. In this gathering and arranging, we will discover the consistency, the unity, the cohesive message of the various passages. Furthermore, this book is not exhaustive. It does not pretend to include every prophetic passage in the Bible, but it covers enough and discusses enough to form a platform of understanding. The length of this book reflects the breadth of biblical prophetic coverage rather than the depth of my treatment of it.

The inaugural source for the content of this work is the Bible. I have written from the perspective that Holy Scripture is God's infallible word, totally trustworthy, divinely true. If you are not of this belief, I invite you to read anyway with an open mind, for prophecy is a powerful defense of biblical validity. It may be that studying from prophecy will change your mind, and I would be especially gratified if this writing helped do so. Any such influence will lie in the scripture passages themselves.

One intention I had throughout the writing of this book was to maintain a demeanor, a spirit in the text, consistent with the disposition found in the scripture being studied. Where loving grace is presented, I tried to write with that same graciousness. Where the scripture is ominous or stern, I tried not to soften that manner in my commentary.

You will find many pauses for recorded prayer scattered throughout this writing. They may sometimes seem to come at odd places. Most of them reflect an actual halt in my writing, for prayer. The enormity of many of these passages frequently caused me to lay aside the books, drop the computer mouse, and simply worship. Some of those prayers are recorded here. I have chosen not to move or edit them much. I pray your reading will experience this same devotional fervor. One can read prophetic scripture as a spectator, looking on from a distance, but this level of study won't accomplish the purpose which I hope to promote in this book. But if you truly desire to know more fully the author of prophecy, then read on. If you are willing to hear His words, pregnant with glory, judgment, salvation, fear and joy, then they will bring you to a new appreciation of who God is, and what He is doing. When these prayers come, I invite you to share them, and to bring your own prayers into His presence.

Finally, I could not imagine embarking on this writing project without requesting in prayer that my writing and your reading were being motivated and guided by the Holy Spirit. Only He can bring the kind of heavenly wisdom that is needed to probe this topic.

> Oh Lord God, speak to me through your Spirit the great themes you would have me write about, and to this reader what you would have him understand. Lead us together into meditations that would draw us to you. Where our natural inclinations seek to know things that are not for us to know, things that distract rather than contribute, forgive us Father, and guide our motives back to solid footing. Make yourself known to us, we pray. Through your word, reveal Jesus in his glory. We seek to know as much of YOU as our mortal souls can endure. Amen.

Scripture Convention

In order to make this study as readable as possible, scripture text is included in the book text. Scriptural quotations are indented and italicized to clearly identify them, like this:

Matthew 13:16 (NKJV)
[16] "But blessed are your eyes for they see, and your ears for they hear; [17] for assuredly, I say to you that many prophets and righteous men desired to see what you see, and did not see it, and to hear what you hear, and did not hear it.

Scripture quoted as part of the commentary text is italicized without quotation marks, like this: 'That day is coming. It is called in scripture, *the day of the Lord*. But . . .'

Many scriptures are herein quoted out of context. To assist contextual understanding, I occasionally insert comments into scriptural quotations using brackets like this: *My prayer is not for them* [the apostles] *alone.*

I have studied several reference sources. References are listed in a Bibliography at the end of the text. From this list, you will see that I have studied varied views and a wide range of sources. By presenting this listing, I am neither necessarily recommending the references, nor implicitly endorsing the views in them.

Mike Brown

PART 1
EMBRACING BIBLE PROPHECY

1
A PASSION FOR HIS RETURN

I remember anticipating Cheryl's arrival in Rome that winter day in 1977. We had been separated for several weeks as business had taken me to the Middle East. I recall the endless days and nights, the longing to see her face, to share a meal and talk with her. A phone call home from there was next to impossible back then. Her embrace was so long past that it required imagination to rehearse it in my mind. My work being completed, we planned to meet in Rome and have a European second honeymoon, and so there I waited. It was her first international flight so I had arrived a day ahead to wait for her.

Then it began. Her plane was delayed, first for an hour, then another. This continued throughout the day. Finally I learned that her flight had left New York late, and after flying an hour, had returned to New York where it underwent engine repair, before resuming flight. The passengers had been kept on the plane throughout the whole ordeal. Cheryl finally did arrive, twelve hours late, and bearing a migraine headache. When she finally ran into my open arms, there was a surge of emotion that welled up between us, borne of eager anticipation, concern, and of physical and emotional exhaustion. It was a sweet reunion, in spite of the headache.

Now, this story could have gone differently. Suppose I arrived at the airport, indifferent about meeting up with her. When her plane was delayed over and over, I might have become annoyed at the inconvenience, and said, "Here I am in Rome. Why waste my time in this airport? I would rather go do some sightseeing than wait for her plane. She is a big girl. She can find her way to the hotel."

If I had not been there to meet her, how would she have felt? How different that reception would have been. There would have been no romance, no shared relief, and no reunion in any real sense. The emotion is gone from this second story. There certainly is no relational passion portrayed in it. This is not a story people would pick up and enjoy reading about. We like the first story because passion is that elusive quality that brings focus to our living and purpose to life. In case you are wondering, the first story is how it happened.

'Romantic' passion is frequently used in scripture as a reflection of the relationship Jesus desires with His people, and for our meeting Him one day, face-to-face. So close is that relationship in God's heart, that it is portrayed in scripture as a marriage, a royal, romantic wedding. In the book of Revelation we read...

> *Revelation 19:6-9 (ESV)*
> *⁶ Then I heard what seemed to be the voice of a great multitude, like the roar of many waters and like the sound of mighty peals of thunder, crying out, "Hallelujah! For the Lord our God the Almighty reigns. ⁷ Let us rejoice and exult and give him the glory, for the marriage of the Lamb has come, and his Bride has made herself ready; ⁸ it was granted her to clothe herself with fine linen, bright and pure"— for the fine linen is the righteous deeds of the saints. ⁹ And the angel said to me, "Write this: Blessed are those who are invited to the marriage supper of the Lamb." And he said to me, "These are the true words of God."*

Yes, that's right. We, the church, are called the *bride* of Christ. This bridegroom metaphor is used several times in Scripture to highlight the loving intimacy that will exist between Christ and his people. For example, Paul wrote...

> *Ephesians 5:31-32 (ESV)*
> *³¹ "Therefore a man shall leave his father and mother and hold fast to his wife, and the two shall become one flesh." ³² This mystery is profound, and I am saying that it refers to Christ and the church.*

The Bible is a book of passion. Why do we call the week before Jesus' crucifixion 'passion week'? The author of Hebrews answers that question:

> *Hebrews 12:2 (NKJV)*
> *² looking unto Jesus, the author and finisher of our faith, who for the joy that was set before Him endured the cross, despising the shame, and has sat down at the right hand of the throne of God.*

It was his passionate desire for relationships yet future that motivated him toward the cross. Now that is passion! That is Joy!

Jesus has promised to return. This return is a pivotal event in prophecy, and we will discuss it at length in chapters 18, 19, and 20. How do you feel about His return? Take a moment to be honest with yourself. Are you the longing, impassioned romantic, or the indifferent, self-absorbed spouse?

Please don't mistake this analogy as a blurring of the different kinds of love. 'Agapeo' is the Greek term (the language of the New Testament) for the selfless love which characterizes God Himself, and is taught as the standard for Christians. 'Eros' is the love of sexual infatuation, and is often the world's model of love. 'Phileo' is also a term for natural affection toward something, from which we get words like philosophy and philanthropy. Without question, in scripture agapeo love stands in stark contrast to the love of the world. Yet with that understood, scripture still presents the marriage analogy to characterize the depth of God's affection for His children. We will revisit this analogy later.

Studying what the Bible says about end-time topics is a sensitive subject for some people, even those who hold a strong faith in Jesus. It makes them nervous. For one thing, it is not an easy read. A casual glossing over it is more troubling than enlightening. Many teachers and even pastors avoid the topic because they are unprepared to invest in the extensive study necessary to probe it.

However, I think the main reason some people avoid studying end-time prophecy is more subtle and profound than these. We are prodded by natural tendencies (which are reinforced by our materialistic culture) to put ourselves at center stage. Even we Christians, while acknowledging in word and conscious thought that Christ is Lord in our lives, still view ourselves at center-stage of all of His plans. Most of us think of our relationship of grace with God as being primarily for our gain. Our view of heaven anticipates something like eternal self-gratification. How often do we ask ourselves, "What is God's purpose and desire in all of this." When we read about end-time prophecy, there is a lot said that may be disturbing. When confronted with the magnitude of God in prophecy, with realities of divine purpose and of ultimate accountability, such passages of scripture seem to rise up and challenge our self-indulging journey.

So, why would I want to study prophecy? I have heard it said, more than once, that we should stick to the 'here and now,' and leave the future to God. It is not any of our business anyway, they say. God will judge us on the basis of how we live now. Their favorite verse of prophecy is …

Matthew 24:36 (NASB77)
^{36} "But of that day and hour no one knows, not even the angels of heaven, nor the Son, but the Father alone.

This sounds like a reasonable attitude, and perhaps it describes a lot of people's perspective. However, it does not square with the teaching of Scripture. This verse is taken out of context. If you read the verses before and after, you get a different conclusion. A few verses later we are told several times to *Watch*.

There was a time when the return of Jesus, and entering heaven, were more prominent, regular fare in the church. When you read through end-time prophecy, you may discover phrases or word pictures you recognize from some of the great old hymns, but never knew they were from end-of-age prophecy. For example, "Holy, Holy. Holy! All the saints adore Thee, casting down their golden crowns around the glassy sea." Remember "In mansions of glory and endless delight," or "Let every Kindred, ev'ry tribe on this terrestrial ball, To Him all majesty ascribe, and crown Him Lord of all." Within evangelicalism, this perspective has gradually faded in our emphasis, although we still claim it in professed doctrine. What should our attitude toward end-time prophecy be? Let us look to Scripture for the answer.

Why Take an Interest in Prophecy?

Our focus is not just on end times, per se. Rather, it is on the big picture, the grand scheme of God's plans given in prophecy, being fulfilled both past and future.

> *Ephesians 1:7-10 (ESV)*
> *[7] In him we have redemption through his blood, the forgiveness of our trespasses, according to the riches of his grace, [8] which he lavished upon us, in all wisdom and insight [9] making known to us the mystery of his will, according to his purpose, which he set forth in Christ [10] as a plan for the fullness of time, to unite all things in him, things in heaven and things on earth.*

Examples

There are a number of reasons for this focus. To begin, let's consider the examples of great men of faith. Abraham is a man known specifically for his faith.

> *Romans 4:3,16 (RSV)*
> *[3] For what does the scripture say? "Abraham believed God, and it was reckoned to him as righteousness." . . . [16] That is why it depends on faith, in order that the promise may rest on grace and be guaranteed to all his descendants -- not only to the adherents of the law but also to those who share the faith of Abraham, for he is the father of us all,*

What was Abraham's world view? He had an eternal perspective, and it permeated his household. We read about it in the 'faith chapter.'

Hebrews 11:8-10, 13-16 (ESV)
⁸ By faith Abraham obeyed when he was called to go out to a place that he was to receive as an inheritance. And he went out, not knowing where he was going. ⁹ By faith he went to live in the land of promise, as in a foreign land, living in tents with Isaac and Jacob, heirs with him of the same promise. ¹⁰ For he was looking forward to the city that has foundations, whose designer and builder is God. . . . ¹³ These all died in faith, not having received the things promised, but having seen them and greeted them from afar, and having acknowledged that they were strangers and exiles on the earth. ¹⁴ For people who speak thus make it clear that they are seeking a homeland. ¹⁵ If they had been thinking of that land from which they had gone out, they would have had opportunity to return. ¹⁶ But as it is, they desire a better country, that is, a heavenly one. Therefore God is not ashamed to be called their God, for he has prepared for them a city.

Job is usually credited with great patience. But where did his patience come from if not from his faith? Yes, Job was foremost a man of faith in God. His knowledge of the hereafter was quite primitive, yet to him, in his suffering, God revealed the concepts of resurrection and eternal life.

Job 19:25-27 (NKJV)
²⁵ For I know that my Redeemer lives, And He shall stand at last on the earth; ²⁶ And after my skin is destroyed, this I know, That in my flesh I shall see God, ²⁷ Whom I shall see for myself, And my eyes shall behold, and not another. How my heart yearns within me!

When we list men of faith, we are bound to include David. He was a *man after God's own heart.* He trusted in the Lord to deliver him from the Philistine, and from all his enemies. In the Psalms, the majority of which were written by David, the word *forever* is used 110 times, and in many others, eternity is clearly in view..

Psalm 33:11-13 (NKJV)
¹¹ The counsel of the LORD stands forever, The plans of His heart to all generations. ¹² Blessed is the nation whose God is the LORD, The people He has chosen as His own inheritance. ¹³ The LORD looks from heaven; He sees all the sons of men.

For all these people of faith, the fulfillment of their faith lays in the future. The list could go on and on. They are examples that God has commended to us. Just because men of faith held such a perspective, should we? Besides their example, why else should we take an interest in end-time prophecy?

The Persistent Quest for Truth

The Bible gives us many concrete reasons for adopting an inquisitive, investigative approach to prophecy. Beyond the examples of men of faith, there is the need to know <u>truth</u>. When Jesus made some politically unpopular statements concerning what it meant to be his disciples, many who followed him turned away and left him. Peter and the other eleven, however, did not leave.

> *John 6:67-68 (NKJV)*
> *67 Then Jesus said to the twelve, "Do you also want to go away?" 68 But Simon Peter answered Him, "Lord, to whom shall we go? You have the words of eternal life.*

John, also one of the twelve, when writing his gospel decades later, records the testimony of John the Baptist, showing his understanding of this matter.

> *John 3:31-35 (NKJV)*
> *31 He who comes from above is above all; he who is of the earth is earthly and speaks of the earth. He who comes from heaven is above all. 32 And what He has seen and heard, that He testifies; and no one receives His testimony. 33 He who has received His testimony has certified that God is true. 34 For He whom God has sent speaks the words of God, for God does not give the Spirit by measure. 35 The Father loves the Son, and has given all things into His hand.*

The urge to know truth, God's truth, should characterize his children, even knowing that it may not always be what we wish to hear, but that it is what we must hear.

If you are a true believer in Jesus, you have already traveled this road. It was by 'coming clean' before God that you received His forgiveness. There was no salvation without genuine repentance, the kind that wrenched the life out of you, and left you limp, and dead to yourself. This experience is not a pleasant one, but painful, if it is genuine. Then you are ready for God to pick you up and make you alive with Christ. It is God who convicts of sin, and Him alone who restores us. As the old hymn says, "'twas grace that taught my heart to fear, and grace my fears relieved." Remember the bliss of that moment when you no longer were crushed by the impossible debt of your sins. Having emerged from the battle with yourself, you stood fresh and open before God, trusting His word, and wanting nothing but His presence.

If you have somehow come into fellowship with believers and blended into the church body without ever reckoning with the sin in your life, perhaps you should revisit the beginnings of your faith. A man I heard about just a couple of days before my writing this suspects he has cancer, but is afraid to visit the doctor because of the diagnosis he might hear. Don't be like him, spiritually. On Pentecost, after Jesus' resurrection, Peter preached his first gospel sermon, a condemning one for his listeners.

Acts 2:37-38 (ESV)
^{37} Now when they heard this they were cut to the heart, and said to Peter and the rest of the apostles, "Brothers, what shall we do?" ^{38} And Peter said to them, "Repent and be baptized every one of you in the name of Jesus Christ for the forgiveness of your sins, and you will receive the gift of the Holy Spirit.

There is something like that in the study of prophecy. In prophecy God reveals divine truth about Himself and His plans found nowhere else. But some of that truth involves tribulation, judgment, wrath, and divine, eternal things that seem a little intimidating. Yet we must know the truth. It is God's ultimate purpose, not my leisurely pleasure in the meantime, that I must set my sights on. It is God's truth that troubles us, and His truth that carries us in faith to the other side, to the ultimate, eternal joy. We cannot read prophecy looking for temporal ease or entertainment. We must read anticipating *Thy kingdom come, Thy will be done.* It must be read with the attitude that it is first, and foremost, about Him, not us. If we read in faith, we will be blessed with hope and peace. If you have never learned what it is to 'carry your cross' in repentance and submission to Jesus, you will have difficulty keeping interest in this study. Only when we have come to the place of putting God's will ahead of our own, will we be ready to handle the truths of prophecy.

People of God have always been hungry for truth about their Messiah, to know Him more accurately and intimately. It has been said that the early New Testament church was focused on two primary topics, the gospel of Jesus' sacrificial death, burial and resurrection, and the anticipation of his return. Many Old Testament saints were infatuated with a desire to know God's plan of redemption. Yet their knowledge was limited. In the New Testament, Jesus told his hearers . . .

Matthew 13:16-17 (KJV)
^{16} But blessed are your eyes, for they see: and your ears, for they hear. ^{17} For verily I say unto you, That many prophets and righteous men have desired to see those things which ye see, and have not seen them; and to hear those things which ye hear, and have not heard them.

Peter later wrote,

1 Peter 1:10-11 (ESV)
¹⁰ Concerning this salvation, the prophets who prophesied about the grace that was to be yours searched and inquired carefully, ¹¹ inquiring what person or time the Spirit of Christ in them was indicating when he predicted the sufferings of Christ and the subsequent glories.

Note that it was in Old Testament times that *the spirit of Christ in them* [the prophets] was pointing and predicting the sufferings and glories of Jesus. What an incentive for us New Testament saints to investigate prophecy. We should consider it a privilege of the highest order to receive revelation from the Creator Himself, especially when we consider the priority others have put on it.

2 Peter 1:19 (NKJV)
¹⁹ And so we have the prophetic word confirmed, which you do well to heed as a light that shines in a dark place, until the day dawns and the morning star rises in your hearts;

When we think of divine truth, as is embodied in scriptural prophecy, we see much more than simply the revealing of information that is true and accurate. We see truth authenticated. I get excited at how prophecy validates scriptural integrity. No stronger argument can be made for the divine origin of Scripture than that of fulfilled prophecy. For example, the book of Daniel contains prophecy about forthcoming world powers and their kings. It gives detailed accounts of military campaigns and political maneuvers that were future to Daniel, but much of which is now history. They are so accurate that biblical skeptics (they have always been around) decided the book had actually been written several hundred years later, after the fulfillment had already taken place. It had to be that way, they said, because of the detailed accuracy. They claimed that a ghost writer in later years posed as Daniel, writing historical events as if they had been predicted much earlier. Then in 1947 an Arab shepherd boy discovered the first of what has become known as the Dead Sea Scrolls. As the cache of these scrolls was unearthed, they included many Old Testament books that predated any existing manuscripts by 1000 years. One such was the prophecy of Daniel. This discovery verified that the book of Daniel was indeed written prior to the events prophesied. The skeptics have since become strangely silent on that subject. Many other examples abound. The bottom line is that biblical prophecy glares of truth. So established is the prophetic record that it serves as a platform of truth on which to defend the validity of the whole scriptural record. It is reinforcement for the faith of believers, and a beacon to any genuine seeker of truth.

Still more compelling, the books of end-time messianic prophecy lead us to truth because they familiarize us with the very source of truth--Jesus. John the apostle was especially intrigued with this aspect of Christ.

John 1:14,17 (KJV)
[14] And the Word was made flesh, and dwelt among us, (and we beheld his glory, the glory as of the only begotten of the Father,) full of grace and truth. [17] For the law was given by Moses, but grace and truth came by Jesus Christ.

John 14:6-7 (NKJV)
[6] Jesus said to him, "I am the way, the truth, and the life. No one comes to the Father except through Me. [7] "If you had known Me, you would have known My Father also; and from now on you know Him and have seen Him."

1 John 5:20 (ESV)
[20] And we know that the Son of God has come and has given us understanding, so that we may know him who is true; and we are in him who is true, in his Son Jesus Christ. He is the true God and eternal life.

In the truth of prophecy, God has staked His claim as sovereign. He says that is how we can know He is Lord—because His prophecies are true and trustworthy.

Isaiah 46:9-10 (RSV)
[9] remember the former things of old; for I am God, and there is no other; I am God, and there is none like me, [10] declaring the end from the beginning and from ancient times things not yet done, saying, `My counsel shall stand, and I will accomplish all my purpose,'

It might be said that the entire Bible is about Christ, directly or indirectly. And prophecy illuminates Christ as the essence of absolute truth like no other part of Scripture. In him truth is glorified; it is given a splendor, unlike the sterile notion of truth that marks men's ideologies. In him truth no longer wafts with the waves of cultural acceptability, but stands unchanging. In prophecy we have the plans of God revealed, and anyone who cares for God should long to know His plans.

When Jesus stood before Pontius Pilate, he had been accused of aspiring to be a king, a challenge to Roman imperialism. Jesus responded with an astounding statement.

> *John 18:37-38 (NKJV)*
> *³⁷ Pilate therefore said to Him, "Are You a king then?" Jesus answered, "You say rightly that I am a king. For this cause I was born, and for this cause I have come into the world, that I should bear witness to the truth. Everyone who is of the truth hears My voice." ³⁸ Pilate said to Him, "What is truth?" . . .*

Jesus came to reveal the most absolute of all truths, the existence, glory, and sovereignty of God. He came to reveal and secure God's redemptive purpose. Truth was an attribute of Jesus, and is an essential characteristic of God in His completeness. When we seek truth, real truth, it always leads us back to its very source—the persona of God Himself. We can refuse to walk that path, and seek truth elsewhere, but nevertheless the beacon of truth is always shining on us. Jesus is a clear manifestation of the Father, the very truth source, and thus calls us to the Father. John said it this way.

> *1 John 2:21-23 (ESV)*
> *²¹ I write to you, not because you do not know the truth, but because you know it, and because no lie is of the truth. ²² Who is the liar but he who denies that Jesus is the Christ? This is the antichrist, he who denies the Father and the Son. ²³ No one who denies the Son has the Father. Whoever confesses the Son has the Father also.*

The quest for truth leads us to Jesus, *the way, the truth and the life*, and thus to the very feet of God in heaven.

The Deep Need of Hope

A third reason to embrace the biblical teaching of end time events is the hope that it offers. This reason doesn't appeal to people who are on top of the world. One junior-high boy told me in Sunday School that he wasn't ready for Christ to return because there were "…too many neat things to do." It is only after we experience some of life's bitterness that we realize the frailty and futility of the human condition. Aches and pains, and the death of loved ones remind us that we ourselves are mortal, and that much of our situation is beyond our personal control. Whether consciously or unconsciously, all of us are affected by the ultimate reality of death. We plan for it, and allow for it. Yet until it affects us head-on, we view it somewhat as a spectator, a bystander. We don't often consciously dwell on death, for it is an unwelcome enemy. Job's friend Bildad called death the *"king of terrors."* About death, Job said…

> *Job 14:7-20 (NKJV)*
> *⁷ "For there is hope for a tree, If it is cut down, that it will sprout again, And that its tender shoots will not cease. ⁸ Though its root may grow old in the earth, And its stump may die in the ground, ⁹ Yet*

at the scent of water it will bud And bring forth branches like a plant. *[10] But man dies and is laid away; Indeed he breathes his last And where is he? [11] As water disappears from the sea, And a river becomes parched and dries up, [12] So man lies down and does not rise. Till the heavens are no more, They will not awake Nor be roused from their sleep. [13] "Oh, that You would hide me in the grave, That You would conceal me until Your wrath is past, That You would appoint me a set time, and remember me! [14] If a man dies, shall he live again? All the days of my hard service I will wait, Till my change comes. [15] You shall call, and I will answer You; You shall desire the work of Your hands. [16] For now You number my steps, But do not watch over my sin. [17] My transgression is sealed up in a bag, And You cover my iniquity. [18] "But as a mountain falls and crumbles away, And as a rock is moved from its place; [19] As water wears away stones, And as torrents wash away the soil of the earth; So You destroy the hope of man. [20] You prevail forever against him, and he passes on; You change his countenance and send him away.*

The prospect of death is perhaps the most compelling motive to seek God. We don't find peace of mind by evading the reality of death. Not far beneath our consciousness the nagging of our mortality stirs at our soul so that hope is elusive. No, distraction is not the solution. A direct invasion of the deep recesses of our mind, ensures us that there is no solution to be found within ourselves. The only solution for this greatest of enemies is to be found in God, and Him alone. As the old hymn says, "While I draw my fleeting breath, when my eyes shall close in death, when I rise to worlds unknown, and behold Thee on Thy throne, Rock of Ages, cleft for me, Let me hide myself in Thee."

John 5:24 (NKJV)
[24] "Most assuredly, I say to you, he who hears My word and believes in Him who sent Me has everlasting life, and shall not come into judgment, but has passed from death into life.

1 Corinthians 15:24-26 (NKJV)
[24] Then comes the end, when He delivers the kingdom to God the Father, when He puts an end to all rule and all authority and power. [25] For He must reign till He has put all enemies under His feet. [26] The last enemy that will be destroyed is death.

Death is the greatest enemy, yet is most of the time remote enough to hide from consciousness. Death's corollaries, on the other hand, inundate us every day. All of life's issues--relational problems, illness, financial worries--cause us to look beyond ourselves for a happy solution.

Romans 8:20-24 (RSV)
²⁰ for the creation was subjected to futility, not of its own will but by the will of him who subjected it in hope; ²¹ because the creation itself will be set free from its bondage to decay and obtain the glorious liberty of the children of God. ²² We know that the whole creation has been groaning in travail together until now; ²³ and not only the creation, but we ourselves, who have the first fruits of the Spirit, groan inwardly as we wait for adoption as sons, the redemption of our bodies. ²⁴ For in this hope we were saved. Now hope that is seen is not hope. For who hopes for what he sees?

On a global scale, when we evaluate the condition of the world around us, we are led to wonder, "How much longer can this continue?" The apparent threats of atomic war, pollution, overpopulation, limited supply of fossil fuels, global warming, increased frequency of natural disasters all raise our natural fears. Furthermore, the degradation of moral and family values and the hatred and strife between ethnic groups worldwide cause us to wonder if the human race might destruct from within. There is this nagging thought that the end of our world, as we know it, could be near, just based on circumstances. That is where end-time prophecy begins. It begins with a world drowning in its own degradation, and then portrays a solution, the only solution. It meets our longing for a happy ending. It leads us to believe that such an ending is not only possible, but certain. It causes us to embrace that solution. That is hope. And so, we believers look for the near return of Jesus as the necessary quench for our world's political, social, economic and material meltdown. Paul, when he spoke of the taking of the saints to glory, ends by saying ...

1 Thessalonians 4:18 (NASB)
¹⁸ Therefore comfort one another with these words.

Peter begins his first letter to the churches of Asia Minor by reminding them of the hope they have, and by tying it to events which occur in the last days. They needed their hope held high as they were bracing for coming persecution.

1 Peter 1:3-5, 8-9 (ESV)
³ Blessed be the God and Father of our Lord Jesus Christ! According to his great mercy, he has caused us to be born again to a living hope through the resurrection of Jesus Christ from the dead, ⁴ to an inheritance that is imperishable, undefiled, and unfading, kept in heaven for you, ⁵ who by God's power are being guarded through faith for a salvation ready to be revealed in the last time. . . . ⁸ Though you have not seen him, you love him. Though you do not now see him, you believe in him and rejoice with joy that is inexpressible and filled

with glory, [9] *obtaining the outcome of your faith, the salvation of your souls.*

Yes, the search for hope is a fundamental need for all men.

The Desperate Search for Purpose

Another motivation to look into the prophecies of God is to find purpose in life. Closely related to hopelessness is a life lived without purpose or significance. Hopelessness is despair over life's dissipation. Purposelessness is despair over life's futility. Solomon, king of Israel, was the wisest and wealthiest man who had ever lived. Solomon's written journal of his quest for meaning and significance in life is found in the Old Testament book of Ecclesiastes. He looked at every area of interest *"under the sun,"* that is, earthly endeavors, leaving God out of the mix. He was unlimited by expense or opportunity. He wrote...

Ecclesiastes 1:14 (NKJV)
[14] I have seen all the works that are done under the sun; and indeed, all is vanity and grasping for the wind.

Ecclesiastes 2:10-11 (NKJV)
[10] Whatever my eyes desired I did not keep from them. I did not withhold my heart from any pleasure, For my heart rejoiced in all my labor; And this was my reward from all my labor. [11] Then I looked on all the works that my hands had done And on the labor in which I had toiled; And indeed all was vanity and grasping for the wind. There was no profit under the sun.

Ecclesiastes 2:7 (NKJV)
[7] I acquired male and female servants, and had servants born in my house. Yes, I had greater possessions of herds and flocks than all who were in Jerusalem before me.

Ecclesiastes 3:10-11 (NKJV)
[10] I have seen the God-given task with which the sons of men are to be occupied. [11] He has made everything beautiful in its time. Also He has put eternity in their hearts, except that no one can find out the work that God does from beginning to end.

Ecclesiastes 3:22 (NKJV)
[22] So I perceived that nothing is better than that a man should rejoice in his own works, for that is his heritage. For who can bring him to see what will happen after him?

The word 'meaningless' occurs thirty-five times in Ecclesiastes, reflecting Solomon's sense of futility. He concludes that, from an earthly perspective, there is no significance to our lives worth the trouble we experience. He speaks of the concept of *eternity,* but considers it unfathomable. In 3:22 he implies that purpose might be found if only a man could know what came *after him* (after he died).

Most of us have entertained the same longing for significance, and come up empty. Apart from God, there is none. Oh, there are temporary counterfeits that lead us there for awhile. But they eventually lead to a dead end. That is what Solomon discovered. But thanks to God, He can save us from such a dismal meaninglessness. He Himself defines His significance and purpose for us, and imparts it to us.

Contrast Solomon with his father David. David was a warrior, not an intellectual. Yet David had a heart for God and an eye for eternity, and God rewarded him with glimpses of glory.

Psalm 145:11-13 (NKJV)
[11] They shall speak of the glory of Your kingdom, And talk of Your power, [12] To make known to the sons of men His mighty acts, And the glorious majesty of His kingdom. [13] Your kingdom is an everlasting kingdom, And Your dominion endures throughout all generations.

There is an insoluble link between ultimate purpose and eternal identity. That desire for life-meaning should send us into the prophetic scriptures, for it is there that we find future eternity on display. It is there we are shown a glimpse of God's purpose for us as it is played out in His scheme of things.

In Obedience

We should be interested in end-time prophecy out of <u>obedience</u>. One man confronted me on this with the words of Daniel. He reminded me that near the end of his life, the Old Testament prophet Daniel was given a prophecy stretching to the end times, then when he asked its meaning, . . .

Daniel 12:9 (NKJV)
[9] And he said, "Go your way, Daniel, for the words are closed up and sealed till the time of the end.

Thus closes the book of Daniel. I explained to the man who confronted me that Daniel was being spoken to prior to the historical redemptive work of Christ, and that the New Testament book of Revelation closes with this . . .

Revelation 22:10 (ESV)
¹⁰ And he said to me, "Do not seal up the words of the prophecy of this book, for the time is near.

We should read Revelation and revisit Daniel and other end-time prophecies because Jesus told us not to seal up the words of the book. They are no longer sealed to our understanding. *The time is near.* In this passage, often referred to as the Olivet Discourse, Jesus talks of this same topic, his return. Six parables are given there with the admonition to *watch*.

Matthew 24:42-44 (NIV2011)
⁴² "Therefore keep watch, because you do not know on what day your Lord will come. ⁴³ But understand this: If the owner of the house had known at what time of night the thief was coming, he would have kept watch and would not have let his house be broken into. ⁴⁴ So you also must be ready, because the Son of Man will come at an hour when you do not expect him.

Matthew 25:13 (NIV2011)
¹³ "Therefore keep watch, because you do not know the day or the hour.

In Revelation we read...

Revelation 2:7 (ESV)
⁷ He who has an ear, let him hear what the Spirit says to the churches. To the one who conquers I will grant to eat of the tree of life, which is in the paradise of God.'

That phrase is repeated again in Revelation 2:11, 2:17, 2:29, 3:6, 3:13 and 3:22. Since we are living on this side of the cross of Christ and call Jesus our Lord, then obedience should motivate us to seek to know all we can about his return.

Out of Love for Christ Jesus

All of these other reasons for studying prophecy are relevant, but they pale compared to the main reason. We should study prophecy out of an infatuating <u>love for the one</u> it is about. The book of Revelation begins...

Revelation 1:1-5 (ESV)
¹ The revelation of Jesus Christ, which God gave him to show to his servants the things that must soon take place. He made it known by sending his angel to his servant John, ² who bore witness to the word of God and to the testimony of Jesus Christ, even to all that he saw. ³ Blessed is the one who reads aloud the words of this

prophecy, and blessed are those who hear, and who keep what is written in it, for the time is near. ⁴ John to the seven churches that are in Asia: Grace to you and peace from him who is and who was and who is to come, and from the seven spirits who are before his throne, ⁵ and from Jesus Christ the faithful witness, the firstborn of the dead, and the ruler of kings on earth. To him who loves us and has freed us from our sins by his blood

My opening story portrayed this idea of love spawning anticipation. When I was on that Middle East trip, I wrote home regularly, and walked each day to the post office to see if I had a letter from home. Suppose I had received letters from Cheryl, but not even bothered to read them. I would have been a real jerk if I had tossed them aside, unopened. Yet, don't many of us do the same thing with the New Testament book of Revelation, for example? Prophecy is about God. It is *"the revelation of Jesus Christ."* He makes it clear that it is his personal message written and addressed specifically from himself to his church.

We have already discussed the marriage analogy being used in scripture to depict our intimacy and security with the Father and with Jesus. In Israel during the time of Jesus' earthly ministry, marriage went something like this. A man or his father would select a young girl to be his wife. The man, sometimes with his father, would go to the father's house of the girl, where they would make a marriage proposal. If the girl's father was in agreement, a dowry would be offered. After certain agreements, the intentions of the two families would be publicly witnessed. This began the betrothal period (a legally binding relationship requiring a formal divorce to repeal). The groom-to-be would then return to his father's home. There he would begin to build a new home. He typically would build an 'insula,' an attachment to the home of his father, and enclosed within the family complex. Depending on the elaborateness of the home, the building period could take quite awhile, and during that time the groom and his future bride would have no social contact with each other. Plans would be made and guests invited, but the date would still be unannounced. When the new home was built and furnished, and the man had developed a supporting trade, then the final, short-notice invitation would go out, followed by the wedding event itself. On the wedding day the groom and his party would march from his house to that of the girl, where they would collect her, her bridesmaids, and her belongings, then parade back to the new house. There the ceremony would commence, and the marriage would be consummated. It was to this traditional procedure that Jesus referred when he said...

John 14:2-3 (NKJV)
² In My Father's house are many mansions; if it were not so, I would have told you. I go to prepare a place for you. ³ And if I go and

prepare a place for you, I will come again and receive you to Myself; that where I am, there you may be also.

During the betrothal period the bride had to be constantly ready. She had to be able to don her wedding garments on fairly short notice. Her belongings were packed and waiting. Her maids were also vigilant and prepared. She would wait patiently but longingly for her man to come. She did not know far in advance the day of his coming, the day of greatest blessing a Jewish girl could experience.

When Jesus was asked what was the greatest commandment, he responded without hesitation,

Matthew 22:37-38 (NASB)
37 And He said to him, " 'YOU SHALL LOVE THE LORD YOUR GOD WITH ALL YOUR HEART, AND WITH ALL YOUR SOUL, AND WITH ALL YOUR MIND.' 38 "This is the great and foremost commandment.

If we do not cherish his whole message, maybe our issue is not about prophecy. It could signal a regard for God that is below what His glory deserves. Many of us adherents of western Christianity have lowered the bar on the magnitude and priority of God in our lives. This is a haze of darkness that has crept into our theology. We who claim to love our Lord Jesus ought also to be looking eagerly for his return, as the longing bride waits to meet her husband. In other words, our eagerness to embrace His glory and fulfilled purposes may be a barometer of our own real esteem for him. A bride who is not eager for her wedding day speaks of a heart not wholly committed to her fiancé. Prophecy portrays a very high and glorious view of God. It portrays Him as totally sovereign and worthy to be worshipped. We should be cultivating a hunger for knowing God Himself in all His glory. Paul wrote . . .

2 Timothy 4:8 (ESV)
8 Henceforth there is laid up for me the crown of righteousness, which the Lord, the righteous judge, will award to me on that Day, and not only to me but also to all who have loved his appearing.

And John captured the essence of eternal life when he quoted Jesus in his last hours, as he prayed aloud:

John 17:3 (NKJV)
3 And this is eternal life, that they may know You, the only true God, and Jesus Christ whom You have sent.

Christ's return will bring euphoric joy and blessing for those eager to know God and to meet Jesus at his return. To nonbelievers, it will be a time of great fear. What about those who call Jesus Lord and Savior, but who have an unromantic apprehension for that day of his return? If, perhaps, you find yourself in that category, I pray that this study of the pertinent scriptures might ignite a change from apathy to eagerness, or from apprehension to romantic enthusiasm in your relationship to your Creator.

When this attitude of excitement for Jesus' return begins to develop, I have discovered that something else happens, as well. There is something invigorating and vitalizing that stems from the anticipation of our Lord's return. A newfound motivation arises within us: a motivation to become mature, to worship more genuinely, to bear witness for Jesus before others, to be about the Lord's business. There is a heightened desire to be holy and to live righteously. This sensitivity occurs as a spontaneous result of our attitude toward God and toward Christ's return.

It is amazing how often the New Testament, makes reference to Jesus' glorious return when motivating its readers to a higher level of holiness or action. Consider the following examples:

2 Peter 3:10-14 (ESV)
[10] But the day of the Lord will come like a thief, and then the heavens will pass away with a roar, and the heavenly bodies will be burned up and dissolved, and the earth and the works that are done on it will be exposed. [11] Since all these things are thus to be dissolved, what sort of people ought you to be in lives of holiness and godliness, [12] waiting for and hastening the coming of the day of God, because of which the heavens will be set on fire and dissolved, and the heavenly bodies will melt as they burn! [13] But according to his promise we are waiting for new heavens and a new earth in which righteousness dwells. [14] Therefore, beloved, since you are waiting for these, be diligent to be found by him without spot or blemish, and at peace.

Hebrews 10:25 (ESV)
[25] not neglecting to meet together, as is the habit of some, but encouraging one another, and all the more as you see the Day drawing near.

Romans 13:12 (RSV)
[12] the night is far gone, the day is at hand. Let us then cast off the works of darkness and put on the armor of light;

Philippians 4:5 (ESV)
⁵ Let your reasonableness be known to everyone. The Lord is at hand;

James 5:8-9 (NKJV)
⁸ You also be patient. Establish your hearts, for the coming of the Lord is at hand. ⁹ Do not grumble against one another, brethren, lest you be condemned. Behold, the Judge is standing at the door!

1 Peter 4:7 (ESV)
⁷ The end of all things is at hand; therefore be self-controlled and sober-minded for the sake of your prayers.

Paul, James, Peter, and the writer of Hebrews share this same perspective. The impending return of our Lord should motivate us for consecrated living. It should not surprise us that they were on the same page. They were simply passing on to their readers the message of Jesus. This message we will explore in following chapters.

> Lord God, open our minds to want to know you, to take you in. Change our hearts so that we find ourselves lovesick and longing for your return, instead of foot-loose and self-indulgent, making up reasons to ignore it. Turn our focus from ourselves, to you, as true love would do. In Jesus' Name We Pray. Amen.

2
PREPARING FOR HIS COMING

Why Prepare?

God is going to be in control anyway, so why should we need to prepare? Why can't we take life as it comes and just trust God for the future? Well, of course, the answer is that certainly we must trust God. But trusting means following direction, and God's command to us is 'prepare.' Let's allow the scriptures themselves to tell us why.

> *Revelation 22:10 (ESV)*
> *[10] And he said to me, "Do not seal up the words of the prophecy of this book, for the time is near.*

The Time is Near
The most prevalent reason given in scripture for looking toward the end is because *"the time is near."* This expression must be understood in light of God's perpetual purpose, not from our western focus on schedules, calendars and time lines. In Chapter 1 we preempted the above passage with one from the book of Daniel.

> *Daniel 12:8-9 (NKJV)*
> *[8] Although I heard, I did not understand. Then I said, "My lord, what shall be the end of these things?" [9] And he said, "Go your way, Daniel, for the words are closed up and sealed till the time of the end.*

This Old Testament prophet was told to *go your way* because it belonged to another time, another era—the *time of the end.* But New Testament passages are never given with instruction to 'seal them up.' All these are opened to the church because they pertain to the church and its age. They are addressed to the church. Revelation says, *"To the churches . . ."* It is telling us that these events will occur during the church age, and could come at any time. We must understand this prophetically. It does not mean near as we might define it. Looking back 2000 years, we would say that is a long time. We must understand it from a dispensational viewpoint. In Daniel's time, Jesus' return was not near because it belonged to a different age. At the time of Jesus' first advent, his second coming was now in view, and belonged to the new age that was just beginning—the church age. This is always the perspective of phrases like *"the time of the end."* The time is always near in this age.

Matthew 24:44 (NASB)
⁴⁴ "For this reason you also must be ready; for the Son of Man is coming at an hour when you do not think He will.

Revelation 16:15 (ESV)
¹⁵ ("Behold, I am coming like a thief! Blessed is the one who stays awake, keeping his garments on, that he may not go about naked and be seen exposed!")

1 Peter 4:7 (ESV)
⁷ The end of all things is at hand; therefore be self-controlled and sober-minded for the sake of your prayers.

Yes, we must anticipate the return of the Lord because the time is near. Furthermore, we must look for it because . . .

The Danger is Great
Passages about his coming again are always stuffed with warning. The warning, for believers, is not about what to fear from the return of Jesus and what he will do. It is about how we will face earthly conditions prior to his return.

Matthew 24:4-13 (NASB)
⁴ And Jesus answered and said to them, "See to it that no one misleads you. ⁵ "For many will come in My name, saying, 'I am the Christ,' and will mislead many. ⁶ "You will be hearing of wars and rumors of wars. See that you are not frightened, for those things must take place, but that is not yet the end. ⁷ "For nation will rise against nation, and kingdom against kingdom, and in various places there will be famines and earthquakes. ⁸ "But all these things are merely the beginning of birth pangs. ⁹ "Then they will deliver you to tribulation, and will kill you, and you will be hated by all nations because of My name. ¹⁰ "At that time many will fall away and will betray one another and hate one another. ¹¹ "Many false prophets will arise and will mislead many. ¹² "Because lawlessness is increased, most people's love will grow cold. ¹³ "But the one who endures to the end, he will be saved.

Jesus predicts persecution for his followers, escalating in the last days. His warning is not about how to avoid such persecution. He has one specific danger in mind. His main concern is not whether we suffer, live or die. The concern is about our faithfulness. Jesus warns about abandoning our faith in the face of persecution. He warns against getting caught up in the hatred and wickedness of the world, and compromising our belief in him. Our faith is of inestimable value in heaven. Regarding trials, Peter wrote:

> *1 Peter 1:7 (ESV)*
> *⁷ so that the tested genuineness of your faith—more precious than gold that perishes though it is tested by fire—may be found to result in praise and glory and honor at the revelation of Jesus Christ.*

There is danger of being robbed of gold and silver. There is much greater danger of being robbed by our world circumstances of our most precious treasure—our faith. This is the danger Jesus warns about.

The time is near, the danger is great. A third reason for looking intently for his coming is because . . .

A Response is Commanded
Throughout prophecy, instructions point toward an appropriate response. The same is true for end-time prophecies. Sometimes the response is implied or left for another passage, like this:

> *Revelation 1:3 (ESV)*
> *³ Blessed is the one who reads aloud the words of this prophecy, and blessed are those who hear, and who keep what is written in it, for the time is near.*

Other times it is more explicit, such as in these passages:

> *2 Peter 3:9-11 (ESV)*
> *⁹ The Lord is not slow to fulfill his promise as some count slowness, but is patient toward you, not wishing that any should perish, but that all should reach repentance. ¹⁰ But the day of the Lord will come like a thief, and then the heavens will pass away with a roar, and the heavenly bodies will be burned up and dissolved, and the earth and the works that are done on it will be exposed. ¹¹ Since all these things are thus to be dissolved, what sort of people ought you to be in lives of holiness and godliness,*

> *Hebrews 10:23-25 (ESV)*
> *²³ Let us hold fast the confession of our hope without wavering, for he who promised is faithful. ²⁴ And let us consider how to stir up one another to love and good works, ²⁵ not neglecting to meet together, as is the habit of some, but encouraging one another, and all the more as you see the Day drawing near.*

We must prepare because the time is near, the danger is great, and a response is commanded. So . . .

How Should We Prepare?

2 Peter 3:11 (ESV)
11 Since all these things are thus to be dissolved, what sort of people ought you to be in lives of holiness and godliness,

What kind of people ought you to be? If we take to heart what the scriptures tell us, then we are not permitted to remain passive regarding the return of Jesus. The biblical record concerning end-time events is not "FYI". This question begs a response. It clearly implies that in light of these truths there is a manner of life and attitude that we should adopt.

Revelation 22:7 (ESV)
7 "And behold, I am coming soon. Blessed is the one who keeps the words of the prophecy of this book."

James 1:23-25 (NKJV)
23 For if anyone is a hearer of the word and not a doer, he is like a man observing his natural face in a mirror; 24 for he observes himself, goes away, and immediately forgets what kind of man he was. 25 But he who looks into the perfect law of liberty and continues in it, and is not a forgetful hearer but a doer of the work, this one will be blessed in what he does.

In what manner and with what attitude should we anticipate the coming of Jesus? Certain natural questions, feelings and tendencies will assuredly arise as we read various prophecies. Those feelings may include uneasiness or apprehension. But I find it very helpful to be instructed by that same Bible as to how to feel about things such as this. Our feelings then become a faith issue which, when nurtured with prayer, draws the seeker into the proper mindset. It awaits only the sure work of the Holy Spirit to align our emotional compass and our self-will with the absolute truth of scripture and the priority of God.

<u>Some Respond in Unbelief</u>
Before investigating the response the believer is to adopt, let's first consider the response of those who choose not to believe. It may seem odd to say that such a response exists, that there is a response associated with unbelief, but there is. This is different than the passive apathy we have already spoken of. This is an aggressive counterattack by those who would scream loudly to drown out the haunting silence of their own empty, Godless life. They protest either internally or openly against the whole idea of a second coming, even against the reality of Jesus himself. Their emptiness seeks fellowship, and so they protest. They secretly detest the true faith and hope

seen in God's people. Their outward mocking may seem rationally founded, but their platform is just a cloak, hiding their real motive.

> *2 Peter 3:3-4 (ESV)*
> *³ knowing this first of all, that scoffers will come in the last days with scoffing, following their own sinful desires. ⁴ They will say, "Where is the promise of his coming? For ever since the fathers fell asleep, all things are continuing as they were from the beginning of creation."*

Peter warns his readers not to listen to this attitude about the subject of his return. The key idea here is that the scoffers are *following their evil desires.* Their motive is their desire to continue in their evil lifestyle, and to avoid accountability to God or man. For them, the question, *What kind of people ought you to be?* is unanswerable in their present condition. They have no excuse. Therefore, they respond by ridiculing those who do believe, questioning their intelligence. Paul agrees:

> *Philippians 3:18-20 (ESV)*
> *¹⁸ For many, of whom I have often told you and now tell you even with tears, walk as enemies of the cross of Christ. ¹⁹ Their end is destruction, their god is their belly, and they glory in their shame, with minds set on earthly things. ²⁰ But our citizenship is in heaven, and from it we await a Savior, the Lord Jesus Christ,*

It is important to know about this response so that when you encounter it, you will recognize it for what it is, and not be led into unscriptural thinking. Now let us see how we believers are instructed to anticipate the Lord's coming. The Bible has volumes to say in this regard.

What Manner of People Ought You to Be?
In regard to his return, Jesus' command to his followers was to *watch*. He repeated the word *watch* four times in Matthew 24-25, but the theme runs continuously for sixty-five consecutive verses spanning these two chapters. This passage is commonly called the 'Olivet Discourse,' since it was taught by Jesus to his disciples on the Mount of Olives, just outside of Jerusalem. The theme of this discourse is future events. It is generally considered to be the single most important prophetic passage in the whole Bible. If you are not intimately familiar with these verses, I suggest you take a break from this chapter, and read that passage of scripture, before resuming this study.

Watch

The major commanded response given in the Olivet Discourse is summed up in one word: *Watch.* What does Jesus mean by his order to *watch*? This long passage contains a series of seven sketches in the form of parables and historical analogies. At first glance, they may appear to be random in content, but closer examination shows that they actually form a progressing view of what it means to *watch*. Each separate sketch reveals a different aspect of *watching*, so we will look at each one, in order.

Pilgrim Alertness
The first of our sketches is known as the parable of the fig tree. Here we are called to an awareness higher than that possessed by unbelieving people.

> *Matthew 24:32-35 (NASB)*
> [32] *"Now learn the parable from the fig tree: when its branch has already become tender and puts forth its leaves, you know that summer is near;* [33] *so, you too, when you see all these things, recognize that He is near, right at the door.* [34] *"Truly I say to you, this generation will not pass away until all these things take place.* [35] *"Heaven and earth will pass away, but My words will not pass away.*

'Watching' means that we are to take note of the signs signaling Jesus' second coming. There are many pre-cursors to the return of Christ spoken of in Matthew 24 that can be observed in our present day. When we see these signs occur, they remind us of the progression of time and events toward the *Day of the Lord*. Furthermore, they serve as rough indicators of the nearness of that time.

Likewise Paul wrote to the Romans...

> *Romans 13:11-12 (RSV)*
> [11] *Besides this you know what hour it is, how it is full time now for you to wake from sleep. For salvation is nearer to us now than when we first believed;* [12] *the night is far gone, the day is at hand. Let us then cast off the works of darkness and put on the armor of light;*

Watching means noting the progression of events toward that day, and lining up our thinking accordingly.

Prepare to Be Surprised
The second in our progression through these *Watch* passages warns against using human wisdom to predict the time of Christ's return. It is the insatiable desire of men to know 'when.' From earliest times predictions have come and failed. One of the most publicized, Hal Lindsey's The Late Great Planet Earth predicted Jesus would come back in or about 1988. It stirred up a lot of interest and sold a lot of books, but when it did not come to pass, it was nothing more than another embarrassment to the prophetic community. Jesus calls on an example from history to demonstrate his point:

Matthew 24:36-42 (NKJV)
³⁶ "But of that day and hour no one knows, not even the angels of heaven, but My Father only. ³⁷ But as the days of Noah were, so also will the coming of the Son of Man be. ³⁸ For as in the days before the flood, they were eating and drinking, marrying and giving in marriage, until the day that Noah entered the ark, ³⁹ and did not know until the flood came and took them all away, so also will the coming of the Son of Man be. ⁴⁰ Then two men will be in the field: one will be taken and the other left. ⁴¹ Two women will be grinding at the mill: one will be taken and the other left. ⁴² Watch therefore, for you do not know what hour your Lord is coming.

This passage, referring back to the time of Noah, tells us that the specific time of Christ's return cannot be predicted. It cannot be pinpointed to the day or hour. In the days of Noah, people did not realize destruction was near. They carried on the routine activities of life right up to the end. Now these were the evil people of Noah's day. What about Noah and, therefore, what about us as God's people of today? He did not know the exact time either, only that it was coming. Jesus said no one, including himself (in the flesh) knew the time. Watching is the antithesis of predicting. To set a date is in direct violation to Jesus' command to *Watch*. Watching means not knowing when, and anticipating being surprised.

Be Vigilant
Matthew 24:43-44 (NASB)
⁴³ "But be sure of this, that if the head of the house had known at what time of the night the thief was coming, he would have been on the alert and would not have allowed his house to be broken into. ⁴⁴ "For this reason you also must be ready; for the Son of Man is coming at an hour when you do not think He will.

In this third story on the subject, the homeowner's vigilance is called to question. If he had known the hour he would be broken into, he would have been on guard. Had he known the time, vigilance would have not been required. He could have slept early, then awakened in time to secure his house. However since he didn't know, he was not on guard, and was robbed. Regarding the time of Jesus' return, three attitudes are available. The first is speculation. We discussed that attitude previously. If prediction fails, a second is indifference. The homeowner became lazy and indifferent about being robbed. Indifference about Christ's return is contrary to his command to *watch*. He wants us to be vigilant continually—the third option.

The Greek word *gregoreuo*, translated *watch*, meant to stay awake. A Roman soldier was not only to take a 'phulake' [watch--a shift for standing guard], but was required under penalty of death to 'gregoreuo' [keep awake and keep vigilant.] The connection between the two words was trained into every sentry's mind. Our Senior Minister once preached a sermon on this entitled, 'A People On Guard.' We are not called to predict the time of his return, but to anticipate it and vigilantly watch for it at all times. This is not a violation of the previous instruction to know the signs. Rather it is an appropriate progression from it.

Remain Loyal
This next parable takes us into the practical side of watching. Until now, the subject has had to do with attitude. From here forward the questions, "How shall I watch; what should I do?" are addressed.

> *Matthew 24:45-50 (NASB)*
> *⁵ "Who then is the faithful and sensible slave whom his master put in charge of his household to give them their food at the proper time? ⁴⁶ "Blessed is that slave whom his master finds so doing when he comes. ⁴⁷ "Truly I say to you that he will put him in charge of all his possessions. ⁴⁸ "But if that evil slave says in his heart, 'My master is not coming for a long time,' ⁴⁹ and begins to beat his fellow slaves and eat and drink with drunkards; ⁵⁰ the master of that slave will come on a day when he does not expect him and at an hour which he does not know,*

There is an obvious analogy between the master leaving on a trip, and Jesus leaving this earth for a period of time, both planning to return in the future. Watching means being faithful and dutiful, even when the master is not there bodily to oversee your work. It means being obedient to the master's instructions. In short, it means continuing to be the servant, rather than usurping the role of the master. This quality of servanthood, in fact, cannot truly be tried until one is left with the opportunity to be unfaithful. That option may be very enticing. It is often tempting to be self-serving when we think that no one will notice. Therefore, this call to watch is a call for the highest level of loyalty to our master.

> *Matthew 25:1-13 (NKJV)*
> *¹ "Then the kingdom of heaven shall be likened to ten virgins who took their lamps and went out to meet the bridegroom. ² Now five of them were wise, and five were foolish. ³ Those who were foolish took their lamps and took no oil with them, ⁴ but the wise took oil in their vessels with their lamps. ⁵ But while the bridegroom was delayed, they all slumbered and slept. ⁶ And at midnight a cry was heard: 'Behold, the bridegroom is coming; go out to meet him!' ⁷ Then all those virgins arose and trimmed their lamps. ⁸ And the foolish said to the wise, 'Give us some of your oil, for our lamps are going out.' ⁹ But the wise answered, saying, 'No, lest there should not be enough for us and you; but go rather to those who sell, and*

buy for yourselves.' ^{10} And while they went to buy, the bridegroom came, and those who were ready went in with him to the wedding; and the door was shut. ^{11} Afterward the other virgins came also, saying, 'Lord, Lord, open to us!' ^{12} But he answered and said, 'Assuredly, I say to you, I do not know you.' ^{13} Watch therefore, for you know neither the day nor the hour in which the Son of Man is coming.

Another aspect of watching for Jesus' return is the imperative to prepare for that day. This is not something for which we should just muddle along, doing our own thing until one day it comes upon us. There is a preparatory mandate clearly presented in this parable.

Notice the finality of the bridegroom's return. This aspect of Christ's second coming being an irreversible impasse is common to all these stories. The fig tree, once ripe with figs, will not return to green. Once the flood came, no one escaped. Once the house was robbed, it was too late for the homeowner to protect his home. Once the master returned and caught the wicked servant overstepping his duty, the damage was done. The age of grace will one day be over. No more chances. When Jesus returns, there will be no opportunity for a decision. It will be too late to repent. Now is the time for decisions. Then will be a time of harvest.

<u>Be Trustworthy Stewards</u>
"What," you ask, "is that preparation?" Notice, if you have not already, that this whole series of passages is a progression from the spiritual to the practical; from the general to the specific. The specifics begin to unfold as we continue on.

Matthew 25:14-30 (NASB)
^{14} "For it is just like a man about to go on a journey, who called his own slaves and entrusted his possessions to them. ^{15} "To one he gave five talents, to another, two, and to another, one, each according to his own ability; and he went on his journey. ^{16} "Immediately the one who had received the five talents went and traded with them, and gained five more talents. ^{17} "In the same manner the one who had received the two talents gained two more. ^{18} "But he who received the one talent went away, and dug a hole in the ground and hid his master's money. ^{19} "Now after a long time the master of those slaves came and settled accounts with them. ^{20} "The one who had received the five talents came up and brought five more talents, saying, 'Master, you entrusted five talents to me. See, I have gained five more talents.' ^{21} "His master said to him, 'Well done, good and faithful slave. You were faithful with a few things, I will put you in charge of many things; enter into the joy of your master.' ^{22} "Also the one who had received the two talents came up and said, 'Master, you entrusted

two talents to me. See, I have gained two more talents.' ²³ *"His master said to him, 'Well done, good and faithful slave. You were faithful with a few things, I will put you in charge of many things; enter into the joy of your master.'* ²⁴ *"And the one also who had received the one talent came up and said, 'Master, I knew you to be a hard man, reaping where you did not sow and gathering where you scattered no seed.* ²⁵ *'And I was afraid, and went away and hid your talent in the ground. See, you have what is yours.'* ²⁶ *"But his master answered and said to him, 'You wicked, lazy slave, you knew that I reap where I did not sow and gather where I scattered no seed.* ²⁷ *'Then you ought to have put my money in the bank, and on my arrival I would have received my money back with interest.* ²⁸ *'Therefore take away the talent from him, and give it to the one who has the ten talents.'* ²⁹ *"For to everyone who has, more shall be given, and he will have an abundance; but from the one who does not have, even what he does have shall be taken away.* ³⁰ *"Throw out the worthless slave into the outer darkness; in that place there will be weeping and gnashing of teeth.*

Here we have another master-servant parable. Again, the master goes away on a journey, and is gone *a long time.* Several servants are given stewardship of a portion of the master's assets. The theme of the parable is investment of the master's entrusted wealth. Since the master was gone so long, we might assume that the entire estate was divided up among a number of servants for oversight. Jesus has been gone quite a while. Before he left, he placed the responsibility of the kingdom on his followers. He gave them responsibility to make disciples, to teach, to be his ambassadors on earth. That responsibility has passed on as a sacred trust to all who believe on his name. We also are called to invest in the kingdom of God. We are called to invest our time, our finances, our efforts, our very selves.

<u>Your Neighbor as Yourself</u>
To be loyal to Jesus can be a somewhat theoretical affair. Since we do not see him face to face, it is easy to emulate love for him, while keeping him at a comfortable distance—not too personal, you know. In this final vignette, Jesus presents the parable of the sheep and the goats. He places us squarely into a responsible relationship with our fellow man. Jesus had taught:

Matthew 22:37-40 (NASB)
⁷ . . . " 'YOU SHALL LOVE THE LORD YOUR GOD WITH ALL YOUR HEART, AND WITH ALL YOUR SOUL, AND WITH ALL YOUR MIND.' ³⁸ *"This is the great and foremost commandment.* ³⁹ *"The second is like it, 'YOU SHALL LOVE YOUR NEIGHBOR AS YOURSELF.'* ⁴⁰ *"On these two commandments depend the whole Law and the Prophets."*

Matthew 25:31-46 (NASB)
³¹ "But when the Son of Man comes in His glory, and all the angels with Him, then He will sit on His glorious throne. ³² "All the nations will be gathered before Him; and He will separate them from one another, as the shepherd separates the sheep from the goats; ³³ and He will put the sheep on His right, and the goats on the left. ³⁴ "Then the King will say to those on His right, 'Come, you who are blessed of My Father, inherit the kingdom prepared for you from the foundation of the world. ³⁵ 'For I was hungry, and you gave Me something to eat; I was thirsty, and you gave Me something to drink; I was a stranger, and you invited Me in; ³⁶ naked, and you clothed Me; I was sick, and you visited Me; I was in prison, and you came to Me.' ³⁷ "Then the righteous will answer Him, 'Lord, when did we see You hungry, and feed You, or thirsty, and give You something to drink? ³⁸ 'And when did we see You a stranger, and invite You in, or naked, and clothe You? ³⁹ 'When did we see You sick, or in prison, and come to You?' ⁴⁰ "The King will answer and say to them, 'Truly I say to you, to the extent that you did it to one of these brothers of Mine, even the least of them, you did it to Me.' ⁴¹ "Then He will also say to those on His left, 'Depart from Me, accursed ones, into the eternal fire which has been prepared for the devil and his angels; ⁴² for I was hungry, and you gave Me nothing to eat; I was thirsty, and you gave Me nothing to drink; ⁴³ I was a stranger, and you did not invite Me in; naked, and you did not clothe Me; sick, and in prison, and you did not visit Me.' ⁴⁴ "Then they themselves also will answer, 'Lord, when did we see You hungry, or thirsty, or a stranger, or naked, or sick, or in prison, and did not take care of You?' ⁴⁵ "Then He will answer them, 'Truly I say to you, to the extent that you did not do it to one of the least of these, you did not do it to Me.' ⁴⁶ "These will go away into eternal punishment, but the righteous into eternal life."

Many students of prophecy see in this parable a complete departure from the thesis of the previous passages. They take this passage to be about an end-of-tribulation judgment by Jesus on the earth's nations, on the basis of their treatment of Israel during the tribulation period. Israel is *the least of these brothers of mine*. The nations are literal political nations. For me, the problem with this view is the ending statement, *Then they will go away to eternal punishment, but the righteous to eternal life.* This is not a limited earthly judgment of temporary consequences. This last phrase describes a jurisdiction that can only be applicable to that great final Judgment.

I see a different meaning in this passage. I believe it is not a change of subject at all, but is, in fact, the next and final logical step in the progression of what it means to *watch*. We now arrive at a final barometer of whether a person is a faithful, prepared, invested disciple of Christ, or an imposter. If we, like Jesus himself, show love and compassion to those around us, then we show ourselves to be loyal to him. On that day of judgment, our loyalty to Jesus will be evidenced by our treatment of other people. This last parable seems to parallel the day of reckoning that was called by the master in the previous parable when he returned to his servants, after his long journey.

In Summary
There we have it. To *watch* means to heed the signs of the times, to avoid speculating on the exact time, but instead to remain constantly vigilant, to keep an attitude of servanthood, to prepare for the day of his arrival, to invest ourselves in the kingdom, and to show love to our fellow man.

Although Jesus did not tell his disciples specifically the time of his return, we see in these passages a hint of valuable information. Note the phrases: *But suppose that servant is wicked and says to himself, 'My master is staying away a long time / The bridegroom was a long time in coming / After a long time the master of those servants returned and settled accounts with them.* It has now been 2000 years. Suppose Jesus had told his disciples that it would be at least 2000 years before his return. What do you think that would have done to their morale? They expected him to come soon. He never disputed that notion. Jesus wanted his disciples to live with anticipation for his return. The same holds true with us. He wants us to expect his any-minute return. He does not want us speculating about it, but rather to be vigilant and well-prepared for that time.

Watch Eagerly

Many prophetic scriptures depict people on earth cringing in terror at the return of Jesus. The message to non-believers is truly that they have good reason to fear. But that is not the attitude Jesus wanted his followers to have. A distinction is made regarding the perspective of his disciples. We will see the same signs, but rather than being overcome with fear, we are to eagerly anticipate the near return of our Lord.

> *Luke 21:25-28 (ESV)*
> *⁵ "And there will be signs in sun and moon and stars, and on the earth distress of nations in perplexity because of the roaring of the sea and the waves, ²⁶ people fainting with fear and with foreboding of what is coming on the world. For the powers of the heavens will be shaken. ²⁷ And then they will see the Son of Man coming in a cloud with power and great glory. ²⁸ Now when these things begin to take place, straighten up and raise your heads, because your redemption is drawing near."*

Our *redemption is drawing near*. That for which we say we have always waited is coming to pass. How can we mourn with the world? We cannot. We must not. We are told to look eagerly to the heavens, so to speak, waiting for our Lord.

Philippians 3:20-4:1 (ESV)
[20] But our citizenship is in heaven, and from it we await a Savior, the Lord Jesus Christ, [21] who will transform our lowly body to be like his glorious body, by the power that enables him even to subject all things to himself. [1] Therefore, my brothers, whom I love and long for, my joy and crown, stand firm thus in the Lord, my beloved.

Romans 8:15-17 (RSV)
[5] For you did not receive the spirit of slavery to fall back into fear, but you have received the spirit of sonship. When we cry, "Abba! Father!" [6] it is the Spirit himself bearing witness with our spirit that we are children of God, [17] and if children, then heirs, heirs of God and fellow heirs with Christ, provided we suffer with him in order that we may also be glorified with him.

Even the Old Testament prophet depicts this view, and amidst warnings of doom and gloom concerning the *Day of the Lord*, encourages people of faith to long for their day of salvation.

Isaiah 25:7-9 (RSV)
[7] And he will destroy on this mountain the covering that is cast over all peoples, the veil that is spread over all nations. [8] He will swallow up death for ever, and the Lord GOD will wipe away tears from all faces, and the reproach of his people he will take away from all the earth; for the LORD has spoken. [9] It will be said on that day, "Lo, this is our God; we have waited for him, that he might save us. This is the LORD; we have waited for him; let us be glad and rejoice in his salvation."

Yes, the coming of the Lord will bring many fearful results for those who do not name his name. Yes, there is an element of unknown in what will happen, and yes, there is a natural tendency to be apprehensive of the unknown. Yes, everything will be changed in one way or another. But his promises to us are that we are destined for glory. This is his objective, and he wants it to be ours also. Therefore he wants us to anticipate his return with eagerness, an eagerness that is born of faith.

> Dear Lord, our natural minds long to know the things that are in store for us. With all you have told us, there is still an element of the unknown. Our first impulse is to fear. But Lord, it is our faith in your grace that we wish

to live by, not our natural feelings. Therefore we say with resolve, 'Whatever is your desire is our desire.' We believe in your good intentions toward us, and we put our faith in your plan of redemption with all its implications. It is you that we trust, only you.

Finally, if you are not a believer in Jesus the Christ, but are sincere enough to seek truth wherever it is found, then I heartily invite you to read on. Be advised however that, while I am trying to write objectively from a biblical foundation, my motive toward you is not objective; I strongly desire that you too might be a believer. I believe that the whole topic of end-time prophecy is the most compelling assault on apathy or agnosticism, and represents God's ultimate appeal. To you, I leave this scripture…

Hebrews 12:25 (ESV)
[25] See that you do not refuse him who is speaking. For if they did not escape when they refused him who warned them on earth, much less will we escape if we reject him who warns from heaven.

3
UNDERSTANDING PROPHECY

What is Prophecy?

I am guessing that by now you are getting anxious to get into the prophecy itself. Enough with preliminary thoughts. However, if you are not accustomed to reading prophecy, it will be most helpful to consider some characteristics of it that can help our understanding. I will say even further that it will be essential to grasp these principles in order to embrace the interpretations I am going to set forth later on. These characteristics are somewhat inconsistent with the pragmatic way we usually think. Hang with me as we look together at these critical and unique distinctives of biblical prophecy.

Throughout biblical history certain men have been raised up by God to proclaim direct communication from Himself to His people. These were the prophets. All biblical writers were inspired by God's spirit to write what they wrote, but the messages of the prophets were distinct. They usually contained information very specific to a time and circumstance, were predictive in essential makeup, and were imperative in their thrust, instructing the hearer to a particular course of action.

It is especially helpful to look to the Old Testament prophets when we want to learn how to understand end-time prophecies. Many of the Old Testament prophecies have already been fulfilled, so we can see how the spirit and character of the prophet's message was interpreted, and how it played out historically.

The Hebrew words most commonly translated 'prophet' or 'prophecy' come from the root word *naba'* which Strong's concordance describes "speak (or sing) by inspiration (in prediction or simple discourse)." Prophets were also called *roeh*, that is 'shepherds,' and *tsaphah*, meaning 'watchman,' stemming from a word that literally means to 'peer into the distance.' These words somewhat describe the role and accountability of the prophet. They were often charged by God to prophesy under penalty of personal responsibility.

Ezekiel 3:17-19 (NASB)
[17] "Son of man, I have appointed you a watchman to the house of Israel; whenever you hear a word from My mouth, warn them from Me. [18] "When I say to the wicked, 'You will surely die,' and you do not warn him or speak out to warn the wicked from his wicked way that he may live, that wicked man shall die in his iniquity, but his blood I will require at your hand. [19] "Yet if you have warned the wicked and he does not turn from his wickedness or from his wicked way, he shall die in his iniquity; but you have delivered yourself.

The messages of the Old Testament prophets varied somewhat, depending on the need. Most of them can be summarized into a few categories. Perhaps the prophetic message most prevalent as you read through the Old Testament is the call of His people to repentance. As typical examples, consider . . .

Isaiah 58:1 (RSV)
"Cry aloud, spare not, lift up your voice like a trumpet; declare to my people their transgression, to the house of Jacob their sins.

Micah 3:8-12 (NASB)
[8] On the other hand I am filled with power— With the Spirit of the LORD— And with justice and courage To make known to Jacob his rebellious act, Even to Israel his sin. [9] Now hear this, heads of the house of Jacob And rulers of the house of Israel, Who abhor justice And twist everything that is straight, [10] Who build Zion with bloodshed And Jerusalem with violent injustice. [11] Her leaders pronounce judgment for a bribe, Her priests instruct for a price And her prophets divine for money. Yet they lean on the LORD saying, "Is not the LORD in our midst? Calamity will not come upon us." [12] Therefore, on account of you Zion will be plowed as a field, Jerusalem will become a heap of ruins, And the mountain of the temple will become high places of a forest.

In some cases, prophets spoke condemnation on enemies of God's chosen people.

Jeremiah 48:1 (NKJV)
[1] Against Moab. Thus says the LORD of hosts, the God of Israel: "Woe to Nebo! For it is plundered, Kirjathaim is shamed and taken; The high stronghold is shamed and dismayed--

Sometimes the message was one of comfort and forgiveness.

> *Isaiah 40:2 (RSV)*
> *² Speak tenderly to Jerusalem, and cry to her that her warfare is ended, that her iniquity is pardoned, that she has received from the LORD's hand double for all her sins.*

Sometimes it brought promises of hope for Israel, plans for a future of blessing and joy.

> *Isaiah 54:4-7 (RSV*
> *⁴ "Fear not, for you will not be ashamed; be not confounded, for you will not be put to shame; for you will forget the shame of your youth, and the reproach of your widowhood you will remember no more. ⁵ For your Maker is your husband, the LORD of hosts is his name; and the Holy One of Israel is your Redeemer, the God of the whole earth he is called. ⁶ For the LORD has called you like a wife forsaken and grieved in spirit, like a wife of youth when she is cast off, says your God. ⁷ For a brief moment I forsook you, but with great compassion I will gather you.*

Finally, and most importantly, they brought the promise of a messiah. From the earliest prophets to the latest, this assurance occurred, and set the stage for the coming of Jesus.

> *Isaiah 9:6-7 (RSV)*
> *⁶ For to us a child is born, to us a son is given; and the government will be upon his shoulder, and his name will be called "Wonderful Counselor, Mighty God, Everlasting Father, Prince of Peace." ⁷ Of the increase of his government and of peace there will be no end, upon the throne of David, and over his kingdom, to establish it, and to uphold it with justice and with righteousness from this time forth and for evermore. The zeal of the LORD of hosts will do this.*

The Inspiration of Prophecy

As we have seen, the prophets were given a binding charge to proclaim their message. They were told that the safety of Israel was on their shoulders. But where did their message come from? How did they find their inspiration? We are given small snapshots of this process in scripture. For example . . .

> *Numbers 12:6 (NASB)*
> *⁶ He said, "Hear now My words: If there is a prophet among you, I, the LORD, shall make Myself known to him in a vision. I shall speak with him in a dream.*

2 Peter 1:20-2:1 (ESV)
[20] knowing this first of all, that no prophecy of Scripture comes from someone's own interpretation. [21] For no prophecy was ever produced by the will of man, but men spoke from God as they were carried along by the Holy Spirit. [1] But false prophets also arose among the people, just as there will be false teachers among you, who will secretly bring in destructive heresies, even denying the Master who bought them, bringing upon themselves swift destruction.

A common warning throughout both Old and New Testaments is to beware of false prophets and false teachers. This is not just a warning against error. Error can happen, even with the best of intentions. Rather it is a warning against those who, under the prodding of the evil one, continually promote their own self-serving philosophy as if it were from God. There were times in Israel's history when there were more false prophets than true prophets. It was then that the loyalty of the people was put to the test.

Jeremiah 23:16-22 (NKJV)
[16] Thus says the LORD of hosts: "Do not listen to the words of the prophets who prophesy to you. They make you worthless; They speak a vision of their own heart, Not from the mouth of the LORD. [17] They continually say to those who despise Me, 'The LORD has said, "You shall have peace" '; And to everyone who walks according to the dictates of his own heart, they say, 'No evil shall come upon you.' " [18] For who has stood in the counsel of the LORD, And has perceived and heard His word? Who has marked His word and heard it? [19] Behold, a whirlwind of the LORD has gone forth in fury-- A violent whirlwind! It will fall violently on the head of the wicked. [20] The anger of the LORD will not turn back Until He has executed and performed the thoughts of His heart. In the latter days you will understand it perfectly. [21] "I have not sent these prophets, yet they ran. I have not spoken to them, yet they prophesied. [22] But if they had stood in My counsel, And had caused My people to hear My words, Then they would have turned them from their evil way And from the evil of their doings.

Real prophets did not speak from their own wisdom, or of their own initiative. It was God who designated them as His speakers, and He who spoke through them. In fact, they often did not understand the very words they spoke.

1 Peter 1:10-12 (ESV)
[0] Concerning this salvation, the prophets who prophesied about the grace that was to be yours searched and inquired carefully, [11] inquiring what person or time the Spirit of Christ in them was indicating when he predicted the sufferings of Christ and the

> *subsequent glories.* [12] *It was revealed to them that they were serving not themselves but you, in the things that have now been announced to you through those who preached the good news to you by the Holy Spirit sent from heaven, things into which angels long to look.*

Perhaps the greatest testimony to the validity of the prophets is found in the many references Jesus made to them, and the frequency with which he quoted them. In his days on earth, he used the words of the prophets, which the Pharisees and the common people embraced unquestioningly, to validate his own claims about himself. In our day, we can reverse this, and use His words, which we hold to be true, to give validity to the words of the prophets.

> *Matthew 5:17-18 (NASB)*
> [17] *"Do not think that I came to abolish the Law or the Prophets; I did not come to abolish but to fulfill.* [18] *"For truly I say to you, until heaven and earth pass away, not the smallest letter or stroke shall pass from the Law until all is accomplished.*

> *Matthew 12:39-40 (NASB)*
> [39] *But He answered and said to them, "An evil and adulterous generation craves for a sign; and yet no sign will be given to it but the sign of Jonah the prophet;* [40] *for just as JONAH WAS THREE DAYS AND THREE NIGHTS IN THE BELLY OF THE SEA MONSTER, so will the Son of Man be three days and three nights in the heart of the earth.*

> *Matthew 24:15-16 (NASB)*
> [15] *"Therefore when you see the ABOMINATION OF DESOLATION which was spoken of through Daniel the prophet, standing in the holy place (let the reader understand),* [16] *then those who are in Judea must flee to the mountains.*

> *Mark 9:11-12 (ESV)*
> [11] *And they asked him, "Why do the scribes say that first Elijah must come?"* [12] *And he said to them, "Elijah does come first to restore all things. And how is it written of the Son of Man that he should suffer many things and be treated with contempt?*

Yes, Jesus validated the prophets by continually quoting them and teaching from them.

Biblical Arrangement of Prophetic Scripture

Prophets of the Bible are often categorized as either writing or non-writing. Non-writing prophets such as Nathan, Elijah and Elisha verbally spoke their message, but left no written contribution to scripture. They are written about in the Bible, in the third person, and were highly influential to the people of their day. The writing prophets, in addition to their verbal proclamations, also wrote down their messages from God which have since come down to us as the biblical books of prophecy. In the Old Testament there are thirty-nine books, the last seventeen of which are designated as prophecy. Of the New Testament's twenty-seven books, only the last one, Revelation, is principally prophetic.

The Old Testament prophetic books are further categorized as 'major' and 'minor' prophets, a rough inference to the relative length of each book, nothing more. The first five prophetic books are major prophets. The last twelve are the minor prophets.

However, not all prophecy is relegated to those books formally classified as prophecy. Prophetic discourses are found in nearly every book of the Bible, spoken by many men of God, some whose primary role was other than that of a prophet. King David, for example, was never classed as a prophet. Yet many of his psalms are highly prophetic. The words of Jesus are found in the gospels, yet some of it is prophecy of the highest order. This widespread distribution of our source material is one of the things that makes study of end-time prophecy seem daunting. To ease this hurdle, I have gathered scriptures from all over the Bible that are pertinent to each topic being discussed.

Although prophecy is sprinkled throughout the Bible, there are three major passages that are especially pertinent to our study of the end-times: the book of Daniel, the 'Olivet Discourse' by Jesus (found in Matthew 24, Mark 13, Luke 21) and the book of Revelation. I recommend you read these sections entirely, and more than once, throughout the course of your study. I have included scripture excerpts in this text to make the study easier. However, reading these entire blocks of prophetic scripture will give a sense of their overall message, and the flavor of their style.

Difficulties in Reading Jewish Prophecy

Jewish prophecy differs from what most of us are used to reading. These unfamiliar characteristics need to be understood if we hope to correctly interpret what we read. Here are a few issues I have run across, and how they are understood by many prophecy students. The examples I have chosen are from the Old Testament, and are either partially or completely fulfilled. These fulfilled prophecies serve to show the principles that we can later apply to predictive prophecy whose fulfillment is yet future.

Double-Take

I list this issue first because I think it is perhaps the most important key to learning how to interpret and understand prophecy. Please take particular note of this, as it heavily affects the way we will interpret certain passages. Simply put, this characteristic is the fact that Jewish prophecy often has more than one fulfillment, a fact not necessarily obvious when first prophesied. This multiple meaning is confusing to us western-world readers, especially those like myself who tend to be somewhat analytical in our approach to learning things. Understanding this principle will help remove the cultural blinders.

It is prevalent for Jewish prophecy to have both a near term fulfillment, and much later, a second fulfillment. In Jewish prophecy, the near term fulfillment is typically narrower in scope and inferior in significance to the later fulfillment. The first fulfillment serves as a 'type' or preview of the later one, pointing to the later fulfillment as the intended focal point. In this, God seems to be saying, "If I was right about the first fulfillment, you can have confidence I will be right about the second one as well." This is of particular interest to us in this study because many of the prophecies we will study have been partially fulfilled already, but seem to be awaiting a future final fulfillment. The validity for this understanding lies in the fact that, for many Old Testament prophecies, both stages of fulfillment are now history, and we can see this pattern clearly. For example, consider . . .

Isaiah 7:5-8,14-16 (RSV)
⁵ Because Syria, with E'phraim and the son of Remali'ah, has devised evil against you, saying, ⁶ "Let us go up against Judah and terrify it, and let us conquer it for ourselves, and set up the son of Ta'be-el as king in the midst of it," ⁷ thus says the Lord GOD: It shall not stand, and it shall not come to pass. ⁸ For the head of Syria is Damascus, and the head of Damascus is Rezin. (Within sixty-five years E'phraim will be broken to pieces so that it will no longer be a people.) . . .¹⁴ Therefore the Lord himself will give you a sign. Behold, a young woman shall conceive and bear a son, and shall call his name Imman'u-el. ¹⁵ He shall eat curds and honey when he knows how to refuse the evil and choose the good. ¹⁶ For before the child knows how to refuse the evil and choose the good, the land before whose two kings you are in dread will be deserted.

This prophecy was given by Isaiah to Ahaz, the faithless king of Judah, in the face of imminent invasion by his enemies. A virgin (or young woman of marriageable age) known to both Ahaz and Isaiah, would become pregnant and bear a son whose name would be *Immanuel*. Before the boy became a young man, Judah's enemies would disappear. This provided a rough time frame for the fulfillment. When Ahaz saw that happen, he should have recognized the hand of God, and given Him the praise for his deliverance, but sadly he did not. While Judah was temporarily delivered from their enemy, they did not repent of their sins of idolatry into which Ahaz had led them. That is the near-term fulfillment. However, verse 14 is recognizable as one commonly read at Christmas.

> *Matthew 1:21-23 (NASB)*
> *[21] "She will bear a Son; and you shall call His name Jesus, for He will save His people from their sins." [22] Now all this took place to fulfill what was spoken by the Lord through the prophet: [23] "BEHOLD, THE VIRGIN SHALL BE WITH CHILD AND SHALL BEAR A SON, AND THEY SHALL CALL HIS NAME IMMANUEL," which translated means, "GOD WITH US."*

The first fulfillment was short term, and speaks of a temporary deliverance. The second fulfillment occurred about 750 years later at the birth of Jesus. It speaks of a deliverance that is eternal. How subtle, yet powerful is the imagery. This long-term fulfillment could not have been predicted from the context and content of the original prophecy. Yet when the gospel writer viewed it in hindsight, he saw a vivid fulfillment of both an event and the purpose behind the event, and he wanted us to see it too. The prophecy thus serves to validate the divine intention of the events at hand.

Another example is found in Isaiah 61. Here the prophet speaks of things that were fulfilled during the re-population of Judah under Ezra and Nehemiah, a period that occurred from about 170 to 280 years later.

> *Isaiah 61:1-4 (RSV)*
> *[1] The Spirit of the Lord GOD is upon me, because the LORD has anointed me to bring good tidings to the afflicted; he has sent me to bind up the brokenhearted, to proclaim liberty to the captives, and the opening of the prison to those who are bound; [2] to proclaim the year of the LORD's favor, and the day of vengeance of our God; to comfort all who mourn; [3] to grant to those who mourn in Zion -- to give them a garland instead of ashes, the oil of gladness instead of mourning, the mantle of praise instead of a faint spirit; that they may be called oaks of righteousness, the planting of the LORD, that he may be glorified. [4] They shall build up the ancient ruins, they shall raise up the former devastations; they shall repair the ruined cities, the devastations of many generations.*

Clearly in view here is the return from exile of the Jewish people. However, a long range plan of God is revealed when Jesus spoke in the synagogue at Nazareth, quoting from these verses...

Luke 4:17-21 (ESV)
[17] And the scroll of the prophet Isaiah was given to him. He unrolled the scroll and found the place where it was written, [18] "The Spirit of the Lord is upon me, because he has anointed me to proclaim good news to the poor. He has sent me to proclaim liberty to the captives and recovering of sight to the blind, to set at liberty those who are oppressed, [19] to proclaim the year of the Lord's favor." [20] And he rolled up the scroll and gave it back to the attendant and sat down. And the eyes of all in the synagogue were fixed on him. [21] And he began to say to them, "Today this Scripture has been fulfilled in your hearing."

The restoration of Israel in the days of the return from exile embodied a historical, temporal fulfillment, but in Jesus the eternal restoration of men by God is revealed. The messianic purpose is the central focus of this passage. Notice that when Jesus quoted from Isaiah 61, he did not quote the entire passage. He left off the portion about rebuilding the walls, or about them being blessed in the land. He also omitted apocalyptic portions of it. The restoration of all things would certainly come, but he wanted to focus on the part that characterized the deliverer.

Carried Away
This is similar to the 'double-take' principle. Often a prophetic discourse will begin in a manner that is consistent with the temporal circumstances. Then as the writer continues, a strange thing happens. He begins talking beyond his current situation, about things unknown to himself, of things yet future, or of things supernatural. Some of the psalms have this characteristic. When David was on the run, his enemies chasing him, he often cried out to God for deliverance from his pursuers. This was a common theme in the psalms. The twenty-second psalm is such a cry. Yet notice how it soon turns into something much more…

Psalm 22:1, 7-8, 16-18 (NKJV)
[1] My God, My God, why have You forsaken Me? Why are You so far from helping Me, And from the words of My groaning? . . . [7] All those who see Me ridicule Me; They shoot out the lip, they shake the head, saying, [8] "He trusted in the LORD, let Him rescue Him; Let Him deliver Him, since He delights in Him!" . . . [16] For dogs have surrounded Me; The congregation of the wicked has enclosed Me. They pierced My hands and My feet; [17] I can count all My bones. They look and stare at Me. [18] They divide My garments among them, And for My clothing they cast lots.

We easily identify this with the crucifixion of Jesus, for when he was on the cross, we read…

Mark 15:34 (ESV)
³⁴ And at the ninth hour Jesus cried with a loud voice, "Eloi, Eloi, lema sabachthani?" which means, "My God, my God, why have you forsaken me?"

But how could David have known over 1000 years earlier? Crucifixion was not even invented at that time. Of course the answer is, he couldn't. It was God speaking as His Holy Spirit directed the thoughts and pen of David. By quoting this one line, Jesus was, in a sense, applying the whole original discourse to himself. And of course we know that his hands and feet were pierced, and they did divide his garments and cast lots for his outer cloak. This prophetic eruption from seemingly contemporary contexts is common in the Old Testament, and there is no reason to think it might not apply in end-time prophecy, as well.

Time Lines, or Maybe Not
Another issue that gives us a problem is the timing of things, the sequence, the order. Our objective minds like time lines and charts. Yet Jewish literature is not always written that way. It is written to a more subjective audience. Poetic imagery was comfortably received by the ancient oriental mind, and by the mind of the early Jewish Christian. Prophetic scripture is no exception. It is often confusing because it is not always chronological or consecutive. For example, this prophecy of Joel seems to imply a sequence of events that occur in the approximate time frame of end-time judgment.

Joel 2:28-31 (NKJV)
²⁸ "And it shall come to pass afterward That I will pour out My Spirit on all flesh; Your sons and your daughters shall prophesy, Your old men shall dream dreams, Your young men shall see visions. ²⁹ And also on My menservants and on My maidservants I will pour out My Spirit in those days. ³⁰ "And I will show wonders in the heavens and in the earth: Blood and fire and pillars of smoke. ³¹ The sun shall be turned into darkness, And the moon into blood, Before the coming of the great and awesome day of the LORD.

However, on the day of Pentecost, forty days after Jesus' crucifixion, burial and resurrection from the dead, the Holy Spirit was poured out on his disciples, enabling them to speak the gospel in the foreign languages of all the Jerusalem visitors. When the onlookers criticized them, Peter said this...

Acts 2:14-21, 31-33 (ESV)
¹⁴ But Peter, standing with the eleven, lifted up his voice and addressed them: "Men of Judea and all who dwell in Jerusalem, let this be known to you, and give ear to my words. ¹⁵ For these people are not drunk, as you suppose, since it is only the third hour of the

> day. ¹⁶ *But this is what was uttered through the prophet Joel:* ¹⁷ *"'And in the last days it shall be, God declares, that I will pour out my Spirit on all flesh, and your sons and your daughters shall prophesy, and your young men shall see visions, and your old men shall dream dreams;* ¹⁸ *even on my male servants and female servants in those days I will pour out my Spirit, and they shall prophesy.* ¹⁹ *And I will show wonders in the heavens above and signs on the earth below, blood, and fire, and vapor of smoke;* ²⁰ *the sun shall be turned to darkness and the moon to blood, before the day of the Lord comes, the great and magnificent day.* ²¹ *And it shall come to pass that everyone who calls upon the name of the Lord shall be saved.' . . .* ³¹ *he foresaw and spoke about the resurrection of the Christ, that he was not abandoned to Hades, nor did his flesh see corruption.* ³² *This Jesus God raised up, and of that we all are witnesses.* ³³ *Being therefore exalted at the right hand of God, and having received from the Father the promise of the Holy Spirit, he has poured out this that you yourselves are seeing and hearing.*

Peter told the audience that the Joel prophecy was being fulfilled right then in their presence. Yet, the verses about shaking of heavenly bodies and of end-time judgment were not fulfilled at that time, nor have they yet been fulfilled. Now an easy explanation might be to draw a line between verses 18 and 19, and separate the part about the pouring out of the Spirit from those verses describing end-time events. However, neither Joel nor Peter made this division. In the ancient Jewish mind, time is not the issue. The wide-angle view of the purpose of God was revealed, as though in a timeless economy. The absoluteness of the events, and correctly responding to them, are the focus. Completely ignored is the span of time between Pentecost and the end (now approaching 2000 years) because the two events were inseparably linked by a purpose that transcends the ages.

Another example is found in the Old Testament Book of Daniel. At the beginning of Daniel, chapter 6, we are told of events that occurred during the reign of Darius, the king of the Medo-Persian Empire.

> *Daniel 6:1-3 (NKJV)*
> ¹ *It pleased Darius to set over the kingdom one hundred and twenty satraps, to be over the whole kingdom;* ² *and over these, three governors, of whom Daniel was one, that the satraps might give account to them, so that the king would suffer no loss.* ³ *Then this Daniel distinguished himself above the governors and satraps, because an excellent spirit was in him; and the king gave thought to setting him over the whole realm.*

At the beginning of chapter 7 we read of Belshazzar, king of Babylon.

Daniel 7:1 (NKJV)
¹ In the first year of Belshazzar king of Babylon, Daniel had a dream and visions of his head while on his bed. Then he wrote down the dream, telling the main facts.

However the Medo-Persian kingdom was not established in Babylon until the fall of the Babylonian kingdom, a sequence described in chapter 12 of this book.

Daniel 5:30-31 (NKJV)
³⁰ That very night Belshazzar, king of the Chaldeans, was slain. ³¹ And Darius the Mede received the kingdom, being about sixty-two years old.

So the chronological order for these events is chapter 7, then 5, then 6. Sequences are not always as defining as we would like them to be, when there are no time-related transitions connecting them, like, *immediately after* . . . or, *Then* . . . Even with such transitions we must be careful. In Revelation we often read, *Then I saw* . . . or something similar. Such a phrase tells the sequence of the vision, not necessarily the sequential order of events being symbolized.

Reruns
Another characteristic of biblical prophecy is that the same historical event is often visualized more than once, each time using different imagery. Whether for emphasis, for clarity, or to add further meaning, this practice can be confusing. This is a major factor in studying prophecy that is yet unfulfilled. An Old Testament example of this style can be found in the book of Daniel. The first vision, found in Daniel chapter 2, was an interpretation by Daniel, from God, of a prophetic dream that God had sent to the Babylonian king. It showed him the sequence of empires that would follow the one he was currently living under.

Daniel 2:1, 31-33, 37-40 (NKJV)
¹ Now in the second year of Nebuchadnezzar's reign, Nebuchadnezzar had dreams; and his spirit was so troubled that his sleep left him. ³¹ "You, O king, were watching; and behold, a great image! This great image, whose splendor was excellent, stood before you; and its form was awesome. ³² This image's head was of fine gold, its chest and arms of silver, its belly and thighs of bronze, ³³ its legs of iron, its feet partly of iron and partly of clay . . . ³⁷ You, O king, are a king of kings. For the God of heaven has given you a kingdom, power, strength, and glory; ³⁸ and wherever the children of men dwell, or the beasts of the field and the birds of the heaven, He has given them into your hand, and has made you ruler over them all--you are this head of gold. ³⁹ But after you shall arise another

kingdom inferior to yours; then another, a third kingdom of bronze, which shall rule over all the earth. [40] And the fourth kingdom shall be as strong as iron, inasmuch as iron breaks in pieces and shatters everything; and like iron that crushes, that kingdom will break in pieces and crush all the others.

In chapter 7 we are told of a vision Daniel himself had, predicting the same sequence of empires.

Daniel 7:2-7 (NKJV)
[2] Daniel spoke, saying, "I saw in my vision by night, and behold, the four winds of heaven were stirring up the Great Sea. [3] And four great beasts came up from the sea, each different from the other. [4] The first was like a lion, and had eagle's wings. I watched till its wings were plucked off; and it was lifted up from the earth and made to stand on two feet like a man, and a man's heart was given to it. [5] And suddenly another beast, a second, like a bear. It was raised up on one side, and had three ribs in its mouth between its teeth. And they said thus to it: 'Arise, devour much flesh!' [6] After this I looked, and there was another, like a leopard, which had on its back four wings of a bird. The beast also had four heads, and dominion was given to it. [7] After this I saw in the night visions, and behold, a fourth beast, dreadful and terrible, exceedingly strong. It had huge iron teeth; it was devouring, breaking in pieces, and trampling the residue with its feet. It was different from all the beasts that were before it, and it had ten horns.

These four beasts symbolized the same four empires portrayed in the previous vision. We will look at the content and application of these visions later, but the point here is to demonstrate how two different prophetic images portrayed the same events. If a person did not recognize them as pertaining to the same sequence of events, this could add much confusion to their understanding.

Jewish Imagery
The prophecies of the Old and New Testaments alike are Jewish in authorship and original audience. In all the Bible, Luke (author of the Gospel of Luke, and of Acts) is the only Gentile (non-Jewish) writer. Obviously, some of the New Testament books were letters written to churches and readers outside of geographical Israel, places like Ephesus and Rome. But even those letters always had in view the reality that many, if not most, of the readers in those places were Jewish. It is not surprising to find that the style and flavor is very Jewish. Likewise, we must recognize that occasionally the imagery used in prophecy is Jewish, as well. For example, this prophecy given by Isaiah . . .

Isaiah 5:1-6 (RSV)
¹ Let me sing for my beloved a love song concerning his vineyard: My beloved had a vineyard on a very fertile hill. ² He digged it and cleared it of stones, and planted it with choice vines; he built a watchtower in the midst of it, and hewed out a wine vat in it; and he looked for it to yield grapes, but it yielded wild grapes. ³ And now, O inhabitants of Jerusalem and men of Judah, judge, I pray you, between me and my vineyard. ⁴ What more was there to do for my vineyard, that I have not done in it? When I looked for it to yield grapes, why did it yield wild grapes? ⁵ And now I will tell you what I will do to my vineyard. I will remove its hedge, and it shall be devoured; I will break down its wall, and it shall be trampled down. ⁶ I will make it a waste; it shall not be pruned or hoed, and briers and thorns shall grow up; I will also command the clouds that they rain no rain upon it.

An unenlightened reader might think it is a nursery rhyme about a vineyard. Or he might have realized it is symbolic, and wondered what it meant. Fortunately for the reader, this particular analogy is explained in the very next verse.

Isaiah 5:7 (RSV)
⁷ For the vineyard of the LORD of hosts is the house of Israel, and the men of Judah are his pleasant planting; and he looked for justice, but behold, bloodshed; for righteousness, but behold, a cry!

However, a Hebrew reader of that day might have already known what was meant, for the nation of Israel had long been symbolized by the grape vine. Over the doors of the Temple was an engraved vine. David spoke in this way about the nation Israel...

Psalm 80:8 (NKJV)
⁸ You have brought a vine out of Egypt; You have cast out the nations, and planted it.

This same symbolism is in view when Jesus told his Jewish apostles that he, not their Jewish pedigree, would connect them with God.

John 15:1 (NKJV)
¹ "I am the true vine, and My Father is the vinedresser.

We will see many instances of Jewish imagery as we go. This brief introduction will hopefully prepare your mind to recognize and accept this literary feature in prophecy when we encounter it. Otherwise, it may seem that the interpreter is trying to force-fit the interpretation to support a preconceived opinion.

The Messianic Dilemma

This concept was a huge perplexity for the Jews of Jesus' day. The collective prophetic scriptures of the Old Testament seemed to paint two portraits of the Messiah. The first was that of a conquering warrior, a mighty king, a powerful ruler, a wise judge. When the Roman Empire had swept into Palestine and conquered Jerusalem in 63 BC, the autonomy of Israel was once again crushed. They groaned under the heathen Roman occupation. Taxes were unbearable, and the common people were oppressed by their presence. From a religious point of view, the Romans were considered idolatrous and vulgar. It was a generally accepted premise among the Pharisees, and the people in the street, that this Roman 'plague' was God's punishment on Israel for her unfaithfulness. It became increasingly apparent that they were not going to escape this bondage by their own strength, or their own holiness. They began looking with escalating eagerness for the arrival of their prophesied conquering-king from God. The prophetic book of Daniel had given a messianic timetable specific enough that the expectation was focused on the very time of Jesus' incarnation.

The second portrait of the Messiah was less prevalent in Old Testament scripture, but was unmistakably there. It was characterized by servanthood, suffering and sacrificial death. This model did not fit the perceived needs of the people, and was less popular. Various speculations for the harmony of these two portraits were put forth by the rabbis. One such proposal was that there were to be two Messiahs, one a king, the other a pious religious leader, both appearing at the same time. It never occurred to them that the same Messiah could appear twice, at different times, fulfilling both portraits.

When Jesus came the first time, he fulfilled the prophecies of a suffering-servant messiah. When he rode into Jerusalem for the last time, about 30AD, just before his crucifixion, the people expected him to rise up and exercise his supernatural authority to destroy the Romans. Instead of riding in as a king, he rode in as the Prince of Peace. Then he suffered and died to secure our peace with God.

> Oh Lord Jesus, how is it that you knew what was coming, and yet willingly gave yourself unto death? you planned it, promised it, performed it--all for your own good pleasure. What a thrill that we actually are redeemed for your pleasure. What could give us a more positive outlook? How blessed we are!

But what happened to those conquering-king prophecies? The way we answer this question figures heavily into the way we interpret much of future prophetic scripture. We will address this in more detail in later chapters.

4
THE INTERPRETATION OF PROPHECY

For the interested student, there is no shortage of books on end-time Bible prophecy. If you dig into them, you will soon discover that there are widely varying ideas about how to interpret it, and what its implications are. This fact alone can be discouraging to would-be students of prophecy. Worse, when you read one view, it is frequently difficult to get past the antagonism that seems to exist for competing views. An animosity often goes past objective comparison, making the study an almost mean-spirited attack on the character of those holding other views. The whole approach calls to question the solidarity of the view being defended, if such tactics must be taken.

Now don't suppose, from this, that I plan to remain neutral on the interpretive scheme. I will certainly present my own opinions about interpretation. However, some areas in prophecy are not as clearly described as we would wish, and to interpret them requires a level of (well, let's just admit it) speculation. Regarding certain topics, we may believe one way very strongly, but until fulfillment occurs, we cannot say without a doubt that our own interpretation is absolutely correct. We certainly should not make speculative matters in prophecy a condition of fellowship with other believers, which sadly, has occurred in some instances. To be that dogmatic is to presume to know beyond what scripture teaches. I personally know several people who have studied prophecy as I have, and who hold different views than I. I also can say, without reservation, that I have complete confidence in the walk these people have with God, even though we may disagree on this subject. Besides, I imagine we will all be in for some surprises when prophecies are ultimately fulfilled.

Now before I fall off a slippery path, let me lean the other way a little. There are many issues that are so clearly and consistently proclaimed in prophecy that there is no reasonable ground for speculation to the contrary. Yet there are people who deny even these most foundational teachings. To do so is to deny the divine inspiration and infallibility of scripture. For some, the second coming of Jesus is not to be taken literally, for example. Such views are not to be entertained as options of interpretation. They spring from unbelief. Most of us know and accept this situation in other areas of Christian faith, but in the area of prophecy, it seems more difficult to distinguish heresy. I hope somehow to stay between being too dogmatic on controversial details and being too tolerant of faithless distractions masquerading as doctrine.

Significant Interpretive Issues

What are the legitimate issues that affect prophecy interpretation? I have tried to summarize, in the following paragraphs, those concerns that often seemed problematic to me.

Literal or Figurative?
When we read Bible prophecy, there is little doubt that much of it is symbolic. There also is much that could be more literal in its interpretation, and direct in its application. Some scholars believe everything to be literal that can be reasonably taken so. Others take everything as figurative. Others are somewhere between, and often disagree on a verse-by-verse evaluation as to where to draw the line.

Neither extreme is appropriate. Too many exceptions can be found either way. I am content to leave obscure and as-yet-unfulfilled passages hanging, without knowing whether they are literally or figuratively fulfilled. I may not know, for instance, whether the swarm of weird, satanic locusts in Revelation chapter 9 are exactly that, whether they are a vision of military helicopters as some have speculated, or symbolic of satanic dominion and influence. Yet, while I have an opinion, I am okay with not knowing. The underlying message in such passages is often more clear than the imagery, and that is what we will seek.

However, a refusal to adopt any opinion about interpretation will lead nowhere. The issue of how literally to interpret prophecy would well be approached by considering prophecy that has already been fulfilled. It is often claimed that the ancient Hebrews were a poetic, visionary people, and that symbolism and illusion characterized their primary perspective on things such as prophecy. That view, however, is not borne out in their interpretation of prophecy. Sure, there are many times when symbolism is used, and was understood as such. However, when a prophecy was not clearly symbolic, how was it interpreted? How was it fulfilled?

A good illustration is the account from Matthew's gospel of King Herod seeking to know where the promised Christ-child was to have been born. He consulted the chief priests and teachers of the law. They quoted the prophecy from Hosea 11 that told of a ruler who would come from Bethlehem, and thus their answer was *thou Bethlehem . . . out of thee shall come a Governor, that shall rule my people Israel. (KJV)* Now other prophecies told them that the Messiah was to be a descendant of David who was also born in Bethlehem. They could have taken the reference in Hosea indirectly, and assumed that this was a way of saying that the lineage of

Messiah began in Bethlehem (with David) and that his descendant (not necessarily from Bethlehem) would be the everlasting king. Or they could have interpreted Hosea figuratively to be saying that a Messiah after the order of David of Bethlehem would be the everlasting king. They did neither. They took it literally. Herod slaughtered hundreds of babies in Bethlehem, based solely on their literal and direct interpretation, which, as it turns out, was the correct one.

Again, it is clear that much symbolism is used in Revelation and in other end-time prophecies, but this should not be an excuse to reject the entire book as indeterminate. A sober approach to such passages that looks first for a literal fulfillment is most consistent with Old Testament Jewish understanding of their scriptures, and also with the approach taken by the church of the first century.

Chronological, Synchronous or Timeless?
The question of time is huge in the interpretation of Bible prophecy. Our total experience in this life is within a framework of time and space. Time travel is for science fiction. Time warp is for physicists. The fact is, it is difficult to even imagine outside the box of chronological, continuous time. We want to know when things are going to happen, which events come first, which ones are far away and which ones may be near. This is a universal desire. When Jesus spoke prophetically about the future, his disciples wanted to know when.

Matthew 24:3 (NASB)
³ As He was sitting on the Mount of Olives, the disciples came to Him privately, saying, "Tell us, when will these things happen, and what will be the sign of Your coming, and of the end of the age?"

Have certain prophecies already been fulfilled or are they yet future? We want to know what might happen in our lifetime.

As we have already seen, biblical prophecy is not always chronological, but then again, sometimes it is. We would like to lay things out consecutively. Many scholars read Revelation and see in it a relatively chronological sequence of events. Others see a series of events repeated several times from different viewpoints. Some read the Olivet discourse in Matthew 24, Mark 13, and Luke 21, and see in it the historical (already fulfilled in 70 AD) destruction of Jerusalem. Others read those same verses and see in them a future event heralding the end of the present age. Both views have distinct and specific elements in that passage. We will address this later, but suffice it now to serve as an example of the difficulty and importance of time in the interpretation of Bible prophecy.

Who is Israel?

As related in the Old Testament, the nation Israel was created by God to be a chosen and special people. She was like an espoused bride to Him, we are told, like the church is today. It was through Israel that God was to be revealed to the world in glory. The people of Israel were to tell of Him to the nations, to give testimony of Him through keeping the Law of Moses, through the temple worship, through the prophets, and finally through the Jewish Messiah. Great promises of favor and glory and peace were made to Israel by God, promises stretching into the distant future. These promises were worldwide in their scope. Literally dozens of these promises can be found. Here are two examples:

Isaiah 2:2-5 (RSV)
² It shall come to pass in the latter days that the mountain of the house of the LORD shall be established as the highest of the mountains, and shall be raised above the hills; and all the nations shall flow to it, ³ and many peoples shall come, and say: "Come, let us go up to the mountain of the LORD, to the house of the God of Jacob; that he may teach us his ways and that we may walk in his paths." For out of Zion shall go forth the law, and the word of the LORD from Jerusalem. ⁴ He shall judge between the nations, and shall decide for many peoples; and they shall beat their swords into plowshares, and their spears into pruning hooks; nation shall not lift up sword against nation, neither shall they learn war any more. ⁵ O house of Jacob, come, let us walk in the light of the LORD.

Psalm 102:13-22 (NKJV)
¹³ You will arise and have mercy on Zion; For the time to favor her, Yes, the set time, has come. ¹⁴ For Your servants take pleasure in her stones, And show favor to her dust. ¹⁵ So the nations shall fear the name of the LORD, And all the kings of the earth Your glory. ¹⁶ For the LORD shall build up Zion; He shall appear in His glory. ¹⁷ He shall regard the prayer of the destitute, And shall not despise their prayer. ¹⁸ This will be written for the generation to come, That a people yet to be created may praise the LORD. ¹⁹ For He looked down from the height of His sanctuary; From heaven the LORD viewed the earth, ²⁰ To hear the groaning of the prisoner, To release those appointed to death, ²¹ To declare the name of the LORD in Zion, And His praise in Jerusalem, ²² When the peoples are gathered together, And the kingdoms, to serve the LORD.

However, when Jesus came, he was not accepted by the Jewish leaders as the promised Messiah. He was not believed to be the Son of God, as he claimed to be. They crucified him, and by doing so, sealed their rejection of him. That death was the sacrificial death that became the payment for our sins, mine and yours. It was a substitutionary death that, by rights, should have been ours. On the third day after his death and burial, he arose from death, and showed himself alive to many people over the next forty days. But because of Israel's rejection of her Messiah, God did two things. He opened the door of grace to Gentiles (non-Jews), and he brought punishment on Israel. As punishment, the nation was destroyed by Imperial Rome, and her people were exiled and widely dispersed among the nations of the Roman Empire.

Apostolic and post-apostolic Christian church fathers believed the nation Israel would again be brought back from this exile (called the 'Diaspora') to again inhabit the land of Palestine. They recalled the great intervention of God on their behalf to bring them out of the land of Egypt and give them the land of Canaan. They remembered how He restored them from the land of Babylon to which they had been exiled for 70 years. They still expected God to fulfill those promises to the Jewish people. However, as years went by and there was no word from God, faith waned, and another view arose within the church. About 350 years after the death of Christ, during what is called the Nicene period, the concept was developed that since Israel had rejected her Messiah and had therefore been rejected by God, all the unfulfilled promises were transferred to the Christian church. The basis for this idea was scripture that seemed to make the church a substitute for faithless Israel, such as ...

Romans 4:16 (RSV)
[16] That is why it depends on faith, in order that the promise may rest on grace and be guaranteed to all his descendants -- not only to the adherents of the law but also to those who share the faith of Abraham, for he is the father of us all,

Romans 9:8 (RSV)
[8] This means that it is not the children of the flesh who are the children of God, but the children of the promise are reckoned as descendants.

When it appeared impossible that the promises could be fulfilled to literal Israel, this 'transfer theology' became popular. It was a stopgap to the decline in faith of many, caused by this apparent failure of God. Transfer theology has been the most prevalent belief of the church from that time until fairly recently.

The Zionist movement was a small minority who clung to hope of a literal fulfillment of the promises for Israel, and maintained that Israel must again be restored to her land. Its influence was first felt about the end of the nineteenth century, and became more significant after each of the World Wars. It culminated in the legalized recognition of the sovereign State of Israel in 1948, after World War II. Only some of the prophecies are fulfilled about Israel. But now the stage is set, whereas before 1948 such a belief defied logic. What once seemed impossible, now looks very plausible. Now the pendulum has swung considerably. The belief that literal Israel will be the recipient of these promises made by God has now become a popular view among evangelical Christians.

This controversy about Israel's role in the prophetic future bears heavily on how we interpret many prophetic passages, and on our whole outlook on end-time prophecy. Those who believe in a fulfillment of promises to literal, political Israel see the geo-political events of this last century as a miraculous manifestation of the hand of God. It is true that no other people group in history has ever maintained their identity that long in exile, and been so restored. They say this is the beginning of a fulfillment right in our day, before our very eyes, of the prophecy of Isaiah...

Isaiah 11:11-12 (RSV)
^{11} In that day the Lord will extend his hand yet a second time to recover the remnant which is left of his people, from Assyria, from Egypt, from Pathros, from Ethiopia, from Elam, from Shinar, from Hamath, and from the coastlands of the sea. ^{12} He will raise an ensign for the nations, and will assemble the outcasts of Israel, and gather the dispersed of Judah from the four corners of the earth.

Those who hold to a *transfer theology* view say present-day Israel's return to their land is coincidental and insignificant. It is embraced by a systematic theological position called 'Covenant Theology'. The view which sees the return and re-establishment of national Israel as a fulfillment of prophetic prediction is adopted by a competing position known as 'Dispensational Theology.' Dispensationalism has a more fundamental definition, but its most notable application is its belief in a fully functioning Jewish religious system in the last days of this age. I believe the literal restoration of Israel to Palestine so closely fits the various prophecies that a literal fulfillment can be expected. We will discuss this in more detail in chapter 21.

To Summarize
There are a number of interpretive issues that can cloud our understanding of Bible prophecy. We westerners have trouble evaluating scripture from any context other than our native western culture. We need to condition ourselves to consider the perspective of the original readers.

Because of the difficulties, a number of different interpretive views have evolved. These are most strictly applied to the Book of Revelation, but, of course, this directly relates to much of our understanding of other prophetic passages. It is good to understand the various views.

The Major Interpretive Views of Revelation

Given these factors that affect our understanding of prophecy, it is not surprising that more than one scheme of interpretation exists. The most extensive block of unfulfilled prophecy in the Bible is the book of Revelation. At least as important in the understanding of end-time chronology is the Olivet discourse. Add to those the prophecies from Psalms, Daniel, Isaiah, Ezekiel and nearly all the minor prophets, and they make up that part of prophecy that is still looking for future fulfillment. For the purpose of understanding interpretation, I believe Revelation can be roughly divided into five parts,. These are:

Part	Revelation Chapters	Topic
1	1	First portrait of the glorified Christ in the church age
2	2-3	Letters to the churches
3	4-19	Second portrait, tribulation, Christ's return
4	20	Millennial kingdom
5	21-22	The ultimate reward--heaven

When someone asks, "What is your view of Revelation?" what they usually are asking about is your stance on the fourth section, the so-called Millennium. However, there is just as wide a divergence of opinion about the second and third sections. The first and fifth sections, while discussing things subject to much intrigue, are not as controversial in interpretation. Thus, the second, third and fourth sections compartmentalize prophecy students and scholars into the various interpretive views that exist today. Here are tree-top summaries of how the five sections are variously interpreted.

First Section
The first section is introductory and foresees the rest of the book. While profound in content, this section, for the most part, does not generate differing interpretive approaches.

Second Section
The letters to the seven churches found in Revelation chapters 2 and 3 are taken by some to be no more than a collection of seven letters, each one to a specific church existing at that time in Asia Minor. Others say that, in addition to being letters to historical churches, the principles set forth in them are timeless for churches throughout the church age. Still others see them as applying to individuals or individual congregations in the church. Finally, many believe that, in addition to being all of the above, the seven churches addressed are also representative of seven successive ages of church history. If that is the case, they are both instructional and prophetic.

Third Section
The third section covered by Revelation chapters 4 through 19 has four main schools of interpretation, and several variations of each. These are, in a nutshell:

- *Preterist View* - This view believes that the chapters included in this section were prophetic of events that occurred in the first century, beginning soon after the writing of the book. Preterists necessarily date the writing of Revelation early, before the fall of Jerusalem to the Romans in 70 AD, and say that it pertains to that destruction. The intended audience of the prophecy was the infant church.

- *Historical View* - Advocates of this view say that these chapters begin with the introduction of the gospel, and extend to the second coming of Jesus. They see this portion of the book as corresponding with the church age, and its various wars, plagues, and tribulations as symbolic of historical events, including right up through the present time and into the future. They seek to identify the visionary symbol with its corresponding event. There is much disagreement among proponents about what events are represented. As an example, Revelation 8:10-11 says:

   > *Revelation 8:10-11 (ESV)*
   > *[10] The third angel blew his trumpet, and a great star fell from heaven, blazing like a torch, and it fell on a third of the rivers and on the springs of water. [11] The name of the star is Wormwood. A third of the waters became wormwood, and many people died from the water, because it had been made bitter.*

   A widely accepted Historicist interpretation holds that the blazing star is Attila the Hun. With his 800,000 man army he swept down upon the Roman world in 440 AD along the inland rivers, leaving an estimated 300,000 corpses in the Rhine, Upper Danube, and Po rivers, making them undrinkable. Many died from drinking their polluted water.

   According to this view, we are currently living in the midst of that period. Some Historicists hold that the events are chronological as written. Others take a synchronous approach, insisting that the various visions are the same historical events, repeated from different perspectives. Historicists believe the book was written to the 'new Israel,' the church.

- *Futurist View* - Futurists believe that the events of this section of Revelation are pointing to a future time, one characterized by great tribulation on the earth. Futurists take a relatively literal approach to interpretation, where it makes sense to do so. There are differences of opinion as to the timing of the resurrection of the church, and therefore, as to the applicability of this period of time to the church. They believe the book of Revelation was written about 90 AD, after the fall of Jerusalem. They believe it was written for both Jewish and Gentile believers.

- *Spiritual View* - There is a segment of scholarship that sees everything in Revelation as being highly symbolic of personal spiritual struggles, but having no tie to specific historical events, past or future. The visions are allegories, nothing more. Their symbolism is typically general in nature. A Spiritual interpretation of the above passage from Revelation 8 sees it as pertaining generally to natural resources necessary to sustain life. It sees, in the passage, God's punishment for sin by causing those very resources to occasionally turn against him, such as by flooding, pollution, etc.

Note that the first three views attach a historical significance to events being symbolized. They differ only with regard to the time frame of the historical event being symbolized. The spiritual view detaches the symbols from history altogether. There may be elements in each of these views that have merit, but as a comprehensive interpretive approach, the futurist position is the only one that takes the Bible as meaning literally what it says, when it makes sense to do so, in the realm of prophecy. Many Christians hold to a strict scriptural foundation for all other areas of their life and doctrine, but abandon this principle when it comes to prophecy. Adopting a spiritual view leaves the door wide open to the interpreter's speculation, and hides any divinely-intended meaning. Most such views are tradition-based rather than being founded on scripture, having arisen during periods of apostasy. In this book, we will consider the prophecies to be literal except where symbolism is clearly in view. We will compare scripture with scripture, and let scripture interpret itself. Applying the same principles of understanding to prophecy as we would to any other part of scripture, I hold the futurist view, and that is the position from which this book is written.

Of those who hold the futurist view, there are still further differences of interpretation within the ranks, such as concerning the significance of the present nation of Israel, or the timing of an event referred to as the 'rapture of the church.' We will discuss these matters later, after we have defined the issues and laid some groundwork.

Fourth Section
The fourth section, that which pertains to the millennium, is interpreted in one of three primary ways.

- *Premillennial View* - These folks believe in a literal period of time, following the church age, when Christ will establish a bodily earthly reign, headquartered in Jerusalem. They believe his return will precede and usher in the millennium, thus the prefix "pre-." Both pre-millennialism and post-millennialism are consistent with a futurist view of the third section, but pre-millennialism is much more widely held.

- *Post-Millennial View* - Those holding this view also believe in a literal time of spiritual triumph on earth, but they believe the return of Christ will not occur until the end of the Millennium. The worldwide spread of the gospel of Jesus Christ will finally be complete, resulting in the conversion of a majority of earth's inhabitants to Christianity through evangelization. This view has lost ground. The trend of reality seems to be that the world is becoming more hostile to Christianity, even as the gospel is being spread. The fact of two 'World Wars,' among other factors, has caused most to abandon this idea of an upward spiral of global allegiance to Christ and adherence to biblical principles.

- *A-Millennial View* - This view is consistent with a Spiritual view of the third section. It holds that there is no separate 1000 years, but that the millennium refers to Christians living in the church age, the number 1000 not taken literally.

I believe in a premillennial interpretation, and am writing from that point of view. I will not attempt a systematic defense of this view, but some of the reasons will become self-evident as we discuss them. I hold this view because it best fits a direct, literal interpretation of scripture.

Fifth Section
This section gives a tremendous view of our eternal home. As with Section 1, it is not divisively controversial in its interpretation.

I feel that the most important benefits from a study of end-time prophecy are not dependent on those areas obscured by questionable interpretation. If we truly wish to expand our knowledge of Jesus Christ, we will find him prominently exhibited in prophecy. May we seek to discover a portrait of Jesus that is revealed to us in prophecy. Let us make him our focus, and knowing him our objective. Yes, we may wade ankle-deep into the conjectural, but that will only be the wallpaper on which we hang the portrait. It will not enlarge the portrait, only make a favorable setting for its viewing. There is enough definitive detail in the prophetic forecast to give all the information we need for our own preparedness, without embellishing it by speculative imagination.

A Chronology of the Second Coming

God's purposes are timeless, but His application of those purposes is brought about within a time-space creation. In order to rightly anticipate the return of Jesus, it is helpful to see it in a sequential framework with other end-time events. At this early point in introducing prophetic interpretation, it seems a good time to set forth a very basic sequence of events that define a futurist, pre-millennial view of end-of-the-age events. This will be the foundation of interpretation in this book. Within this sequence there are still interpretive differences to be faced, but this bare-bones sequence is a starting framework. I will present just enough scriptures to give foundation for the postulates being made. Once the sequence is understood, more scriptures will be added in later chapters to support the proposed chronology. Not much description is given to the various events here, leaving the reader to continue through later chapters for more information. So prepare to jump into this elemental chronology.

The Tribulation
Just prior to the return of Christ, scripture tells us that there will be a time of terrible hardship on the earth.

> *Matthew 24:21 (NASB)*
> *[21] "For then there will be a great tribulation, such as has not occurred since the beginning of the world until now, nor ever will.*

> *Revelation 3:10 (ESV)*
> *[10] Because you have kept my word about patient endurance, I will keep you from the hour of trial that is coming on the whole world, to try those who dwell on the earth.*

There are many names given to this period of time in the scriptures. We will call it by its best-known name, the 'Tribulation.'

Christ's Second Coming
In the NIV translation of Mark's account of the Olivet Discourse, the term is *distress*. After a lengthy discourse about this tribulation time, we read:

> *Mark 13:24-26 (ESV)*
> *[24] "But in those days, after that tribulation, the sun will be darkened, and the moon will not give its light, [25] and the stars will be falling from heaven, and the powers in the heavens will be shaken. [26] And then they will see the Son of Man coming in clouds with great power and glory.*

Thus we see the tribulation immediately preceding the second coming of Jesus.

Armageddon

The tribulation will culminate in this greatest of all battles ever fought. The buildup to it will begin before Christ comes, but the battle itself will be fought by him, immediately upon, or shortly after, his coming. He will be the victor.

Revelation 19:17-21 (ESV)
[17] Then I saw an angel standing in the sun, and with a loud voice he called to all the birds that fly directly overhead, "Come, gather for the great supper of God, [18] to eat the flesh of kings, the flesh of captains, the flesh of mighty men, the flesh of horses and their riders, and the flesh of all men, both free and slave, both small and great." [19] And I saw the beast and the kings of the earth with their armies gathered to make war against him who was sitting on the horse and against his army. [20] And the beast was captured, and with it the false prophet who in its presence had done the signs by which he deceived those who had received the mark of the beast and those who worshiped its image. These two were thrown alive into the lake of fire that burns with sulfur. [21] And the rest were slain by the sword that came from the mouth of him who was sitting on the horse, and all the birds were gorged with their flesh.

The Millennium

Revelation 20:1-4 (ESV)
[1] Then I saw an angel coming down from heaven, holding in his hand the key to the bottomless pit and a great chain. [2] And he seized the dragon, that ancient serpent, who is the devil and Satan, and bound him for a thousand years, [3] and threw him into the pit, and shut it and sealed it over him, so that he might not deceive the nations any longer, until the thousand years were ended. After that he must be released for a little while. [4] Then I saw thrones, and seated on them were those to whom the authority to judge was committed. Also I saw the souls of those who had been beheaded for the testimony of Jesus and for the word of God, and those who had not worshiped the beast or its image and had not received its mark on their foreheads or their hands. They came to life and reigned with Christ for a thousand years.

Following the victory at Armageddon, Christ will establish an earthly reign lasting (either literally or figuratively) a thousand years. Natural laws will still be in effect. The earth will still be under the curse during this time, but because Jesus *will rule with an iron scepter*, and because Satan will be bound and gagged, a glorious life will be experienced on earth.

Final Rebellion and Final Judgment
Revelation 20:7-15 (ESV)
⁷ And when the thousand years are ended, Satan will be released from his prison ⁸ and will come out to deceive the nations that are at the four corners of the earth, Gog and Magog, to gather them for battle; their number is like the sand of the sea. ⁹ And they marched up over the broad plain of the earth and surrounded the camp of the saints and the beloved city, but fire came down from heaven and consumed them, ¹⁰ and the devil who had deceived them was thrown into the lake of fire and sulfur where the beast and the false prophet were, and they will be tormented day and night forever and ever. ¹¹ Then I saw a great white throne and him who was seated on it. From his presence earth and sky fled away, and no place was found for them. ¹² And I saw the dead, great and small, standing before the throne, and books were opened. Then another book was opened, which is the book of life. And the dead were judged by what was written in the books, according to what they had done. ¹³ And the sea gave up the dead who were in it, Death and Hades gave up the dead who were in them, and they were judged, each one of them, according to what they had done. ¹⁴ Then Death and Hades were thrown into the lake of fire. This is the second death, the lake of fire. ¹⁵ And if anyone's name was not found written in the book of life, he was thrown into the lake of fire.

Following the millennial kingdom reign of Jesus, a final rebellion will occur. Satan will be unbound, battled, and disposed of forever. Then all men will face final judgment.

Heaven
Following Judgment, the ultimate reward is introduced. The eternal dwelling is portrayed here as a mystical dream-city appearing from heaven.

Revelation 21:1-4 (ESV)
¹ Then I saw a new heaven and a new earth, for the first heaven and the first earth had passed away, and the sea was no more. ² And I saw the holy city, new Jerusalem, coming down out of heaven from God, prepared as a bride adorned for her husband. ³ And I heard a loud voice from the throne saying, "Behold, the dwelling place of God is with man. He will dwell with them, and they will be his people, and God himself will be with them as their God. ⁴ He will wipe away every tear from their eyes, and death shall be no more, neither shall there be mourning, nor crying, nor pain anymore, for the former things have passed away."

In Summary

Among premillennialists, this sequence is the accepted view. It can be summarized in this order:

- CHURCH AGE
- TRIBULATION
- RETURN OF JESUS
- ARMAGEDDON
- MILLENNIUM
- FINAL REBELLION AND FINAL JUDGMENT
- HEAVEN

There are other important events besides these, such as the resurrection and rapture, the conversion of Israel, the wedding supper of the lamb, and others. These also need to fit into the chronology. Because their placement is controversial, and needs more discussion, I will address their timing in later chapters. Here we have a skeleton premillennial chronology for end-time events and time periods on which this book is based.

> Oh Lord how we, in our feeble capacity, grasp for comprehension. We pray just now that we may sidestep the errors of men, dispense promptly with obscure and speculative trifles, and draw reverently and purposefully into your presence as we seek you in prophecy. May your Holy Spirit guide our discernment. May he show us what is vital. May the portrait of Christ in prophecy enlarge our knowledge of him, and deepen our intimacy with him. Lead us past the technical, into the relational, we pray. Amen

PART 2
PROPHETIC UNVEILING OF HIS GLORY

5
A FIRST PORTRAIT OF CHRIST EXALTED

In chapter 1 we discussed several reasons for embracing the message of prophecy. There were the examples of past saints, the quest for truth, the need of hope, the search for purpose, obedience, and our love of Jesus. Which of these is your greatest motivation? All are valid motives. All but the last one are centered on our needs. It is very difficult to take ourselves out of our focus, isn't it? I suggest that the last one, love for Jesus himself, is perhaps the closest to God's purpose. As we consider these next two chapters, and truths about Jesus that God has made known to us, I pray that together we discover a heightened motivation that is increasingly filled with God's purpose for the ages.

The book of Revelation begins, *The revelation of Jesus Christ* . . . Jesus is the one being revealed. It does not say 'The revelation by Jesus Christ.' He is not just the one doing the revealing. He is that which is being revealed. It's all about him. "But," you may protest, "How can he be revealed? I already know Jesus. He is my Savior and Lord. I have read all about him in the gospels. I pray to him, and in his name, to the Father."

I began the first lesson of our Sunday School series through Revelation with this question to the class. "Imagine the Sunday school classroom door swings open, and in walks Jesus. You recognize him. He walks in and greets each of you. How would you describe him?" I now ask you the same question. I'm not looking for a theological thesis, but for your spontaneous impression of his appearance. That Sunday as different ones spoke up, each contributed verbally to an imaginary portrait that was visualized by everyone. They described his robe, his hair and beard. Someone mentioned the nail prints in his hands. Without exception, everyone related impressions of his appearance when he walked the shores of Galilee in about 30 AD.

That is a valid portrait for us to imagine because that is how he came--made in the likeness of a man. We are told that he was called a *son of man*, meaning in one sense, simply, a real human being. It is difficult for anyone to be his disciple who has not vicarious walked down the Mount of Olives with him, eaten bread and fish with him, sat on the windswept hillside watching him heal and teach, gone night-fishing with him. We have thrilled as we read these accounts over and over in scripture, and imagined ourselves being there. In his humanness he revealed the Father to each of us. Through this earthly man, we fell in love with God the Son, and through him, God the Father. To love someone, we must know him, and that earthly life is what we best know of him. After we have relived these biographical sketches many times, we may feel we know him quite well.

I imagine the apostles thought they knew Jesus very well too, especially those who seemed to enjoy the closest relationship with him: Peter, James and John. They three alone had seen his transfiguration. They were chosen from the rest to go further with him in Gethsemane as he prayed. Of them, John had been at Jesus right side when they ate the last supper, and it was him alone who followed boldly into the courtyard of the high priest after Jesus was arrested. It was John to whom Jesus committed the care of Mary, his mother, as he hung on the cross. In writing his gospel account, John referred to himself as *that disciple whom Jesus loved.* We get the idea he was a close earthly friend to Jesus. Not only that, but they had known the resurrected Jesus. He had appeared to them, eaten with them, and taught them. Now when John had his first vision, which he relates in the book or Revelation, he had an unexpected encounter with his old friend. You might expect that he ran up to Jesus and threw his arms around him. What did he actually do?

> *Revelation 1:12-17 (ESV)*
> *[12] Then I turned to see the voice that was speaking to me, and on turning I saw seven golden lampstands, [13] and in the midst of the lampstands one like a son of man, clothed with a long robe and with a golden sash around his chest. [14] The hairs of his head were white, like white wool, like snow. His eyes were like a flame of fire, [15] his feet were like burnished bronze, refined in a furnace, and his voice was like the roar of many waters. [16] In his right hand he held seven stars, from his mouth came a sharp two-edged sword, and his face was like the sun shining in full strength. [17] When I saw him, I fell at his feet as though dead. But he laid his right hand on me, saying, "Fear not, I am the first and the last,*

Have you ever failed to recognize someone you knew fairly well when you saw him at an unanticipated time and place, or dressed in an uncharacteristic manner? This is way more than that. John had known the human Jesus, but now he was seeing the exalted, glorified Christ, and his natural mind was not prepared for what he was experiencing. This John who had seen miracles, seen Jesus transfigured, even seen him resurrected, now fell at his feet as though dead. He was about to be shown much more of his Savior than his imagination had ever dreamed. He was about to know a side of Jesus that he had not known before. After he saw, he wrote for us what he saw, so that we too could know.

To love someone more completely means to know him more fully. As precious as the earthly Jesus is to us, it is not the finished portrait. To stop there in our perception of him is to view just a corner of the portrait, while much of it remains hidden under the artist's veil. In this chapter we will remove the veil and view all that is made available to us in the great prophetic scriptures.

To gain a greater view of Christ, we are invited by Jesus himself to consider him in his glory. For this we must see him as he was before his incarnation, and since his ascension. About this glory that characterizes the eternal fullness of Jesus, let's listen in on Jesus' prayer, just before his arrest and crucifixion which he knew were imminent.

> *John 17:1-5 (NKJV)*
> *[1] Jesus spoke these words, lifted up His eyes to heaven, and said: "Father, the hour has come. Glorify Your Son, that Your Son also may glorify You, [2] as You have given Him authority over all flesh, that He should give eternal life to as many as You have given Him. [3] And this is eternal life, that they may know You, the only true God, and Jesus Christ whom You have sent. [4] I have glorified You on the earth. I have finished the work which You have given Me to do. [5] And now, O Father, glorify Me together with Yourself, with the glory which I had with You before the world was.*

About Christ's glory Paul writes...

> *Philippians 2:8-11 (ESV)*
> *[8] And being found in human form, he humbled himself by becoming obedient to the point of death, even death on a cross. [9] Therefore God has highly exalted him and bestowed on him the name that is above every name, [10] so that at the name of Jesus every knee should bow, in heaven and on earth and under the earth, [11] and every tongue confess that Jesus Christ is Lord, to the glory of God the Father.*

"The Revelation of Jesus Christ..." After ascending to the Father, Jesus was not only restored to his original glory because of *who he is*, but he was elevated even higher in our esteem because of *what he had done*. It is this highly exalted, splendid view of him that is revealed to us.

Are we prepared for this encounter? It drove John to faint at his master's feet. Heavenly glory seems to have that effect on men. It happened to Isaiah. It happened to Daniel. It happened to Paul. It may, indeed it should, unsettle us when we come face to face with his consuming holiness.

If you have picked up Revelation only to lay it aside with a sense of dread, then you know just how John felt. It is the natural human reaction.

If you are not a believer and follower of Jesus, then the message of this fear is that you must repent. You must respond in faith to the message of the gospel. Otherwise the fear you feel will continue to nag you, and those fears will someday become reality. In fact, the book of Revelation is, first and foremost, an evangelistic appeal. The book ends with this statement:

> *Revelation 22:17 (ESV)*
> *17 The Spirit and the Bride say, "Come." And let the one who hears say, "Come." And let the one who is thirsty come; let the one who desires take the water of life without price.*

If you are already a Christian, don't be surprised to find that you too experience this same fear. We still are very much aware of the sin nature that battles within us. We are aware of our natural unfitness to be in his holy presence. Don't let this fear keep you from his truth. Let Jesus do for you what he did for John.

> *Revelation 1:17-18 (ESV)*
> *17 When I saw him, I fell at his feet as though dead. But he laid his right hand on me, saying, "Fear not, I am the first and the last, 18 and the living one. I died, and behold I am alive forevermore, and I have the keys of Death and Hades.*

Every genuine relationship with God and with His Son must, at its outset, experience this fear of the Holy.

> *Matthew 5:3-6 (NASB)*
> *3 "Blessed are the poor in spirit, for theirs is the kingdom of heaven. 4 "Blessed are those who mourn, for they shall be comforted. 5 "Blessed are the gentle, for they shall inherit the earth. 6 "Blessed are those who hunger and thirst for righteousness, for they shall be satisfied.*

After we become poor in spirit, and mourn our futile condition, and recognize our helplessness to becoming worthy, and after we seek with relentless pursuit the righteousness that will not offend God, and have tasted the joy of accepted genuine humility before Him, and after we become knowledgeable of Jesus in his exalted state, will we have attained our ultimate objective? Is there more in store for us? Yes, knowing is a step in the direction of Christ, and it prepares us for the ultimate relationship to him. But we are not destined to just see him with our imagination through scriptural images, or even just to know him with a yearning and embracing faith. The Christian's hope is not based on philosophical concepts. It is based on ultimate (but presently unseen) reality. The ultimate goal of our calling is beyond those, and lies in the future. It lies in that time when we shall stand face-to-face with him bodily.

1 John 3:2 (ESV)
² Beloved, we are God's children now, and what we will be has not yet appeared; but we know that when he appears we shall be like him, because we shall see him as he is.

This is what we are aspiring for. Are you ready to explore this exalted Jesus? Let's prepare.

First Portrait of the Exalted Christ: His Essence

Chapter 1 of Revelation, after initial introductions, wastes no time going to this foundational vision. The gospels closed with Jesus having risen back to life from the dead. In the first chapter of Acts we see his ascension into heaven, and the apostles joyfully proclaiming the good news. Yet here on earth what we see with our natural eyes is not a Christ who was victorious over his enemies, but a Christ who escaped from them. Through faith and understanding of the inspired letters of the other biblical writers, we understand that the sacrificial death of Jesus was a victory of love over hate, a victory of God's grace over Satan's treachery. But still, at the close of the biographical/historical books of the New Testament, we see the people responsible for his death continuing to do evil. Where is justice? Where is righteousness realized? Where is victory over all of his enemies? Must these be forfeited to gain the other? The answer found throughout scripture points to a time yet future to the writers. It is yet future to us too. For many, it is a time wrapped in mystique--vague and obscure. We read in the gospels that after his ascension Jesus was told to sit at the right hand of the Father until He had made his *enemies his footstool*. So what is he doing in the meantime? Is he hiding behind the throne of God, licking his wounds, so to speak, while the Father solves his problems? This is the question answered in this first vision. Let us read.

Revelation 1:10-19 (ESV)
¹⁰ I was in the Spirit on the Lord's day, and I heard behind me a loud voice like a trumpet ¹¹ saying, "Write what you see in a book and send it to the seven churches, to Ephesus and to Smyrna and to Pergamum and to Thyatira and to Sardis and to Philadelphia and to Laodicea." ¹² Then I turned to see the voice that was speaking to me, and on turning I saw seven golden lampstands, ¹³ and in the midst of the lampstands one like a son of man, clothed with a long robe and with a golden sash around his chest. ¹⁴ The hairs of his head were white, like white wool, like snow. His eyes were like a flame of fire, ¹⁵ his feet were like burnished bronze, refined in a furnace, and his

voice was like the roar of many waters. ¹⁶ In his right hand he held seven stars, from his mouth came a sharp two-edged sword, and his face was like the sun shining in full strength. ¹⁷ When I saw him, I fell at his feet as though dead. But he laid his right hand on me, saying, "Fear not, I am the first and the last, ¹⁸ and the living one. I died, and behold I am alive forevermore, and I have the keys of Death and Hades. ¹⁹ Write therefore the things that you have seen, those that are and those that are to take place after this.

What a tremendous, powerful opening scene we are immediately confronted with. Who is this 'someone' among the lampstands before whom John fell on his face? He was *like a son of man*. Technically this phrase could simply mean 'human-like,' and is so used many times in scripture of many people. However it is reminiscent of the title Jesus often used of himself while alive on earth, and seems to be intentionally so used here. More compelling, the person speaking claimed to be him who had been dead, but was now alive. There is no doubt this refers to Jesus. But the description of him is nothing like how we suppose he appeared during his earth-walk. This is Jesus as he was revealed to John in his glorified state. For Jesus, glory is the normal state.

The Old Testament prophet Daniel had a similar vision while he was in exile in Babylon. He saw a messenger from God having much the same appearance as John here describes. His reaction was also similar. He writes...

Daniel 10:4-12 (NKJV)
⁴ Now on the twenty-fourth day of the first month, as I was by the side of the great river, that is, the Tigris, ⁵ I lifted my eyes and looked, and behold, a certain man clothed in linen, whose waist was girded with gold of Uphaz! ⁶ His body was like beryl, his face like the appearance of lightning, his eyes like torches of fire, his arms and feet like burnished bronze in color, and the sound of his words like the voice of a multitude. ⁷ And I, Daniel, alone saw the vision, for the men who were with me did not see the vision; but a great terror fell upon them, so that they fled to hide themselves. ⁸ Therefore I was left alone when I saw this great vision, and no strength remained in me; for my vigor was turned to frailty in me, and I retained no strength. ⁹ Yet I heard the sound of his words; and while I heard the sound of his words I was in a deep sleep on my face, with my face to the ground. ¹⁰ Suddenly, a hand touched me, which made me tremble on my knees and on the palms of my hands. ¹¹ And he said to me, "O Daniel, man greatly beloved, understand the words that I speak to you, and stand upright, for I have now been sent to you." While he was speaking this word to me, I stood trembling. ¹² Then he said to me, "Do not fear, Daniel, for from the

first day that you set your heart to understand, and to humble yourself before your God, your words were heard; and I have come because of your words.

> Oh Lord, as we view in our mind these great visions, may we, like Daniel, and like John, be of such humility before you, and so set our hearts on understanding, that you would reveal to us your glory as you did for these men. We risk the trauma that may overwhelm us when we confront your glory, for we must see you. Amen

What is glory? Is it an intrinsic characteristic of God, or is it our perception of his divine nature? Asked another way, does He have glory even if there is no one around to see it? The answer is, 'it is both.' The concept of glory in many passages portrays the sum total of God's attributes. His attributes are well beyond our understanding. In other scriptures, glory is something we render to Him. We perceive those attributes, and express them back to Him in praise. Thus, we give Him glory. We glorify Him. It is perfectly valid for us to 'bring Him glory.'

As we approach this vision of John's, we must ask ourselves, "Is this what Jesus really looks like in glory, or is this a symbolic presentation given to highlight certain attributes?" We need only read to the fourth chapter of Revelation to find another vision of him, and there his appearance is different altogether. Therefore, it seems good not to extract too rigid a visual likeness from this vision, but rather to look for the spiritual and authoritative attributes that are accentuated. This is not a denial of the validity of what John saw, and wrote down. Certainly John clearly saw a visual likeness, which he is describing, but the portrait is not intended to be observed with only the natural eyes. The visible attributes are the means by which God displays things that can't be seen.

Christ the Great High Priest
Revelation 1:12-18 (ESV)
[12] Then I turned to see the voice that was speaking to me, and on turning I saw seven golden lampstands, [13] and in the midst of the lampstands one like a son of man, clothed with a long robe and with a golden sash around his chest.

Here we have a scene very similar to a Jewish temple worship setting. In the temple, the Jews had their menorah, which is a large lampstand holding seven lamps on a single central pedestal. There were many symbolic representations of the presence of God in the temple, and many priests whose job it was to attend to the practicality of administering them. Sacrifices, burning of incense and ceremonial washings kept a whole platoon of priests busy daily. However, it was the job of the high priest to keep the lamps of the menorah burning. The seven lamps burned olive oil. They could easily go out, and need to be rekindled. It was necessary to constantly add more oil. In these following Old Testament passages, we see the symbols initiated.

Exodus 27:20-21 (NASB)
[20] *"You shall charge the sons of Israel, that they bring you clear oil of beaten olives for the light, to make a lamp burn continually.* [21] *"In the tent of meeting, outside the veil which is before the testimony, Aaron and his sons shall keep it in order from evening to morning before the LORD; it shall be a perpetual statute throughout their generations for the sons of Israel.*

Exodus 28:2-6 (NASB)
[2] *"You shall make holy garments for Aaron your brother, for glory and for beauty.* [3] *"You shall speak to all the skillful persons whom I have endowed with the spirit of wisdom, that they make Aaron's garments to consecrate him, that he may minister as priest to Me.* [4] *"These are the garments which they shall make: a breastpiece and an ephod and a robe and a tunic of checkered work, a turban and a sash, and they shall make holy garments for Aaron your brother and his sons, that he may minister as priest to Me.* [5] *"They shall take the gold and the blue and the purple and the scarlet material and the fine linen.* [6] *"They shall also make the ephod of gold, of blue and purple and scarlet material and fine twisted linen, the work of the skillful workman.*

We have in this vision a semblance of that Jewish high priest. It is not that Christ in this vision was a likeness or representation of the Jewish temple reality. Rather conversely, it was the Jewish role of high priest that was a forward-looking representation of a heavenly reality to come, namely, this resurrected and ascended Jesus standing in the heavenly sanctuary. He has now returned to heaven as our great high priest. This is the real thing. This is eternal reality.

Hebrews 9:24 (ESV)
[24] *For Christ has entered, not into holy places made with hands, which are copies of the true things, but into heaven itself, now to appear in the presence of God on our behalf.*

Hebrews 4:14-16 (ESV)
[14] *Since then we have a great high priest who has passed through the heavens, Jesus, the Son of God, let us hold fast our confession.* [15] *For we do not have a high priest who is unable to sympathize with our weaknesses, but one who in every respect has been tempted as we*

are, yet without sin. [16] Let us then with confidence draw near to the throne of grace, that we may receive mercy and find grace to help in time of need.

We are encouraged because our perfect high priest is our constant advocate before the throne of the Father. It is not that we must live perfectly holy to make ourselves worthy of heaven. No! Living holy lives is our response of gratitude, our very desire, for the grace that has been given for us. Our holiness before God is effected by the sacrificial death of Jesus cleansing us from all sin. It is a more perfect holiness than we could even conceive, much less achieve.

Here we see the Lord as our high priest walking among seven lampstands. The implication is that he is tending the lamps, keeping them burning. This was the duty of the Old Testament high priest. He holds in his hands seven stars. What is represented by the stars and lampstands? We are told clearly in verse 20.

> *Revelation 1:20 (ESV)*
> *[20] As for the mystery of the seven stars that you saw in my right hand, and the seven golden lampstands, the seven stars are the angels of the seven churches, and the seven lampstands are the seven churches.*

It is a picture of Christ taking care of his churches. Here instead of the seven lamps of the single menorah we seem to have seven separate lamps. There was only one Jewish temple at any one time, and Judaism was complete with that. But there are many churches making up the complete universal church. Here we have this frighteningly overwhelming picture of him, yet from within his awesome glory, the first impression described has to do with him lovingly and purposefully ensuring the well being of his churches. From this same glory he already has picked John up and told him, *"Do not be afraid."*

Why *seven* stars and candlesticks? This is one of fifty-six uses of the number seven in the book of Revelation. It is used eleven times in the first chapter alone, so you don't have to read far to sense the significance and deliberateness of it. The number seven in scripture seems to be associated with God Himself, and applies to things of God, especially with regard to their completeness or ideal suitability. (God created, then rested on the seventh day. The Jewish Sabbath was proclaimed the last day of each seven-day week.) In these groups of sevens we are having revealed to us the completed work of Christ at the end of this age.

> Dear Lord Jesus, we see you now as our high priest, ministering for us with tireless concentration and fidelity.

We know you must have a purpose for us that stretches into eternity, else why would you be doing this? We are overcome with humility that You, the creator of the universe, would pay attention to us, much less invest so freely of Yourself for us. How weak and dependent we are. Help us to realize this, and to cooperate with your working in our lives by submitting to you in all things. Take away our stubborn self-will, and replace it with a consecrated heart. Where we are unfaithful, give us faith. Where we are sinful, make us holy. Where we are impatient, give us peace. In short, Lord, we are looking for you to make up for all of our shortcomings. As we stand in the radiance of your great glory, even a commitment on our part seems shallow, considering our own weakness. The only appropriate response is to be overwhelmed by your majesty, and by your care for us. Our intention to be devoted to you should be instinctive at this point. How great you are. How great is the love of the Father. Amen

His Appearance

Awesome and Ominous
It is an amazingly secure thought that we are gently cared for by The One in the position of ultimate eternal power. After all, of what benefit is it to us if our God is compassionate, but impotent. We revel to know that He who is our advocate *holds the keys to death and Hades.*

Revelation 1:14-16 (ESV)
14 The hairs of his head were white, like white wool, like snow. His eyes were like a flame of fire, 15 his feet were like burnished bronze, refined in a furnace, and his voice was like the roar of many waters. 16 In his right hand he held seven stars, from his mouth came a sharp two-edged sword, and his face was like the sun shining in full strength.

First there is the snow-white head and hair. The Old Testament prophet Daniel saw a similar vision of the Lord in His end-time authority.

Daniel 7:9 (KJV)
9 I beheld till the thrones were cast down, and the Ancient of days did sit, whose garment was white as snow, and the hair of his head like the pure wool: his throne was like the fiery flame, and his wheels as burning fire.

Then, as now, this appearance of white hair depicts aged wisdom, but then it did so in a culture where such age was much more esteemed than in our present western society. It was a limited symbol of the unlimited eternal nature of God. His infinite wisdom and eternal self-existence are here in view.

Next we encounter the feet of bronze. The King James translation says, *His feet were like fine brass, as if they burned in a furnace. . .* In the original Greek, the language emphasizes the radiant brilliance of the metal, hinting that perhaps it is still glowing from the heat of the furnace. This symbolism occurs other places in scripture, and points to impending judgment. For example, these visions of heavenly beings...

> *Ezekiel 1:4-7 (NASB)*
> *⁴ As I looked, behold, a storm wind was coming from the north, a great cloud with fire flashing forth continually and a bright light around it, and in its midst something like glowing metal in the midst of the fire. ⁵ Within it there were figures resembling four living beings. And this was their appearance: they had human form. ⁶ Each of them had four faces and four wings. ⁷ Their legs were straight and their feet were like a calf's hoof, and they gleamed like burnished bronze.*

> *Ezekiel 40:3 (NASB)*
> *³ So He brought me there; and behold, there was a man whose appearance was like the appearance of bronze, with a line of flax and a measuring rod in his hand; and he was standing in the gateway.*

> *Daniel 10:5-6 (NKJV)*
> *⁵ I lifted my eyes and looked, and behold, a certain man clothed in linen, whose waist was girded with gold of Uphaz! ⁶ His body was like beryl, his face like the appearance of lightning, his eyes like torches of fire, his arms and feet like burnished bronze in color, and the sound of his words like the voice of a multitude.*

Here is our first indication of what is about to be revealed. This *One among the lampstands* is prepared for judgment. There are dreadful and glorious things to follow. This symbolism would not have been lost to John. He knew the Old Testament scriptures and the promises that one day the Lord would come in person judging earth's inhabitants. For example:

> *Daniel 7:9-14 (NKJV)*
> *⁹ "I watched till thrones were put in place, And the Ancient of Days was seated; His garment was white as snow, And the hair of His*

head was like pure wool. His throne was a fiery flame, Its wheels a burning fire; ¹⁰ *A fiery stream issued And came forth from before Him. A thousand thousands ministered to Him; Ten thousand times ten thousand stood before Him. The court was seated, And the books were opened.* ¹¹ *"I watched then because of the sound of the pompous words which the horn was speaking; I watched till the beast was slain, and its body destroyed and given to the burning flame.* ¹² *As for the rest of the beasts, they had their dominion taken away, yet their lives were prolonged for a season and a time.* ¹³ *"I was watching in the night visions, And behold, One like the Son of Man, Coming with the clouds of heaven! He came to the Ancient of Days, And they brought Him near before Him.* ¹⁴ *Then to Him was given dominion and glory and a kingdom, That all peoples, nations, and languages should serve Him. His dominion is an everlasting dominion, Which shall not pass away, And His kingdom the one Which shall not be destroyed.*

Isaiah 13:6-8,13 (RSV)
⁶ *Wail, for the day of the LORD is near; as destruction from the Almighty it will come!* ⁷ *Therefore all hands will be feeble, and every man's heart will melt,* ⁸ *and they will be dismayed. Pangs and agony will seize them; they will be in anguish like a woman in travail. They will look aghast at one another; their faces will be aflame. . .* ¹³ *Therefore I will make the heavens tremble, and the earth will be shaken out of its place, at the wrath of the LORD of hosts in the day of his fierce anger.*

The Mighty Sound of His Voice

He speaks with a voice so powerful and authoritative that it is compared with the thunderous roar of a torrent of floodwaters. If you have been near a large waterfall, you can relate to this imagery. Ezekiel used similar language when he heard the Lord's voice.

Ezekiel 43:2 (NASB)
² *and behold, the glory of the God of Israel was coming from the way of the east. And His voice was like the sound of many waters; and the earth shone with His glory.*

The psalmist wrote this of the Lord...

Psalm 93:3-4 (NKJV)
³ *The floods have lifted up, O LORD, The floods have lifted up their voice; The floods lift up their waves.* ⁴ *The LORD on high is mightier Than the noise of many waters, Than the mighty waves of the sea.*

You know how riveting it is when a bolt of lightning strikes very close. Your whole concentration is momentarily on it. This will be nothing compared with the speaking of the Lord in judgment. So compelling was this voice in the understanding of biblical writers, that the idea of the *word* issuing from the Lord's mouth was symbolized by a weapon--a sword.

Out of his mouth came a *sharp double-edged sword*. In biblical times the sword was the symbol of war. It was the offensive weapon with which every soldier was equipped. *Killed by the sword* was an axiom meaning to die in battle. Decapitation with a sword was also the Roman means of execution for its own citizens sentenced to death, or for war criminals. In scripture, the sword is symbolic of the piercing word of God.

Hebrews 4:12 (ESV)
[12] For the word of God is living and active, sharper than any two-edged sword, piercing to the division of soul and of spirit, of joints and of marrow, and discerning the thoughts and intentions of the heart.

The word of God is able to separate evil from good within us. Even that which has stayed hidden from our own conscience, when confronted by the Word of God, is dredged up and becomes a cancerous, spiritually painful tumor. Then this *sword* is able to perform spiritual surgery by bringing us under conviction, and driving us to God's salvation. Likewise, Isaiah's description of the judging, reigning Messiah yet to come spoke in this manner.

Isaiah 11:3-4 (RSV)
[3] And his delight shall be in the fear of the LORD. He shall not judge by what his eyes see, or decide by what his ears hear; [4] but with righteousness he shall judge the poor, and decide with equity for the meek of the earth; and he shall smite the earth with the rod of his mouth, and with the breath of his lips he shall slay the wicked.

This same imagery recurs throughout Revelation, as in the following verses:

Revelation 2:12-16 (ESV)
[12] "And to the angel of the church in Pergamum write: 'The words of him who has the sharp two-edged sword . . . [16] Therefore repent. If not, I will come to you soon and war against them with the sword of my mouth.

Revelation 19:15,21 (ESV)
[15] From his mouth comes a sharp sword with which to strike down the nations, and he will rule them with a rod of iron. He will tread the winepress of the fury of the wrath of God the Almighty . . . [21] And

the rest were slain by the sword that came from the mouth of him who was sitting on the horse, and all the birds were gorged with their flesh.

What is meant by the word *"word"*? Through the ages, God has spoken in various ways. Before the fall, to Adam and Eve, He spoke directly somehow. To men and women everywhere, He has spoken through his creative perfection. To Moses, He spoke from His glory. He spoke to David in his spirit. Through the prophets, he spoke by putting his words into their mouths, and into their pens. He has, on rare occasion, spoken audibly so that many heard his voice, but sometimes mistook it as thunder in their dull spiritual awareness. It is the sum of God's self-revelation to us. Finally and foremost, He speaks through Jesus Christ. In Jesus, the *Word became flesh and dwelt among us. (John 1:14)*

Hebrews 1:1-3 (ESV)
[1] Long ago, at many times and in many ways, God spoke to our fathers by the prophets, [2] but in these last days he has spoken to us by his Son, whom he appointed the heir of all things, through whom also he created the world. [3] He is the radiance of the glory of God and the exact imprint of his nature, and he upholds the universe by the word of his power . . .

Jesus is the final revelation of God to men during this present age. It is this total body of revealed knowledge of God for which men and women are accountable. It is t his available understanding by which they will finally be judged.

Before judgment is brought by God, the word itself judges the individual heart by bringing a self-conviction upon the one who seeks to know it. It is there that the self-sufficient soul discovers he is not qualified to enter into God's presence. It is at this point that many recoil in their prideful affront, and thrust it aside, before it might cause them to lose sleep. But those who truly seek God will venture on, perhaps in anguish. The word is not finished yet with having convicted one's soul. Once a person convicted, this same word leads the seeker to the source of salvation, again Jesus himself. It introduces him to the one who *holds the keys to death...(v18).* It instructs how to approach God for the first time. It then trains the regenerate person in the ways of righteousness. This word is the textbook and the Holy Spirit is the tutor. The word of scripture is the very voice of God, and as such, soon becomes in itself a companion to the believer. In it the believer finds fellowship with his Creator.

Ephesians 6:17 (ESV)
[17] and take the helmet of salvation, and the sword of the Spirit, which is the word of God,

Psalm 119:103-106 (NKJV)
[103] How sweet are Your words to my taste, Sweeter than honey to my mouth! [104] Through Your precepts I get understanding; Therefore I hate every false way. [105] Your word is a lamp to my feet And a light to my path. [106] I have sworn and confirmed That I will keep Your righteous judgments.

The voice of the Lord is heard throughout his creation. It is not mute or camouflaged, but loud and clear, so that on judgment day men will have no excuse. The time to hear the voice of the Lord is now, while he still speaks an invitation. A time will come, not of our choosing, when no further invitation will be offered.

Acts 17:30-31 (ESV)
[30] The times of ignorance God overlooked, but now he commands all people everywhere to repent, [31] because he has fixed a day on which he will judge the world in righteousness by a man whom he has appointed; and of this he has given assurance to all by raising him from the dead."

Piercing Vision

Next we are told of *eyes like blazing fire*. At the time we began studying this vision in Sunday School class, a comic came out in the newspaper that I cut out for an introduction to the lesson. It consisted of one single landscape-like picture, showing a large elevated platform in the middle-distance, surrounded by a sea of people down on a lower level, looking up. On the platform was a throne and a very old and wise looking person with white hair and long beard and flowing robe. Over the stage was suspended a large marquee that read, "Judgment Day." In the foreground, and seemingly at the back of this huge crowd, stood the two main characters. One says to the other, "The trick is to not catch His eye."

Hebrews 4:13 (ESV)
[13] And no creature is hidden from his sight, but all are naked and exposed to the eyes of him to whom we must give account.

Revelation 6:16 (ESV)
[16] calling to the mountains and rocks, "Fall on us and hide us from the face of him who is seated on the throne, and from the wrath of the Lamb,

God's eyes not only see far and wide, but they see deep--deep within the heart. They penetrate past the outer façade, even past the psyche, to the very spirit. They see what the eyes of men cannot see. They even see in us what we cannot see in ourselves. The Old Testament saints, too, shared this belief that God sees all, knows all. The term *in the eyes of the Lord* became an axiom for this concept, occurring eighty-eight times.

> *Deuteronomy 12:28 (NKJV)*
> ^{28} *Observe and obey all these words which I command you, that it may go well with you and your children after you forever, when you do what is good and right in the sight of the LORD your God.*

> *Judges 2:11 (ESV)*
> ^{11} *And the people of Israel did what was evil in the sight of the LORD and served the Baals.*

> *Job 34:21-22 (NKJV)*
> ^{21} *"For His eyes are on the ways of man, And He sees all his steps.*
> ^{22} *There is no darkness nor shadow of death Where the workers of iniquity may hide themselves.*

> *Proverbs 15:3 (RSV)*
> ^{3} *The eyes of the LORD are in every place, keeping watch on the evil and the good.*

Many hope to not catch His eye when that day arrives. It won't happen. We might ignore Him in this life, but He will not be ignored on that day.

> *Revelation 20:11 (ESV)*
> ^{11} *Then I saw a great white throne and him who was seated on it. From his presence earth and sky fled away, and no place was found for them.*

> O Lord, how awesome are your attributes. We know that before you our every thought, word and deed will be brought to light. Thank you for being lovingly disposed toward all who call on your name; for your forgiveness of those who acknowledge their sin and who repent of it before you. Thank you for your invitation to leave a life of hiding from you, for we know the futility of trying to escape your gaze. Thank you for your word that speaks to us so clearly, and with such power that we cannot be honest with ourselves and say we did not hear it. We know that your relentless pursuit of us proceeds out of your great love for us. Keep seeing, and speaking and pursuing, Lord, we pray. Amen

The explicit theme in this first vision is the holy glory of Christ exalted. Yet the very persona of his being implicitly portrays several of his roles.

We have seen him in his attentive high priestly role. But this is no ordinary priest. We saw him as a judging priest, as he stood before all creation in glowing sovereignty. We cannot escape the imagery of impending judgment. The purpose here is to concentrate on this fearfully magnificent and ominously imposing portrait of Jesus. We do not want to be distracted from the Judge, by details of judgment, at this time. Let us focus hard on Christ, as revealed here.

I stated earlier that prophecy thrusts us full-force into a crucible of an unfamiliar encounter with God. If you have already felt it, you are in good company—that of men like John. In fact, if you haven't felt any sense of holy dread as you looked at this portrait, check your spiritual pulse to see if you have one. But before you let yourself be overtaken with apprehension, read on, for only by knowing the whole truth, our fear is turned to unspeakable joy.

Christ the Holder of the Keys

John certainly was filled with holy dread, at this point.

> *Revelation 1:17-18 (ESV)*
> *17 When I saw him, I fell at his feet as though dead. But he laid his right hand on me, saying, "Fear not, I am the first and the last, 18 and the living one. I died, and behold I am alive forevermore, and I have the keys of Death and Hades.*

Abruptly, the mood of the vision changes. This one who walks among the lampstands with greatest attentiveness, who frightens speechless with his imposing aspect, who troubles with impending judgment, this same Jesus with equally surprising contrast speaks tenderly to John. With words powerfully comforting, he nurtures his soul. First, He assures him he has nothing to fear from Him. *"Do not be afraid."* This was the first thing John needed to know. Nothing else was ahead of this. How could the demeanor of judgment be so easily drawn aside when he talked to His beloved apostle? It is because John was not one for whom the penalty of judgment was intended. The basis for this is found throughout scripture, and will be developed later. For now, we need only observe and know that the Christ of judgment said that John had nothing to fear from Him.

This experience of John thrusts us into a profound dilemma found in scripture, and perhaps in our hearts as well. One of the most often repeated phrases in the Bible is the admonition to *"fear not."* There are many things we are instructed not to fear. Some of those times it means not being afraid in God's presence, as it does here. On the other hand, another of the most often repeated phrases in the Bible is *"the fear of the Lord."* We are called to have a fear of the Lord.

Proverbs 9:10 (RSV)
[10] The fear of the LORD is the beginning of wisdom, and the knowledge of the Holy One is insight.

Acts 9:31 (ESV)
[31] So the church throughout all Judea and Galilee and Samaria had peace and was being built up. And walking in the fear of the Lord and in the comfort of the Holy Spirit, it multiplied.

The fully exposed holiness of God is said to be a terrifying encounter before which no mortal man can stand. The instinctive impulse of a soul confronted by holiness is terror. Like Ezekiel and Jeremiah, John didn't consult his doctrinal notes to decide how to react. It was automatic. Likewise, when we read these scriptures and meditate on God's glory, we may be tempted to close our Bible and divert our minds to more leisurely thoughts.

Are we called to fear God, or to not fear? Some may attempt to explain it away by diluting down the meaning of "fear." I submit that 'fear' in scripture means fear, plain and simple. The simple answer seems to be that yes, we certainly are to fear Him. When we do, we then allow Him to be the One to remove that fear. Remember again "'twas grace that taught my heart to fear, and grace my fears relieved." If there is anything we are gaining from this study, I hope it is that the glory of God is greater than we imagine it to be, and fear is the appropriate first reaction. We 'fear' Him because of his holiness. Our fear is relieved not by diminishing His holiness, but by Him alone saying "Do not be afraid." Because of His grace, we do not remain in fear. His grace relieves our fears.

The same tender overture is made today to all who call on the name of Jesus as Savior and Lord. Just as we are about to be consumed with dread, at this stunning vision and its implications of judgment, we are told "Do not be afraid." If you are troubled by the judgmental role of Christ, know that His anger and punishment is not aimed toward his followers.

1 Thessalonians 5:9-11 (NASB)
[9] For God has not destined us for wrath, but for obtaining salvation through our Lord Jesus Christ, [10] who died for us, so that whether we are awake or asleep, we will live together with Him. [11] Therefore encourage one another and build up one another, just as you also are doing.

We will investigate this in prophetic detail later. For now, let us simply look at the kind regard of Jesus toward us in the last moments before his arrest and crucifixion. Note the love he already feels toward those who believe in him, even future believers, and of which John himself recorded as he recounted Christ's prayer to the Father.

> *John 17:20-24 (NIV2011)*
> [20] *"My prayer is not for them* [the twelve apostles] *alone. I pray also for those who will believe in me through their message,* [21] *that all of them may be one, Father, just as you are in me and I am in you. May they also be in us so that the world may believe that you have sent me.* [22] *I have given them the glory that you gave me, that they may be one as we are one—* [23] *I in them and you in me—so that they may be brought to complete unity. Then the world will know that you sent me and have loved them even as you have loved me.* [24] *"Father, I want those you have given me to be with me where I am, and to see my glory, the glory you have given me because you loved me before the creation of the world.*

John is further comforted with the reminder that Jesus is eternal himself, and holds the keys to *death and Hades.* This identity leaves no doubt who it was speaking these powerful words. He was the one who was dead, but now was alive forever. No other identification was needed for John to recognize his risen Lord. John was himself a prisoner of Rome at the time these visions were given to him. He was in exile on an island called Patmos, where he, even at his very old age, performed hard labor in the rock quarries. Death probably seemed to loom near with regularity. Now Jesus tells him it is He, and He alone, who holds the keys to death. That message is also for us. From earth's perspective, death is the end. Jesus assures that from the perspective of God's view, it is not the end at all. Since He holds the keys, He decides the end, or abolishes it at His own choosing.

There we have it. Christ Jesus glorified. Christ asked the Father while he was in the flesh that his disciples might see his glory. It was during his prayer the night of his betrayal.

> *John 17:24 (NKJV)*
> [24] *Father, I desire that they also whom You gave Me may be with Me where I am, that they may behold My glory which You have given Me; for You loved Me before the foundation of the world.*

In a limited way, that request is granted in this vision given to us through John's vision. It was Jesus' passion. It should be ours as well, to see him and know him in every way possible. If we do not take in this vision, we, in a sense, are preventing Jesus from having his last stated earthly desire with us. Of course he was referring to us being in heaven with him, and seeing him in his glory. But if we will not take in this sneak preview of his glory offered in this life, what will we have to say for ourselves when we see his real glory in that day?

His Intimate Encounter

Imposing glory and endearing grace in this vision are set against a very strategic backdrop of personal, solitary confrontation. No Roman guards entered with John into this vision. There are no angels accompanying Jesus in it. There are no other believers looking on. It is just Jesus and John. Soon John will be shown great rolling panoramas, vast marching armies, unidentified creatures, and drama, drama, drama. But here, we first see him in intimate encounter with his glorified Lord. Others may have been physically near, but they were shut out from this engagement. True worship is always an intimate encounter. It may take place in a well-crowded worship service, but it is--it must be--a connection of an individual soul with his or her Lord. Jesus said it like this:

> *John 4:21-24 (NKJV)*
> *[21] Jesus said to her, "Woman, believe Me, the hour is coming when you will neither on this mountain, nor in Jerusalem, worship the Father. [22] You worship what you do not know; we know what we worship, for salvation is of the Jews. [23] But the hour is coming, and now is, when the true worshipers will worship the Father in spirit and truth; for the Father is seeking such to worship Him. [24] God is Spirit, and those who worship Him must worship in spirit and truth."*

And Jesus was quoting Isaiah in teaching his hearers that worship must be from the heart.

> *Mark 7:6 (ESV)*
> *[6] And he said to them, "Well did Isaiah prophesy of you hypocrites, as it is written, "'This people honors me with their lips, but their heart is far from me;*

Corporate worship done correctly is a shared and witnessed collection of worshippers, each having an intimate dialog with their God. The reception of the corporate appeal depends on the dominion of God within each individual heart.

We are temporarily finished with this first vision-portrait of Christ. Do not lay its concept or its content too far aside, for this portrait is the backdrop for what follows.

> Lord Jesus, you have given us a supreme gift. You have shown us your glory, in advance, this same glory that we will share with you. We stand between fright and longing as we survey your countenance. By your promise of grace towards us, we are made bold to embrace it.

Like Jacob of old, we wrestle with your self-revelation, trembling yet persisting, waiting to be blessed. Make this image of glory a benchmark for our hope, an applause for our faith and a spring of joy. Amen

6
A SECOND PORTRAIT OF CHRIST EXALTED

In Revelation's first vision of Christ, his glory exploded upon us like a bright light turned on in a dark place. It emanated from his very essence, our perception of his intrinsic characteristics of divine holiness and power. Knowing nothing more of him from the vision than simply to behold this awesome manifestation caused us to bow before him in worship. If that were all we had of him, it alone should compel us to honor him. Confronted with his holiness, our sinful selves should instinctively shrink back in shame. Encountering his power and absolute authority, our defenseless souls recoil in fear. Then when his hand of mercy assures us of his goodwill towards us, we were left in joyful exhilaration. In this we see his most magnanimous attribute—that of his merciful compassion. All that, just by being in his presence. We worshipped him in our minds because of who he is, and for the very essence of his character.

God on His Throne

In Revelation chapters 4 and 5 we encounter a second compelling vision. Again John was shown another out-of-this-world scene--the Heavenly Throne Room. We read...

> *Revelation 4:1-8 (ESV)*
> *¹ After this I looked, and behold, a door standing open in heaven! And the first voice, which I had heard speaking to me like a trumpet, said, "Come up here, and I will show you what must take place after this." ² At once I was in the Spirit, and behold, a throne stood in heaven, with one seated on the throne. ³ And he who sat there had the appearance of jasper and carnelian, and around the throne was a rainbow that had the appearance of an emerald. ⁴ Around the throne were twenty-four thrones, and seated on the thrones were twenty-four elders, clothed in white garments, with golden crowns on their heads. ⁵ From the throne came flashes of lightning, and rumblings and peals of thunder, and before the throne were burning seven torches of fire, which are the seven spirits of God, ⁶ and before the throne there was as it were a sea of glass, like crystal. And around the throne, on each side of the throne, are four living creatures, full of eyes in front and*

behind: *⁷ the first living creature like a lion, the second living creature like an ox, the third living creature with the face of a man, and the fourth living creature like an eagle in flight. ⁸ And the four living creatures, each of them with six wings, are full of eyes all around and within, and day and night they never cease to say, "Holy, holy, holy, is the Lord God Almighty, who was and is and is to come!"*

The description reads like a script for the ultimate special-effects film. We wonder how literally it is intended to be taken? It is intriguing that this vision is so similar to that described by the Old Testament prophet Ezekiel. In Revelation, the four creatures (created beings) are around the throne, and most of the descriptive text centers on them. In Ezekiel's prophecy, the four creatures are his first topic. He wrote:

Ezekiel 1:1-24 (NASB)
¹ Now it came about in the thirtieth year, on the fifth day of the fourth month, while I was by the river Chebar among the exiles, the heavens were opened and I saw visions of God. ² (On the fifth of the month in the fifth year of King Jehoiachin's exile, ³ the word of the LORD came expressly to Ezekiel the priest, son of Buzi, in the land of the Chaldeans by the river Chebar; and there the hand of the LORD came upon him.) ⁴ As I looked, behold, a storm wind was coming from the north, a great cloud with fire flashing forth continually and a bright light around it, and in its midst something like glowing metal in the midst of the fire. ⁵ Within it there were figures resembling four living beings. And this was their appearance: they had human form. ⁶ Each of them had four faces and four wings. ⁷ Their legs were straight and their feet were like a calf's hoof, and they gleamed like burnished bronze. ⁸ Under their wings on their four sides were human hands. As for the faces and wings of the four of them, ⁹ their wings touched one another; their faces did not turn when they moved, each went straight forward. ¹⁰ As for the form of their faces, each had the face of a man; all four had the face of a lion on the right and the face of a bull on the left, and all four had the face of an eagle. ¹¹ Such were their faces. Their wings were spread out above; each had two touching another being, and two covering their bodies. ¹² And each went straight forward; wherever the spirit was about to go, they would go, without turning as they went.¹³ In the midst of the living beings there was something that looked like burning coals of fire, like torches darting back and forth among the living beings. The fire was bright, and lightning was flashing from the fire. ¹⁴ And the living beings ran to and fro like bolts of lightning. ¹⁵ Now as I looked at the living beings, behold, there was one wheel on the earth beside the living beings, for each of the four of them. ¹⁶ The appearance of the wheels and their

workmanship was like sparkling beryl, and all four of them had the same form, their appearance and workmanship being as if one wheel were within another. [17] Whenever they moved, they moved in any of their four directions without turning as they moved. [18] As for their rims they were lofty and awesome, and the rims of all four of them were full of eyes round about. [19] Whenever the living beings moved, the wheels moved with them. And whenever the living beings rose from the earth, the wheels rose also. [20] Wherever the spirit was about to go, they would go in that direction. And the wheels rose close beside them; for the spirit of the living beings was in the wheels. [21] Whenever those went, these went; and whenever those stood still, these stood still. And whenever those rose from the earth, the wheels rose close beside them; for the spirit of the living beings was in the wheels. [22] Now over the heads of the living beings there was something like an expanse, like the awesome gleam of crystal, spread out over their heads. [23] Under the expanse their wings were stretched out straight, one toward the other; each one also had two wings covering its body on the one side and on the other. [24] I also heard the sound of their wings like the sound of abundant waters as they went, like the voice of the Almighty, a sound of tumult like the sound of an army camp; whenever they stood still, they dropped their wings.

Then at the sound overhead, Ezekiel raises his gaze and his field of vision takes in the throne and the one seated on it:

Ezekiel 1:25-28 (NASB)
[25] And there came a voice from above the expanse that was over their heads; whenever they stood still, they dropped their wings. [26] Now above the expanse that was over their heads there was something resembling a throne, like lapis lazuli in appearance; and on that which resembled a throne, high up, was a figure with the appearance of a man. [27] Then I noticed from the appearance of His loins and upward something like glowing metal that looked like fire all around within it, and from the appearance of His loins and downward I saw something like fire; and there was a radiance around Him. [28] As the appearance of the rainbow in the clouds on a rainy day, so was the appearance of the surrounding radiance. Such was the appearance of the likeness of the glory of the LORD. And when I saw it, I fell on my face and heard a voice speaking.

These two prophecies, although separated by nearly 700 years, portray virtually the same scene. We can say that this is the image of heaven's throne room and of God Himself that He wanted us to have. He wanted us to stand in awe of His own glory. Now we recognize that same powerful glory that we saw in Christ in the first vision. Different setting, same glory.

Lord God, here we are before you in your highest setting as angelic beings dart around the throne, carrying out your wishes. We look for a hiding place from which to watch at a distance. But there is no hiding place. We, like John, find our souls laid bare by your holiness. How we tremble before your throne. Yet strangely, we feel the security of your loving-kindness to us. Our hunger to know you draws us. Is that hunger really you. setting us upright and saying, "FEAR NOT?" Where else can this daring hunger originate? We know it is by your invitation that we are here. What further vision do you have for us, Father?

Heavenly Worship of the Father

What John saw and heard next exceeded the most genuine expressions of collective worship he had ever seen. He, with the other apostles, fell at Jesus' feet after his resurrection. He had stood with the others as Jesus ascended into the clouds of heaven, and they had all rejoiced and praised God. For 60 years John the apostle had evangelized and shepherded many churches with whom he shared daily devotion and corporate worship. But surely this was a pinnacle of worship experience.

> *Revelation 4:9-11 (ESV)*
> *⁹ And whenever the living creatures give glory and honor and thanks to him who is seated on the throne, who lives forever and ever, ¹⁰ the twenty-four elders fall down before him who is seated on the throne and worship him who lives forever and ever. They cast their crowns before the throne, saying, ¹¹ "Worthy are you, our Lord and God, to receive glory and honor and power, for you created all things, and by your will they existed and were created."*

The deluge of the surrounding splendor was drowned out by the unbridled voices and hearts of the elders and angelic beings. The sights were all-consuming. The sound was so powerful, we can imagine that the ground resonated beneath John's feet. Here in unveiled exposure shown the attributes of Him who sits on the throne--His glory, his power and his eternal existence. To stand in such presence and be unconsumed must have felt exhilarating. He was awed by the joy. He himself dared to feel joy, and to be caught up in the worship ecstasy.

Crisis of Faith

Seemingly almost as a result of that worship, the demeanor shifts, and the business at hand becomes a matter of grave and solemn purpose.

> *Revelation 5:1-4 (ESV)*
> *[1] Then I saw in the right hand of him who was seated on the throne a scroll written within and on the back, sealed with seven seals. [2] And I saw a mighty angel proclaiming with a loud voice, "Who is worthy to open the scroll and break its seals?" [3] And no one in heaven or on earth or under the earth was able to open the scroll or to look into it, [4] and I began to weep loudly because no one was found worthy to open the scroll or to look into it.*

As joyful as the worship of the Father had been, this scene turns equally emotional with bitter grief. John seems to understand the significance of the scroll. He recognizes the opening of the seals as the carrying out of God's plans, and the fulfillment of His purposes. Momentarily, it was as though God Himself was stalemated. Could it be that all God had done in creation, and in sustaining his people through the ages--His plans for redemption, conceived in eternity past--had been defeated? John wept bitterly.

Can we not honestly relate to John? Have we not each one entertained fears that our faith was in vain, that God was not who we thought He was, or that salvation was a daydream? In times of depression have there not been fleeting doubts, or maybe lingering fears? Was ever there a time when everything you held as absolute truth seemed to collapse and burn around you? Walk on with John.

Sovereign Solution

> *Revelation 5:5-6 (ESV)*
> *[5] And one of the elders said to me, "Weep no more; behold, the Lion of the tribe of Judah, the Root of David, has conquered, so that he can open the scroll and its seven seals." [6] And between the throne and the four living creatures and among the elders I saw a Lamb standing, as though it had been slain, with seven horns and with seven eyes, which are the seven spirits of God sent out into all the earth.*

The Slain Lamb Triumphant

John's vision was turned aside, perhaps buried in his arms as he sobbed. *Look* said one of the elders. He told John not to weep for the Lion of Judah had prevailed and was able to break the seals and open the scroll. John redirected his sight toward the throne, expecting to see a lion. What he saw was a lamb, bearing the outward markings of having been slain for sacrifice, yet living.

The Lamb was none other than John's Lord and Master, Jesus, although he doesn't identify him. His appearance was a shocking reminder of the sacrificial nature of his ministry. There was nothing pleasant about the atoning sacrificial procedure. It was a ghastly reminder of the seriousness of our sin. We, like John, want to flinch at the gruesome sight. Yet we are face-to-face with the whole truth of God. We take it in, realizing as if for the first time the price that was paid for our salvation. The vivid imagery thrusts the price of our redemption ever before us, lest we might at some time think of it trivially. The seven horns demonstrate the omnipotence of Christ. The seven eyes are understood to be represent his omniscience. The seven spirits of God are a reference to his omnipresent Holy Spirit.

In the first vision we were dazzled with the essential qualities of the glorified Christ. Now we are presented with an obligatory reason for adoring him--gratitude.

> *2 Corinthians 5:14 (NASB)*
> *[14] For the love of Christ controls us, having concluded this, that one died for all, therefore all died;*

We are here presented an exhibition of the ultimate in God's grace. This kind of grace obligates us to love Him. It obligates us to love Jesus even if we are not in his glorified presence. We still find ourselves in his indebtedness. In fact, even though it is this obligation of love that has captured most Christians; relatively few are as familiar with the glorified Jesus.

The sad fact is that the obligation is missed by many. Some tinker with it curiously, never being struck down by the gravity of its truth, nor responding appropriately to such an overt act of love. When this occurs, it is no less than to spurn the divine love, so graciously poured out to us. This realization highlights a spiritual principle that is found throughout scripture, but nowhere more strongly demonstrated than in Revelation. It is this: where the grace of God is most graciously offered, the penalty for rejecting it is the greater. Put another way...

> *Luke 12:47-48 (ESV)*
> *[47] And that servant who knew his master's will but did not get ready or act according to his will, will receive a severe beating. [48] But the one who did not know, and did what deserved a beating, will receive a light beating. Everyone to whom much was given, of him much will be required, and from him to whom they entrusted much, they will demand the more.*

As for us:

Matthew 13:16-17 (NASB)
¹⁶ "But blessed are your eyes, because they see; and your ears, because they hear. ¹⁷ "For truly I say to you that many prophets and righteous men desired to see what you see, and did not see it, and to hear what you hear, and did not hear it.

We in this age, with the completed scriptural record, have more opportunity and evidence than those of ages past. Thus in Revelation we have a final appeal. If anyone rejects it...

Revelation 22:11 (ESV)
¹¹ Let the evildoer still do evil, and the filthy still be filthy, and the righteous still do right, and the holy still be holy."

In other words, as Revelation closes, the Lord closes his appeal. All that can be said, has been said. No stronger persuasion than this can be made to reach the hard hearts of some. Hopefully the first vision will have served to soften a heart, making it vulnerable to this second one. This second vision is equally powerful, but its power lies in the manifested love of the Father and of His Son.

<u>Heavenly Worship of the Son</u>
How was this lamb received?

Revelation 5:7-14 (ESV)
⁷ And he went and took the scroll from the right hand of him who was seated on the throne. ⁸ And when he had taken the scroll, the four living creatures and the twenty-four elders fell down before the Lamb, each holding a harp, and golden bowls full of incense, which are the prayers of the saints. ⁹ And they sang a new song, saying, "Worthy are you to take the scroll and to open its seals, for you were slain, and by your blood you ransomed people for God from every tribe and language and people and nation, ¹⁰ and you have made them a kingdom and priests to our God, and they shall reign on the earth." ¹¹ Then I looked, and I heard around the throne and the living creatures and the elders the voice of many angels, numbering myriads of myriads and thousands of thousands, ¹² saying with a loud voice, "Worthy is the Lamb who was slain, to receive power and wealth and wisdom and might and honor and glory and blessing!" ¹³ And I heard every creature in heaven and on earth and under the earth and in the sea, and all that is in them, saying, "To him who sits on the throne and to the Lamb be blessing and honor and glory and might forever and ever!" ¹⁴ And the four living creatures said, "Amen!" and the elders fell down and worshiped.

"You are worthy!" they shouted. Of course the pre-incarnate Christ had always been worthy. He was God, after all. But now those who previously worshipped Him for his essential nature have a new verse of praise. They worship Him for what He has done in redemption. No wonder they are rejoicing. The euphoria of their celebration is appropriately poured out. To them, it is even more evident than to us, that this sacrificial death and its attending burial and resurrection are the pivotal historical episode in the entire history of mankind. The rise and fall of nations and kingdoms is tedious droning compared with this.

The Revelation of God's Eternal Purpose
The drama heightens in chapter 5 of Revelation. Here we are shown an innumerable crowd of people and every cognitive creature who has picked up the celebration.

> *Revelation 5:9 (ESV)*
> *⁹ And they sang a new song, saying, "Worthy are you to take the scroll and to open its seals, for you were slain, and by your blood you ransomed people for God from every tribe and language and people and nation,*

Not only are those worshipping who had previously worshipped his essential holiness and glory. "Every creature" is seen worshipping Christ. This is the goal that God has set for His Son. It certainly has not yet happened on earth. But a time will come when it will happen *on earth as it is in heaven.*

Listen and hear the words of the worshippers. Why are they pouring out their very souls in excited adoration? Because the slain lamb is "WORTHY." The theme of this worship is the worthiness of the lamb. Why was he worthy of such unrestrained praise? *". . . for you were slain, and by your blood you ransomed people for God from every tribe and language and people and nation. . ."* It is here in this very scene that we are shown the grand purpose of the redemptive plan, the grand purpose of all creation. The whole of biblical history and wisdom find their fulfillment right here. And this glorious scene, above all others, depicts the intended focus of this book you are reading. God's redemptive purpose is revealed right here! In this scene, God is gathering eternal worshippers from *every tribe and language and people and nation!* His attributes of mercy and grace could only be extolled by redeemed sinners. Angels could worship as awestruck spectators, but only recipients of extravagant grace could worship from the heart, a heart created in God's own image for this very day.

In this chapter, we learn that not only is Jesus worthy, but ONLY Jesus is worthy. No one else in heaven or earth was worthy, because no one else could fulfill the needs of redemption. No one else was able to open the scroll. Only Jesus was and is worthy. Righteousness is imputed to us on the basis of Christ's satisfactory payment for our sin. However, worthiness cannot be imputed. 'Worthy' means 'deserving.' No one is deserving of Christ's life in exchange for our own. And so we add our own voices to the chorus, *"Worthy is the Lamb, who was slain, to receive power and wealth and wisdom and strength and honor and glory and praise!"*

Notice that the song was one of praise, and there is no language directly expressing thanksgiving. That seems strange to us. Our first inclination might be toward gratitude. I have no doubt the hearts of those worshippers were filled to overflowing with gratitude. Yet the expressions are purely praise. Gratitude is an appropriate response to God's blessing, but it measures it in the context of one's own benefit. Perhaps if we could truly stand before the full glory of God, as these heavenly worshippers are, our focus would lift from ourselves and be so fully directed toward Him that nothing else—no other motivation—would find place in us. Then perhaps, we too would overflow with unmixed praise.

What song did they sing? They sang a "new song." This phrase is used nine times in the Old and New Testaments, and carries a strong reference to God's mighty power to save. The psalmists saw a song of redemption being sung that would be new and different.

> *Psalm 96:1-4 (NKJV)*
> *¹ Oh, sing to the LORD a new song! Sing to the LORD, all the earth.*
> *² Sing to the LORD, bless His name; Proclaim the good news of His salvation from day to day. ³ Declare His glory among the nations, His wonders among all peoples. ⁴ For the LORD is great and greatly to be praised; He is to be feared above all gods.*

The psalmist did not know the words of that new song, but he looked for a novel theme. From our perspective on this side of the cross, we see how the sacrificial death and resurrection of Jesus was that new and pivotal theme for a song of redemption. Paul said it this way,

> *2 Corinthians 5:17 (NASB)*
> *¹⁷ Therefore if anyone is in Christ, he is a new creature; the old things passed away; behold, new things have come.*

The lamb, Jesus, is worthy of the highest praise because he literally bought your life with his blood, and with his very life. This was not just a symbolic connection between Jesus' death and your salvation. It is a real, genuine, directly-dependent umbilical between you and eternity. It was not only a demonstration of God's love for you. It is the execution of it on your behalf, and at great cost to Himself. Do you see how great is the love that the Father has exercised for you? Do you see the rebuff that is made to His grace by all who do not embrace, with all their soul, this offering of love? How many times will a groom propose marriage?

Universal Worship of Jesus

In the scene we just considered, we saw the courts of heaven praising Jesus because of his redemption of people from every nation. Shortly thereafter we are presented another vision scene--that of the very redeemed themselves. They are those from every nation, every people group, every language, from the distant past, right up to the end. They are gathered in ecstatic worship of God, and of the lamb!

> *Revelation 7:9-12 (ESV)*
> *⁹ After this I looked, and behold, a great multitude that no one could number, from every nation, from all tribes and peoples and languages, standing before the throne and before the Lamb, clothed in white robes, with palm branches in their hands, ¹⁰ and crying out with a loud voice, "Salvation belongs to our God who sits on the throne, and to the Lamb!" ¹¹ And all the angels were standing around the throne and around the elders and the four living creatures, and they fell on their faces before the throne and worshiped God, ¹² saying, "Amen! Blessing and glory and wisdom and thanksgiving and honor and power and might be to our God forever and ever! Amen."*

Note they don't just say words or sing songs. They 'cry out in a loud voice' the praises of their redeemer. Imagine the roar of all those voices in unison. At this sound, even the angelic beings fell facedown before the throne of God. Truly this is the grand fulfillment of the grand purpose of the ages. This will inaugurate eternal worship. It was toward this that all history paraded. In this, men and women will join all creation to find their most excellent fulfillment. They will realize it was for this that they were created, and to experience it will be ecstatic joy and satisfaction of the highest order!!

To more fully appreciate the fulfilling nature of this scene, we look very briefly at the big picture of the redemptive initiative of God from the very beginning. He revealed it to Adam and Eve in the curse.

> *Genesis 3:14-15 (RSV)*
> *¹⁴ The LORD God said to the serpent, "Because you have done this, cursed are you above all cattle, and above all wild animals; upon your belly you shall go, and dust you shall eat all the days of your life. ¹⁵ I will put enmity between you and the woman, and between your seed and her seed; he shall bruise your head, and you shall bruise his heel."*

This is the first mention of the redemptive purpose of God in scripture. It is also the first mention of the spiritual conflict with which we would have to contend. Much later, God spoke to Abraham, and made a covenant with him.

> *Genesis 28:14 (NCV)*
> *14 Your descendants will be as many as the dust of the earth. They will spread west and east, north and south, and all the families of the earth will be blessed through you and your descendants.*

This blessing was not just a prediction. It was God's purpose being revealed. It was much more than descendants and land for Israel. It was the promise that all nations would be blessed through Abraham's seed. Jesus is that seed. When Jesus gave his departing instructions to his disciples he said . . .

> *Matthew 28:19-20 (NASB)*
> *19 "Go therefore and make disciples of all the nations, baptizing them in the name of the Father and the Son and the Holy Spirit, 20 teaching them to observe all that I commanded you; and lo, I am with you always, even to the end of the age."*

Worship from all nations is clearly in view from the start, and is traceable throughout both old and new testaments. These few serve to show continuity of purpose in the revealed plans of God. And now we are shown this tremendous glimpse of fulfillment.

<u>Unending Praise</u>
This adoration before the throne is just the beginning. It continues throughout eternity. It recurs many times throughout the book of Revelation.

> *Revelation 11:15-18 (ESV)*
> *15 Then the seventh angel blew his trumpet, and there were loud voices in heaven, saying, "The kingdom of the world has become the kingdom of our Lord and of his Christ, and he shall reign forever and ever." 16 And the twenty-four elders who sit on their thrones before God fell on their faces and worshiped God, 17 saying, "We give thanks to you, Lord God Almighty, who is and who was, for you have taken your great power and begun to reign. 18 The nations raged, but your wrath came, and the time for the dead to be judged, and for rewarding your servants, the prophets and saints, and those who fear your name, both small and great, and for destroying the destroyers of the earth."*

Revelation 14:2-3 (ESV)
² And I heard a voice from heaven like the roar of many waters and like the sound of loud thunder. The voice I heard was like the sound of harpists playing on their harps, ³ and they were singing a new song before the throne and before the four living creatures and before the elders. No one could learn that song except the 144,000 who had been redeemed from the earth.

Revelation 15:2-4 (ESV)
² And I saw what appeared to be a sea of glass mingled with fire—and also those who had conquered the beast and its image and the number of its name, standing beside the sea of glass with harps of God in their hands. ³ And they sing the song of Moses, the servant of God, and the song of the Lamb, saying, "Great and amazing are your deeds, O Lord God the Almighty! Just and true are your ways, O King of the nations! ⁴ Who will not fear, O Lord, and glorify your name? For you alone are holy. All nations will come and worship you, for your righteous acts have been revealed."

Revelation 19:1-6 (ESV)
¹ After this I heard what seemed to be the loud voice of a great multitude in heaven, crying out, "Hallelujah! Salvation and glory and power belong to our God, ² for his judgments are true and just; for he has judged the great prostitute who corrupted the earth with her immorality, and has avenged on her the blood of his servants." ³ Once more they cried out, "Hallelujah! The smoke from her goes up forever and ever." ⁴ And the twenty-four elders and the four living creatures fell down and worshiped God who was seated on the throne, saying, "Amen. Hallelujah!" ⁵ And from the throne came a voice saying, "Praise our God, all you his servants, you who fear him, small and great." ⁶ Then I heard what seemed to be the voice of a great multitude, like the roar of many waters and like the sound of mighty peals of thunder, crying out, "Hallelujah! For the Lord our God the Almighty reigns.

The Grand Finale

In this creation-wide worship, Jesus is receiving what is due him. Paul describes this victorious occasion in his letter to the Philippians:

Philippians 2:9-11 (ESV)
⁹ Therefore God has highly exalted him and bestowed on him the name that is above every name, ¹⁰ so that at the name of Jesus every knee should bow, in heaven and on earth and under the earth, ¹¹ and every tongue confess that Jesus Christ is Lord, to the glory of God the Father.

Christ exalted! Eternal kingdom fulfilled! God is glorified! But wait, there is more. We find one more major event in completing the fulfillment of the redemptive process. One last, grand finale. Jesus, the name above all names, defers to the Father.

> *1 Corinthians 15:24,28 (NKJV)*
> *²⁴ Then comes the end, when He delivers the kingdom to God the Father, when He puts an end to all rule and all authority and power. . . ²⁸ Now when all things are made subject to Him, then the Son Himself will also be subject to Him who put all things under Him, that God may be all in all.*

Jesus will present his secure kingdom to the Father. He will resume his place in the Godhead that he had always had. He does this without reservation, but joyfully. In my career I have participated in a number of corporate transitions, from restructure to new ownership. It is always a difficult time. Experienced, reputable people are replaced and eliminated. Layoffs occur. Some employees will bail out on their own initiative. It is never seamless, no matter how ingratiating the new management tries to make it. It won't be like that when the Son passes the role of ultimate authority over creation to the Father. With unity and in one accord, the Trinity will complete the transition amidst divine and angelic joy.

The Two Faces of Christ

In these two visions, we have portrayed two essential characteristics of the glorified Jesus, who is the exact image of the Father. We saw him in splendid eternal holiness, ready for judgment against the unholiness of the creation. In His holiness, judgment is an essential, for perfect holiness must not compromise, or its perfection is corrupted. This is the dilemma with which Satan thought to destroy the paradise of God by the introduction of sin.

Second, we saw his sacrificial grace. It was this grace that exceeds logic that overcame the dilemma of sin. The grace of God should be the sweetest, most welcome blessing conceivable in the mind of man. That God made a way for me when I could not, is the most hopeful message in the world.

It is strange, but both of these components of God are often rejected by men. Many reject the concept of a God who would not accept everyone into heaven. On the other hand, there are many 'religious' people who reject God's grace, because their pride will not allow them to consider themselves unworthy of being in God's presence. How naïve. Instead, men design God to their own liking, one that suits their lifestyle. This is no different than one who sits and carves an idol. He too seeks to make a god who will accommodate his own wishes. Sin promotes these excuses, so that a person will not think long enough about his condition to sense the condemnation, and then receive the gracious gift of salvation at the hand of Jesus. If these visions have not spoken loudly enough, what more can be said? There is no apology or softening of the truths we have seen. This is Jesus Christ, the one who lives eternally with the Father. Those who the Spirit of God will call, will reach for these attributes of Jesus, embracing them joyfully. Those who are at odds with God will be offended by these visions.

There are many other glorious visions of Christ in the book of Revelation, and we shall explore them going forward in this book. However the dichotomy shown in these first two visions serves to highlight the characteristics of God, which Satan tries to attack in the heavenly conflict which is now being battled out on earth. It is this war that we engage in daily. God wonderfully reveals Himself to us as our trailblazer and our assurance of victory through this war zone.

> Dear Lord, many have loved you from having known the Jesus of the gospels. But now you have also given us another vision of him. We have seen him in glory. May these visions cause this reader to stand face-to-face with you, and having done so, to rightly scrutinize more than before his need of your grace. Superlatives fail us as we attempt to respond to these great visions. May our superlative simply be the obedience of a wholly consecrated life. May we embrace you in your holiness and in your love. We want to know you--all of you. Amen

PART 3
REDEMPTION PROPHESIED

7
ATONEMENT PROPHESIED

In the last section we saw the two faces of God as revealed in His glorified Son. One is perfect holiness, uncompromised. The other is grace, unrestrained. John spoke of Jesus as being *full of grace and truth*. These two facets of Jesus reflect characteristics of the Father. These two attributes of God are central themes in scripture. We are called to recognize God as being both. We see these demonstrated over and over again in Old Testament stories, and we see them thrust into the limelight in the New Testament.

We even see them symbolized. For example, the ancient city of Jerusalem was built on two mountains. That is, two mountain ranges run parallel through the city. One is called Zion, the other Moriah. Just about everything inside the city walls was on one or the other of these two mountains. Zion was where the king's palace and other government buildings were located. It was the sovereign mountain, the mountain of political authority. Moriah was where the temple was located; it was the mountain of God's grace. Often in scripture the name Zion is used as a synonym for Jerusalem, and always with an exalted view of her supremacy. The city of God symbolizes the characteristics of God in this way.

These two attributes are often seemingly conflicting concepts. In the mind of man, these attributes appear to be contradictory, but in God, they are perfectly harmonized. The apparent conflict is not within God Himself, but in his dealing with sinful mankind. The two attributes are synchronized, with regard to God's dealing with man, in a scheme invented by God which we call 'atonement.' To probe into the doctrine of atonement may, at first glance, seem somewhat removed from the subject of biblical prophecy, but in fact, it is the very focus of the whole prophetic agenda.

The Conflict

In the epic stage play Camelot, 'sin' is exposed in the royal family. The accusation is made by an illegitimate step son. The idealistic justice of Camelot is thrust into direct conflict with Arthur's love for Guinevere, his wife and queen. Justice versus love. Truth against compassion. By this conflict, the kingdom is shaken from its utopian foundation, and divided in civil war. Finally, at the last moment, Sir Lancelot arrives to rescue Queen

Guinevere. Like the step son, Satan seeks to destroy the heavenly kingdom, planned by the Father for eternity, by putting the holiness of God in conflict with His love toward His creation. He does this over the issue of sin by accusing us before God. Satan is portrayed as the accuser many places in scripture. For example, notice these passages from both the Old and New Testaments.

> *Job 1:9-11 (NKJV)*
> *⁹ So Satan answered the LORD and said, "Does Job fear God for nothing? ¹⁰ Have You not made a hedge around him, around his household, and around all that he has on every side? You have blessed the work of his hands, and his possessions have increased in the land. ¹¹ But now, stretch out Your hand and touch all that he has, and he will surely curse You to Your face!"*

> *Zechariah 3:1 (RSV)*
> *¹ Then he showed me Joshua the high priest standing before the angel of the LORD, and Satan standing at his right hand to accuse him.*

> *Revelation 12:10 (ESV)*
> *¹⁰ . . . for the accuser of our brothers has been thrown down, who accuses them day and night before our God.*

In the gospels we see the adversaries of Jesus constantly trying to trap him into having to choose one or the other of these attributes and abandon the other, either to choose truth and abandon grace, or choose grace and abandon truth. Consider this example:

> *Mark 3:1-6 (ESV)*
> *¹ Again he entered the synagogue, and a man was there with a withered hand. ² And they watched Jesus, to see whether he would heal him on the Sabbath, so that they might accuse him. ³ And he said to the man with the withered hand, "Come here." ⁴ And he said to them, "Is it lawful on the Sabbath to do good or to do harm, to save life or to kill?" But they were silent. ⁵ And he looked around at them with anger, grieved at their hardness of heart, and said to the man, "Stretch out your hand." He stretched it out, and his hand was restored. ⁶ The Pharisees went out and immediately held counsel with the Herodians against him, how to destroy him.*

The religious leaders knew Jesus was a man of compassion, and would be hard-pressed to overlook a needy person. It was the Sabbath. Could they get Jesus to break the Sabbath traditions, and thus find reason in their own pathetic hearts to accuse him as being evil? Consider another example:

John 8:2-11 (NKJV)
² Now early in the morning He came again into the temple, and all the people came to Him; and He sat down and taught them. ³ Then the scribes and Pharisees brought to Him a woman caught in adultery. And when they had set her in the midst, ⁴ they said to Him, "Teacher, this woman was caught in adultery, in the very act. ⁵ Now Moses, in the law, commanded us that such should be stoned. But what do You say?" ⁶ This they said, testing Him, that they might have something of which to accuse Him. But Jesus stooped down and wrote on the ground with His finger, as though He did not hear. ⁷ So when they continued asking Him, He raised Himself up and said to them, "He who is without sin among you, let him throw a stone at her first." ⁸ And again He stooped down and wrote on the ground. ⁹ Then those who heard it, being convicted by their conscience, went out one by one, beginning with the oldest even to the last. And Jesus was left alone, and the woman standing in the midst. ¹⁰ When Jesus had raised Himself up and saw no one but the woman, He said to her, "Woman, where are those accusers of yours? Has no one condemned you?" ¹¹ She said, "No one, Lord." And Jesus said to her, "Neither do I condemn you; go and sin no more."

Would Jesus deny the Mosaic Law and show mercy, or would he deny mercy and hold to the truth of the Old Testament scriptures? The religious leaders thought to create an impossible dilemma for Jesus, but he responded in a way that both exposed their illicit motives, and elevated the character of God who offers mercy and grace without compromising His own holiness.

Through atonement, God's holiness and His lovingkindness toward sinful mankind are perfectly reconciled. Perhaps this satisfying of both facets of the Lord's being was in the mind of the psalmist as he prophetically peered into the future . . .

Psalm 85:10 (NKJV)
¹⁰ Mercy and truth have met together; Righteousness and peace have kissed.

Truth and *righteousness* represent that side of God that is holy and perfectly just, prepared for judgment, and which tends toward fear in our relationship with Him. They are the Zion of God. *Mercy* and *peace* present a loving God who is approachable, and encourages intimacy. The God of Moriah. The psalmist envisioned a time when they were seen perfectly reconciled on earth. Yet the mechanism of this reconciliation did not appear until hundreds of years later.

Whenever we sin, we recreate this dilemma. It sets up a scenario which tries to pit God's love and grace against His holiness and righteousness, and the blood of Jesus must resolve the dilemma once again and rescue us from the consequences of it. This is the Christian's motivation to live a life of righteousness.

When Jesus came bodily to live among us, he came for the purpose of reconciling us with our God. He came to harmonize God's grace with His truth in regard to our hopeless, helpless condition. We will return to this conflict shortly, but first, let's consider the first advent of Jesus--his atoning work--as it was foretold in Old Testament prophecy.

Original Sin, Curse, and Redemption Initiated

In the garden, after Adam and Eve allowed Satan to seduce them into disobedience, God pronounced a curse on the creation. A curse is a predestination of dissipation and destruction. He pronounced that they would not live forever in their sinful state. Yet even while he pronounced the curse, God revealed His plan of redemption. He first revealed the conflict. As part of that curse, God told the serpent-embodied Satan:

> *Genesis 3:15 (NKJV)*
> *[15] And I will put enmity Between you and the woman, And between your seed and her Seed; He shall bruise your head, And you shall bruise His heel."*

In the New Testament Paul makes reference to this passage and adds his explanation in his letter to the Galatians:

> *Galatians 3:16 (NKJV)*
> *[16] Now to Abraham and his Seed were the promises made. He does not say, "And to seeds," as of many, but as of one, "And to your Seed," who is Christ.*

So we see that the plan of redemption in the *seed* was introduced way back in Genesis 3. It originated in the mind of God long before this, as seen in other passages such as this one.

> *Revelation 13:8 (ESV)*
> *[8] . . . everyone whose name has not been written before the foundation of the world in the book of life of the Lamb who was slain.*

A Messianic Lineage Prophesied

A number of books have been written claiming to have uncovered some divinely-originated hidden pattern or code in scriptural text. This is not new, but has proliferated with the use of computers to do the searching.

The authors claim that certain secret messages lurk behind the obvious meaning of scripture. I believe this mentality flies in the face of what scripture is declared to be—a revelation of God to His people.

There are some things in scripture, however, that are somewhat obscure if viewed from a microscopic perspective. They are only known to us when we take a comprehensive view of scripture, seeing passages in the context of the big picture. Thus they are somewhat like a code to us until we begin to grasp that overall purpose of the Bible. Understanding God's purpose for the ages allows us to crack open that code. Looking back from a New Testament perspective, allows us to gain that perspective.

Such is the doctrine of the messianic lineage. We may find it hard to get excited about genealogies in the Bible. Yet when we understand their significant purpose in the plan of redemption, they can become interesting and even a bit fascinating. Don't worry; we won't look into them microscopically, but we do need to gain a general appreciation for them. The curse of Genesis 3:15 includes a prophetic statement about the *seed* of the woman. As God pronounced the curse, this God who knows *the end from the beginning* for all things, tells a very important and foundational truth. He tells of the seed of Eve who would be the ultimate victor, and that the serpent would be destroyed by him. Paul identifies the seed as Jesus, the seed of Eve, the one we know as the *Son of Man*. God already had his plan of redemption in mind when Adam and Eve fell from innocence. He already knew it would involve conflict between His Son and Satan. Paul referred to this Genesis passage and its predicted conflict in his Roman letter:

Romans 16:20 (RSV)
[20] *then the God of peace will soon crush Satan under your feet . . .*

The Genesis 3:15 and Galatians 3:16 passages demonstrate God's intended direct connection between Adam and Jesus. There were many generations between Adam and Jesus, and many, many offspring in each generation. However, there was only one direct genealogical line between Adam and Jesus and that genealogy is called by Bible students the 'messianic lineage.' In the messianic lineage we see God's plan of redemption. In this lineage we learn about God himself. We see Him as sovereign over both the redemptive big picture, and over the details. Amazing!

At certain points, we see this messianic lineage further confined. For example, as Jacob pronounced his blessing on each of his twelve sons, he spoke with a spirit of prophecy. In his blessing, he narrowed the messianic lineage to a specific branch on the family tree.

> *Genesis 49:10 (RSV)*
> [10] *The scepter shall not depart from Judah, nor the ruler's staff from between his feet, until he comes to whom it belongs; and to him shall be the obedience of the peoples.*

This messianic lineage is evident many places in the Old Testament, but its prominence as a major theme is illuminated greatly by the New Testament writers. For example, the genealogies of Matthew 1 and Luke 3 trace the connecting generations through specific people. Now that Messiah had come, the genealogies gave evidence that Jesus was in the valid lineage. Then in Paul's letter to the Romans, he refers back to the days of the patriarchs:

> *Romans 9:8-11 (ESV)*
> [8] *This means that it is not the children of the flesh who are the children of God, but the children of the promise are counted as offspring.* [9] *For this is what the promise said: "About this time next year I will return, and Sarah shall have a son."* [10] *And not only so, but also when Rebekah had conceived children by one man, our forefather Isaac,* [11] *though they were not yet born and had done nothing either good or bad—in order that God's purpose of election might continue, not because of works but because of him who calls—*

Abraham had two sons, Ishmael and Isaac. Isaac was God's chosen link in the lineage. Isaac had twin sons, Esau and Jacob. Paul points out that God specifically identified Jacob as the son of promise. In both cases, the younger son was God's choice, contrary to the prevailing custom of that day in which the first son was prominent. Thus, his purpose in election was made clear in the messianic lineage. Thus the boundaries of the lineage were repeatedly confined.

David, the youngest among twelve sons, was in that lineage, and through the providence of God, became king in Israel. Later, while David ruled as king in Israel, God revealed to him through Nathan the prophet a further narrowing of the lineage.

> *2 Samuel 7:4-5, 15-17 (ESV)*
> [4] *But that same night the word of the LORD came to Nathan,* [5] *"Go and tell my servant David, 'Thus says the LORD: Would you build me a house to dwell in?. . .* [15] *but my steadfast love will not depart from him, as I took it from Saul, whom I put away from before you.* [16] *And your house and your kingdom shall be made sure forever before me. Your throne shall be established forever.'"* [17] *In accordance with all these words, and in accordance with all this vision, Nathan spoke to David.*

So the lineage was focused on the lineage of David, and was firmly established, being spoken by Nathan.

The lineages of both Joseph and Mary are given in the gospels. Both lineages were from the tribe of Judah. This prominence given to the messianic lineage of prophecy, shows that there is significance in it, and a message for us.

This lineage of promise has been a target of Satan throughout biblical history. This will be discussed in a little more detail in chapter 10. In short, Satan has attempted many times, throughout history, to either destroy the Jewish race, or to destroy the messianic branch. In many cases, he came very close, but always God preserved this lineage. In fact, the preservation of this lineage is so central in Old Testament purpose that it significantly helps explain many of the historical events, and why they are included in scripture.

Sacrifice

While it is true that Paul and the New Testament saints understood that the *seed* of Genesis 3:15 was Jesus, no such clear understanding was evident to Adam and those that followed him in Old Testament times. Yet, to Adam and his sons, a special practice having a veiled representation of Jesus, was given; a representation that carried a prophetic message. It was the practice of animal sacrifice.

Both Cain and Abel presented a sacrifice to God. A sacrificial offering was an offering that cost something of the worshipper. Both an animal sacrifice and a grain sacrifice were offered, according to each man's vocation. Later on, under the Law given to Moses, Jews continued to bring both kinds of sacrifices to the altar. Offerings of produce, such as grain, were primarily to express thanksgiving for God's continued blessing, or to celebrate their special fellowship with God. Animal sacrifices accompanied prayers of repentance, and were offered as an appeasement for the sins of the people.

<u>Animal Sacrifice</u>
Animal sacrifices were offered from earliest times. Abel offered an animal sacrifice in Genesis 4:

Genesis 4:4 (RSV)
⁴ and Abel brought of the firstlings of his flock and of their fat portions. And the LORD had regard for Abel and his offering,

How did Abel know to do this? No doubt he learned it from Adam and Eve. Where did they learn it? They learned it firsthand from God.

> *Genesis 3:7,21 (RSV)*
> *⁷ Then the eyes of both were opened, and they knew that they were naked; and they sewed fig leaves together and made themselves aprons. . . ²¹ And the LORD God made for Adam and for his wife garments of skins, and clothed them.*

God Himself performed the first animal sacrifice to cover their sinful nature. They saw and understood that the innocent animal had died the world's first death for their sin. So this they learned to do. This practice was passed down to successive generations.

As time went on, men began to abandon their knowledge of the Almighty God known to Adam. Instead, they worshipped false gods or inferior representations of God, fashioned as idols. This led to a perversion of sacrificial worship. Their view of God became so corrupted that some tribes practiced child sacrifice.

It was out of such an idolatrous culture that God called Abraham to separate himself. Thus, the Hebrew people had their beginning. Abraham offered sacrifices in his worship of God. His son and grandson did the same. Much later, Moses led the enslaved Hebrews out of Egypt, and they were given the Law. In the expanded details of the Law provided by Yahweh God, lengthy and specific details about animal sacrifices were commanded, such as these:

> *Leviticus 4:23-26 (ESV)*
> *²³ or the sin which he has committed is made known to him, he shall bring as his offering a goat, a male without blemish, ²⁴ and shall lay his hand on the head of the goat and kill it in the place where they kill the burnt offering before the LORD; it is a sin offering. ²⁵ Then the priest shall take some of the blood of the sin offering with his finger and put it on the horns of the altar of burnt offering and pour out the rest of its blood at the base of the altar of burnt offering. ²⁶ And all its fat he shall burn on the altar, like the fat of the sacrifice of peace offerings. So the priest shall make atonement for him for his sin, and he shall be forgiven.*

> *Leviticus 14:19-20 (ESV)*
> *¹⁹ The priest shall offer the sin offering, to make atonement for him who is to be cleansed from his uncleanness. And afterward he shall kill the burnt offering. ²⁰ And the priest shall offer the burnt offering and the grain offering on the altar. Thus the priest shall make atonement for him, and he shall be clean.*

Sacrifices continued and eventually were allocated to the tabernacle and later to the Jerusalem temple after it was built. That site then became the only legitimate location at which the Jewish ritual sacrifices could be made. Today, national Israel is back in their homeland, but they do not possess the plot of land where the temple must be built. It is occupied by the Islamic mosque called 'the Dome of the Rock.' Therefore, they are not currently able to practice their system of temple worship.

Substitution
What is an animal sacrifice? Why did their worship include such a gruesome practice? One reason was to teach God'ss people the seriousness of their sins. Although we do not practice animal sacrifice today, we are given this same message through our understanding of the historical context. The animal was slaughtered right before the eyes of the worshipper, then offered as a burnt offering. I believe if I were to observe the trauma of the animal, it would be a vivid reminder that it was for my sin this animal had to die. Being that close to death would cause me to consider how serious my sin was before holy God.

An even more stark realization would have been knowing that the death being witnessed should have been mine. The animal was a substitute for the person bringing the sacrifice. The penitent person recognized that he was guilty of sin before God. He also recognized that the sacrificial animal was innocent of that sin. His sin was seen as being transferred to the animal, while he, himself, was cleansed. By his carrying out of the sacrifice, he was confessing that he deserved to die as that animal died. The idea of substitution is intrinsic to the concept of atonement as understood by both Old Testament Jews and New Testament saints.

An Acceptable Sacrifice, Prophesied

The writer of Hebrews points out that the blood of bulls and goats, offered in sacrifice, had no cleansing power.

> *Hebrews 10:1-4 (ESV)*
> *¹ For since the law has but a shadow of the good things to come instead of the true form of these realities, it can never, by the same sacrifices that are continually offered every year, make perfect those who draw near. ² Otherwise, would they not have ceased to be offered, since the worshipers, having once been cleansed, would no longer have any consciousness of sins? ³ But in these sacrifices there is a reminder of sins every year. ⁴ For it is impossible for the blood of bulls and goats to take away sins.*

So why were they offered? God commanded their offering in Old Testament times as a symbol. When the Jews obeyed His command, He pardoned them on the basis of two facts: a) their faith, as demonstrated in heartfelt obedience, and b) a pardon of a different kind, which they were unknowingly symbolizing in their practice of animal sacrifice. This 'different' sacrifice was unknown to them because historically it had not occurred yet. It was introduced much later. When John the Baptist announced the presence of Jesus, centuries later, he spoke of him this way:

John 1:29 (NKJV)
[29] The next day John saw Jesus coming toward him, and said, "Behold! The Lamb of God who takes away the sin of the world!

When Jesus died on the cross, he became the acceptable substitutionary sacrifice for the sins of the whole world--for whoever would respond to him in true faith. This connection was recognized by New Testament saints after Jesus' death and resurrection, and they wrote and spoke about it:

1 Peter 1:18-19 (ESV)
[18] knowing that you were ransomed from the futile ways inherited from your forefathers, not with perishable things such as silver or gold, [19] but with the precious blood of Christ, like that of a lamb without blemish or spot.

Hebrews 9:13-14 (ESV)
[13] For if the blood of goats and bulls, and the sprinkling of defiled persons with the ashes of a heifer, sanctify for the purification of the flesh, [14] how much more will the blood of Christ, who through the eternal Spirit offered himself without blemish to God, purify our conscience from dead works to serve the living God.

The Hebrews writer also quotes from an Old Testament prophet's portrayal of a conversation between the Father and the Son, as the Son is preparing to enter the mainstream of humanity at his first coming. His sacrificial mission is in clear view:

Hebrews 10:3-5 (ESV)
[3] But in these sacrifices there is a reminder of sins every year. [4] For it is impossible for the blood of bulls and goats to take away sins. [5] Consequently, when Christ came into the world, he said, "Sacrifices and offerings you have not desired, but a body have you prepared for me;

Revelation 5:9 (ESV)
[9] And they sang a new song, saying, "Worthy are you to take the scroll and to open its seals, for you were slain, and by your blood you ransomed people for God from every tribe and language and people and nation,

After his resurrection, Jesus spoke to two of his disciples, as he built up their faith.

> *Luke 24:25-27 (ESV)*
> *²⁵ And he said to them, "O foolish ones, and slow of heart to believe all that the prophets have spoken! ²⁶ Was it not necessary that the Christ should suffer these things and enter into his glory?" ²⁷ And beginning with Moses and all the Prophets, he interpreted to them in all the Scriptures the things concerning himself.*

And later that same day, with the apostles, in an upper room . . .

> *Luke 24:44-45 (ESV)*
> *⁴⁴ Then he said to them, "These are my words that I spoke to you while I was still with you, that everything written about me in the Law of Moses and the Prophets and the Psalms must be fulfilled." ⁴⁵ Then he opened their minds to understand the Scriptures,*

According to Jesus' own words, his atoning death was prophesied by 1) the Law of Moses, 2) the prophets, and 3) the psalms. The Old Testament Scripture points to it from every direction.

Jesus in the Law of Moses

How did the Law foretell of Jesus? The 'Law of Moses' in its broad sense may be taken to refer to the entire group of Moses writings known as the Torah or Pentateuch, that is, the biblical books of Genesis, Exodus, Leviticus, Numbers and Deuteronomy. With this broad view, we understand that the *Law* embodied much more than just the rules of the commandments. It embodied the very initiating elements of God's revelation of Himself to mankind. As we proceed through the narrative, we encounter many such elements. Following are a few notable examples of narrated events that were prophetic of Jesus.

In the early days of Abraham's dwelling in the promised land, after God had revealed His promises to Abraham, we read this:

> *Genesis 15:6-18 (ESV)*
> *⁶ And he believed the LORD, and he counted it to him as righteousness. ⁷ And he said to him, "I am the LORD who brought you out from Ur of the Chaldeans to give you this land to possess." ⁸ But he said, "O Lord GOD, how am I to know that I shall possess it?" ⁹ He said to him, "Bring me a heifer three years old, a female goat three years old, a ram three years old, a turtledove, and a young pigeon." ¹⁰ And he brought him all these, cut them in half, and laid each half over against the other. But he did not cut the birds in half.*

¹¹ And when birds of prey came down on the carcasses, Abram drove them away. ¹² As the sun was going down, a deep sleep fell on Abram. And behold, dreadful and great darkness fell upon him. ¹³ Then the LORD said to Abram, "Know for certain that your offspring will be sojourners in a land that is not theirs and will be servants there, and they will be afflicted for four hundred years. ¹⁴ But I will bring judgment on the nation that they serve, and afterward they shall come out with great possessions. ¹⁵ As for you, you shall go to your fathers in peace; you shall be buried in a good old age. ¹⁶ And they shall come back here in the fourth generation, for the iniquity of the Amorites is not yet complete." ¹⁷ When the sun had gone down and it was dark, behold, a smoking fire pot and a flaming torch passed between these pieces.¹⁸ On that day the LORD made a covenant with Abram, saying, "To your offspring I give this land, from the river of Egypt to the great river, the river Euphrates,

In ancient times in this region, two people would make a covenant in this way. After they had agreed upon terms, they would separate halves of an animal and both parties would walk between the carcass halves. They were each saying, 'If I violate the terms of this oath, then I offer my very life as surety.' However, this covenant was unconditional on Abraham. He was not called to do anything, except believe. The fire pot and torch together in this vision represent God Himself. Only God passed between the carcasses. Only God ratified the covenant. The terms of this covenant were set by God; Abraham was to walk in upright obedience before God. Thus, God was saying, in effect, 'If either one of us violates this covenant, I give my life in restitution. Of course, God did not violate the covenant, but Abraham and his descendants have, and regularly do, violate it. All men violate it. About 1900 years later, God made good His promise to give His life when Jesus was crucified. On the cross, the Abrahamic covenant was satisfied. We are justified along with Abraham by believing and embracing Jesus' sacrificial death as payment for our sins. The cross was being prophetically symbolized in the Abrahamic covenant. That covenant was pointing forward to the cross of redemption.

Later, after Isaac was born and had grown into a young man, God visited Abraham again with this message.

Genesis 22:2-14 (RSV)
² He said, "Take your son, your only son Isaac, whom you love, and go to the land of Mori'ah, and offer him there as a burnt offering upon one of the mountains of which I shall tell you." ³ So Abraham rose early in the morning, saddled his ass, and took two of his young men with him, and his son Isaac; and he cut the wood for the burnt offering, and arose and went to the place of which God had told him. ⁴ On the third day Abraham lifted up his eyes and saw the place afar

off. ⁵ *Then Abraham said to his young men, "Stay here with the ass; I and the lad will go yonder and worship, and come again to you."* ⁶ *And Abraham took the wood of the burnt offering, and laid it on Isaac his son; and he took in his hand the fire and the knife. So they went both of them together.* ⁷ *And Isaac said to his father Abraham, "My father!" And he said, "Here am I, my son." He said, "Behold, the fire and the wood; but where is the lamb for a burnt offering?"* ⁸ *Abraham said, "God will provide himself the lamb for a burnt offering, my son." So they went both of them together.* ⁹ *When they came to the place of which God had told him, Abraham built an altar there, and laid the wood in order, and bound Isaac his son, and laid him on the altar, upon the wood.* ¹⁰ *Then Abraham put forth his hand, and took the knife to slay his son.* ¹¹ *But the angel of the LORD called to him from heaven, and said, "Abraham, Abraham!" And he said, "Here am I."* ¹² *He said, "Do not lay your hand on the lad or do anything to him; for now I know that you fear God, seeing you have not withheld your son, your only son, from me."* ¹³ *And Abraham lifted up his eyes and looked, and behold, behind him was a ram, caught in a thicket by his horns; and Abraham went and took the ram, and offered it up as a burnt offering instead of his son.* ¹⁴ *So Abraham called the name of that place The LORD will provide; as it is said to this day, "On the mount of the LORD it shall be provided."*

This story cannot be appreciated in isolation. Note the parallels with the crucifixion of Jesus. Just as Isaac had been born through a miracle, Jesus was born of a virgin. Jesus was the son of covenant, just like Isaac was the birthright Son. As Isaac climbed a mountain, Jesus climbed Golgotha's hill. The mountains of Moriah where Abraham took Isaac were the very location where Jesus would one day be crucified. Just as the servants (who might have tried to rescue Isaac) were left behind, so Jesus' disciples fled, leaving him alone. Just as Isaac bore the wood of his sacrifice, Jesus bore his own cross. Just as Isaac did not resist, Jesus did not resist. The sacrifice of Isaac was halted when God provided a ram, just like he provides our atoning sacrifice today in Jesus.

In this emotion-packed narrative, God uses the near-sacrifice of Isaac to portray for us the intense passion of His own heart in sending His one-and-only Son to redeem us from the penalty of sin. We are thrust into weighing the cost of our Creator's own sacrifice. We are in awe as we plumb the depths of His love and fail to find its limit.

> Oh God Almighty! Oh God our Creator! Oh Savior! Our minds are engulfed by the extent of your love for us. How you loved us as you allowed your heart to break in anguish for our redemption. Teach us the seriousness of sin. Teach us quickly of your tenacious love for us, a love

that overcomes the debt and penalty of our sin. Thank you Lord.

This narrative is a prophecy in 'history.' Like many prophecies, the fulfillment is only clear when the reality is revealed. On this side of the cross, we can see this picture, and be stricken by the intensity of the passion of God that He shows us.

In another Old Testament example, many generations later when the Hebrews were enslaved in Egypt, God used a series of plagues to demonstrate His sovereignty to Pharaoh and the Egyptian people. The last of these plagues was the death of the firstborn in each family. The plagues were aimed at Egypt. To prevent the plague from affecting them, the Hebrews were given these instructions:

Exodus 11:1-7,12:3-7,12:12-13 (NASB)
^{1} Now the LORD said to Moses, "One more plague I will bring on Pharaoh and on Egypt; after that he will let you go from here. When he lets you go, he will surely drive you out from here completely. ^{2} "Speak now in the hearing of the people that each man ask from his neighbor and each woman from her neighbor for articles of silver and articles of gold." ^{3} The LORD gave the people favor in the sight of the Egyptians. Furthermore, the man Moses himself was greatly esteemed in the land of Egypt, both in the sight of Pharaoh's servants and in the sight of the people. ^{4} Moses said, "Thus says the LORD, 'About midnight I am going out into the midst of Egypt, ^{5} and all the firstborn in the land of Egypt shall die, from the firstborn of the Pharaoh who sits on his throne, even to the firstborn of the slave girl who is behind the millstones; all the firstborn of the cattle as well. ^{6} 'Moreover, there shall be a great cry in all the land of Egypt, such as there has not been before and such as shall never be again. ^{7} 'But against any of the sons of Israel a dog will not even bark, whether against man or beast, that you may understand how the LORD makes a distinction between Egypt and Israel.' . . . $^{12:2}$ "This month shall be the beginning of months for you; it is to be the first month of the year to you. ^{3} "Speak to all the congregation of Israel, saying, 'On the tenth of this month they are each one to take a lamb for themselves, according to their fathers' households, a lamb for each household. ^{4} 'Now if the household is too small for a lamb, then he and his neighbor nearest to his house are to take one according to the number of persons in them; according to what each man should eat, you are to divide the lamb. ^{5} 'Your lamb shall be an unblemished male a year old; you may take it from the sheep or from the goats. ^{6} 'You shall keep it until the fourteenth day of the same month, then the whole assembly of the congregation of Israel is to kill it at twilight. ^{7} 'Moreover, they shall take some of the blood and put it on the two

doorposts and on the lintel of the houses in which they eat it. . . . [12] *'For I will go through the land of Egypt on that night, and will strike down all the firstborn in the land of Egypt, both man and beast; and against all the gods of Egypt I will execute judgments—I am the LORD.* [13] *'The blood shall be a sign for you on the houses where you live; and when I see the blood I will pass over you, and no plague will befall you to destroy you when I strike the land of Egypt.*

Thus God instituted the Passover. In that symbolism, we see the people being saved from death by the blood of the sacrificial lamb. In the same way, Christ is our Passover lamb. Again, the symbolic backdrop of the historical account is prophetic of the atoning work of Christ, which would not take place for 1500 years. On the night Jesus was betrayed, he celebrated the Passover meal with his disciples for the last time before his death. As he administered the meal with them . . .

Luke 22:19-20 (ESV)
[19] *And he took bread, and when he had given thanks, he broke it and gave it to them, saying, "This is my body, which is given for you. Do this in remembrance of me."* [20] *And likewise the cup after they had eaten, saying, "This cup that is poured out for you is the new covenant in my blood.*

Jesus was saying, 'when you celebrate Passover from this day forward, realize all of this was pointing to me. I am the real Passover lamb.'

The God-instituted practice of animal sacrifice by the Hebrews in the tabernacle, and later in the temple, was a prophetic forecast of the real and perfect sacrifice that would come. It was not spoken through a prophet, but through a priest that regularly performed this duty. It is prophecy in symbolism. With the exception of the promises made at the pronouncement of the curse in Genesis 4, animal sacrifice is the oldest 'prophecy' about Jesus' redemptive ministry of which we have record.

Often, it seems we tend to see the Old Testament sacrifices as something that was later copied into New Testament theology, as though Jesus was just trying to create a link to the past. It is clear from scripture that just the opposite is true. Jesus has always been the sacrificial lamb since before creation. History is sliced in two by his sacrificial death and resurrection. That is the <u>real</u> substitute. Preceding animal sacrifices were veiled references to that real sacrifice.

In the Torah, we encounter Moses' own prophetic words:

Deuteronomy 18:15 (NKJV)
[15] "The LORD your God will raise up for you a Prophet like me from your midst, from your brethren. Him you shall hear,

Moses spoke of one who would come at a future time with the authority of God, just as God had clearly demonstrated his authority in the role given to Moses.

Jesus in the Prophets

The atoning work of Jesus, at his first coming, was prophesied by Israel's writing prophets. Vivid accounts, such as the following, baffled the Jewish scholars. They did not know what to do with this 'suffering servant' person spoken of by their prophets:

Isaiah 53:4-7 (RSV)
[4] Surely he has borne our griefs and carried our sorrows; yet we esteemed him stricken, smitten by God, and afflicted. [5] But he was wounded for our transgressions, he was bruised for our iniquities; upon him was the chastisement that made us whole, and with his stripes we are healed. [6] All we like sheep have gone astray; we have turned every one to his own way; and the LORD has laid on him the iniquity of us all. [7] He was oppressed, and he was afflicted, yet he opened not his mouth; like a lamb that is led to the slaughter, and like a sheep that before its shearers is dumb, so he opened not his mouth.

Daniel 9:26 (NKJV)
[26] "And after the sixty-two weeks Messiah shall be cut off, but not for Himself; And the people of the prince who is to come Shall destroy the city and the sanctuary. The end of it shall be with a flood, And till the end of the war desolations are determined.

Zechariah 13:7 (RSV)
[7] "Awake, O sword, against my shepherd, against the man who stands next to me," says the LORD of hosts. "Strike the shepherd, that the sheep may be scattered; I will turn my hand against the little ones.

Jesus spoke of his impending three days in the grave being prophesied by Jonah in the belly of the fish three days. This was prophecy by demonstration. Speaking to the religious leaders who had asked him for a sign . . .

Matthew 12:39-41 (NASB)
[39] But He answered and said to them, "An evil and adulterous generation craves for a sign; and yet no sign will be given to it but

the sign of Jonah the prophet; [40] *for just as JONAH WAS THREE DAYS AND THREE NIGHTS IN THE BELLY OF THE SEA MONSTER, so will the Son of Man be three days and three nights in the heart of the earth.* [41] *"The men of Nineveh will stand up with this generation at the judgment, and will condemn it because they repented at the preaching of Jonah; and behold, something greater than Jonah is here.*

The number of messianic prophecies in the writings of the Old Testament prophets is huge. We have only considered a very small sampling of the prophecies on this subject. Just when you think maybe you have exhausted most of them, several more come to recognition. In fact, the Messiah, the coming eternal king, is the common thread that all prophecy has in common. Directly, or indirectly, all Old Testament prophecy pointed, and still points, to Jesus.

Jesus in the Psalms

In the psalms, the atoning death of Jesus is envisioned in the distant future, described in Technicolor and Surround Sound, and woven mystically into the psalmist's own cry for his God.

Psalm 22: 1,7-8,12-18 (NKJV)
[1] *My God, My God, why have You forsaken Me? Why are You so far from helping Me, And from the words of My groaning? . . .* [7] *All those who see Me ridicule Me; They shoot out the lip, they shake the head, saying,* [8] *"He trusted in the LORD, let Him rescue Him; Let Him deliver Him, since He delights in Him!" . . .* [12] *Many bulls have surrounded Me; Strong bulls of Bashan have encircled Me.* [13] *They gape at Me with their mouths, Like a raging and roaring lion.* [14] *I am poured out like water, And all My bones are out of joint; My heart is like wax; It has melted within Me.* [15] *My strength is dried up like a potsherd, And My tongue clings to My jaws; You have brought Me to the dust of death.* [16] *For dogs have surrounded Me; The congregation of the wicked has enclosed Me. They pierced My hands and My feet;* [17] *I can count all My bones. They look and stare at Me.* [18] *They divide My garments among them, And for My clothing they cast lots.*

When David penned these words, he was being led by the Holy Spirit. As he began to write about his own desperate situation, suddenly the imagery departs from David, to another. David never experienced these things. We recognize these words as applying to the crucifixion of Jesus. Note these New Testament narrative accounts of the crucifixion.

Matthew 27:33-35 (NASB)
[33] And when they came to a place called Golgotha, which means Place of a Skull, [34] they gave Him wine to drink mixed with gall; and after tasting it, He was unwilling to drink. [35] And when they had crucified Him, they divided up His garments among themselves by casting lots.

Matthew 27:39-43 (NASB)
[39] And those passing by were hurling abuse at Him, wagging their heads [40] and saying, "You who are going to destroy the temple and rebuild it in three days, save Yourself! If You are the Son of God, come down from the cross." [41] In the same way the chief priests also, along with the scribes and elders, were mocking Him and saying, [42] "He saved others; He cannot save Himself. He is the King of Israel; let Him now come down from the cross, and we will believe in Him. [43] "HE TRUSTS IN GOD; LET GOD RESCUE Him now, IF HE DELIGHTS IN HIM; for He said, 'I am the Son of God.'"

Matthew 27:46 (NASB)
[46] About the ninth hour Jesus cried out with a loud voice, saying, "ELI, ELI, LAMA SABACHTHANI?" that is, "MY GOD, MY GOD, WHY HAVE YOU FORSAKEN ME?"

John 19:28 (NKJV)
[28] After this, Jesus, knowing that all things were now accomplished, that the Scripture might be fulfilled, said, "I thirst!"

In the psalms we see pictures of the rigged trial before the Sanhedrin:

Psalm 35:11-12,15-21 (NKJV)
[11] Fierce witnesses rise up; They ask me things that I do not know. [12] They reward me evil for good, To the sorrow of my soul. . . . [15] But in my adversity they rejoiced And gathered together; Attackers gathered against me, And I did not know it; They tore at me and did not cease; [16] With ungodly mockers at feasts They gnashed at me with their teeth. [17] Lord, how long will You look on? Rescue me from their destructions, My precious life from the lions. [18] I will give You thanks in the great assembly; I will praise You among many people. [19] Let them not rejoice over me who are wrongfully my enemies; Nor let them wink with the eye who hate me without a cause. [20] For they do not speak peace, But they devise deceitful matters Against the quiet ones in the land. [21] They also opened their mouth wide against me, And said, "Aha, aha! Our eyes have seen it."

[New Testament Fulfillment]
Mark 14:56-64 (ESV)
[56] For many bore false witness against him, but their testimony did not agree. [57] And some stood up and bore false witness against him, saying, [58] "We heard him say, 'I will destroy this temple that is made with hands, and in three days I will build another, not made with hands.'" [59] Yet even about this their testimony did not agree. [60] And the high priest stood up in the midst and asked Jesus, "Have you no answer to make? What is it that these men testify against you?" [61] But he remained silent and made no answer. Again the high priest asked him, "Are you the Christ, the Son of the Blessed?" [62] And Jesus said, "I am, and you will see the Son of Man seated at the right hand of Power, and coming with the clouds of heaven." [63] And the high priest tore his garments and said, "What further witnesses do we need? [64] You have heard his blasphemy. What is your decision?" And they all condemned him as deserving death.

In the psalms we read of an earthquake:

[Psalm]
Psalm 18:2-7 (NKJV)
[2] The LORD is my rock and my fortress and my deliverer; My God, my strength, in whom I will trust; My shield and the horn of my salvation, my stronghold. [3] I will call upon the LORD, who is worthy to be praised; So shall I be saved from my enemies. [4] The pangs of death surrounded me, And the floods of ungodliness made me afraid. [5] The sorrows of Sheol surrounded me; The snares of death confronted me. [6] In my distress I called upon the LORD, And cried out to my God; He heard my voice from His temple, And my cry came before Him, even to His ears. [7] Then the earth shook and trembled; The foundations of the hills also quaked and were shaken, Because He was angry.

[New Testament Fulfillment]
Matthew 27:50-51 (NASB)
[50] And Jesus cried out again with a loud voice, and yielded up His spirit. [51] And behold, the veil of the temple was torn in two from top to bottom; and the earth shook and the rocks were split.

When we read these psalms against the backdrop of the New Testament accounts of the crucifixion, we easily recognize their prophetic nature and their fulfillment. How did God know all this would happen? How could He predict? God didn't just know. He didn't only predict. He caused it to happen that way and told us of it ahead of time so that we would believe. It was all in His divine plan since before we were created.

> *1 Peter 1:18-20 (ESV)*
> *[18] knowing that you were ransomed from the futile ways inherited from your forefathers, not with perishable things such as silver or gold, [19] but with the precious blood of Christ, like that of a lamb without blemish or spot. [20] He was foreknown before the foundation of the world but was made manifest in the last times for the sake of you*

There are literally hundreds of references in the Old Testament that can be seen as metaphorically pointing to Jesus. These few serve to make the case that Jesus is the focus of the Old Testament scriptures.

The Messiah of Promise

As the early church emerged out of first century Judaism, its evangelical message was, "Jesus is the long awaited Messiah of scripture."

> *Deuteronomy 18:15 (NKJV)*
> *[15] "The LORD your God will raise up for you a Prophet like me from your midst, from your brethren. Him you shall hear,*

These passages we have been looking at are the very ones they read to see if this were true. As we look in the Book of Acts, we find this to be the case. When Peter preached on Pentecost in Acts 2, what message did he preach? It was the Old Testament scriptures.

> *Acts 2:22-32 (ESV)*
> *[22] "Men of Israel, hear these words: Jesus of Nazareth, a man attested to you by God with mighty works and wonders and signs that God did through him in your midst, as you yourselves know— [23] this Jesus, delivered up according to the definite plan and foreknowledge of God, you crucified and killed by the hands of lawless men. [24] God raised him up, loosing the pangs of death, because it was not possible for him to be held by it. [25] For David says concerning him, "'I saw the Lord always before me, for he is at my right hand that I may not be shaken; [26] therefore my heart was glad, and my tongue rejoiced; my flesh also will dwell in hope. [27] For you will not abandon my soul to Hades, or let your Holy One see corruption. [28] You have made known to me the paths of life; you will make me full of gladness with your presence.' [29] "Brothers, I may say to you with confidence about the patriarch David that he both died and was buried, and his tomb is with us to this day. [30] Being therefore a prophet, and knowing that God had sworn with an oath to him that he would set one of his descendants on his throne, [31] he foresaw and spoke about the resurrection of the Christ, that he*

was not abandoned to Hades, nor did his flesh see corruption. [32] This Jesus God raised up, and of that we all are witnesses.

[... referring to Psalm 16]
Psalm 16:8-10 (NKJV)
[8] I have set the LORD always before me; Because He is at my right hand I shall not be moved. [9] Therefore my heart is glad, and my glory rejoices; My flesh also will rest in hope. [10] For You will not leave my soul in Sheol, Nor will You allow Your Holy One to see corruption.

In Acts 3 when Peter healed a man crippled from birth, his message to the onlookers was that Jesus was the man's healer, and the Christ of Prophecy.

Acts 3:15-20 (ESV)
[15] and you killed the Author of life, whom God raised from the dead. To this we are witnesses. [16] And his name—by faith in his name—has made this man strong whom you see and know, and the faith that is through Jesus has given the man this perfect health in the presence of you all. [17] "And now, brothers, I know that you acted in ignorance, as did also your rulers. [18] But what God foretold by the mouth of all the prophets, that his Christ would suffer, he thus fulfilled. [19] Repent therefore, and turn back, that your sins may be blotted out, [20] that times of refreshing may come from the presence of the Lord, and that he may send the Christ appointed for you, Jesus,

In Acts 8, when Philip encountered the Ethiopian eunuch, the prophecy of Isaiah became the foundation for presenting the gospel of Jesus, and the eunuch believed.

Acts 8:30-38 (ESV)
[30] So Philip ran to him and heard him reading Isaiah the prophet and asked, "Do you understand what you are reading?" [31] And he said, "How can I, unless someone guides me?" And he invited Philip to come up and sit with him. [32] Now the passage of the Scripture that he was reading was this: "Like a sheep he was led to the slaughter and like a lamb before its shearer is silent, so he opens not his mouth. [33] In his humiliation justice was denied him. Who can describe his generation? For his life is taken away from the earth." [34] And the eunuch said to Philip, "About whom, I ask you, does the prophet say this, about himself or about someone else?" [35] Then Philip opened his mouth, and beginning with this Scripture he told him the good news about Jesus. [36] And as they were going along the road they came to some water, and the eunuch said, "See, here is water! What prevents me from being baptized?" [38] And he

commanded the chariot to stop, and they both went down into the water, Philip and the eunuch, and he baptized him.

The cases go on and on. Paul relied heavily on reference to prophecy when preaching to Jews or Gentiles with Jewish association. After he preached in Berea, we read:

Acts 17:11 (ESV)
[11] Now these Jews were more noble than those in Thessalonica; they received the word with all eagerness, examining the Scriptures daily to see if these things were so.

Of course "the Scriptures" they examined were those of the Old Testament. In the Old Testament we see Jesus prophesied in written foretelling, in Jewish symbolism, and in historical demonstrational circumstances. It is clear that Jesus was the promised Messiah, the Christ. In this forth-telling of His plans and purposes, we come face to face with a God who cares for us passionately. We see in these prophecies that the entirety of the Old Testament was focused on the plan of redemption, a plan already established in the mind of God. It is the plan more fully revealed in the New Testament. We see in prophecy the common focus on redemption running through all of scripture. In fact, as we study the Bible thoroughly, we come to realize Jesus the Messiah is the central theme from Genesis through Revelation. Thus, in prophecy we are led to celebrate God's plan for the ages.

Atonement Defends God's Holiness

Atonement is the application of God's grace to redeem sinful man. However, it is not only the application of grace. It is more. If mercy and grace were God's only agenda, then he could have just dismissed the guilt of our sin, at no cost to himself. But God is not only full of grace. He is also full of truth. He is holy, righteous, and just. To show mercy and grace to the exclusion of His holiness would violate His very character. We must not diminish this facet of His person. In fact, *Holy* is the only adjective used in scripture to describe God that is repeated three times in succession, and that occurs twice, both times by angels.

Isaiah 6:1-3 (KJV)
[1] In the year that king Uzziah died I saw also the Lord sitting upon a throne, high and lifted up, and his train filled the temple. [2] Above it stood the seraphims: each one had six wings; with twain he covered his face, and with twain he covered his feet, and with twain he did fly. [3] And one cried unto another, and said, Holy, holy, holy, is the LORD of hosts: the whole earth is full of his glory.

Revelation 4:8 (ESV)
⁸ And the four living creatures, each of them with six wings, are full of eyes all around and within, and day and night they never cease to say, "Holy, holy, holy, is the Lord God Almighty, who was and is and is to come!"

God's holiness does not take a backseat to his mercy and grace. It cannot be compromised by our sins. Thus, we see clearly in prophecy that the dilemma between truth and grace is brought to the forefront of cosmic issues by God's response to our sins.

As we saw in the beginning of this chapter, this is the apparent dilemma which the atoning work of Jesus satisfied. This same dilemma was evidenced in our second vision in Revelation when John was told to look for the Lion of Judah, and turned to see a slain Lamb which was alive. Lion and lamb. Truth and Grace, joined together in Jesus.

Jesus became our atoning sacrifice for sin. Our sin has been paid for. Thus, for those who believe, God no longer holds our sin against us. He would be acting unjustly to continue our guilt after already exacting the due penalty for it. That is why John could write:

1 John 1:9 (ESV)
⁹ If we confess our sins, he is faithful and just to forgive us our sins and to cleanse us from all unrighteousness.

Notice John does not say God is 'merciful and graceful' to forgive our sins, but that He is *faithful and just*. Because of atonement, God's just and holy nature is fully satisfied, and He necessarily shows us mercy as a result. Atonement is all about God's 'truth' side, while giving way to His mercy.

What Atonement Does
When animal sacrifices were performed in Old Testament times, the sins of the worshipper were understood as being transferred to the animal, and thus, they were blotted out of the worshipper's account. The scholarly term for this is 'imputed.' That is exactly what happens when Jesus' sacrificial death is applied to our life. Our sins are imputed to him. But something else is also imputed—a most wonderful reality. Not only are our sins imputed from us to Christ, but his righteousness is imputed to us! It is a two-way exchange.

2 Corinthians 5:21 (NASB)
²¹ He made Him who knew no sin to be sin on our behalf, so that we might become the righteousness of God in Him.

Philippians 3:9 (ESV)
⁹ and be found in him, not having a righteousness of my own that comes from the law, but that which comes through faith in Christ, the righteousness from God that depends on faith—

Creation is God's. He owes us nothing. He is not obligated, by any external principle, to love and redeem us. But He has obligated himself through His covenants and promises. That He has chosen to redeem us when we were so undeserving, is a call to praise for the loving kindness of God. The manner in which He has redeemed us through atonement is a call to praise the holiness, righteousness and justness of God. We should be eternally grateful for both facets of God's being.

> Lord, cause us to take pause at your purpose in redemption. Make us to know and stand in awe of your eternal plans. Help us to see you at work in history, especially, now in prophetic history. Our gratitude to you is without adequate words. Your grace brings us to our knees in humility. We are grateful, too, for your unchanging holiness and truth and justice. We are thankful to be seeking such an absolute and perfect God. Thank you for redeeming us through the sacrificial death of Jesus. May we never again lean on self-styled attempts at virtue, but only on your provisional way. With gladness we celebrate Your Love, oh God. In hope and faith we celebrate you, oh God! Great are You, oh God of prophecy. Great are You, oh God of the Bible. Great are you, and worthy of our praise.

8
RESURRECTION

Life has been good for me. I take joy in life, and look forward to each day. This is not to say that I have lived a utopian life, or have been oblivious to problems along the way, but still, I'm glad to be on board. It is not that the circumstances of every day bring joy. I live in the same world you do. No, but the joy and contentment comes from within. I understand from scripture that God's indwelling Holy Spirit brings a sense of well-being that transcends my environment.

Romans 14:17 (RSV)
[17] For the kingdom of God is not food and drink but righteousness and peace and joy in the Holy Spirit;

Romans 15:13 (RSV)
[13] May the God of hope fill you with all joy and peace in believing, so that by the power of the Holy Spirit you may abound in hope.

I am not claiming a special contentment, but describing a contentment that is available to every Christian. It should be the common blessing of His followers. It is not a Pollyanna mentality that everything will be easy or happy, but the work of the Spirit. He lifts us beyond our circumstances. He does this by constantly reminding us of our eternal destiny with God, if, in fact, we are His and therefore have the indwelling of His Holy Spirit.

For those who do not know the Lord Jesus Christ, there is a futility that casts a certain pall over their mental landscape. This futility is characteristic, consciously or unconsciously, of those who have no hope. At the root of this futility is a certain specific obstacle. Without Jesus, that obstacle frustrates any purpose, any peace, any contentment. But through Jesus, God promises victory over this obstacle. What is this futility, this obstacle?

For me, it was one of those benchmark experiences that you never forget. I was probably about four or five years old. I was playing with my best friends, three brothers. The oldest was a year older than me, and carried the virtue of aged wisdom. Somehow the subject came up, and he told me what no one had told me before--that all people die sooner or later. Oh, I knew that death existed. I knew you could get shot by a gunslinger or killed in a car wreck. But I guess I thought that if I were careful, I could live forever.

When he told me this, I remember crying, and his mother coming out and trying to comfort me, but when I asked her about it, she confirmed that awful truth. I remember it vividly, and to this day, could point to the exact spot where I was standing. That was the day I learned the truth of my mortality.

Death

The greatest obstacle in life is death. Job's friend Bildad called it *the king of terrors*. We condition ourselves not to think about it. This is especially true in our modern western culture. Death is seldom a welcome topic of discussion. When someone does die, we have the body whisked away by a coroner, who tries to make it look as alive as possible. Closure is difficult while we nurture denial. In the past, burial preparation was made by family and friends of the deceased. Today there is a general detachment from the reality of it. Some deny that death is significant to them because they are not consciously thinking about it most of the time. They are unaware of the unseen bondage of death upon natural man. However, scripture teaches that all who have flesh and blood live in a subliminal fear of death. The writer of the book of Hebrews said:

> *Hebrews 2:14-15 (ESV)*
> *^{14} Since therefore the children share in flesh and blood, he himself likewise partook of the same things, that through death he might destroy the one who has the power of death, that is, the devil, ^{15} and deliver all those who through fear of death were subject to lifelong slavery.*

At the same time, there exists a subculture which entertains an unhealthy enamor with death. At its extreme are those involved in the occult. At the other end are those influenced by its dark shadow. In short, this is not the kind of acquaintance with death that the scriptures recommend.

Though death may be avoided in conscious thought and conversation, it subconsciously manipulates the fabric of our lives. How many people eighty years old begin a college education? Why does life insurance get more expensive as we get older? Why are there so few professional athletes over forty years old? Why do I need a magnifying glass to read the fine print? We live our lives against the backdrop of our own mortality. The death of a friend or loved one reminds us of our own impending demise. ". . . Never send to know for whom the bell tolls; It tolls for thee," wrote John Donne. We are held captive all our lives by this reality, and a burdensome bondage it is.

There are also beneficial ways that death affects us. The prospect of death causes us to look for purpose and meaning in life. After all, how can we live this life, filled with a sense of our existence, only to cease to exist? If we vanish, what was the reason for our life? Death adds a sense of urgency to accomplish whatever we set out to do. Most important of all, death causes us to look for the source of life. It motivates us to go to God. If there were no death, who would seek his maker? As Moses wrote, in the only psalm attributed to him:

Psalm 90:12 (NKJV)
[12] So teach us to number our days, That we may gain a heart of wisdom.

And as David said...

Psalm 39:4-7 (NKJV)
[4] "LORD, make me to know my end, And what is the measure of my days, That I may know how frail I am. [5] Indeed, You have made my days as handbreadths, And my age is as nothing before You; Certainly every man at his best state is but vapor. Selah [6] Surely every man walks about like a shadow; Surely they busy themselves in vain; He heaps up riches, And does not know who will gather them. [7] "And now, Lord, what do I wait for? My hope is in You.

From earliest times, man has sought relief from the burden of death. He has searched for immortality in his own way. A sense of immortality has been found through procreation, our children and grandchildren being seen as an extension of ourselves. This view shaped the thinking of the early people groups living in family and tribal structures. Some have sought immortality in the minds of their survivors through a legacy left for the future. Still others have custom-designed a religion to deal with death. Reincarnation is a man-crafted philosophy about death prevalent in eastern religions such as Hinduism, but finding acceptance in western culture, as well. Ponce de Leon led early American expeditions in search of the Fountain of Youth.

<u>What is Death?</u>
Clinically the validation of death must satisfy certain criteria. We used to check for a pulse and for breathing. Now we search for brain waves and other 'vital signs.' The Bible also addresses death in terms of vital signs. Mark's narrative of the death of Jesus says, simply:

Mark 15:37 (ESV)
[37] And Jesus uttered a loud cry and breathed his last.

But spiritually speaking, what is death? Old and New Testaments alike describe death as a separation of a person's spirit from his body. For example...

Psalm 146:4 (NKJV)
⁴ His spirit departs, he returns to his earth; In that very day his plans perish.

Ecclesiastes 12:7-8 (NKJV)
⁷ Then the dust will return to the earth as it was, And the spirit will return to God who gave it. ⁸ "Vanity of vanities," says the Preacher, "All is vanity."

James 2:26 (NKJV)
²⁶ For as the body without the spirit is dead . . .

Whereas Mark described Jesus' death clinically as he *breathed his last*, gospel writers Matthew and John address His death spiritually:

Matthew 27:50 (NASB)
⁵⁰ And Jesus cried out again with a loud voice, and yielded up His spirit.

John 19:30 (NKJV)
³⁰ So when Jesus had received the sour wine, He said, "It is finished!" And bowing His head, He gave up His spirit.

Luke, the doctor, includes both perspectives:

Luke 23:46 (ESV)
⁴⁶ Then Jesus, calling out with a loud voice, said, "Father, into your hands I commit my spirit!" And having said this he breathed his last.

We all know what happens to the body after its spirit departs. What about the spirit and the soul? First let us look at the origin of death.

The Birth of Death
Scripture teaches us that death originated at the command of God. In the original creation there was no sin and no death. Man, by disobeying the direct command of God, introduced sin into the world. At that point God cursed the world, that is, He dedicated it for destruction. Along with it, He cursed man who had initiated sin.

Genesis 3:16-17,22 (RSV)
¹⁶ To the woman he said, "I will greatly multiply your pain in childbearing; in pain you shall bring forth children, yet your desire shall be for your husband, and he shall rule over you." ¹⁷ And to Adam he said, "Because you have listened to the voice of your wife, and have eaten of the tree of which I commanded you, 'You shall not eat of it,' cursed is the ground because of you; in toil you shall eat of

it all the days of your life . . . ^{22} Then the LORD God said, "Behold, the man has become like one of us, knowing good and evil; and now, lest he put forth his hand and take also of the tree of life, and eat, and live forever" --

A humanist interpretation of man's relationship to God is that in the beginning there was no knowledge of God. After man became more civilized and intelligent, he began to question his existence and purpose, and eventually came to believe in a god. But the Bible is clear that this is not the case at all. From the beginning, man knew about God, but due to his own sinful rebellious nature, he chose to ignore Him. His relationship with God deteriorated.

> *Romans 1:21,28 (RSV)*
> *^{21} for although they knew God they did not honor him as God or give thanks to him, but they became futile in their thinking and their senseless minds were darkened . . . ^{28} And since they did not see fit to acknowledge God, God gave them up to a base mind and to improper conduct.*

In this passage we see the downward path to which sin lures us. It is essentially an irreversible course. No man or woman is able by his own virtue to separate himself from this headlong plunge, to rise above his own sinful tendencies. As long as we live in this body, in this world, our nature will be corrupt. Christians are not exempt from this inner struggle. In fact, that is where the struggle begins. There really is no struggle until one is introduced to holiness, and seeks to live therein.

> *Romans 7:21-24 (RSV)*
> *^{21} So I find it to be a law that when I want to do right, evil lies close at hand. ^{22} For I delight in the law of God, in my inmost self, ^{23} but I see in my members another law at war with the law of my mind and making me captive to the law of sin which dwells in my members. ^{24} Wretched man that I am! Who will deliver me from this body of death?*

Death--God's Cure for Sin

In His mercy, God did not allow sinful man to live forever in the downward spiral of degradation He knew would follow. Instead, He devised a plan whereby, through faith, a sinful man dies, and is redeemed a new man from the old. According to this plan, Jesus, became the means by which our sins were paid for, or 'atoned.' In his first letter to the Corinthians, Paul addressed the dissipating life of sin. He speaks of Adam through whom sin entered the world, and Jesus as the *last Adam* through whom eternal life came:

1 Corinthians 15:45-50 (NKJV)
45 And so it is written, "The first man Adam became a living being." The last Adam became a life-giving spirit. 46 However, the spiritual is not first, but the natural, and afterward the spiritual. 47 The first man was of the earth, made of dust; the second Man is the Lord from heaven. 48 As was the man of dust, so also are those who are made of dust; and as is the heavenly Man, so also are those who are heavenly. 49 And as we have borne the image of the man of dust, we shall also bear the image of the heavenly Man. 50 Now this I say, brethren, that flesh and blood cannot inherit the kingdom of God; nor does corruption inherit incorruption.

Romans 6:20-23 (RSV)
20 When you were slaves of sin, you were free in regard to righteousness. 21 But then what return did you get from the things of which you are now ashamed? The end of those things is death. 22 But now that you have been set free from sin and have become slaves of God, the return you get is sanctification and its end, eternal life. 23 For the wages of sin is death, but the free gift of God is eternal life in Christ Jesus our Lord.

I remember as a young Christian, frustrated by my failed attempts at holiness, praying for the Lord to overpower my self-will and forcibly take control of my mind and body. I longed for rest from the struggle against sinful tendencies. Of course in my immaturity, I did not understand that what He wanted was my surrendered self, offered daily, continually. Yes, we long for a time when our transgressions no longer blemish our relationship with God. That is what He wants too, and death is part of His plan to bring about that very thing.

Resurrection

Many people are confused about the meaning and significance of resurrection. In my adult Sunday school class when I taught on this topic, I divided the members into two teams. To one of these teams I gave four scriptures, and to the other I gave four different scriptures. The assignment was for them to read the assigned scriptures in the group, then determine and report back as to when life-after-death begins. The first scriptures were these:

Luke 16:19-31 (ESV)
19 "There was a rich man who was clothed in purple and fine linen and who feasted sumptuously every day. 20 And at his gate was laid a poor man named Lazarus, covered with sores, 21 who desired to be fed with what fell from the rich man's table. Moreover, even the dogs came and licked his sores. 22 The poor man died and was carried by

the angels to Abraham's side. The rich man also died and was buried, ²³ and in Hades, being in torment, he lifted up his eyes and saw Abraham far off and Lazarus at his side. ²⁴ And he called out, 'Father Abraham, have mercy on me, and send Lazarus to dip the end of his finger in water and cool my tongue, for I am in anguish in this flame.' ²⁵ But Abraham said, 'Child, remember that you in your lifetime received your good things, and Lazarus in like manner bad things; but now he is comforted here, and you are in anguish. ²⁶ And besides all this, between us and you a great chasm has been fixed, in order that those who would pass from here to you may not be able, and none may cross from there to us.' ²⁷ And he said, 'Then I beg you, father, to send him to my father's house— ²⁸ for I have five brothers—so that he may warn them, lest they also come into this place of torment.' ²⁹ But Abraham said, 'They have Moses and the Prophets; let them hear them.' ³⁰ And he said, 'No, father Abraham, but if someone goes to them from the dead, they will repent.' ³¹ He said to him, 'If they do not hear Moses and the Prophets, neither will they be convinced if someone should rise from the dead.'"

Luke 23:40-43 (ESV)
⁴⁰ But the other rebuked him, saying, "Do you not fear God, since you are under the same sentence of condemnation? ⁴¹ And we indeed justly, for we are receiving the due reward of our deeds; but this man has done nothing wrong." ⁴² And he said, "Jesus, remember me when you come into your kingdom." ⁴³ And he said to him, "Truly, I say to you, today you will be with me in Paradise."

Matthew 22:31-32 (NASB)
³¹ "But regarding the resurrection of the dead, have you not read what was spoken to you by God: ³² 'I AM THE GOD OF ABRAHAM, AND THE GOD OF ISAAC, AND THE GOD OF JACOB'? He is not the God of the dead but of the living."

Philippians 1:22-23 (ESV)
²² If I am to live in the flesh, that means fruitful labor for me. Yet which I shall choose I cannot tell. ²³ I am hard pressed between the two. My desire is to depart and be with Christ, for that is far better.

This group reported back that the after-life begins immediately after death. From these scriptures they concluded that we are fully conscious immediately after death. At the same time, the following scriptures were given to the other team:

John 6:39-40 (NKJV)
³⁹ This is the will of the Father who sent Me, that of all He has given Me I should lose nothing, but should raise it up at the last day. ⁴⁰

> *And this is the will of Him who sent Me, that everyone who sees the Son and believes in Him may have everlasting life; and I will raise him up at the last day."*
>
> *1 Corinthians 15:21-23 (NKJV)*
> *[21] For since by man came death, by Man also came the resurrection of the dead. [22] For as in Adam all die, even so in Christ all shall be made alive. [23] But each one in his own order: Christ the firstfruits, afterward those who are Christ's at His coming.*
>
> *1 Thessalonians 4:15-17 (NASB)*
> *[15] For this we say to you by the word of the Lord, that we who are alive and remain until the coming of the Lord, will not precede those who have fallen asleep. [16] For the Lord Himself will descend from heaven with a shout, with the voice of the archangel and with the trumpet of God, and the dead in Christ will rise first. [17] Then we who are alive and remain will be caught up together with them in the clouds to meet the Lord in the air, and so we shall always be with the Lord.*
>
> *2 Timothy 2:18 (ESV)*
> *[18] who have swerved from the truth, saying that the resurrection has already happened. They are upsetting the faith of some.*

The group with the second set of scriptures reported back that the after-life begins at some unknown point in the future when Christ returns. The two conclusions are in direct contradiction with each other. I believe this confusion is widespread among Christian believers.

Both groups correctly concluded the timing set forth in their groups of scriptures. The timing is unquestionable. The problem was a weak understanding of biblical concepts concerning death and life after. The team members failed to distinguish between 'life-after-death' and 'resurrection.' Everyone in class took them to be equivalent concepts, and therefore arrived at conflicting conclusions.

Life After Death
Remember that the biblical understanding of death is the separation of body and spirit. The term *spirit* is used in these verses to include both spirit and soul. If immediately after death the soul lives and is fully conscious and in fellowship with God, then we can conclude eternal life has already begun. This seems to be what is in view in the first set of scriptures.

In our fairytale mentality, we might think it would be adventurous to be a spirit and move anywhere instantly and effortlessly. To see the spirit realm as well as this physical world would certainly broaden our intelligence.

However, apparently we were not created to be permanent spirits. Apparently we will remain incomplete in this state. Paul expressed it when writing to the Corinthians.

> *2 Corinthians 5:1-5 (NASB)*
> *[1] For we know that if the earthly tent which is our house is torn down, we have a building from God, a house not made with hands, eternal in the heavens. [2] For indeed in this house we groan, longing to be clothed with our dwelling from heaven, [3] inasmuch as we, having put it on, will not be found naked. [4] For indeed while we are in this tent, we groan, being burdened, because we do not want to be unclothed but to be clothed, so that what is mortal will be swallowed up by life. [5] Now He who prepared us for this very purpose is God, who gave to us the Spirit as a pledge.*

The *earthly tent* is our physical body in this life. However he says that when our earthly tent *is destroyed* (when we die and the body decays) we (our living spirits) will be given a *building from God, a house not made with hands, eternal in the heavens.* Furthermore *we do not want to be unclothed but to be clothed,* What is this *building from God* that we long for? In his first letter to Corinth Paul described a new body that will be given.

> *1 Corinthians 15:35-44 (NKJV)*
> *[35] But someone will say, "How are the dead raised up? And with what body do they come?" [36] Foolish one, what you sow is not made alive unless it dies. [37] And what you sow, you do not sow that body that shall be, but mere grain--perhaps wheat or some other grain. [38] But God gives it a body as He pleases, and to each seed its own body. [39] All flesh is not the same flesh, but there is one kind of flesh of men, another flesh of animals, another of fish, and another of birds. [40] There are also celestial bodies and terrestrial bodies; but the glory of the celestial is one, and the glory of the terrestrial is another. [41] There is one glory of the sun, another glory of the moon, and another glory of the stars; for one star differs from another star in glory. [42] So also is the resurrection of the dead. The body is sown in corruption, it is raised in incorruption. [43] It is sown in dishonor, it is raised in glory. It is sown in weakness, it is raised in power. [44] It is sown a natural body, it is raised a spiritual body. There is a natural body, and there is a spiritual body.*

This new body, the 'resurrection body,' is reserved for the people of God. All others will be resurrected too, but scripture speaks little of the kind of body they will receive. The word *resurrection* in scripture always refers to our spirit receiving our new, heavenly body.

Until resurrection occurs, our spirits live, but while they enjoy blissful peace and fellowship with God, they will nevertheless still be *unclothed,* and will nurture anticipation for the day when they will be clothed. This spiritual state after death and before resurrection is often called the intermediate state, or the disembodied state. In our scripture passage of Jesus telling about the rich man and Lazarus, we read that Lazarus was taken by the angels to *Abraham's side,* or *Abraham's bosom,* as the KJV puts it. When the penitent thief on the cross begged Jesus to remember him, he was told, *"Today you will be with me in paradise."* What is this paradise, this place at Abraham's side? It is thought to be a 'place' in heaven where the disembodied saints reside. It seems from these scriptures to be a place of blessing. Not much else is said about this condition.

There are other interpretations about what the Bible means by these scriptures, and about what happens at death and thereafter. This view, however, is the most comprehensive and compatible, explaining the dilemma we discussed earlier, and removing some of the problems we would otherwise confront when we study end-time prophecy. I agree with this interpretation because it seems to satisfy all the reference scriptures about death.

The Resurrection of the Righteous

The resurrection of the saints (Christians) was envisioned by John the apostle, and recorded in the book of Revelation. He writes...

> *Revelation 20:4-6 (ESV)*
> [4] *. . . I saw the souls of those who had been beheaded for the testimony of Jesus and for the word of God, . . . They came to life and reigned with Christ for a thousand years.* [5] *. . . This is the first resurrection.* [6] *Blessed and holy is the one who shares in the first resurrection! Over such the second death has no power. . .*

Paul was given insight into the coming resurrection, and he described it in more detail than any other scripture writer. I Corinthians 15 is often called the 'resurrection chapter' of scripture because the entire text of this long chapter deals with the topic. We have already looked at excerpts from it, and here is another:

> *1 Corinthians 15:50-55 (NKJV)*
> [50] *Now this I say, brethren, that flesh and blood cannot inherit the kingdom of God; nor does corruption inherit incorruption.* [51] *Behold, I tell you a mystery: We shall not all sleep, but we shall all be changed--* [52] *in a moment, in the twinkling of an eye, at the last trumpet. For the trumpet will sound, and the dead will be raised incorruptible, and we shall be changed.* [53] *For this corruptible must put on incorruption, and this mortal must put on immortality.* [54] *So*

when this corruptible has put on incorruption, and this mortal has put on immortality, then shall be brought to pass the saying that is written: "Death is swallowed up in victory." ^{55} "O Death, where is your sting? O Hades, where is your victory?"

In this passage Paul deals with two groups of faithful, believing people. On that day when the *last trumpet* sounds, there will be those who are alive on the earth and those who have already died. Those already dead will be resurrected or *raised imperishable*. *We* (referring to those still living) *will be changed*. The living will undergo a transformation. Both will put on the imperishable. Both will become immortal by the process of resurrection.

Christ's victory over death harkens back to the vision of salvation's completion shown to the prophet Isaiah, speaking of a time yet future for him and for us:

Isaiah 25:6-9 (KJV)
^{6} And in this mountain shall the LORD of hosts make unto all people a feast of fat things, a feast of wines on the lees, of fat things full of marrow, of wines on the lees well refined. ^{7} And he will destroy in this mountain the face of the covering cast over all people, and the vail that is spread over all nations. ^{8} He will swallow up death in victory; and the Lord GOD will wipe away tears from off all faces; and the rebuke of his people shall he take away from off all the earth: for the LORD hath spoken it. ^{9} And it shall be said in that day, Lo, this is our God; we have waited for him, and he will save us: this is the LORD; we have waited for him, we will be glad and rejoice in his salvation.

The pall or veil that covers mortal men will be removed forever. In the first resurrection, Christ will be shown victorious over the kingdoms of this world, but even more importantly, over death. I certainly want to be on the winning side of this issue of eternal life or everlasting death. I want to be on the side of the one who beat the grave.

<u>Resurrection Roots</u>
We know that Jesus taught there would be a resurrection at the end of the age. However the hope of resurrection was already an established doctrine in first century Israel. This is demonstrated in an exchange Jesus had with some Sadducees.

Matthew 22:23 (NASB)
^{23} On that day some Sadducees (who say there is no resurrection) came to Jesus and questioned Him,

The beliefs of the Sadducees and Pharisees on this matter is more distinctly stated later by Luke in his book of Acts . . .

> *Acts 23:6-8 (ESV)*
> *⁶ Now when Paul perceived that one part were Sadducees and the other Pharisees, he cried out in the council, "Brothers, I am a Pharisee, a son of Pharisees. It is with respect to the hope and the resurrection of the dead that I am on trial." ⁷ And when he had said this, a dissension arose between the Pharisees and the Sadducees, and the assembly was divided. ⁸ For the Sadducees say that there is no resurrection, nor angel, nor spirit, but the Pharisees acknowledge them all.*

We do not know the details of how the concept of resurrection became known among the Hebrew people. It is mentioned rarely in the Old Testament, but one example is quite vivid . . .

> *Job 19:25-27 (NKJV)*
> *²⁵ For I know that my Redeemer lives, And He shall stand at last on the earth; ²⁶ And after my skin is destroyed, this I know, That in my flesh I shall see God, ²⁷ Whom I shall see for myself, And my eyes shall behold, and not another. How my heart yearns within me!*

. . . but this does not necessarily indicate an existing, well-developed concept of resurrection by Job. It seems to be a divine prophetic revelation. Likewise Isaiah writes:

> *Isaiah 26:19 (RSV)*
> *¹⁹ Thy dead shall live, their bodies shall rise. O dwellers in the dust, awake and sing for joy! For thy dew is a dew of light, and on the land of the shades thou wilt let it fall.*

Certainly a belief in eternal life existed very early on, being seen in the patriarchs' yearning for a heavenly city, told to us by the writer of Hebrews..

> *Hebrews 11:14-16 (ESV)*
> *¹⁴ For people who speak thus make it clear that they are seeking a homeland. ¹⁵ If they had been thinking of that land from which they had gone out, they would have had opportunity to return. ¹⁶ But as it is, they desire a better country, that is, a heavenly one. Therefore God is not ashamed to be called their God, for he has prepared for them a city.*

But resurrection was not spoken of clearly in Old Testament scripture. Some believe the concept of bodily resurrection developed into a doctrine while the Jews were in exile in Babylon. Perhaps, just as God used the evil Babylonians to discipline His chosen people, He may have worked through the pagan religions of Babylon and Persia to reveal components that would eventually develop into the dogma of the Pharisees. This included a belief not only in resurrection, but in the supernatural, in general.

Whatever the origins of resurrection awareness might have been, there is no question it was comprehended and embraced by many in Jesus' day.

> *John 11:23-24 (NKJV)*
> *²³ Jesus said to her, "Your brother will rise again." ²⁴ Martha said to Him, "I know that he will rise again in the resurrection at the last day."*

Jesus himself taught often about it. He spoke of it as a future certainty for the righteous:

> *Luke 14:13-14 (ESV)*
> *¹³ But when you give a feast, invite the poor, the crippled, the lame, the blind, ¹⁴ and you will be blessed, because they cannot repay you. For you will be repaid at the resurrection of the just."*

> *Luke 20:34-36 (ESV)*
> *³⁴ And Jesus said to them, "The sons of this age marry and are given in marriage, ³⁵ but those who are considered worthy to attain to that age and to the resurrection from the dead neither marry nor are given in marriage, ³⁶ for they cannot die anymore, because they are equal to angels and are sons of God, being sons of the resurrection.*

> *John 11:25-26 (NKJV)*
> *²⁵ Jesus said to her, "I am the resurrection and the life. He who believes in Me, though he may die, he shall live. ²⁶ And whoever lives and believes in Me shall never die. Do you believe this?"*

He taught about his own upcoming death, burial and resurrection:

> *Matthew 16:21 (NASB)*
> *²¹ From that time Jesus began to show His disciples that He must go to Jerusalem, and suffer many things from the elders and chief priests and scribes, and be killed, and be raised up on the third day.*

> *Matthew 17:9 (NASB)*
> *⁹ As they were coming down from the mountain, Jesus commanded them, saying, "Tell the vision to no one until the Son of Man has risen from the dead."*

Luke 24:6-8 (ESV)
⁶ He is not here, but has risen. Remember how he told you, while he was still in Galilee, ⁷ that the Son of Man must be delivered into the hands of sinful men and be crucified and on the third day rise." ⁸ And they remembered his words,

First Christ

The premise for resurrection of the saints was (and is) founded upon the resurrection of Christ himself. We recall this scripture that we read earlier in which Paul said:

1 Corinthians 15:22-23 (NKJV)
²² For as in Adam all die, even so in Christ all shall be made alive. ²³ But each one in his own order: Christ the firstfruits, afterward those who are Christ's at His coming.

What does Paul mean by calling the resurrection of Christ '*firstfruits*?' This is a beautiful picture. In Israel's agrarian economy, the third of their many annual feasts was the festival of firstfruits. All were called to bring the very first of the year's produce, typically barley, and offer it to the Lord on this day. They could not eat of their produce until after firstfruits were offered. It was always held the day after a Sabbath. This festival was a thanksgiving for God's bounty in the harvest yet to come.

In the first century AD, the term had come to represent any blessing of God given as a first installment of more to come. Paul spoke of the indwelling Holy Spirit in this way, that is, as the anticipatory promise of one day being bodily in the very presence of God.

Romans 8:23 (RSV)
²³ and not only the creation, but we ourselves, who have the first fruits of the Spirit, groan inwardly as we wait for adoption as sons, the redemption of our bodies.

It also had the connotation of the most excellent, or crowning emblem of a larger group. James speaks with this meaning.

James 1:18 (NKJV)
¹⁸ Of His own will He brought us forth by the word of truth, that we might be a kind of firstfruits of His creatures.

It is in this understanding of *firstfruits* meaning 'preeminence' that in 1 Corinthians 15 Paul is making reference to the festival of firstfruits to demonstrate that just as Jesus was resurrected, so shall we also be resurrected. Read again, together with verse 20.

1 Corinthians 15:20,23 (NKJV)
[20] But now Christ is risen from the dead, and has become the firstfruits of those who have fallen asleep . . . [23] But each one in his own order: Christ the firstfruits, afterward those who are Christ's at His coming.

When the Feast of Firstfruits was celebrated in Old Testament times, it was a foreshadowing portrayal of Jesus' resurrection being a firstfruits of a bountiful harvest to come--the resurrection to eternal life of those saved by faith. They were celebrating Jesus' firstfruits resurrection without realizing it.

Other New Testament passages present the same concept, without making specific reference to the firstfruits analogy.

Acts 26:23 (ESV)
[23] that the Christ must suffer and that, by being the first to rise from the dead, he would proclaim light both to our people and to the Gentiles."

Colossians 1:18 (ESV)
[18] And he is the head of the body, the church. He is the beginning, the firstborn from the dead, that in everything he might be preeminent.

Revelation 1:5 (ESV)
[5] and from Jesus Christ the faithful witness, the firstborn of the dead, and the ruler of kings on earth. To him who loves us and has freed us from our sins by his blood

Resurrection is not just another of several tenets of the Christian faith. It was, and is, foundational in Jesus' teaching and in that of his disciples. We see this centrality of resurrection in Paul's writings.

1 Corinthians 15:3-4 (NKJV)
[3] For I delivered to you first of all that which I also received: that Christ died for our sins according to the Scriptures, [4] and that He was buried, and that He rose again the third day according to the Scriptures,

1 Corinthians 15:16-20 (NKJV)
[16] For if the dead do not rise, then Christ is not risen. [17] And if Christ is not risen, your faith is futile; you are still in your sins! [18] Then also those who have fallen asleep in Christ have perished. [19] If in this life only we have hope in Christ, we are of all men the most

> pitiable. [20] But now Christ is risen from the dead, and has become the firstfruits of those who have fallen asleep.

When the Roman governor Festus conveyed his case against Paul to Herod Agrippa II, he said . . .

> Acts 25:18-19 (ESV)
> [18] When the accusers stood up, they brought no charge in his case of such evils as I supposed. [19] Rather they had certain points of dispute with him about their own religion and about a certain Jesus, who was dead, but whom Paul asserted to be alive.

The death and resurrection of Jesus was the defining feature of Christianity, so much so that even the Roman leaders understood its centrality to this 'sect'. Today, it must likewise be at the heart of our belief. It cannot be denied or made a sideline issue by any congregation or group, without distancing themselves from God. It is at the heart of the gospel message.

Religion Smorgasbord
Consider what the doctrine of resurrection means. To highlight it, let's compare it to the alternatives that existed in the world of Jesus' day, for they are similar to the options we have before us today. Begin with the premise that people want immortality. They want to live forever (free from the burdens of this life, of course).

There were many religions out there. Besides Judaism, there were Roman and Greek mythologies, Greek philosophies and eastern mysticism. Imagine yourself an Epicurean, and believe that there is no afterlife. You believe in annihilation of the soul at death. You simply cease to exist. This philosophy is still with us—"You only go 'round once in life. Ya gotta grab for all the gusto you can get." In this ideology, you try to define God out of the picture and therefore eliminate any accountability. When death looms near this is not a very comforting position, it seems to me.

The Stoics, another group of Greek philosophers believed that each person had within him a spark of the essence of god, and at death, that spark was absorbed back into the nature-continuum that was itself god. You didn't cease to exist; you just lost your identity. Today's New Age beliefs are very similar. These philosophies, though originating far away, had infiltrated the land of Palestine, and indeed the whole Roman world of that time.

Eastern mystery religions introduced strange concepts such as the teaching that we today call reincarnation. At death you did not lose your existence or your identity, but your characterizing personality. After death the soul was seen to live on, but it was assigned a new form in which to live. No distinction was made between men and animals. You might be a wealthy man in one life, but come back as a fruit fly.

Christianity embraces the doctrine of a bodily resurrection. In resurrection the dead body is replaced with a new body, which reunites with the person's soul and spirit. After this reunion, the whole person will retain his existence, his identity, his essential personality. He will be recognizable.

Now let us personalize this. When YOU are resurrected, YOU will be made complete in Christ Jesus. YOU will still be you, but without the veil of mortality attached. What an awesome and comforting thought. What a joyful expectation. What a motivation to do our best to live here and now like we hope to live then.

<u>The Resurrection Body</u>
When we speak of a bodily resurrection, what do we mean? What type of body will we have? Paul addressed this question as as much as it was revealed to him:

> *1 Corinthians 15:35-49 (NIV2011)*
> *[35] But someone will ask, "How are the dead raised? With what kind of body will they come?" [36] How foolish! What you sow does not come to life unless it dies. [37] When you sow, you do not plant the body that will be, but just a seed, perhaps of wheat or of something else. [38] But God gives it a body as he has determined, and to each kind of seed he gives its own body. [39] Not all flesh is the same: People have one kind of flesh, animals have another, birds another and fish another. [40] There are also heavenly bodies and there are earthly bodies; but the splendor of the heavenly bodies is one kind, and the splendor of the earthly bodies is another. [41] The sun has one kind of splendor, the moon another and the stars another; and star differs from star in splendor. [42] So will it be with the resurrection of the dead. The body that is sown is perishable, it is raised imperishable; [43] it is sown in dishonor, it is raised in glory; it is sown in weakness, it is raised in power; [44] it is sown a natural body, it is raised a spiritual body. If there is a natural body, there is also a spiritual body. [45] So it is written: "The first man Adam became a living being"; the last Adam, a life-giving spirit. [46] The spiritual did not come first, but the natural, and after that the spiritual. [47] The first man was of the dust of the earth; the second man is of heaven. [48] As was the earthly man, so are those who are of the earth; and as is the heavenly man, so also are those who are of heaven. [49] And just as we have borne the image of the earthly man, so shall we bear the image of the heavenly man.*

The essence of our new bodies are not defined because we have no frame of reference in glory to which they can be compared. He simply emphasizes the contrast of different 'bodies' from our natural experiences. The central idea is that what you harvest is not a replica of what was sown, but is exceedingly more excellent. Yet, amazingly the old is in the identity of the new. The resurrected person bears distinguishing uniqueness with the old, just as the full grown plant shares the same DNA as the seed. It would seem our new selves will be recognizable as transformations of our former selves.

> Praise be to you, Oh Lord God, for You raised your son back to life. You restored him to a bodily existence. You preserved his identity and his personality. Great are You, Father!! Great are you!!! Raise us up like Jesus was raised, we pray and anticipate. We fully recognize that the immortality we long for is not within us, but is a gift from you. Thank you. Thank you for this priceless gift. Amen

Redemption

The resurrection of the righteous means more than being raised to eternal life. In this life 'being good' is a struggle against temptation and fear. Our sinful nature that still resides within us in this life wars against us. Paul describes this burdensome dilemma.

> *Romans 7:21-25 (RSV)*
> [21] *So I find it to be a law that when I want to do right, evil lies close at hand.* [22] *For I delight in the law of God, in my inmost self,* [23] *but I see in my members another law at war with the law of my mind and making me captive to the law of sin which dwells in my members.* [24] *Wretched man that I am! Who will deliver me from this body of death?* [25] *Thanks be to God through Jesus Christ our Lord! So then, I of myself serve the law of God with my mind, but with my flesh I serve the law of sin.*

The *body of death* refers to our mortal body, plagued with an incurable malady known as the *sinful nature*. If we were raised to immortality only to continue struggling forever with our old sinful nature, that might not be a blessing at all.

The blessing of resurrection is that we will be made new. When we came to faith in Jesus, we were told that we were a new creation--and so we were. At salvation the Holy Spirit came to reside within us, and to put God's will within our mind. But while we had peace with God, we found we had a struggle with ourselves, just like Paul. The Holy Spirit is a deposit against what is to come. He does not control us forcibly, but in cooperation with our own will. We never rise completely above our old self as long as we are in this body.

Ephesians 4:30 (ESV)
30 And do not grieve the Holy Spirit of God, by whom you were sealed for the day of redemption.

Ephesians 1:13-14 (ESV)
13 In him you also, when you heard the word of truth, the gospel of your salvation, and believed in him, were sealed with the promised Holy Spirit, 14 who is the guarantee of our inheritance until we acquire possession of it, to the praise of his glory.

Paul saw not only the personal struggle against sin, but through the perspective of God's ultimate purpose for His creation, he saw a global struggle:

Romans 8:19-23 (RSV)
19 For the creation waits with eager longing for the revealing of the sons of God; 20 for the creation was subjected to futility, not of its own will but by the will of him who subjected it in hope; 21 because the creation itself will be set free from its bondage to decay and obtain the glorious liberty of the children of God. 22 We know that the whole creation has been groaning in travail together until now; 23 and not only the creation, but we ourselves, who have the first fruits of the Spirit, groan inwardly as we wait for adoption as sons, the redemption of our bodies.

In resurrection, we will be made new in the ultimate sense. We will be made into the likeness of Jesus in holiness.

Philippians 3:20-21 (ESV)
20 But our citizenship is in heaven, and from it we await a Savior, the Lord Jesus Christ, 21 who will transform our lowly body to be like his glorious body, by the power that enables him even to subject all things to himself.

1 John 3:2 (ESV)
2 Beloved, we are God's children now, and what we will be has not yet appeared; but we know that when he appears we shall be like him, because we shall see him as he is.

2 Timothy 4:8 (ESV)
⁸ Henceforth there is laid up for me the crown of righteousness, which the Lord, the righteous judge, will award to me on that Day, and not only to me but also to all who have loved his appearing.

Are we expectantly awaiting His return? Are we the passionate romantic or the self-focused spouse? In the resurrection we will not only put on immortality, but we will put on a crown of righteousness--the likeness of Jesus. In all of this, God's purpose for us is fulfilled:

Romans 8:29-30 (RSV)
²⁹ For those whom he foreknew he also predestined to be conformed to the image of his Son, in order that he might be the first-born among many brethren. ³⁰ And those whom he predestined he also called; and those whom he called he also justified; and those whom he justified he also glorified.

Knowing our citizenship is already in heaven, and knowing our redemption is sealed, knowing the day of resurrection is coming when we will be like him, we are motivated and empowered to live a resurrected life. That is, we should and can, live a life consistent with the hope within us. The likeness of Christ is already being formed within us. Paul wrote:

2 Corinthians 3:18 (NASB)
¹⁸ But we all, with unveiled face, beholding as in a mirror the glory of the Lord, are being transformed into the same image from glory to glory, just as from the Lord, the Spirit.

Thus, resurrection finalizes both our immortality and our transformation into the likeness of Christ, those characteristics with which we enter eternal life.

9
A HIDDEN MYSTERY REVEALED

When we delve into prophecy, we expect to have things revealed to us. However, in times past, prophecy often concealed rather than revealed. The gospel of redemption is the primary theme of prophecy. It is clearly presented over and over again in the New Testament. It was also presented in the Old Testament, as we saw in a previous chapter, and will see further in this chapter. It was presented in such a way that it was veiled in Old Testament times, and concealed from their understanding. It is not because it was not spoken of in the Old Testament, as we shall show, but because God presented His message in a way they could not grasp. It suited His purpose to delay understanding. This is a reality we must understand in studying prophecy. It is helpful, in studying prophecy, to recognize what the contemporary recipients did not understand, as well as to know what they did understand. We will see this in this chapter.

In New Testament language, the original Greek word *musterion* means 'that which is not understood,' and is translated by our English word 'mystery.' In Greek, it is not quite like our English usage. To us, if something is mysterious, it often implies something unknowable with a sort of dark connotation. In biblical usage, it speaks of things that simply haven't been revealed yet, or that haven't yet become understood. This is by God's intention. He both conceals and reveals things at a time of His choosing.

God's intentional revealing and concealing in the Old Testament is clearly seen. For example, we already noted in Chapter 1 of this book that the Old Testament prophet Daniel was shown a glimpse of things to come, but when he inquired further...

> *Daniel 12:8-9 (NKJV)*
> [8] *Although I heard, I did not understand. Then I said, "My lord, what shall be the end of these things?"* [9] *And he said, "Go your way, Daniel, for the words are closed up and sealed till the time of the end.*

In the closing book of the New Testament, a different command is given to John for believers:

> *Revelation 22:10 (ESV)*
> *¹⁰ And he said to me, "Do not seal up the words of the prophecy of this book, for the time is near.*

What was veiled and sealed up in Daniel's day, has been unsealed and revealed in John's day. The difference-maker for these two occasions is the cross and resurrection of Jesus. Daniel lived before the cross, in Old Testament times. John lived in the first century, continuing after the death and resurrection of Christ, in New Testament times.

What is this mystery theme? In the New Testament, it is called the *mystery of the gospel*. Jesus began to unveil the mystery to his disciples when he said:

> *Matthew 13:16-17 (KJV)*
> *¹⁶ But blessed are your eyes, for they see: and your ears, for they hear. ¹⁷ For verily I say unto you, That many prophets and righteous men have desired to see those things which ye see, and have not seen them; and to hear those things which ye hear, and have not heard them.*

As we have said, the mystery was not a mystery because God had not mentioned it in times past. The fact is, its various aspects are referred to often in the Old Testament, as we shall see. It was a mystery because references to it were like puzzle pieces that hadn't been put into place. From their perspective, rooted before the cross, Jewish people could not understand the mind and plans of God.

Looking from this side of the cross, we see a clear purpose of God in His redemptive scheme. But those living before the cross could not fathom these passages, and so they remained veiled, in ages past. Ancient scholars took note of them, but could not figure out how to fit the puzzle pieces together. Thus, for them they became perimeter passages rather than figuring directly into God's redemptive plan.

What exactly is the *mystery of the gospel*? Whatever it is, Paul considered it worth sacrificing his freedom and his very life for.

> *Colossians 4:3 (ESV)*
> *³ At the same time, pray also for us, that God may open to us a door for the word, to declare the mystery of Christ, on account of which I am in prison—*

Paul is the most outspoken of New Testament writers regarding this mystery. He uses the word fifteen times in his writings that now make up a major part of the New Testament. The mystery encompasses several bombshell concepts that were not understood in Old Testament times. They were bombshells because they ran contrary to contemporary Jewish understanding and customs of the culture. They were bombshells because they were inflammatory to the status quo. The whole package of the mystery was put into operation leading up to a final goal. Paul wrote:

> *Ephesians 1:9-10 (ESV)*
> *⁹ making known to us the mystery of his will, according to his purpose, which he set forth in Christ ¹⁰ as a plan for the fullness of time, to unite all things in him, things in heaven and things on earth.*

Christ must have the preeminence. He must be sovereign over all. But prior to that, he said and did some things that created quite a stir. What are these bombshell concepts imbedded in this mystery? Following are the major facets of it that emerge as we read the passages.

Jesus is the Way

> *1 Timothy 3:16 (NKJV)*
> *¹⁶ And without controversy great is the mystery of godliness: God was manifested in the flesh, Justified in the Spirit, Seen by angels, Preached among the Gentiles, Believed on in the world, Received up in glory.*

From a redemptive doctrine point of view, the mystery of the gospel was the sacrificial death and resurrection of God's incarnate Son, Christ Jesus. The idea that God Himself would enter the human race and give his life to ransom sinful mankind was beyond the wildest imagination of the Jewish mind of Jesus' day. In this newly revealed agenda of God's, the way to righteousness—the way to reconciliation with God—is through faith and acceptance of the substitutionary death of Jesus, as we discussed in chapter 7. This was the message of all the apostles.

> *1 John 5:11-13 (NKJV)*
> *¹¹ And this is the testimony: that God has given us eternal life, and this life is in His Son. ¹² He who has the Son has life; he who does not have the Son of God does not have life. ¹³ These things I have written to you who believe in the name of the Son of God, that you may know that you have eternal life, and that you may continue to believe in the name of the Son of God.*

> *John 14:6 (NKJV)*
> *⁶ Jesus said to him, "I am the way, the truth, and the life. No one comes to the Father except through Me.*

Acts 4:12 (NKJV)
[12] Nor is there salvation in any other, for there is no other name under heaven given among men by which we must be saved."

By God's grace alone, we may come to a salvation relationship with God through His Son. In Old Testament times, even the prophets themselves were without full understanding, as witnessed by Peter:

1 Peter 1:10-12,18-20 (NKJV)
[10] Of this salvation the prophets have inquired and searched carefully, who prophesied of the grace that would come to you, [11] searching what, or what manner of time, the Spirit of Christ who was in them was indicating when He testified beforehand the sufferings of Christ and the glories that would follow. [12] To them it was revealed that, not to themselves, but to us they were ministering the things which now have been reported to you through those who have preached the gospel to you by the Holy Spirit sent from heaven--things which angels desire to look into . . . [18] knowing that you were not redeemed with corruptible things, like silver or gold, from your aimless conduct received by tradition from your fathers, [19] but with the precious blood of Christ, as of a lamb without blemish and without spot. [20] He indeed was foreordained before the foundation of the world, but was manifest in these last times for you

This novel way to God bypassed Jewish identity, Jewish law and tradition, and Jewish heritage. Naturally, there was tremendous opposition to this Gospel by the Jewish leadership. Nevertheless, this is the truth that the apostles preached.

Jesus is the Long-Awaited Messiah
The resurrection was the pivot point of understanding, bolstered by the post-resurrection teachings of Jesus, and the coming of the Holy Spirit at Pentecost. A microcosm of how this before-the-resurrection and after-the-resurrection perspective made the difference in understanding is seen in the lives of the apostles themselves. After Jesus' arrest and prior to his resurrection, Jesus' disciples were in complete confusion and dismay. After his resurrection was made evident, they began to put the whole puzzle together. The seemingly disjointed prophecies of the Old Testament suddenly fell into place. The eternal agenda became cohesive, consistent, and unified. The Messiah had indeed come! The Messiah had completed his plan, and fulfilled his purpose. Jesus was the long-awaited Messiah.

Romans 3:21-24 (RSV)
[21] But now the righteousness of God has been manifested apart from law, although the law and the prophets bear witness to it, [22] the righteousness of God through faith in Jesus Christ for all who

believe. For there is no distinction; ^{23} *since all have sinned and fall short of the glory of God,* ^{24} *they are justified by his grace as a gift, through the redemption which is in Christ Jesus,*

This is central to the gospel mystery. It is the core of the plan put in place from the mind of God *before creation*. Messiah was not a liberator of national Israel from Roman bondage. In his incarnation, Messiah was the author of spiritual salvation in an eternal sense. Jesus was the long-awaited Messiah, who was *chosen before the creation of the world, but was revealed in these last times for your sake.* Jesus is the mystery Messiah. Peter wrote this of him . . .

2 Peter 1:16-19 (ESV)
^{16} For we did not follow cleverly devised myths when we made known to you the power and coming of our Lord Jesus Christ, but we were eyewitnesses of his majesty. ^{17} For when he received honor and glory from God the Father, and the voice was borne to him by the Majestic Glory, "This is my beloved Son, with whom I am well pleased," ^{18} we ourselves heard this very voice borne from heaven, for we were with him on the holy mountain. ^{19} And we have the prophetic word more fully confirmed, to which you will do well to pay attention as to a lamp shining in a dark place, until the day dawns and the morning star rises in your hearts,

Peter's readers of the first century were told that they would do well to pay attention to the words of the prophets because it is the prophecies that laid the undeniable groundwork for Jesus to be recognized as the Messiah of promise. The apostles were eyewitnesses of God's verbal confirmation of his identity. For them, their experience solidified the words of the prophets. Prophecies are also laying groundwork for his second coming. Peter's message is for us too. We would do well to pay attention to what lies ahead, as prophesied.

The Mystery Nature of Messiah
The personal identity of Messiah was not the only messianic mystery. Jews of the first century were looking for a Messiah. Prophecy was converging on the timeline of those days. The air was buzzing with the hope of Messiah's soon arrival. The culture was electrified with expectation. The possibly imminent coming of Messiah was not a mystery. The mystery was that they didn't know exactly what to expect in him. What they didn't know about him was the nature of his being. Most expected a man whom God would endow with His Spirit, but was otherwise an ordinary man. Some looked for a warrior. Some looked for a prophet after the pattern of the Old Testament prophets. Some thought he would actually be an Old Testament prophet such as Isaiah or Elijah, resurrected in their day. Some even thought he might be an angel. Speculation ran high on the subject. When

John the Baptist exploded onto the scene, great crowds came to him in the desert to hear him and to be baptized by him.

Luke 3:15-17 (RSV)
[15] As the people were in expectation, and all men questioned in their hearts concerning John, whether perhaps he were the Christ, [16] John answered them all, "I baptize you with water; but he who is mightier than I is coming, the thong of whose sandals I am not worthy to untie; he will baptize you with the Holy Spirit and with fire. [17] His winnowing fork is in his hand, to clear his threshing floor, and to gather the wheat into his granary, but the chaff he will burn with unquenchable fire."

John 1:19-23 (NKJV)
[19] Now this is the testimony of John, when the Jews sent priests and Levites from Jerusalem to ask him, "Who are you?" [20] He confessed, and did not deny, but confessed, "I am not the Christ." [21] And they asked him, "What then? Are you Elijah?" He said, "I am not." "Are you the Prophet?" And he answered, "No." [22] Then they said to him, "Who are you, that we may give an answer to those who sent us? What do you say about yourself?" [23] He said: "I am 'The voice of one crying in the wilderness: "Make straight the way of the LORD," ' as the prophet Isaiah said."

The people were expecting something big to happen. They were expecting someone great to come. They were not expecting God Himself. When Jesus began to reveal his divine nature to them, it created an identity crisis. Many were not prepared to hear such a thing. If they had taken seriously the prophecies of Isaiah, they would not have been surprised by this. He proclaimed the nature of the Messiah clearly.

Isaiah 7:14 (RSV)
[14] Therefore the Lord himself will give you a sign. Behold, a young woman shall conceive and bear a son, and shall call his name Imman'u-el.

(The meaning of the word Immanuel is explained in the New Testament telling of this prophecy.)

Matthew 1:22-23 (NASB)
[22] Now all this took place to fulfill what was spoken by the Lord through the prophet: [23] "BEHOLD, THE VIRGIN SHALL BE WITH CHILD AND SHALL BEAR A SON, AND THEY SHALL CALL HIS NAME IMMANUEL," which translated means, "GOD WITH US."

Isaiah 9:6-7 (RSV)
⁶ For to us a child is born, to us a son is given; and the government will be upon his shoulder, and his name will be called "Wonderful Counselor, Mighty God, Everlasting Father, Prince of Peace." ⁷ Of the increase of his government and of peace there will be no end, upon the throne of David, and over his kingdom, to establish it, and to uphold it with justice and with righteousness from this time forth and for evermore. The zeal of the LORD of hosts will do this.

Isaiah 40:9-11 (RSV)
⁹ Get you up to a high mountain, O Zion, herald of good tidings; lift up your voice with strength, O Jerusalem, herald of good tidings, lift it up, fear not; say to the cities of Judah, "Behold your God!" ¹⁰ Behold, the Lord GOD comes with might, and his arm rules for him; behold, his reward is with him, and his recompense before him. ¹¹ He will feed his flock like a shepherd, he will gather the lambs in his arms, he will carry them in his bosom, and gently lead those that are with young.

The prophesied Messiah was called "God with us," "Mighty God," and "Sovereign Lord." Still, in spite of all these prophecies and many others, it came as a mystery to them. They still did not understand. When Jesus proclaimed before the Sanhedrin his divine identity, they tore their clothes and cried, "*blasphemy.*" When he died the death of a criminal on the cross, they were certain he was not God. They were certain, but they were wrong. The prophet predicted this error, and the apostles pointed to this in supporting their claims of Jesus as Messiah.

Isaiah 8:13-14(NKJ)
¹³ The LORD of hosts, Him you shall hallow; let Him be your fear, and let Him be your dread. ¹⁴He will be as a sanctuary, but a stone of stumbling and a rock of offense to both the houses of Israel, as a trap and a snare to the inhabitants of Jerusalem.

Isaiah 28:16(NKJ)
¹⁶ Therefore thus says the Lord GOD: "Behold, I lay in Zion a stone for a foundation, a tried stone, a precious cornerstone, a sure foundation; whoever believes will not act hastily.

Matthew 21:42(NKJ)
⁴² Jesus said to them, "Have you never read in the Scriptures: 'The stone which the builders rejected has become the chief cornerstone. This was the Lord's doing, and it is marvelous in our eyes'?

Romans 9:31-33(NKJ)
[31] but Israel, pursuing the law of righteousness, has not attained to the law of righteousness. [32] Why? Because they did not seek it by faith, but as it were, by the works of the law. For they stumbled at that stumbling stone. [33] As it is written: "Behold, I lay in Zion a stumbling stone and rock of offense, and whoever believes on Him will not be put to shame."

1 Peter 2:7-8(NKJ)
[7] Therefore, to you who believe, He is precious; but to those who are disobedient, "The stone which the builders rejected has become the chief cornerstone," [8] and "A stone of stumbling and a rock of offense." They stumble, being disobedient to the word, to which they also were appointed.

In the newly formed church, the incarnation of God in Jesus was taught consistently by the apostles, and is a foundational doctrine of Christianity, as expressed in the following.

John 1:1,14 (NKJV)
[1] In the beginning was the Word, and the Word was with God, and the Word was God. . . [14] And the Word became flesh and dwelt among us, and we beheld His glory, the glory as of the only begotten of the Father, full of grace and truth.

Philippians 2:5-7 (ESV)
[5] . . . Christ Jesus, [6] who, though he was in the form of God, did not count equality with God a thing to be grasped, [7] but emptied himself, by taking the form of a servant, being born in the likeness of men.

Of course the New Testament is replete with passages attesting to the truth of the incarnation of the Word. To the Jews of Jesus' day, it was an offense; a stumbling block. Nevertheless, understanding of this fundamental truth was, and is, a necessity of redeeming faith. It is the mystery that divides mankind.

2 Corinthians 2:15-16 (NASB)
[15] For we are a fragrance of Christ to God among those who are being saved and among those who are perishing; [16] to the one an aroma from death to death, to the other an aroma from life to life. And who is adequate for these things?

The Mystery of a Different Kind of Kingdom

The concept of a new kingdom to be ushered in by Messiah was the common expectation of the day. This was not a surprise. However the nature of the kingdom that Jesus brought and proclaimed was very different from the typical Jewish expectation. It is very different from the kingdoms men build today. This kingdom was not anticipated. Jesus spoke of the *secrets of the kingdom* while teaching in parables.

> *Luke 8:10 (ESV)*
> *¹⁰ he said, "To you it has been given to know the secrets of the kingdom of God, but for others they are in parables, so that 'seeing they may not see, and hearing they may not understand.'*

And when he stood before Pilot at his trial:

> *John 18:36 (NKJV)*
> *³⁶ Jesus answered, "My kingdom is not of this world. If My kingdom were of this world, My servants would fight, so that I should not be delivered to the Jews; but now My kingdom is not from here."*

The nature of the kingdom of God was a mystery to Jewish people of Old Testament times and remained a mystery in Jesus' day, and that fact alone blinded them from his truth. Much space is given in the New Testament to teaching about *the kingdom of heaven*, also called *the kingdom of God*. The average Jew of Jesus' day was familiar with the concept and the promises of a kingdom ruled by God himself. In a prophetic vision, Daniel had been told about it.

> *Daniel 2:44 (NKJV)*
> *⁴⁴ And in the days of these kings the God of heaven will set up a kingdom which shall never be destroyed; and the kingdom shall not be left to other people; it shall break in pieces and consume all these kingdoms, and it shall stand forever.*

Yet, his understanding was clouded by long-standing traditions and national elitism. He had difficulty embracing a kingdom bigger than earthly Israel. Furthermore, the nature of that kingdom was not clear, just as the nature of Messiah himself had not been clear. They could only conceive of a kingdom that operated on the same principles as other kingdoms. When Jesus introduced the precepts of the kingdom, they seemed like foolishness. The kingdom Jesus revealed seemed not only contrary to Jewish tradition, but also to natural human logic; happy are the poor, happy are those that mourn, happy are the persecuted. It was so different that it was difficult to be unveiled in their minds. And so the kingdom was part of the *mystery of the gospel*.

> *Ephesians 1:9-10 (ESV)*
> *⁹ making known to us the mystery of his will, according to his purpose, which he set forth in Christ ¹⁰ as a plan for the fullness of time, to unite all things in him, things in heaven and things on earth.*

God's intention to bring everything into willful submissive relationship with Jesus has now been revealed to us and it is our focus as we celebrate God's purpose for the ages.

The Mystery of the Indwelling Spirit

Another mystery treasure in the gospel was the indwelling of the Holy Spirit. Paul wrote this to the church at Colossae:

> *Colossians 1:25-27 (ESV)*
> *²⁵ of which I became a minister according to the stewardship from God that was given to me for you, to make the word of God fully known, ²⁶ the mystery hidden for ages and generations but now revealed to his saints. ²⁷ To them God chose to make known how great among the Gentiles are the riches of the glory of this mystery, which is Christ in you, the hope of glory.*

Christ in you! In scripture, the Holy Spirit is also called *the Spirit of God* and *the Spirit of Christ*. Thus, Paul could say *Christ in you* with respect to the indwelling of the Holy Spirit. In the same way Jesus could say:

> *John 14:26,28a (NKJV)*
> *²⁶ But the Helper, the Holy Spirit, whom the Father will send in My name, He will teach you all things, and bring to your remembrance all things that I said to you . . .²⁸ You have heard Me say to you, 'I am going away and coming back to you.' . . .*

The context indicates his *coming back* to them in this passage was not referring to Christ's second coming, but was anticipating the Holy Spirit's coming, and *Christ in you* in the preceding scripture is speaking of the indwelling of the Spirit. All this to show that the indwelling Spirit was an integral part of the mystery of the gospel. Notice the involvement of all three members of the Trinity here.

This indwelling was initiated on Pentecost, fifty days after Passover and after the death and resurrection of Jesus. In the history of the human race, this had never before been a reality. Certain men, prophets, kings, and priests had, on occasion, received the direct, temporary intervention of the Holy Spirit as God made His will known to them. However, once the prophetic discourse was finished, they were left alone again. But now, under the new covenant, the Spirit indwells all who accept in faith the atoning work of Jesus, and there is no departure as in Old Testament times. This was foreseen by the Old Testament prophet Joel and others.

> *Joel 2:28-29 (NKJV)*
> *[28] "And it shall come to pass afterward That I will pour out My Spirit on all flesh; Your sons and your daughters shall prophesy, Your old men shall dream dreams, Your young men shall see visions. [29] And also on My menservants and on My maidservants I will pour out My Spirit in those days.*

> *Isaiah 32:14-15 (RSV)*
> *[14] For the palace will be forsaken, the populous city deserted; the hill and the watchtower will become dens forever, a joy of wild asses, a pasture of flocks; [15] until the Spirit is poured upon us from on high, and the wilderness becomes a fruitful field, and the fruitful field is deemed a forest.*

> *Isaiah 44:3 (RSV)*
> *[3] For I will pour water on the thirsty land, and streams on the dry ground; I will pour my Spirit upon your descendants, and my blessing on your offspring.*

> *Ezekiel 39:29 (NASB)*
> *[29] "I will not hide My face from them any longer, for I will have poured out My Spirit on the house of Israel," declares the Lord GOD.*

In spite of these predictions by Israel's prophets, no one quite knew what to make of them. But on the day of Pentecost following Jesus' ascension, when the Holy Spirit filled the believers in Jerusalem, some onlookers accused them of being drunk. Peter stood up and defended them, stating that this was the fulfillment of Joel's prophecy.

> *Acts 2:15-18 (ESV)*
> *[15] For these people are not drunk, as you suppose, since it is only the third hour of the day. [16] But this is what was uttered through the prophet Joel: [17] "'And in the last days it shall be, God declares, that I will pour out my Spirit on all flesh, and your sons and your daughters shall prophesy, and your young men shall see visions, and your old men shall dream dreams; [18] even on my male servants and female servants in those days I will pour out my Spirit, and they shall prophesy.*

The idea of the indwelling and abiding presence of God's Spirit was a brand new human experience. It is this reality that enables genuine believers in

New Testament times to live God-focused lives—holy lives, honoring Him. Jesus said:

> *Matthew 11:28-30 (ESV)*
> [28] Come to me, all who labor and are heavy laden, and I will give you rest. [29] Take my yoke upon you, and learn from me, for I am gentle and lowly in heart, and you will find rest for your souls. [30] For my yoke is easy, and my burden is light."

What yoke was Jesus referring to? What was his light burden? It is the yoke of his lordship, his kingship in our lives. It is the burden of denying ourselves, and following him. Later, John wrote:

> *1 John 5:3 (ESV)*
> [3] For this is the love of God, that we keep his commandments. And his commandments are not burdensome.

Why are the commands of Jesus not burdensome? Why is his yoke easy? Is it because his commands were easier than those of the old covenant? No! Just the opposite is true. Jesus said,

> *Matthew 5:20-22a (NASB)*
> [20] "For I say to you that unless your righteousness surpasses that of the scribes and Pharisees, you will not enter the kingdom of heaven. [21] "You have heard that the ancients were told, 'YOU SHALL NOT COMMIT MURDER' and 'Whoever commits murder shall be liable to the court.' [22] "But I say to you that everyone who is angry with his brother shall be guilty before the court . . .

Jesus continued on to apply the principles of the kingdom to immorality, divorce, honesty, and love for enemies. He got past the external practices to the heart of a person. No, he didn't lower the standard of righteousness. He elevated it. It is true that a king can put a heavy burden on his subjects if his demands are too great. The Old Testament law was a burden on the Jews because they were unable to completely fulfill it. This is attested to in the New Testament, when the council of Jerusalem convened with the apostles and Paul and Barnabas present. They discussed the 'burden' of the law:

> *Acts 15:10,28 (ESV)*
> [10] Now, therefore, why are you putting God to the test by placing a yoke on the neck of the disciples that neither our fathers nor we have been able to bear? . . . [28] For it has seemed good to the Holy Spirit and to us to lay on you no greater burden than these requirements:

So how could John say that *his commands are not burdensome* if the bar is raised on righteous standards in the new kingdom? It is because of this mystery of the indwelling of the Holy Spirit. Laws are burdensome when they legislate against our personal desires. Under the leading of the Holy Spirit, our own wills and desires are being transformed to be like God's. Therefore, keeping his commands is now something we delight in doing, not something that wars against our will. It is not burdensome. No other way could have preserved His will in us. How wise He is.

The Mystery of Redemption for the Nations

This was the most flagrant mystery to the Jewish traditionalists of Jesus' day. This teaching could have started a riot or gotten a person stoned to death in first century Palestine. The Jews of Old Testament times were very aware of their uniqueness in God's redemptive plan. Instead of understanding their uniqueness as a mandate for outreach, they saw it as a privilege to be guarded. They developed an exclusive spirit that barred any non-Jew from participating in the revealed knowledge of God with which they had been entrusted. Into this mentality exploded the *mystery of the gospel*. In Paul's perspective, this was the most veiled and misunderstood aspect of the mystery. This is the characteristic of the mystery that he repeatedly displays in his writings. This was his mystery of mysteries.

> *Romans 16:25-27 (RSV)*
> *[25] Now to him who is able to strengthen you according to my gospel and the preaching of Jesus Christ, according to the revelation of the mystery which was kept secret for long ages [26] but is now disclosed and through the prophetic writings is made known to all nations, according to the command of the eternal God, to bring about the obedience of faith -- [27] to the only wise God be glory for evermore through Jesus Christ! Amen.*

Whenever scripture speaks of *"nations,"* it is talking about Gentile nations, nations outside the nation Israel. We see God's purpose here to encompass all mankind in His redemptive plan. How would the nations be included? Would the nations be as conquered slaves to redeemed Israel, worshipping Israel's God in fear? Would they merely be in an outer court looking in, so to speak—worshipping, but never fully included? Paul writes:

> *Ephesians 3:1-12 (ESV)*
> *[1] For this reason I, Paul, a prisoner for Christ Jesus on behalf of you Gentiles— [2] assuming that you have heard of the stewardship of God's grace that was given to me for you, [3] how the mystery was made known to me by revelation, as I have written briefly. [4] When you read this, you can perceive my insight into the mystery of Christ, [5] which was not made known to the sons of men in other generations as it has now been revealed to his holy apostles and*

> *prophets by the Spirit. ⁶ This mystery is that the Gentiles are fellow heirs, members of the same body, and partakers of the promise in Christ Jesus through the gospel. ⁷ Of this gospel I was made a minister according to the gift of God's grace, which was given me by the working of his power. ⁸ To me, though I am the very least of all the saints, this grace was given, to preach to the Gentiles the unsearchable riches of Christ, ⁹ and to bring to light for everyone what is the plan of the mystery hidden for ages in God who created all things, ¹⁰ so that through the church the manifold wisdom of God might now be made known to the rulers and authorities in the heavenly places. ¹¹ This was according to the eternal purpose that he has realized in Christ Jesus our Lord, ¹² in whom we have boldness and access with confidence through our faith in him.*

No, the Gentiles would not be included as slaves or as onlookers, but on equal standing with the faithful of Israel.

> *Hebrews 11:40 (NKJV)*
> *⁴⁰ God having provided something better for us* [New Testament Christians], *that they* [the faithful of Old Testament Israel] *should not be made perfect apart from us.*

This mystery is that through the gospel the Gentiles are heirs together with Israel, members together of one body, and sharers together in the promise in Christ Jesus. It began in the mind of God long before the redemptive initiative of Jesus was set into motion. Through prophetic revelation, we have a unique, remarkable, and magnificent little window into a heavenly dialog taking place between the Father and the Son, prior to his incarnation. How great in scope is this.

> *Isaiah 49:6 (RSV)*
> *⁶ he says: "It is too light a thing that you should be my servant to raise up the tribes of Jacob and to restore the preserved of Israel; I will give you as a light to the nations, that my salvation may reach to the end of the earth."*

The redemption of Israel was the great hope of all Jews of that day. But as great as that was, God had a much larger purpose, the redemption of people from all over the world. This is the best news of all for those of us who are not Jewish. This changes everything for us! But, how could this be? How could those who did not have the Law, the patriarchs, the temple, the old covenants—how could they be included? Let's revisit this passage.

> *Colossians 1:26-27 (ESV)*
> *²⁶ the mystery hidden for ages and generations but now revealed to his saints. ²⁷ To them God chose to make known how great among*

the Gentiles are the riches of the glory of this mystery, which is Christ in you, the hope of glory.

As with the other aspects of the mystery, the inclusion of Gentiles was also prophesied in the Old Testament period, but the message was not heeded by a Jewish nation that preferred to be elitists rather than evangelists. It should have been clear, but it was veiled to the Jews. Here are some of the references in which God's purpose was prophesied in the Old Testament. First, the call of Abraham:

Genesis 12:1-3 (NCV)
[1] The LORD said to Abram, "Leave your country, your relatives, and your father's family, and go to the land I will show you. [2] I will make you a great nation, and I will bless you. I will make you famous, and you will be a blessing to others. [3] I will bless those who bless you, and I will place a curse on those who harm you. And all the people on earth will be blessed through you."

In this calling of Abram, notice that God here reveals his intention to bless *all nations*. God reiterated this prophetic promise over and over in his word so that it would not be forgotten.

Genesis 18:18 (NCV)
[18] Abraham's children will certainly become a great and powerful nation, and all nations on earth will be blessed through him.

Genesis 22:18 (NCV)
[18] Through your descendants all the nations on the earth will be blessed, because you obeyed me.'

Genesis 26:4 (NCV)
[4] I will give you many descendants, as hard to count as the stars in the sky, and I will give them all these lands. Through your descendants all the nations on the earth will be blessed.

Genesis 28:14 (NCV)
[14] Your descendants will be as many as the dust of the earth. They will spread west and east, north and south, and all the families of the earth will be blessed through you and your descendants.

Psalm 9:11 (NKJV)
[11] Sing praises to the LORD, who dwells in Zion! Declare His deeds among the people.

Psalm 22:27 (NKJV)
²⁷ All the ends of the world Shall remember and turn to the LORD, And all the families of the nations Shall worship before You.

Psalm 45:17 (NKJV)
¹⁷ I will make Your name to be remembered in all generations; Therefore the people shall praise You forever and ever.

Psalm 57:9-11 (NKJV)
⁹ I will praise You, O Lord, among the peoples; I will sing to You among the nations. ¹⁰ For Your mercy reaches unto the heavens, And Your truth unto the clouds. ¹¹ Be exalted, O God, above the heavens; Let Your glory be above all the earth.

Psalm 67:4-5 (NKJV)
⁴ Oh, let the nations be glad and sing for joy! For You shall judge the people righteously, And govern the nations on earth. Selah ⁵ Let the peoples praise You, O God; Let all the peoples praise You.

God's intention should have been clear. And remember that the prophet Jonah was called by God to go and preach to Nineveh, a Gentile city. Remember too when John the Baptist beheld Jesus for the first time . . .

John 1:29 (NKJV)
²⁹ The next day John saw Jesus coming toward him, and said, "Behold! The Lamb of God who takes away the sin of the world!

John the Baptist proclaimed that Jesus was sent to take away the *sin of the world*, not just the sin of Israel. The purpose of worldwide redemption was imbedded in John's decree. Later, in his letter to the believers in Galatia, Paul wrote:

Galatians 3:6-9 (NKJV)
⁶ just as Abraham "believed God, and it was accounted to him for righteousness." ⁷ Therefore know that only those who are of faith are sons of Abraham. ⁸ And the Scripture, foreseeing that God would justify the Gentiles by faith, preached the gospel to Abraham beforehand, saying, "In you all the nations shall be blessed." ⁹ So then those who are of faith are blessed with believing Abraham.

The inclusion of Gentiles in God's redemptive plan was certainly told in Old Testament prophecy, but it was a bombshell in Jesus' day because they had not understood. Finally we come to the scene that we saw from Revelation chapter 7 where men and women from every tribe and nation stand before the throne in heaven worshipping God and His Son.

The Mystery of a Second Coming of Messiah

In the later part of his earthly ministry, Jesus taught often that he would be leaving the disciples, but that he would later return to usher in God's glory. This is universal Christian understanding today. We understand that he came the first time as the suffering servant to make atonement for our sins. We understand his second coming will be as conquering king, bringing judgment and justice to the earth. John said Jesus was *full of grace and truth*. We saw these two portraits of Jesus' character manifested in glory in chapters 5 and 6 of this book. We see his two comings as demonstrating both of these characteristics. At his first coming, he brought grace. One day in the future, he will come again inaugurating truth on earth.

While the idea of two advents may be familiar to us, it was not on the radar screen in first century Israel. The Jewish scholars were well aware of the scriptures supporting both portraits of the Messiah, but had no idea how to integrate them. The scriptures presenting him as King are much greater in number than those portraying him as a suffering Servant. That, together with the seemingly-hopeless political dilemma in which Israel was embroiled at the start of the first century, thrust the 'king' portrait to the forefront of popular hope and thinking, and relegated the 'servant' portrait to top-shelf storage for future reference.

Thus, the Jewish populace was primed for the coming of their warrior-savior who would lead their escape from Roman imperialism. Their prevailing understanding of the end-of-the-age scenario was that when this conquering Messiah came, he would lead a revolt, and Armageddon would immediately follow. All this would usher in Israel's glory days and their rightful king would take his throne. No one envisioned a first and second coming of Messiah. No one anticipated a delay in the fulfillment of things lasting at least 2000 years.

Why two comings? And why this long gap between the first and second coming of Christ? It was with great purpose that it happened that way. Two comings with a long gap between them were included in God's sovereign plan in order to bring salvation beyond the boundaries of national Israel, to the ends of the earth. Since Israel rejected her Messiah, the gospel was now taken to Gentiles. As Paul told the Roman believers:

> *Romans 11:25 (RSV)*
> [25] *Lest you be wise in your own conceits, I want you to understand this mystery, brethren: a hardening has come upon part of Israel, until the full number of the Gentiles come in,*

God extended his grace to all who would follow the Son, no longer limited to Jews, but freely given to Gentiles as well. From the time of Jesus' resurrection until the yet-future 'end of the age,' God has been pushing his message to every tribe and every language. Thus, the concept of two advents of Christ is an intrinsic part of his plan to bring the gospel to all people. Less than forty years after Jesus rejection and death by the Jewish leaders, Israel was attacked and exiled by the Romans. Jerusalem was overtaken and overrun by Gentiles. In his recounting of Jesus' Olivet Discourse, Luke calls this gap the *times of the Gentiles*.

> *Luke 21:24 (ESV)*
> *[24] They will fall by the edge of the sword and be led captive among all nations, and Jerusalem will be trampled underfoot by the Gentiles, until the times of the Gentiles are fulfilled.*

And so there is this pre-ordained gap in time, these *times of the Gentiles*, that was completely hidden from Old Testament saints. They were blinded from it, but it is now revealed to us who are recipients of that grace. This is part of the *mystery of the gospel*.

Cheryl and I were privileged to visit Israel in 2008. As Gentile tourists, we *trampled* Jerusalem *underfoot* for several days. It was with a great awareness of prophetic destiny that we participated first-hand in this state of affairs. If judgment had come when Jesus came the first time, only a handful of Jews would have had faith unto salvation. The whole objective for this gap is so Gentiles might be included in God's salvation. *"It is too light a thing that you should be my servant to raise up the tribes of Jacob and to restore the preserved of Israel; I will give you as a light to the nations, that my salvation may reach to the end of the earth."*

> *Romans 3:29 (RSV)*
> *[29] Or is God the God of Jews only? Is he not the God of Gentiles also? Yes, of Gentiles also,*

> *Romans 9:23-24 (RSV)*
> *[23] in order to make known the riches of his glory for the vessels of mercy, which he has prepared beforehand for glory, [24] even us whom he has called, not from the Jews only but also from the Gentiles?*

Thus, the concept of a first and second coming is an integral part of the mysterious purpose of God to extend salvation to the ends of the earth. What an awesome purpose!

The Mystery of the Missional Command

The gap in time was not foreseen by prophets and righteous men of old, but it was not a late addition to the plan. It was always God's plan to open His grace up to all mankind. The divine intent is revealed clearly as early as the call of Abraham when God told him his posterity would be a blessing to all nations, as we have already read. Now we see that promise fulfilled in the person of Jesus. He is the one who is bringing salvation to *the ends of the earth* through his atoning sacrificial death and resurrection.

When Jesus gave his 'great commission' just before he ascended, he was passing along the task of bringing the gospel message to *all nations*. He was passing it to us, the church. Matthew records it like this:

> *Matthew 28:18-20 (NASB)*
> *[18] And Jesus came up and spoke to them, saying, "All authority has been given to Me in heaven and on earth. [19] "Go therefore and make disciples of all the nations, baptizing them in the name of the Father and the Son and the Holy Spirit, [20] teaching them to observe all that I commanded you; and lo, I am with you always, even to the end of the age."*

The divine plan of salvation for the nations is now passed from the eternally secure hand of God to the frail and often-tentative hands of the church. Yet the frailty causes men to rely on God, and our weakness serves to magnify His power and grace. In the power of the Holy Spirit, the greatness of His grace is seen as the advancement of the gospel prevails against the resistance of the devil, taking the battle deep into his territory. Satan is the adversary. The world of unredeemed human beings is his domain. Like Jesus, we are commissioned to go into attack mode. We are called to take it to him. Our beliefs are grace, love and truth, the characteristics of God Himself. Our strategies and tactics are compassion, obedience, and love for others. Our motive is love for God and for Jesus, the one who is worthy of our gratitude and praise.

> *Matthew 24:14 (NASB)*
> *[14] "This gospel of the kingdom shall be preached in the whole world as a testimony to all the nations, and then the end will come.*

When I was a young man and a young Christian, and read in scripture that the objective of missions is to reach *all nations* with the gospel message, I thought that must surely be a figure of speech. It seemed too far out of reach to be literally realistic. Now I am amazed at how the message has exploded across the world, largely during my lifetime. Literally thousands of mission-sending groups have sprung up. Churches around the globe are both sending evangelists and raising up nationals in the faith. Now, most overseas missions are formed with the goal of instilling national believers with the initiative of leadership. Overseas nationals are also heeding the mandate to evangelize. Today, a significant thrust of evangelism comes at the hands of those nationals previously converted.

The New Testament Greek word 'ethnos' is translated *nations* in our modern English translations. It literally means 'ethnic groups.' It is not restricted to political nations, but rather has in view groups of people sharing culture and language. Indonesia today is one country, but consists of hundreds of sub-cultures. This is true to a slightly lesser degree of India, China, and many other countries. Yet today, a huge inroad has been made toward making the message of the Bible available in their native languages through translation, oral storytelling, and visual interpretive means. Note that the targeted result is not that all people will hear and believe, but that all people will hear and have the opportunity to believe.

Jesus' mandate to spread the knowledge of the gospel to all nations is at the heart of God's purpose for the ages. In the hair-raising scene of worldwide worship in Revelation 7 we just considered, the great multitude of people from every nation, tribe, people and language were seen around the throne praising God and praising the Lamb who was slain for their atonement, for their redemption. There we saw a preview of victorious faith fulfilled in eternity. What a powerful motivation for mission. What an encouraging promise for us in times of trouble. The mystery of the gospel is our source of joy in the great hope of eternal fulfillment of all these promises.

Prophetic Revealing and Concealing
All of these different facets of the mystery may seem random, but they all converge in the person of Jesus Christ. Jesus is the fulfillment. In this chapter we have seen how prophecy has both revealed and concealed the purposes of God at the proper time. God often spoke in veiled ways in Old Testament times because his plan was that Israel's unbelief would open the door for the gospel to be taken to the whole world. One day he will use this worldwide opportunity to pierce the dull heart of Israel, awakening smoldering embers of faith into flame. Now, His plans are fully revealed to those who believe. The *mystery* is made known. Regarding this revealing of mysteries, God told the Old Testament prophet Daniel long ago:

Daniel 12:10 (NKJV)
[10] Many shall be purified, made white, and refined, but the wicked shall do wickedly; and none of the wicked shall understand, but the wise shall understand.

God's purposes are opened to all who are redeemed by the blood of Jesus—*they will understand.* Jesus taught his disciples . . .

Matthew 13:52 (NASB)
[52] And Jesus said to them, "Therefore every scribe who has become a disciple of the kingdom of heaven is like a head of a household, who brings out of his treasure things new and old."

The message of the Old Testament is not obsolete. On the contrary, the New Testament illuminates the big picture, showing us the Old Testament passages in light of their ultimate purpose and fulfillment.

> *2 Corinthians 4:5-7 (NASB)*
> *[5] For we do not preach ourselves but Christ Jesus as Lord, and ourselves as your bond-servants for Jesus' sake. [6] For God, who said, "Light shall shine out of darkness," is the One who has shone in our hearts to give the Light of the knowledge of the glory of God in the face of Christ. [7] But we have this treasure in earthen vessels, so that the surpassing greatness of the power will be of God and not from ourselves;*

> *1 John 2:7-8 (ESV)*
> *[7] Beloved, I am writing you no new commandment, but an old commandment that you had from the beginning. The old commandment is the word that you have heard. [8] At the same time, it is a new commandment that I am writing to you, which is true in him and in you, because the darkness is passing away and the true light is already shining.*

The Old Testament prepared the way for the Messiah. It demonstrated the need for him. It pointed forward to him. Now, the New Testament introduces him in full revelation. No more mystery. In historical context, God's prophesied mystery has been revealed.

There is a parallel of this historical sequence in the life of every person who hears the gospel and believes. The gospel presentation begins by establishing the problem of sin, showing the hearer how he falls short of Gods righteous standard. Then comes a personal struggle with sin in which the hearer eventually realizes he is not only hapless and hopeless, but also helpless. In scripture, Israel had to fight this same fight as a nation. Only then is the hearer ready to receive the help he needs from God, the grace of forgiveness at the hand of Jesus Christ, the very God incarnate. Paul expressed this very idea like this:

> *Galatians 4:1-5 (NKJV)*
> *[1] Now I say that the heir, as long as he is a child, does not differ at all from a slave, though he is master of all, [2] but is under guardians and stewards until the time appointed by the father. [3] Even so we, when we were children, were in bondage under the elements of the world. [4] But when the fullness of the time had come, God sent forth His Son, born of a woman, born under the law, [5] to redeem those who were under the law, that we might receive the adoption as sons.*

May this mystery, once hidden but now revealed, bring us to the throne of grace with a heightened astonishment and awe for what the Lord has done for us. Of all the people living throughout history on this earth, we are privileged above them all by living in the age of revelation. May it elevate our praise of Him! May it increase our joy in Him! If you have believed that he is who he said he is, and followed him in the obedience of faith, you too are included in the promises of eternal life in Christ!

> Oh, Lord! How great are your plans. How precious they are to us. Your purpose for the ages brings astonishment to us as we try to fathom what you have done on our behalf. How privileged we are to live at a time when your purpose is revealed. Through your revelation of your plans, you are revealing yourself. You invite us to know you more fully, more intimately. Even our most profound thoughts only plumb the shallows of the deep reservoir of your attributes and your reality. We anticipate eagerly the eventual supreme privilege of knowing you fully when we see you as you are in Jesus—in glory. Teach us to treasure that hope above all else.

**PART 4
THE DAY OF THE LORD**

10
THERE IS AN ENEMY

It is difficult to comprehend how God could have an enemy. Granted, there are those people who do not give Him the time of day, and those who worship Him falsely or inappropriately. But an outright adversary? When He created all things, why did He allow for the possibility of an opponent? Many regard the concept that God has an adversary as a relic from primitive, archaic, beliefs about the origin of evil. We are now more sophisticated than to pursue that kind of thinking, they would say.

We could research man's endless philosophies about the topic, but why? What might we expect to find there? Human understanding can only speculate on such an issue. Let us again turn to the pages of scripture to seek answers to questions beyond our knowledge. The adversary of God is in focus throughout scripture, and is a major theme in biblical prophecy. Therefore let's let the Creator himself tell us about him.

He is Real, He is Personal

We may have trouble grasping the purpose of God in allowing such an enemy. That is no reason to doubt his existence. Jesus told this parable to his followers:

> *Matthew 13:24-30 (NASB)*
> *[24] Jesus presented another parable to them, saying, "The kingdom of heaven may be compared to a man who sowed good seed in his field. [25] "But while his men were sleeping, his enemy came and sowed tares among the wheat, and went away. [26] "But when the wheat sprouted and bore grain, then the tares became evident also. [27] "The slaves of the landowner came and said to him, 'Sir, did you not sow good seed in your field? How then does it have tares?' [28] "And he said to them, 'An enemy has done this!' The slaves said to him, 'Do you want us, then, to go and gather them up?' [29] "But he said, 'No; for while you are gathering up the tares, you may uproot the wheat with them. [30] 'Allow both to grow together until the harvest; and in the time of the harvest I will say to the reapers, "First gather up the tares and bind them in bundles to burn them up; but gather the wheat into my barn."'"*

The landowner did not blame bad luck for his misfortune. He immediately recognized the work of an enemy. That is the theme of this parable. This enemy is not a whimsical metaphor for any bad fate that happens to come upon us. He is not a personification of an evil tendency, or an icon for injustice. He is a distinct, aggressive, destructive being with evil intent, and the power to act. Jesus himself encountered him. When he was tempted in the wilderness, he did not wonder where the temptation came from.

Matthew 4:9-11 (NASB)
⁹ and he said to Him, "All these things I will give You, if You fall down and worship me." ¹⁰ Then Jesus *said to him, "Go, Satan! For it is written, 'YOU SHALL WORSHIP THE LORD YOUR GOD, AND SERVE HIM ONLY.'" ¹¹ Then the devil left Him; and behold, angels came and began to minister to Him.

Jesus spoke of Satan often as a specific being:

Luke 10:17-18 (ESV)
¹⁷ The seventy-two returned with joy, saying, "Lord, even the demons are subject to us in your name!" ¹⁸ And he said to them, "I saw Satan fall like lightning from heaven.

Luke 22:31-32 (ESV)
³¹ "Simon, Simon, behold, Satan demanded to have you, that he might sift you like wheat, ³² but I have prayed for you that your faith may not fail. And when you have turned again, strengthen your brothers."

The apostles held the same view of Satan, the devil, as a real, personal enemy:

2 Corinthians 2:11 (NASB)
¹¹ so that no advantage would be taken of us by Satan, for we are not ignorant of his schemes.

2 Corinthians 11:14 (NASB)
¹⁴ No wonder, for even Satan disguises himself as an angel of light.

1 Peter 5:8 (ESV)
⁸ Be sober-minded; be watchful. Your adversary the devil prowls around like a roaring lion, seeking someone to devour.

1 John 5:18-19 (ESV)
¹⁸ We know that everyone who has been born of God does not keep on sinning, but he who was born of God protects him, and the evil

one does not touch him. *¹⁹ We know that we are from God, and the whole world lies in the power of the evil one.*

Satan's Origin

If Satan is a real personage, a distinct being, then who is he and where did he come from? His origin is somewhat obscure. It is revealed to us woven into the rhetorical fabric of some ancient, history-based prophecies. The Old Testament prophet Ezekiel was given a message of God's judgment against the enemy nations of Israel, among which is this passage:

> *Ezekiel 28:11-17 (NASB)*
> *¹¹ Again the word of the LORD came to me saying, ¹² "Son of man, take up a lamentation over the king of Tyre and say to him, 'Thus says the Lord GOD, "You had the seal of perfection, Full of wisdom and perfect in beauty. ¹³ "You were in Eden, the garden of God; every precious stone was your covering: The ruby, the topaz and the diamond; The beryl, the onyx and the jasper; The lapis lazuli, the turquoise and the emerald; and the gold, the workmanship of your settings and sockets, was in you. On the day that you were created they were prepared. ¹⁴ "You were the anointed cherub who covers, and I placed you there. You were on the holy mountain of God; you walked in the midst of the stones of fire. ¹⁵ "You were blameless in your ways from the day you were created until unrighteousness was found in you. ¹⁶ "By the abundance of your trade you were internally filled with violence, And you sinned; therefore I have cast you as profane from the mountain of God. And I have destroyed you, O covering cherub, from the midst of the stones of fire. ¹⁷ "Your heart was lifted up because of your beauty; You corrupted your wisdom by reason of your splendor. I cast you to the ground; I put you before kings, that they may see you.*

The prophet's lament was addressed to the king of Tyre. Tyre was a major sea port for the country of Phoenicia, Israel's northern enemy. You don't have to read far to realize the target of the lament is beyond just an earthly king. The king of Tyre was just a front for its real recipient, a covering *cherub*.

A cherub (singular of cherubim) is of a high order of angels. They are mentioned many times in the Old Testament, always portrayed in splendor, always associated with God's glory. Take the following short excerpt from another of Ezekiel's heavenly visions:

> *Ezekiel 10:15-18 (KJV)*
> *¹⁵ And the cherubims were lifted up. This is the living creature that I saw by the river of Chebar. ¹⁶ And when the cherubims went, the*

wheels went by them: and when the cherubims lifted up their wings to mount up from the earth, the same wheels also turned not from beside them. ⁱ⁷ When they stood, these stood; and when they were lifted up, these lifted up themselves also: for the spirit of the living creature was in them. ¹⁸ Then the glory of the LORD departed from off the threshold of the house, and stood over the cherubims.

This cherub in Ezekiel 28 was created with great beauty and specially anointed by God. In fact his beauty was *perfect*, that is, the ultimate that God could have given him. He was *anointed*, and *ordained* to be a *guardian cherub*. The main function of the cherubim is to stand guard before the holiness of God.

It is significant that Satan is not on the same level of hierarchy and authority as God. God the Father, Son and Spirit were already there *in the beginning* (John 1:1). As persons of the Holy Trinity they are understood to be eternally self-existent. On the other hand, the cherub was a created being, created by God at a particular point in 'time.' Furthermore, the God of creation included the Son.

John 1:2-3 (NKJV)
² He [Jesus the Son] was in the beginning with God. ³ All things were made through Him, and without Him nothing was made that was made.

So the cherub was created by the Father and the Son. He was holy and exalted until *wickedness was found* in him. Pride in his beauty corrupted him. Perhaps the king of Tyre was especially vulnerable to satanic control, and thus his wickedness was directed by this chief cherub.

As we mentioned in Chapter 3, this grammatical mechanism of starting with familiar earthly things, then progressing into an otherworldly realm, is not uncommon in Hebrew prophecy. This seems to be how we are told of the enemy's origin. Another such prophecy was given to Isaiah, this time in a dirge against the king of Babylon:

Isaiah 14:3-17 (NKJV)
³ It shall come to pass in the day the LORD gives you rest from your sorrow, and from your fear and the hard bondage in which you were made to serve, ⁴ that you will take up this proverb against the king of Babylon, and say: "How the oppressor has ceased, The golden city ceased! ⁵ The LORD has broken the staff of the wicked, The scepter of the rulers; ⁶ He who struck the people in wrath with a continual stroke, He who ruled the nations in anger, is persecuted and no one hinders. ⁷ The whole earth is at rest and quiet; They break forth into singing. ⁸ Indeed the cypress trees rejoice over you,

And the cedars of Lebanon, Saying, 'Since you were cut down, No woodsman has come up against us.' ⁹ *"Hell from beneath is excited about you, to meet you at your coming; it stirs up the dead for you, All the chief ones of the earth; it has raised up from their thrones all the kings of the nations.* ¹⁰ *They all shall speak and say to you: 'Have you also become as weak as we? Have you become like us?* ¹¹ *Your pomp is brought down to Sheol, And the sound of your stringed instruments; the maggot is spread under you, And worms cover you.'* ¹² *"How you are fallen from heaven, O Lucifer, son of the morning! How you are cut down to the ground, You who weakened the nations!* ¹³ *For you have said in your heart: 'I will ascend into heaven, I will exalt my throne above the stars of God; I will also sit on the mount of the congregation on the farthest sides of the north;* ¹⁴ *I will ascend above the heights of the clouds, I will be like the Most High.'* ¹⁵ *Yet you shall be brought down to Sheol, to the lowest depths of the Pit.* ¹⁶ *"Those who see you will gaze at you, and consider you, saying: 'Is this the man who made the earth tremble, who shook kingdoms,* ¹⁷ *who made the world as a wilderness and destroyed its cities, who did not open the house of his prisoners?'*

Nebuchadnezzar, the king of Babylon who invaded Judah, Israel's Southern Kingdom and defeated her, is the named target of this prophecy. Granted, the pagan king did elevate himself as a god-king before his subjects. But the language *How you are fallen from heaven, O Lucifer, son of the morning?* and the references to *God* and *the Most High* clearly transcend the continuum of earthly history. Many take this to be another case where the surpassing reference is to Satan. If so, it describes his downfall. He sought to usurp the throne of God. He thought to become *like the Most High*. There was rebellion in the heavenly ranks.

It seems incredulous that Satan thought he could overthrow the God who effortlessly created the universe, including he (Satan) himself. That is what pride does to people too. It causes us to lose perspective of our own worth and limitations, and to become consumed with ourselves.

Satan's Character

Satan was not passive in his pride, but openly rebelled against the God of heaven. He was soundly defeated, but not destroyed, and today lives and works in the world around us and even in the lives of believers. His purpose is against that of God in all things. Think of all the attributes of God. The devil can be described by the antithesis of those attributes. God is love, Satan is characterized by hate. God is truthful, but Satan is a liar.

John 8:44-45 (NKJV)
⁴⁴ You are of your father the devil, and the desires of your father you want to do. He was a murderer from the beginning, and does not stand in the truth, because there is no truth in him. When he speaks a lie, he speaks from his own resources, for he is a liar and the father of it. ⁴⁵ But because I tell the truth, you do not believe Me.

God makes us free, but the devil attempts to put us in bondage.

2 Timothy 2:26 (ESV)
²⁶ and they may come to their senses and escape from the snare of the devil, after being captured by him to do his will.

God is the creator of life and Jesus came that we *might have life* to the fullest, but Satan is the purveyor of death.

Hebrews 2:14-15 (ESV)
¹⁴ Since therefore the children share in flesh and blood, he himself likewise partook of the same things, that through death he might destroy the one who has the power of death, that is, the devil, ¹⁵ and deliver all those who through fear of death were subject to lifelong slavery.

The list could be extended, but the character of Satan is clearly shown in even a few such passages. He is everything that is opposed to God.

Satan's Earthly Agenda

The devil failed in his attempt to usurp God's throne in heaven. He then set out to destroy the work of God's kingdom in creation.

His First Agenda—Destroy the Messiah

In Revelation, sandwiched between the sounding of the seven trumpets and the pouring out of the seven bowls, we read of a symbolic vision that John was shown:

Revelation 12:1-5 (ESV)
¹ And a great sign appeared in heaven: a woman clothed with the sun, with the moon under her feet, and on her head a crown of twelve stars. ² She was pregnant and was crying out in birth pains and the agony of giving birth. ³ And another sign appeared in heaven: behold, a great red dragon, with seven heads and ten horns, and on his heads seven diadems. ⁴ His tail swept down a third of the stars of heaven and cast them to the earth. And the dragon stood before the woman who was about to give birth, so that when she bore her child he might devour it. ⁵ She gave birth to a male child,

one who is to rule all the nations with a rod of iron, but her child was caught up to God and to his throne,

To analyze this passage, identification of the participants seems the first order of business. The easiest to name is the dragon, because in verse 9 that follows we are plainly told he is the devil.

The male child that was born is Jesus. That is evidenced because he was caught up to heaven, and because he is the one who will *rule all the nations with an iron scepter.* This iron scepter is a symbol associated with the ultimate millennial reign of Christ. Here are a couple of examples of this *iron scepter* terminology in other prophetic scriptures:

Psalm 2:7-9 (NKJV)
[7] "I will declare the decree: The LORD has said to Me, 'You are My Son, Today I have begotten You. [8] Ask of Me, and I will give You The nations for Your inheritance, And the ends of the earth for Your possession. [9] You shall break them with a rod of iron; You shall dash them to pieces like a potter's vessel.' "

Revelation 2:26-28 (ESV)
[26] The one who conquers and who keeps my works until the end, to him I will give authority over the nations, [27] and he will rule them with a rod of iron, as when earthen pots are broken in pieces, even as I myself have received authority from my Father. [28] And I will give him the morning star.

Revelation 19:11,15 (ESV)
[11] Then I saw heaven opened, and behold, a white horse! The one sitting on it is called Faithful and True, and in righteousness he judges and makes war . . . [15] From his mouth comes a sharp sword with which to strike down the nations, and he will rule them with a rod of iron. He will tread the winepress of the fury of the wrath of God the Almighty.

The iron scepter is always a symbol of Christ's sovereignty as it is manifested in end time events. Christ is most assuredly represented by the child.

We will postpone identifying the woman, for now. In Chapter 22 we will take it up again, and try to solve her identity.

In this Revelation vision of the woman giving birth and the dragon, we have the earthly agenda of Satan portrayed in graphic symbolism. His first strategy was to eliminate the prophesied Messiah. As the dragon stood before the pregnant woman to devour her child, likewise Satan worked tirelessly to destroy the redemptive work of Jesus. Actually, his attempts to destroy Christ began in earliest Old Testament times. He tried to destroy the very lineage of Christ by inciting Cain to kill Abel, but God raised up a new lineage in Seth. (Gen 4:8) He prodded Laban to kill his son-in-law Jacob, but God softened Laban's heart. (Gen 31:29) Satan made Esau burn with hatred, and plot to murder his twin brother Jacob, the son of promise, but God changed Esau's heart at the last moment. (Gen 33)

Scripture tells us that Saul, Israel's first king, was sent an evil spirit from the Lord that tormented him. Since God is not the author of evil, and He does not tempt anyone, we understand this in the sense that God gave him over to his own selfish passions. God removed His protection, giving the spirit free access to Saul. Saul became insanely jealous and antagonistic toward David, God's intended heir in the messianic lineage, and tried to kill him on several occasions. God always made a way of escape for David. See I Sam 19:9-10 for one example. (Saul was a Benjamite, not from the prophesied messianic tribe of Judah.)

After David's death, the woman Athaliah attempted to execute all members of the royal lineage. Everyone was murdered except the young child Joash who was hidden away, in God's providence by his handmaid, for six years while Athaliah ruled the land. (II Chron 22:10-11) Under the leadership of the high priest, Joash was later anointed king at the age of seven years, restoring the lineage of David to the throne.

During the exile of the Southern Kingdom of Israel in Babylon, during the reign of Persian monarchy, Satan incited Haman, the Persian king's trusted advisor, to instigate a decree to kill all Jews in Babylon. Again the devil was attacking the messianic lineage. God caused the plan to backfire, and through the bravery of Queen Esther, the Jews were saved and the royal lineage was preserved. (Est 3:1-9:32)

When Jesus was born in Bethlehem, Satan gave Herod an insane paranoia of insecurity. In an attempt to kill his perceived competition--the Messiah, he murdered all baby boys two years old or younger in the vicinity of Bethlehem. God snatched his Son out of the mouth of the dragon once again by sending Mary, Joseph and the baby Jesus into Egypt. (Matt 2) Several times Jesus had to overcome the temptations and the persecutions of the devil, but God spared him. (Lk 4:2-13, 16-30)

Finally, when Jerusalem was filled with pilgrims for the Passover, Satan incited the religious leaders and the people to riot and demand Jesus' execution. He surely thought he had finally succeeded in destroying the redemptive plan of God when Jesus died on that Roman cross. But then something happened. After three days in the grave, Jesus rose from his borrowed tomb. Satan's greatest victory suddenly became his worst nightmare. He had actually promoted God's plan by slaughtering the sacrificial Lamb of God. Thus ended Satan's attack on the messianic agenda.

Satan's Fallback Plan—Destroy the Covenant Relationship

Satan was completely defeated in his attempts to interrupt God's plan of a coming Messiah. Yet he has not been subdued. He continues his work. His purpose to derail God's redemption of mankind is still the motivating force that drives his activities. What are those activities? He is doing all he can to destroy the redemptive plan by attacking the church.

> *Revelation 12:17 (ESV)*
> *[17] Then the dragon became furious with the woman and went off to make war on the rest of her offspring, on those who keep the commandments of God and hold to the testimony of Jesus . . .*

We will revisit this passage in that regard in more detail in Chapter 23 as we study Israel in the Tribulation. Now the dragon attacks *the rest of her offspring--those who obey God's commandments and hold to the testimony of Jesus.* The woman's other offspring is the church, those who *hold to the testimony of Jesus.* Christians are the brothers and sisters of Christ, as the Hebrews writer says:

> *Hebrews 2:11 (ESV)*
> *[11] For he who sanctifies and those who are sanctified all have one source. That is why he is not ashamed to call them brothers,*

Satan pursues the church to destroy it. This brings us to the present time. We are currently in the church age. This struggle will continue until the end of this age. He is driven, by his hatred of the Almighty, to corrupt and destroy the people created in God's image. This physical world is the battlefield on which Satan is attacking the sovereignty of God. Just as this world is the battlefield, people created by God in His image are the target. This is seen in many scripture passages. Just before his death, Jesus prayed this prayer:

> *John 17:15 (ESV)*
> *[15] I do not ask that you take them out of the world, but that you keep them from the evil one.*

When the apostle Peter spoke to his first Gentile audience, he spoke of the bondage with which the devil enslaves people:

> *Acts 10:37-38 (ESV)*
> *[37] you yourselves know what happened throughout all Judea, beginning from Galilee after the baptism that John proclaimed: [38] how God anointed Jesus of Nazareth with the Holy Spirit and with*

power. He went about doing good and healing all who were oppressed by the devil, for God was with him.*

Paul wrote to the church at Ephesus . . .

Ephesians 6:16 (ESV)
¹⁶ In all circumstances take up the shield of faith, with which you can extinguish all the flaming darts of the evil one;

And John recorded the Lord's own spoken words which attributed upcoming persecution to Satan himself.

Revelation 2: 10 (ESV)
¹⁰ Do not fear what you are about to suffer. Behold, the devil is about to throw some of you into prison, that you may be tested, and for ten days you will have tribulation. Be faithful unto death, and I will give you the crown of life.

Satan was present in the Garden of Eden, the home of the first man and woman.

Genesis 3:1 (RSV)
¹ Now the serpent was more subtle than any other wild creature that the LORD God had made. He said to the woman, "Did God say, `You shall not eat of any tree of the garden'?"

He was at work throughout Israel's history.

1 Chronicles 21:1 (NKJV)
¹ Now Satan stood up against Israel, and moved David to number Israel.

One of Satan's main tactics was (and is) to accuse men before God.

Zechariah 3:1 (RSV)
¹ Then he showed me Joshua the high priest standing before the angel of the LORD, and Satan standing at his right hand to accuse him.

And many are familiar with how he accused Job to God.

Job 1:6 (NKJV)
⁶ Now there was a day when the sons of God came to present themselves before the LORD, and Satan also came among them.

So aggressive and destructive is the devil's pursuit of us that Paul likened our defense against it to a soldier in full armor.

> *Ephesians 6:11 (NKJV)*
> *[11] Put on the whole armor of God, that you may be able to stand against the wiles of the devil.*

Our Protection

Scripture calls the devil a *roaring lion*, a *murderer*, *the father of lies*, *the evil one*, a *dragon*, a *serpent* and many other names which attest to his despicable character and ambitious motives. We have learned of his great power and splendor in the spiritual realm. We see that we ourselves are now his target, each one of us. This is enough to make a person lose sleep. It is easy to see from scripture that we are no match for Satan in the game of life and death. But wait! We are no match, but the Holy Spirit of God who indwells us is more than a match. We do not need to fear the power of Satan, as though we were defenseless.

> *John 10:28 (NKJV)*
> *[28] And I give them eternal life, and they shall never perish; neither shall anyone snatch them out of My hand.*

> *1 John 4:4 (ESV)*
> *[4] Little children, you are from God and have overcome them, for he who is in you is greater than he who is in the world.*

> *Romans 8:37 (KJV)*
> *[37] Nay, in all these things we are more than conquerors through him that loved us.*

> *Ephesians 6:10 (NKJV)*
> *[10] Finally, my brethren, be strong in the Lord and in the power of His might.*

> *1 John 5:3-5 (ESV)*
> *[3] For this is the love of God, that we keep his commandments. And his commandments are not burdensome. [4] For everyone who has been born of God overcomes the world. And this is the victory that has overcome the world—our faith. [5] Who is it that overcomes the world except the one who believes that Jesus is the Son of God?*

> *Ephesians 3:16-21 (ESV)*
> *[16] that according to the riches of his glory he may grant you to be strengthened with power through his Spirit in your inner being, [17] so that Christ may dwell in your hearts through faith—that you, being*

rooted and grounded in love, [18] may have strength to comprehend with all the saints what is the breadth and length and height and depth, [19] and to know the love of Christ that surpasses knowledge, that you may be filled with all the fullness of God. [20] Now to him who is able to do far more abundantly than all that we ask or think, according to the power at work within us, [21] to him be glory in the church and in Christ Jesus throughout all generations, forever and ever. Amen.

Ephesians 6:10-12 (ESV)
[10] *Finally, be strong in the Lord and in the strength of his might. [11] Put on the whole armor of God, that you may be able to stand against the schemes of the devil. [12] For we do not wrestle against flesh and blood, but against the rulers, against the authorities, against the cosmic powers over this present darkness, against the spiritual forces of evil in the heavenly places.*

From these and many other scriptures we understand that we have available to us a 'hedge' of protection from God against the attacks of Satan.

Two additional comments--First, this protection does not mean we are exempt from anything bad happening to us. But the only evil that comes our way is that which the Lord allows. We are guarded by the Lord's angels in most situations or we would not survive a single day. But this protection is not promised to be absolute. We are well aware that bad things do happen. Rather it means that God will sustain us through our trials so that we will not lose our faith. His top priority for us is our eternal fitness. Satan's motive is to unseat us from the eternal love of God. Satan's attacks will not be successful in what he intended, that is, he cannot separate us from God.

Matthew 10:28 (ESV)
[28] *And do not fear those who kill the body but cannot kill the soul. Rather fear him who can destroy both soul and body in hell.*

Second, while the protection is available, we can jeopardize its application to our lives by not cooperating with God in our warfare with the enemy. When we sin, we are vulnerable to the temporal consequences of our actions. When Peter challenged Jesus, saying he would not die on a cross, Jesus said, "*Get behind me, Satan.*" Jesus was not calling Peter 'Satan' out of anger or contempt. He knew that Satan was behind Peter's attitude, and Peter was accommodating the enemy. This was not a statement about Peter's eternal standing with God, but an indictment of his momentary act of treason. In that same spirit, John writes:

1 John 3:8 (ESV)
⁸ Whoever makes a practice of sinning is of the devil, for the devil has been sinning from the beginning. The reason the Son of God appeared was to destroy the works of the devil.

Taken in context, this verse is saying that an act of sinning is serving the devil, not God, and is an expression of disloyalty.

> Lord, we don't want to serve the enemy. We want to serve you. We want to remain loyal to you and you alone. Empower us, we pray, to overcome the attacks of the devil, and to be steadfast in our allegiance to you. Amen

11
SATAN'S EARTHLY KINGDOM

Satan has been called *Prince of this world (John 12:31), the ruler of the kingdom of the air (Eph 2:2), prince of demons (Matt 12:24)*. It suited God's eternal plan to allow him to reign on earth for a season. While it is true that the devil is a spiritual being, not personally visible to us, it is also understood from scripture that he operates within our realm of existence. He does not operate alone, but is the ruler over a huge host of demons (fallen angels). The influence of this spiritual army in the affairs of men subjugates them to serve Satan instead of God. Thus, his kingdom includes not only demons, but also men and women who are in bondage under his power, and who, usually unknowingly, serve him as their king. Behind their actions, words, and thoughts a spiritual battle is being waged.

His influence is not only on individuals, but also through the authority structures of this world. Behind the scenes of every political issue, every social groundswell, every military campaign, a spiritual war is being waged. As Christians it is our duty to do our best to always be on God's side of life's situations.

> *Ephesians 6:12 (ESV)*
> *[12] For we do not wrestle against flesh and blood, but against the rulers, against the authorities, against the cosmic powers over this present darkness, against the spiritual forces of evil in the heavenly places.*

By influencing the mind of a dictator, president, governor or senator, Satan can exert tremendous power over large numbers of people. Thus those prophetic passages we just read about the origin of Satan commenced with an earthly king. That is more than just a literary technique. Those kings were appropriate fronts for the devil because they were his operators. Just as individuals unwittingly serve in the devil's kingdom when they conform to his control, so rulers have often inadvertently acted as agents in the devil's kingdom. Certain rulers or cultures or cities are identified with Satan in Scripture. For example:

> *Revelation 2:12-13 (ESV)*
> *[12] "And to the angel of the church in Pergamum write: 'The words of him who has the sharp two-edged sword.* [13] *"'I know where you*

dwell, where Satan's throne is. Yet you hold fast my name, and you did not deny my faith even in the days of Antipas my faithful witness, who was killed among you, where Satan dwells.

It is not unusual, then, to find in biblical prophecy an emphasis on ancient politics. In fact, God uses prophecies about the flow of nations to reveal Satan's kingdom, its growth and destiny. This plays heavily in end-time prophecy, and is an integral component in God's plan of ultimate redemption. There are several such references, but the most important are found in the book of Daniel, or more accurately they are the book of Daniel, for so much of the book deals with that topic. Therefore we will begin there to see the development of Satan's kingdom.

The Rise of the Satanic Kingdom

In about 607 BC Israel's southern kingdom of Judah was overthrown by the Babylonians led by Nebuchadnezzar. Many of the inhabitants were carried into exile in Babylon. Daniel, the Israelite prophet, was among those exiled, and ended up in the service of the pagan King. God gave this king a vision. When he awoke, he was very disturbed by his dream, but could not remember it. Finally, Daniel was called in and given a chance to recall the king's dream and give its interpretation.

> *Daniel 2:26-35 (NKJV)*
> *[26] The king answered and said to Daniel, whose name was Belteshazzar, "Are you able to make known to me the dream which I have seen, and its interpretation?" [27] Daniel answered in the presence of the king, and said, "The secret which the king has demanded, the wise men, the astrologers, the magicians, and the soothsayers cannot declare to the king. [28] But there is a God in heaven who reveals secrets, and He has made known to King Nebuchadnezzar what will be in the latter days. Your dream, and the visions of your head upon your bed, were these: [29] As for you, O king, thoughts came to your mind while on your bed, about what would come to pass after this; and He who reveals secrets has made known to you what will be. [30] But as for me, this secret has not been revealed to me because I have more wisdom than anyone living, but for our sakes who make known the interpretation to the king, and that you may know the thoughts of your heart. [31] "You, O king, were watching; and behold, a great image! This great image, whose splendor was excellent, stood before you; and its form was awesome. [32] This image's head was of fine gold, its chest and arms of silver, its belly and thighs of bronze, [33] its legs of iron, its feet partly of iron and partly of clay. [34] You watched while a stone was cut out without hands, which struck the image on its feet of iron and clay, and broke them in pieces. [35] Then the iron, the clay, the bronze, the silver, and*

the gold were crushed together, and became like chaff from the summer threshing floors; the wind carried them away so that no trace of them was found. And the stone that struck the image became a great mountain and filled the whole earth.

I would love to have seen the look on the king's face. Daniel had Nebuchadnezzar's attention for sure, by reciting to him the dream he himself had forgotten.

Daniel 2:36-47 (NKJV)
[36] "This is the dream. Now we will tell the interpretation of it before the king. [37] You, O king, are a king of kings. For the God of heaven has given you a kingdom, power, strength, and glory; [38] and wherever the children of men dwell, or the beasts of the field and the birds of the heaven, He has given them into your hand, and has made you ruler over them all--you are this head of gold. [39] But after you shall arise another kingdom inferior to yours; then another, a third kingdom of bronze, which shall rule over all the earth. [40] And the fourth kingdom shall be as strong as iron, inasmuch as iron breaks in pieces and shatters everything; and like iron that crushes, that kingdom will break in pieces and crush all the others. [41] Whereas you saw the feet and toes, partly of potter's clay and partly of iron, the kingdom shall be divided; yet the strength of the iron shall be in it, just as you saw the iron mixed with ceramic clay. [42] And as the toes of the feet were partly of iron and partly of clay, so the kingdom shall be partly strong and partly fragile. [43] As you saw iron mixed with ceramic clay, they will mingle with the seed of men; but they will not adhere to one another, just as iron does not mix with clay. [44] And in the days of these kings the God of heaven will set up a kingdom which shall never be destroyed; and the kingdom shall not be left to other people; it shall break in pieces and consume all these kingdoms, and it shall stand forever. [45] Inasmuch as you saw that the stone was cut out of the mountain without hands, and that it broke in pieces the iron, the bronze, the clay, the silver, and the gold--the great God has made known to the king what will come to pass after this. The dream is certain, and its interpretation is sure." [46] Then King Nebuchadnezzar fell on his face, prostrate before Daniel, and commanded that they should present an offering and incense to him. [47] The king answered Daniel, and said, "Truly your God is the God of gods, the Lord of kings, and a revealer of secrets, since you could reveal this secret."

The dream was a prophecy about kingdoms to come. These were not the first empires. They were kingdoms going forward from that time. Let's look at these kingdoms as Daniel reveals them in the interpretation of the dream. The first kingdom was identified as Nebuchadnezzar's own kingdom, existing at the time this prophecy was given. Babylon was a kingdom with a history.

The Head of Gold

You are that head of gold. Nebuchadnezzar was not the first king to build an empire, but the vision started with him since he was then the present king. The vision then prophesied about the kingdoms that would follow. This kingdom of Babylon can be traced back to very early times after the great flood. In those days after Noah, as the vacant earth began to repopulate, men migrated southeastward from the mountains of Ararat between the Black and Caspian Seas, where the ark had come to rest. They followed streams from their headwaters in Ararat down to the fertile plains hugging the mighty Tigris and Euphrates rivers in present day Iraq. There they settled, and a significant post-flood civilization was formed.

> *Genesis 11:1-4 (RSV)*
> *¹ Now the whole earth had one language and few words. ² And as men migrated from the east, they found a plain in the land of Shinar and settled there. ³ And they said to one another, "Come, let us make bricks, and burn them thoroughly." And they had brick for stone, and bitumen for mortar. ⁴ Then they said, "Come, let us build ourselves a city, and a tower with its top in the heavens, and let us make a name for ourselves, lest we be scattered abroad upon the face of the whole earth."*

After the flood, God had given Noah specific instructions for him and his descendants about their life objective:

> *Genesis 9:1,7 (RSV)*
> *¹ And God blessed Noah and his sons, and said to them, "Be fruitful and multiply, and fill the earth. . . ⁷ And you, be fruitful and multiply, bring forth abundantly on the earth and multiply in it."*

He told them to *fill the earth*, that is, to scatter. The desire of the people in Shinar to congregate together rather than to spread out over the land, was contrary to God's plan. Rather than being obedient to His will and His instructions, they were following their own desires. Is this not, after all, the essence of all sin--following our own will, rather than God's?

This organization into a city-like culture did not just happen. It was developed by a man who rose to leadership during that time. His name was Nimrod.

> *Genesis 10:8-13 (RSV)*
> *⁸ Cush became the father of Nimrod; he was the first on earth to be a mighty man. ⁹ He was a mighty hunter before the LORD; therefore*

it is said, "Like Nimrod a mighty hunter before the LORD." [10] *The beginning of his kingdom was Ba'bel, Erech, and Accad, all of them in the land of Shinar.* [11] *From that land he went into Assyria, and built Nin'eveh, Reho'both-Ir, Calah, and* [12] *Resen between Nin'eveh and Calah; that is the great city.* [13] *Egypt became the father of Ludim, An'amim, Leha'bim, Naph-tu'him,*

Nimrod was the great grandson of Noah. He led the people in their disobedience of God. Archaeological investigation has found that this civilization worshipped man-made idols and nature-gods, appeased evil spirits, and built ziggurat-like temples toward the heavens. From these scriptures we see that these practices must have already been widespread just three generations away from faithful Noah. This people rebelled against God, and coalesced their rebellion into an organized unity.

The significance of these events is not the accomplishments of Nimrod. Behind the political ambitions of Nimrod lay a spiritual agenda of one much greater than him. This brief background helps clarify the mysterious intertwining of the political and spiritual we already encountered in Isaiah 14. Let's look again at a broader, but condensed version of the passage.

Isaiah 14:4,9,12,22,24,26-27 (KJV)
[4] *That thou shalt take up this proverb against the king of Babylon, and say, How hath the oppressor ceased! the golden city ceased! . . .*
[9] *Hell from beneath is moved for thee to meet thee at thy coming: it stirreth up the dead for thee, even all the chief ones of the earth; it hath raised up from their thrones all the kings of the nations . . .* [12] *How art thou fallen from heaven, O Lucifer, son of the morning! how art thou cut down to the ground, which didst weaken the nations! . . .* [22] *For I will rise up against them, saith the LORD of hosts, and cut off from Babylon the name, and remnant, and son, and nephew, saith the LORD . . .* [24] *The LORD of hosts hath sworn, saying, Surely as I have thought, so shall it come to pass; and as I have purposed, so shall it stand: . . .* [26] *This is the purpose that is purposed upon the whole earth: and this is the hand that is stretched out upon all the nations.* [27] *For the LORD of hosts hath purposed, and who shall disannul it? and his hand is stretched out, and who shall turn it back?*

Here in early Babylon we see the earliest biblical record of blatant idolatry. This is a significant step in the downward spiral in sin and degradation after the flood. Idolatry would earmark most of the nations that followed. It would one day infect the very people God had called out to be his own: Israel. The practice still thrives in civilized societies today, and even in the church, as people try to 'sculpt' God to be to their own liking. Babylon seems to have the dubious distinction of spawning this detestable practice.

We understand, now, that the ziggurats were built for idolatrous worship, not to draw near to the true God.

> *Genesis 11:5-9 (RSV)*
> *⁵ And the LORD came down to see the city and the tower, which the sons of men had built. ⁶ And the LORD said, "Behold, they are one people, and they have all one language; and this is only the beginning of what they will do; and nothing that they propose to do will now be impossible for them. ⁷ Come, let us go down, and there confuse their language, that they may not understand one another's speech." ⁸ So the LORD scattered them abroad from there over the face of all the earth, and they left off building the city. ⁹ Therefore its name was called Ba'bel, because there the LORD confused the language of all the earth; and from there the LORD scattered them abroad over the face of all the earth.*

God confused the language of this people, causing them to disperse. He did this to limit their evil. It seems when people unify, the opportunity for the devil to exploit them increases. It has been his primary tactic ever since. Many dictators have sought to bring worldwide unity (with themselves in charge, of course). But world unity is contrary to the division of nations that God brought about when he intervened at Babel. This division serves as a check against unlimited evil.

Babylon as a unified kingdom waxed and waned in power over the following centuries under the rule of these people known as Chaldees. About 1500 years after Babylon's beginning, Nebuchadnezzar engineered its rise to supremacy during the time of Daniel. Under his reign it enjoyed unprecedented military success, swallowing up neighboring nations, melding them into an expansive empire. Babylon was steeped in idolatry during this time, consistent with her history and roots. In this pagan empire we see Satan's manipulation of people and, particularly, high-authority leaders. The Babylonian dynasty of this prophecy lasted from about 605 to about 539 BC.

The Chest and Arms of Silver

On the great statue of Nebuchadnezzar's dream, he saw a chest and arms of silver. Daniel revealed to him that the silver arms and chest represented another kingdom, inferior to his, that would arise after Babylon. How unpredictable is that—that an inferior kingdom would conquer a superior one? But that is exactly what happened. That second kingdom was the Medo-Persian Empire. Media and Persia were two other pagan cultures that joined forces to take Babylon from the Chaldees. This invasion occurred while Israel's southern region was still in exile in Babylon. The occasion is recorded in Daniel Chapter 5. This empire lasted from 539 to about 331 BC. The book of Esther in the Old Testament was written during this time.

She played a key, divinely appointed role in the Jews finding favor in the eyes of the Medo-Persians, and eventually being allowed to return to their homeland.

<u>Belly and Thighs of Brass</u>
When Alexander the Great swept across Europe and Asia, he spread the boundaries of the Greek Empire as far east as Medo-Persia. Thus, the region of Babylon came under control of Greece. By this time, the returning exiles of Israel had already vacated Babylon and settled in their homeland of Judah. Israel was also captured by the Greeks. The Greek empire, represented by the brass belly and thighs of the image, stretched from 331 to 168 BC. With the Greek occupation came a new culture. The driving purpose, and lasting mark of the Grecian conquests was the intent to replace prevailing cultures of vanquished nations with the Greek culture. In the Grecian Empire, as in the previous empires, idolatry flourished.

Hellenism was a much more relaxed culture than the Jewish culture of rigid laws and customs. This liberal, 'enlightened' culture appealed to many, and threatened Judaism from within. Age-old traditions were given over to free thinking from the west. This cultural struggle split successive generations of Jews into two distinct, competitive views. The Grecian culture outlasted the Empire. By the time of Christ, Greece was no more than a far away country, but this enduring cultural division had evolved into the sects of the Pharisees (the traditionalists) and Sadducees (the progressives). Thus, the permeating culture of Greece survived the demise of its empire, and influences many of our ways of thinking even today.

<u>Legs of Iron</u>
A fourth kingdom was represented by legs of iron.

> *Daniel 2:40 (NKJV)*
> *^{40} And the fourth kingdom shall be as strong as iron, inasmuch as iron breaks in pieces and shatters everything; and like iron that crushes, that kingdom will break in pieces and crush all the others.*

Alexander died young, and he had no legitimate descendants. His brief, but expansive empire was divided into four quadrants, and given to each of his four field generals. Those smaller empires continued for some time, but eventually were gobbled up by the most powerful empire of all time, the Roman Empire. Rome brought a level of civilization and military might unknown before its time. Just as with all the previous empires, its goal was to unify the world under the banner of Rome. When Jesus was born in Judea, Rome was reigning, led by her imperial Caesars. Rome endured from about 168 BC to 476 AD, first as a republic, then as an imperial dictatorship.

I have vivid memories of visiting the ruins of Rome, particularly those just adjacent the Coliseum and the Forum. I was so intrigued that I went there three times during five days in Rome. While there, I was reminded of the idolatry that prevailed in the culture. There was the idolatry of the emperorship of the Caesars. There was the idolatry of a myriad of gods and goddesses from Roman mythology and from eastern religions. I especially remember the ruins of the Temple of the Vestal Virgins with row upon row of short columns with an idol statuette atop each one. There was idolatry to human accomplishment. The relics of idolatry are abundant there. I had flashbacks of this later when visiting Athens. Ruins of Greek and Roman temples to their deities were there too, validating the linage of idolatry running through these empires.

Rome was not conquered by another single empire. Instead it deteriorated from within, due to corruption, self-indulgence and moral deterioration. Neighboring barbaric clans moved in and took it over bit by bit. Rome, in all her pomp and power, was the epitome of human political accomplishment. She was, in essence, humanism carried to its highest degree. Her demise was a clear picture of humanism's doom.

Feet of Iron and Clay
Babylon, Medo-Persia, Greece and Rome are the first four empires clearly prophesied in Nebuchadnezzar's dream. The dream was interpreted by Daniel in about 570 BC and has come to pass just as predicted. When the Roman Empire disintegrated, it broke into smaller dominions according to the barbaric clan that merged with each part. This agglomeration evolved into present day Europe. Much of the way of life of the preceding Roman culture lived on. In fact, in each of those territories the empire's legacy blended with the pagan practices of the barbarians, and shaped what we today call 'western civilization.' It is still, in many ways, a continuation of the fabric of the Roman Empire.

The western world continues to be a patchwork of individual countries, some powerful in their own right, but never uniting into an empire with the others. This was portrayed in Nebuchadnezzar's image by the feet made of iron mixed with baked clay. The weakness of the clay demonstrates the lack of solidarity within the European community. This is not for lack of attempts to do so through the ages. Charlemagne, Napoleon, the Kaisers, and Hitler, among others, sought to accomplish it. Royal intermarriage, economic pressure and military campaigns have ultimately all failed to fuse these countries back into one empire. This is the current status of western civilization.

Europe is not alone in this unification movement. Globalization has been the agenda of social engineers in the United States for several decades. Unification maneuvers have been continuous, and are ongoing, as seen in institutions such as NATO, the United Nations, and the European Common Market up to, and including, the recent introduction of the Euro as a common currency.

When the ancient and still persisting desire for unification is viewed against the historical backdrop of God's segregating the nations, it is seen as a continuation of man's attempts at self-sufficiency and divine independence. Behind it, we see the work of our enemy, the devil himself.

What will be the success of this globalization? Will we see another major world empire?

> *Daniel 2:43-45 (NKJV)*
> *[43] As you saw iron mixed with ceramic clay, they will mingle with the seed of men; but they will not adhere to one another, just as iron does not mix with clay. [44] And in the days of these kings the God of heaven will set up a kingdom which shall never be destroyed; and the kingdom shall not be left to other people; it shall break in pieces and consume all these kingdoms, and it shall stand forever. [45] Inasmuch as you saw that the stone was cut out of the mountain without hands, and that it broke in pieces the iron, the bronze, the clay, the silver, and the gold--the great God has made known to the king what will come to pass after this. The dream is certain, and its interpretation is sure."*

The prophetic prediction is that there will not be another major empire among those countries that formed the old Roman Empire. The remnants of Rome will continue as they have for many centuries, but their attempts at unification will fail. The next world kingdom will be the kingdom of God, politically established by Christ at his second coming, and continuing through the millennium. It will powerfully displace the authority, the cultures and the humanistic motives of the Roman Empire, and of all those previous empires. It will have no end. This everlasting kingdom will be developed in later chapters.

Just so We Don't Miss it--The Message Confirmed

Another passage from Daniel's prophecy was written later during the reign of Belshazzar, the last king of the Neo-Babylonian Empire, and grandson of Nebuchadnezzar. This time the prophetic vision came to Daniel himself:

> *Daniel 7:1-14 (NKJV)*
> *[1] In the first year of Belshazzar king of Babylon, Daniel had a dream and visions of his head while on his bed. Then he wrote down the dream, telling the main facts. [2] Daniel spoke, saying, "I saw in my*

vision by night, and behold, the four winds of heaven were stirring up the Great Sea. ³ And four great beasts came up from the sea, each different from the other. ⁴ The first was like a lion, and had eagle's wings. I watched till its wings were plucked off; and it was lifted up from the earth and made to stand on two feet like a man, and a man's heart was given to it. ⁵ And suddenly another beast, a second, like a bear. It was raised up on one side, and had three ribs in its mouth between its teeth. And they said thus to it: 'Arise, devour much flesh!' ⁶ After this I looked, and there was another, like a leopard, which had on its back four wings of a bird. The beast also had four heads, and dominion was given to it. ⁷ After this I saw in the night visions, and behold, a fourth beast, dreadful and terrible, exceedingly strong. It had huge iron teeth; it was devouring, breaking in pieces, and trampling the residue with its feet. It was different from all the beasts that were before it, and it had ten horns. ⁸ I was considering the horns, and there was another horn, a little one, coming up among them, before whom three of the first horns were plucked out by the roots. And there, in this horn, were eyes like the eyes of a man, and a mouth speaking pompous words. ⁹ "I watched till thrones were put in place, And the Ancient of Days was seated; His garment was white as snow, And the hair of His head was like pure wool. His throne was a fiery flame, Its wheels a burning fire; ¹⁰ A fiery stream issued And came forth from before Him. A thousand thousands ministered to Him; Ten thousand times ten thousand stood before Him. The court was seated, And the books were opened. ¹¹ "I watched then because of the sound of the pompous words which the horn was speaking; I watched till the beast was slain, and its body destroyed and given to the burning flame. ¹² As for the rest of the beasts, they had their dominion taken away, yet their lives were prolonged for a season and a time. ¹³ "I was watching in the night visions, And behold, One like the Son of Man, Coming with the clouds of heaven! He came to the Ancient of Days, And they brought Him near before Him. ¹⁴ Then to Him was given dominion and glory and a kingdom, That all peoples, nations, and languages should serve Him. His dominion is an everlasting dominion, Which shall not pass away, And His kingdom the one Which shall not be destroyed.

Again, God showed Daniel a vision about four great empires, the same four empires as before, this time represented by four strange-looking beasts. The lion stood for the kingdom of Babylon in its strength and majesty. The bear raised up on one side represented the Medo-Persians, the Persians being stronger than the Medes, and ultimately prevailing. The leopard with four wings like those of a bird portrayed the lightening-quick sweep of Alexander the Great conquering an empire for Greece. The four heads of the leopard were the four divisions of that kingdom at his death.

Finally, Daniel saw a fourth beast, not like any known animal, but described as different from the others. It was exceptionally powerful and brutal. Its ten horns represented ten kings under his authority. There is clearly a parallel symbolism between the ten horns of this vision and the (presumed) ten toes on the feet of the image in the previous vision. Historical interpreters of the book of Revelation apply their frame of reference to this prophecy as well. They believe these ten kings represent ten barbarian tribes that filled the power vacuum when the Roman Empire waned. In these countries the seed of Rome lived on, mingled with the cultures of the barbarian tribes that absorbed them. These ten people-groups have been identified by some interpreters as:

1. Saxons - today's English
2. Franks - French
3. Suevi - Portuguese
4. Visigoths - Spanish
5. Burgundians - Swiss
6. Alamanni - German
7. Lombards - Italian
8. Ostrogoths - indistinct
9. Heruli - indistinct
10. Vandals - indistinct

Futurist interpreters of Revelation parallel this passage about ten kings with some passages from the apocalypse (Revelation), and conclude that they represent ten 'kings' that will emerge in the end-time, not yet identified.

While I am of the futurist view, I see both interpretations in this symbolism. The ten end-time kingdoms are not newly-formed, but continuations of the ten original fragments of the Roman Empire. Granted, some of the originals have become indistinct, and some new ones have formed, but the same people lineages live on under other names. The influence of the Roman Empire lives on in them even today, and in many of their colonial nations, including the United States.

The Greatest Kingdom

Both of these prophecies in Daniel show that there is one more kingdom yet to come after the Roman Empire. It will not originate under the direction of men, but will be established by the *Ancient of Days*. It will be an everlasting kingdom. We shall see in later chapters that the first thousand years of this kingdom will be the millennium, right here on earth. The kingdom will continue on, after the millennium, into eternity.

I believe what we see developing today in the realm of attempted unification in Europe and globalization worldwide shows two truths that we can recognize. First, they are indicators of fulfilled prophecy; that the political scene is shaping up for the end of the age and the return of Christ. Second, in light of the scriptures we have studied, we can see the agenda of Satan being promoted in this world's global politics. World unification is a concept that appeals to men, but is contrary to the will of God at this time. The historically frequent attempts at unification may appear to have been random. They were not. Rather they were part of a conspiracy–not that those who attempted were conscious of being part of such a conspiracy. The conspiracy is in the spiritual realm. It is Satan's conspiracy.

12
THE ANTICHRIST

Revelation 12:17-13:2 (ESV)
17 Then the dragon became furious with the woman and went off to make war on the rest of her offspring, on those who keep the commandments of God and hold to the testimony of Jesus. And he stood on the sand of the sea.1 And I saw a beast rising out of the sea, with ten horns and seven heads, with ten diadems on its horns and blasphemous names on its heads. 2 And the beast that I saw was like a leopard; its feet were like a bear's, and its mouth was like a lion's mouth. And to it the dragon gave his power and his throne and great authority.

In Revelation Chapter 13 we meet a beast which comes out of the sea. He acts as an ambassador for Satan. He is given great satanic power and authority to institute an evil plot on the earth. Who or what is this beast coming *out of the sea*? A little further along in Revelation we read this:

Revelation 17:15 (ESV)
15 And the angel said to me, "The waters that you saw, where the prostitute is seated, are peoples and multitudes and nations and languages.

Assuming the waters in Rev 13:1 and 17:15 are the same (and the context supports this), they represent Gentile people from all over the world. *Nations* in Old Testament literature refers to non-Israelite peoples. The beast is a Gentile man or government who will rise to international power in the end time.

The Rise of Antichrist

The reference to the beast resembling *a leopard,* with *feet like those of a bear and a mouth like that of a lion* clearly identifies it with the first three beasts in Daniel 7. The seven heads, ten horns and ten crowns are like that of the fourth beast, and like the great dragon, Satan. Remember those beasts represented the four successive empires--Babylon, Medo-Persia, Greece and Rome. We saw how the spirit of idolatry permeated those empires, and how they promoted an anti-Yahweh (God) culture. They were both a tool and an emblem of Satan's conspiracy of evil in the affairs of men. The same demonic motivation behind those kingdoms will also be behind this *beast out of the sea*. His kingdom will be a continuation of them in their spiritual sense.

This beast *out of the sea* occupies a significant portion of the book of Revelation. He is also identified variously in several other scripture passages, but under different names and symbolisms. As we piece together all of these references, we see from their content that they all seem to converge in a single person.

One of the most fertile sources for information on him is the prophet Daniel. Picking up on our passage, already studied, from Daniel 7:

> *Daniel 7:7-8,16,19-25 (NIV2011)*
> [7] *"After that, in my vision at night I looked, and there before me was a fourth beast—terrifying and frightening and very powerful. It had large iron teeth; it crushed and devoured its victims and trampled underfoot whatever was left. It was different from all the former beasts, and it had ten horns.* [8] *"While I was thinking about the horns, there before me was another horn, a little one, which came up among them; and three of the first horns were uprooted before it. This horn had eyes like the eyes of a human being and a mouth that spoke boastfully . . .* [16] *I approached one of those standing there and asked him the meaning of all this. "So he told me and gave me the interpretation of these things: . . .* [19] *"Then I wanted to know the meaning of the fourth beast, which was different from all the others and most terrifying, with its iron teeth and bronze claws—the beast that crushed and devoured its victims and trampled underfoot whatever was left.* [20] *I also wanted to know about the ten horns on its head and about the other horn that came up, before which three of them fell—the horn that looked more imposing than the others and that had eyes and a mouth that spoke boastfully.* [21] *As I watched, this horn was waging war against the holy people and defeating them,* [22] *until the Ancient of Days came and pronounced judgment in favor of the holy people of the Most High, and the time came when they possessed the kingdom.* [23] *"He gave me this explanation: 'The fourth beast is a fourth kingdom that will appear on earth. It will be different from all the other kingdoms and will devour the whole earth, trampling it down and crushing it.* [24] *The ten horns are ten kings who will come from this kingdom. After them another king will arise, different from the earlier ones; he will subdue three kings.* [25] *He will speak against the Most High and oppress his holy people and try to change the set times and the laws. The holy people will be delivered into his hands for a time, times and half a time.*

Rome, according to tradition, was founded on seven hills by seven princes. Out of Rome came ten kingdoms. We have talked about these ten kings being the ten kingdoms that arose on the soil of the deteriorating Roman Empire during the latter part of the third century and much of the fourth. The barbaric invasions resulted in the ten *nations*. These ten eventually became today's Europe.

The passage says another king would rise up and subdue three kings. Many futurists believe this is speaking of events yet to come. This king will arise out of the nations, will assume great spiritual and political authority given him by Satan, and will arrogantly and defiantly assert himself over the affairs of men and in the affairs of God. He will overthrow three 'kings' of the ten somewhat-unified Mediterranean conglomerate members, the offspring of the ancient Roman Empire. Then he will attempt to usurp the honor and sovereignty that belongs to God alone. In other words, he will set himself up as God.

We also understand that he will persecute *the saints*. Throughout the New Testament *the saints* refers exclusively to the church. The saints will be under his oppression *for a time, times and half a time*. This phrase is a specific time period. Its meaning and significance will be developed in Chapter 13.

He will *try to change the set times and the laws*. Since we are considering a dictator in the international community where laws and customs will already vary from country to country, this seems to refer to major changes in basic codes of human conduct that transcend political boundaries, perhaps to norms embraced by all civilizations since the beginning. Thus we are informed about a man referred to by prophecy students as the 'little horn of Daniel 7.' Another title is given to him in Paul's New Testament letters to the Thessalonians where he is called the *man of lawlessness*.

> *2 Thessalonians 2:3-12 (ESV)*
> *³ Let no one deceive you in any way. For that day will not come, unless the rebellion comes first, and the man of lawlessness is revealed, the son of destruction, ⁴ who opposes and exalts himself against every so-called god or object of worship, so that he takes his seat in the temple of God, proclaiming himself to be God. ⁵ Do you not remember that when I was still with you I told you these things? ⁶ And you know what is restraining him now so that he may be revealed in his time. ⁷ For the mystery of lawlessness is already at work. Only he who now restrains it will do so until he is out of the way. ⁸ And then the lawless one will be revealed, whom the Lord Jesus will kill with the breath of his mouth and bring to nothing by the appearance of his coming. ⁹ The coming of the lawless one is by the activity of Satan with all power and false signs and wonders, ¹⁰*

and with all wicked deception for those who are perishing, because they refused to love the truth and so be saved. *¹¹* Therefore God sends them a strong delusion, so that they may believe what is false, *¹²* in order that all may be condemned who did not believe the truth but had pleasure in unrighteousness.

And John writes:

1 John 2:18,22 (ESV)
¹⁸ Children, it is the last hour, and as you have heard that antichrist is coming, so now many antichrists have come. Therefore we know that it is the last hour . . . *²²* Who is the liar but he who denies that Jesus is the Christ? This is the antichrist, he who denies the Father and the Son.

This beast, the little horn, the lawless one, is the infamous antichrist. This term, antichrist, is used only in the letters of John, but not in his writing of Revelation. There he is portrayed symbolically as *the beast*.

Here both Paul and John recognize that the *spirit of antichrist,* that will one day empower the person of the antichrist, is already at work, for it is none other than Satan himself. There have been many forerunners of antichrist. The evil of Satan has often been personified in certain humans who, because of their evil character, portray his likeness and become his servants to do evil. He empowers them for evil, and scripts them with his agenda.

Scripture portrays them as Satan's agents. In some cases their lives so closely parallel the prophesied antichrist that they are considered to be prophetic replicas of him. Theologians call these figures 'types.' Types are prophecies embodied in actual historical events or people. For example, figures like the serpent in the Garden of Eden, Nimrod who established Babylon and many other ancient Babylonian and Assyrian cities contrary to God's commands, Pharaoh of Egypt, Sennacherib the king of Assyria, Nebuchadnezzar king of Babylon, and the entire Herod lineage have often been cited, along with many others.

There is one historical figure that stands out as a type of antichrist more than any other, and actually was called so by Jesus. Here is how it unfolds, beginning in the Old Testament prophecies. In Daniel 9 we read of a vision that Daniel had. We will consider it in some detail later, but note for now that in verse 27 he refers to a pagan king who will make an *abomination that causes desolation* in the Jerusalem temple. Perhaps about four years later Daniel had another vision, recorded in Chapter 10 of his book. There we are given an extremely detailed prophecy of the rise and breakup of a kingdom. In that passage he predicts a king who would set up the *abomination which causes desolation.*

When Alexander the Great died, his vast Grecian empire was divided between his four generals, forming four smaller empires. Two of the four empires, the Selucids (Syrians) and Ptolemies (Egyptians) engaged in a long-standing battle for territory. That disputed territory included the land of Israel. (These historical events all occurred during the 'silent period' between the Old and New Testaments.) Israel was caught in the middle. For one hundred years the land of promise was occupied alternately by Egypt and Syria. During one stretch when Syria was in control, a very powerful, unscrupulous and ruthless man named Antiochus IV Epiphanes came to power. He viciously persecuted the Jews. In total defiance against them and their God, he defiled the temple by entering it himself, setting up an idol, and roasting a pig on the altar. So offensive was this to the Jews that they rebelled and were put down in a devastating bloodbath in the streets of Jerusalem. This abomination that certainly resulted in desolation occurred about 350 years after Daniel wrote of it. The prophetic description of military campaigns and political schemes unmistakably describes these historical events. Details are accurate beyond belief. (Read Daniel 11 to appreciate the intricacy of the prophecy.) Prophecy fulfilled--right? Not completely.

If all we had was this, we could certainly assume the fulfillment was complete. But yet 215 years later Jesus told his listeners:

Matthew 24:15-16 (NASB)
[15] "Therefore when you see the ABOMINATION OF DESOLATION which was spoken of through Daniel the prophet, standing in the holy place (let the reader understand), [16] then those who are in Judea must flee to the mountains.

The event with Antiochus Epiphanes was now past history. Jesus, however, clearly spoke to a time in the future, giving his disciples valuable information about this event. Matthew adds gravity to this prophecy by Jesus when he inserts the admonition *let the reader understand.* In Luke's version of this discourse, he records Jesus as saying,

Luke 21:20-21 (ESV)
[20] "But when you see Jerusalem surrounded by armies, then know that its desolation has come near. [21] Then let those who are in Judea flee to the mountains, and let those who are inside the city depart, and let not those who are out in the country enter it,

If all we had to go on was Luke's version, this would have been most amazingly fulfilled in 70 AD. At that time because of a rebellion by Jewish freedom fighters led by rabbi Simon bar Kokhba, the Roman army, under General Titus, laid siege to Jerusalem and finally captured it, slaughtering thousands of Jews. But while the Roman army did destroy the temple, there is no evidence that they desecrated it like Antiochus had done. Yes, this event was certainly in view as Jesus makes his predictions. But neither Antiochus Epiphanes nor Titus were the ultimate fulfillment to Daniel's prophecy. Both Matthew and Luke, a few verses later, speak specifically of events associated with the second coming of Christ. A major portion of Revelation is about earthly tribulation prior to the return of Christ. And in Matt 24 just after the passage describing the abomination of desolation, we read . . .

> *Matthew 24:29-30 (ESV)*
> *²⁹ "Immediately after the tribulation of those days the sun will be darkened, and the moon will not give its light, and the stars will fall from heaven, and the powers of the heavens will be shaken. ³⁰ Then will appear in heaven the sign of the Son of Man, and then all the tribes of the earth will mourn, and they will see the Son of Man coming on the clouds of heaven with power and great glory.*

The real antichrist will be a person who lives and exercises great authority just prior to the return of Jesus. His reign and self-revelation will escalate during a time of *great tribulation*.

The Olivet Discourse of Matthew 24 (and Mark 13 and Luke 21) seems to present a chronology of events with its beginning in the fall of Jerusalem that subsequently occurred in 70 AD, but with its ending clearly anchored in some yet future time. To overcome this, the tendency of many scholars is to divide the passage, making everything before the dividing line pertain to 70 AD and everything after it pertain to a future event. Several different dividing lines have been proposed.

The fact that there are several historical events that seem to have been clearly predicted by Daniel's prophecy often leads to confusion. Scholars dispute which was the intended fulfillment. Jewish interpreters would point to the desecration of Antiochus. Preterist Christian interpreters point to 70 AD events; futurists say it is all about an end-time event.

God is not the *author of confusion*. Instead of seeing contradiction and confusion, it seems more appropriate to be looking for comprehensiveness and consistency. It was not to create confusion that God orchestrated things this way. It was intentional on His part, in order to expose an underlying truth. By so accurately predicting the earlier partial fulfillments it seems God is showing us a couple of things.

First, He underscores the trustworthiness of His prophecy. Our western minds want a single distinct meaning, a one-for-one correlation between prophecy and fulfillment. In ancient oriental cultures such as that of the

Hebrews, the perception is much different. These partial–fulfillments are often seen as indicators of what is to follow. Because the shorter-term fulfillments were so literally accurate, we can confidently assert that this prophecy is from God who knows the beginning from the end. Therefore we have valid evidence to believe in the end-time complete fulfillment.

Second, He shows us the consistency of Satan's evil schemes. Although these multiple partial fulfillments are distinct historical events separated by hundreds of years, they demonstrate an evil spiritual continuum running through the ages. In prophecy's wide-angle scope we see a comprehensive network of evil, showing its single primal source. From the serpent of Eden, in the murder of Abel by Cain, in the prevailing evil during Noah's day, in the idolatry of the early post-flood cultures, and right on down the line, we find the spirit of antichrist, Satan himself. In this regard it is best to regard the scriptural record as a panoramic portrayal of antichrist's program.

A straightforward interpretation of these prophecies is that antichrist will be a specific man who will appear in the last days prior to Christ's return. He is also a pervasive spirit, already here and always trying to lead us away from Christ.

The Deceit of Antichrist

If Satan is the *father of* lies, then it is no surprise that the antichrist, his ambassador, will be a deceiver. His deceit is used to cause men to worship him rather than God. Actually he will be happy for men to worship anyone other than God. He is glad to share the honor, so long as God does not get it. Therefore he will have already sent many counterfeit messiahs to attract the attention of men. In the Olivet Discourse . . .

> *Matthew 24:4-5, 23-26 (NASB)*
> *[4] And Jesus answered and said to them, "See to it that no one misleads you. [5] "For many will come in My name, saying, 'I am the Christ,' and will mislead many . . . [23] "Then if anyone says to you, 'Behold, here is the Christ,' or 'There He is,' do not believe him. [24] "For false Christs and false prophets will arise and will show great signs and wonders, so as to mislead, if possible, even the elect. [25] "Behold, I have told you in advance. [26] "So if they say to you, 'Behold, He is in the wilderness,' do not go out, or, 'Behold, He is in the inner rooms,' do not believe them.*

The final antichrist will be the consummate deceiver. He will mimic many of the signs and wonders that Jesus had done. Satan will empower him, and he will deceive many people into thinking he is divine, and ultimately that he is the one and only god. Refer again to the passage:

> *2 Thessalonians 2:9-10 (ESV)*
> *⁹ The coming of the lawless one is by the activity of Satan with all power and false signs and wonders, ¹⁰ and with all wicked deception for those who are perishing, because they refused to love the truth and so be saved.*

One specific miracle he will perform is described in our Revelation passage. Just as Jesus was resurrected on the third day after his death, the antichrist or some portion of him or his reign will appear dead, then will be raised to life, to the marveling wonder of many:

> *Revelation 13:3-4 (ESV)*
> *³ One of its heads seemed to have a mortal wound, but its mortal wound was healed, and the whole earth marveled as they followed the beast. ⁴ And they worshiped the dragon, for he had given his authority to the beast, and they worshiped the beast, saying, "Who is like the beast, and who can fight against it?"*

Antichrist's Arrogance

The result of this deceit will be that men will worship antichrist because of the show of authority he displays. Out of fear and awe, they will honor him as supreme. He will gladly accept this praise. He will compound his arrogance by speaking with unthinkable heresies and insults against the true God and all that is holy.

> *Revelation 13:5-6 (ESV)*
> *⁵ And the beast was given a mouth uttering haughty and blasphemous words, and it was allowed to exercise authority for forty-two months. ⁶ It opened its mouth to utter blasphemies against God, blaspheming his name and his dwelling, that is, those who dwell in heaven.*

For *forty-two months* (3-1/2 years), antichrist will exert his blasphemous attack on God's sovereignty.

Antichrist's Persecution of the Saints

This blasphemous attitude will, of course, place the upstart leader in direct opposition to the saints and any who fear God. This conflict of loyalty will bring about hostility, and the saints will be persecuted.

> *Revelation 13:7-10 (ESV)*
> *⁷ Also it was allowed to make war on the saints and to conquer them. And authority was given it over every tribe and people and language*

and nation, ⁸ and all who dwell on earth will worship it, everyone whose name has not been written before the foundation of the world in the book of life of the Lamb who was slain. ⁹ If anyone has an ear, let him hear: ¹⁰ If anyone is to be taken captive, to captivity he goes; if anyone is to be slain with the sword, with the sword must he be slain. Here is a call for the endurance and faith of the saints.

The antichrist will appear to be winning the battle because any Christians who stand in their faith will be persecuted. Many will be imprisoned, others killed. Jesus also warned of this time:

Matthew 24:9-11 (NASB)
⁹ "Then they will deliver you to tribulation, and will kill you, and you will be hated by all nations because of My name. ¹⁰ "At that time many will fall away and will betray one another and hate one another. ¹¹ "Many false prophets will arise and will mislead many.

The Mark of the Beast

Even people who know nothing about prophecy have some reaction to this phrase, *the mark of the beast*. Films have been made around this topic. Articles upon articles have been written about it. It makes the hair on our necks stand up. Sends chills down our spine. So, what is it? Some say it is symbolic of falling away from the faith. Some say it represents some particular sin, but is a spiritual mark, not a literal mark. Still others say it is literal.

The antichrist will rule over many nations. He will seek global dominion. According to scripture, to promote this agenda he will instigate a mark of loyalty that will ultimately be required to trade for goods on the open market.

Revelation 13:16-18 (ESV)
¹⁶ Also it causes all, both small and great, both rich and poor, both free and slave, to be marked on the right hand or the forehead, ¹⁷ so that no one can buy or sell unless he has the mark, that is, the name of the beast or the number of its name. ¹⁸ This calls for wisdom: let the one who has understanding calculate the number of the beast, for it is the number of a man, and his number is 666.

That mark is either the antichrist's name or the number of his name which is given as 666. This number is assumedly based on the then-prevalent practice of assigning a number from the alphabet to each letter of a name, then adding them up. Preterist and historical interpreters have tried to identify a historical antichrist on this basis. This may sound like a good clue for identifying him. However, there are problems with this.

First, it is not clear what language is intended. Some of the suggested solutions are satisfied using the Hebrew language, since John was Hebrew, while others insist that it must be based on Greek, since the book was originally written in Greek. The practice of assigning numbers to letters, and thus representing a name with a number, was practiced both in the Greek and the Hebrew language.

Another problem is that word forms can be varied slightly so that subtle changes in spelling can be used to force-fit many names. Using this 'tool' makes it relatively easy to find a name or combination of names and titles that will give this value. Using names of the past, over 100 suggestions have been proposed. Perhaps some of the better matches for those views are 'Caesar Nero' (for the preterest view) and 'Lateinos' (meaning Roman Empire from the historical view). The problem here is that there are too many matches, so that none of them seems uniquely credible on this basis alone.

It is interesting that the number 666 has symbolic significance in itself. Since creation, the number six has been associated with animals and with man, since they were created on the 6th day. Seven is the number associated with God and His perfection. Man was created in the image of God, and placed above the animals, but beneath God. He was given dominion over animals, but his affections were to be toward God. When he listened to the serpent (a created being) in the Garden of Eden, he was turning away from God.

The number six is often used symbolically by the biblical writers to symbolize underlying evil in real situations. For example, the idolatrous image that Nebuchadnezzar made is described like this:

Daniel 3:1 (KJV)
[1] Nebuchadnezzar the king made an image of gold, whose height was threescore [60] cubits, and the breadth thereof six cubits: he set it up in the plain of Dura, in the province of Babylon.

In another example, when the children of Israel were preparing to enter the promised land, they were given this warning:

Deuteronomy 17:14-17 (NASB)
[14] "When you enter the land which the LORD your God gives you, and you possess it and live in it, and you say, 'I will set a king over me like all the nations who are around me,' [15] you shall surely set a king over you whom the LORD your God chooses, one from among your countrymen you shall set as king over yourselves; you may not put a foreigner over yourselves who is not your countryman. [16]

> *"Moreover, he shall not multiply horses for himself, nor shall he cause the people to return to Egypt to multiply horses, since the LORD has said to you, 'You shall never again return that way.'* [17] *"He shall not multiply wives for himself, or else his heart will turn away; nor shall he greatly increase silver and gold for himself.*

Later Solomon became Israel's third King. We know he was exceedingly rich, and had 700 wives and 300 concubines. About him we read . . .

2 Chronicles 9:13 (ESV)
[13] *Now the weight of gold that came to Solomon in one year was 666 talents of gold,*

One more example relates to Goliath, the heathen giant who defiantly challenged Israel and her God. Of him we read:

1 Samuel 17:4-7 (KJV)
[4] *And there went out a champion out of the camp of the Philistines, named Goliath, of Gath, whose height was six cubits and a span.* [5] *And he had an helmet of brass upon his head, and he was armed with a coat of mail; and the weight of the coat was five thousand shekels* [some manuscripts say six thousand shekels] *of brass.* [6] *And he had greaves of brass upon his legs, and a target of brass between his shoulders.* [7] *And the staff of his spear was like a weaver's beam; and his spear's head weighed six hundred shekels of iron: and one bearing a shield went before him.*

Note the repeated use of the number six to emphasize the evil represented in this man. The idea seems to be the same in all of these examples. Six often symbolizes moral or spiritual wickedness, in conflict with God's holiness. It testifies to the unseen spiritual war being fought behind the scenes, in which we are, often unknowingly, involved. There are underlying spiritual implications for earthly struggles. The hardships here on earth are symptoms of the spiritual conflict being waged in the spiritual realms for our souls.

Scholars of the spiritual method of interpretation will say this is strictly symbolic in prophecy. However, just as the number six was used by God to symbolize evil in real historical situations, there is no reason to dismiss a somewhat literal and real meaning as it relates to the mark of the beast.

In modern times many Futurist speculators have assigned contemporary and fanciful identities to antichrist such as Kaiser Wilhelm, Adolph Hitler, Winston Churchill, Henry Kissinger and dozens of others. None proved correct, of course. Perhaps the lesson to be learned from all this is to be alert to evil, discerning the times, but not too eager to speculate about the identity of the antichrist. We do not know how far evil will be allowed to go before Christ finally intervenes. If we stay close to him, we will not need to fear being deceived. When the antichrist is revealed, we will recognize him if we know our God.

The False Prophet

As powerful as the antichrist will be, he does not work alone. He will be the political ruler. At his side will be a different kind of *beast*. This second beast has great power, and speaks with the same authority as the first beast.

> *Revelation 13:11-15 (ESV)*
> *[11] Then I saw another beast rising out of the earth. It had two horns like a lamb and it spoke like a dragon. [12] It exercises all the authority of the first beast in its presence, and makes the earth and its inhabitants worship the first beast, whose mortal wound was healed. [13] It performs great signs, even making fire come down from heaven to earth in front of people, [14] and by the signs that it is allowed to work in the presence of the beast it deceives those who dwell on earth, telling them to make an image for the beast that was wounded by the sword and yet lived. [15] And it was allowed to give breath to the image of the beast, so that the image of the beast might even speak and might cause those who would not worship the image of the beast to be slain.*

Who is this second beast? Later we read:

> *Revelation 19:20a (ESV)*
> *[20] And the beast was captured, and with it the false prophet who in its presence had done the signs by which he deceived those who had received the mark of the beast and those who worshiped its image.*

He is identified simply as the *false prophet*. He is symbolized as having *two horns like a lamb, but he spoke like a dragon*. He will not come wielding military power. However, his speech reveals that inwardly he has the evil spirit of the dragon, just like the first beast. He will speak with great authority--that of the dragon himself. Many believe he will be a religious figure. He will perform many miracles. He will cause fire to fall from the sky. As a result of his miraculous abilities, he will be given more power and will have tremendous influence.

To promote worship of antichrist, he will erect a huge image of him, presumably a statue of some sort. Then he will perform a miracle before the eyes of the world by causing the image to seem to come alive and speak. Like a flood, homage will pour in for the image and for the antichrist. Emboldened by his swelling popularity, he will require all men to pay homage to the image.

> *Revelation 13:15-17 (ESV)*
> [15] *And it was allowed to give breath to the image of the beast, so that the image of the beast might even speak and might cause those who would not worship the image of the beast to be slain.* [16] *Also it causes all, both small and great, both rich and poor, both free and slave, to be marked on the right hand or the forehead,* [17] *so that no one can buy or sell unless he has the mark, that is, the name of the beast or the number of its name.*

It is actually the false prophet who will administer the *mark of the beast*. His motive and agenda will be to cause people to be drawn into the net of loyalty to antichrist.

The dragon, the first beast (antichrist) and the second beast (false prophet) will engineer a powerful conspiracy that will intoxicate wayward people and capture the mindless souls of those who live in self-gratification. Just as God is manifest in the Father, the Son and the Holy Spirit, so this satanic trio will promote the antichristian kingdom at the end of the age.

What is the destiny of the dragon, antichrist, and the false prophet? We will defer this discussion for a later chapter because it is tightly interwoven into the fabric of the Tribulation and its final war.

In Summary

Satan is the arch-enemy of God and of Jesus Christ. He is not the equal of God, having been created an angel. He tried to usurp the throne of God and was defeated and thrown out of heaven. In his rebellion he took a large number of rebellious angels with him. He has waged war in the spiritual realm against the people of God. In the Old Testament times, that war was focused on the nation Israel. In the New Testament period, Satan adds the church to his hit list.

We can recognize the work of the devil in the events of everyday life. His influence is seen in human behavior all around us. His seduction is in every form of media. His treachery is seen in the tragedies of this life. Yet we are told in the Bible that if we are *in Christ*, we have God's power to make us victorious against him. Nevertheless, we are told to be aware of his strategies and tactics so that we can be prepared in scriptural understanding and in holiness. That is why Paul said:

> *Ephesians 6:11-13 (ESV)*
> *[11] Put on the whole armor of God, that you may be able to stand against the schemes of the devil. [12] For we do not wrestle against flesh and blood, but against the rulers, against the authorities, against the cosmic powers over this present darkness, against the spiritual forces of evil in the heavenly places. [13] Therefore take up the whole armor of God, that you may be able to withstand in the evil day, and having done all, to stand firm.*

In the events of the end time, Satan will work through his agents, the antichrist and the false prophet. They will form an evil Trinitarian coalition, bringing powerful delusion to deceive men, and an authoritarian force to compel them to pay loyalty, homage and worship to the antichrist. Their primary agenda is to again usurp the rightful place of the God of heaven, this time on his earthly turf. This sets the stage and introduces some of the actors for the next chapter.

> Lord, we recognize our enemy. He is wholly bent on separating us from you. We know in the arm of flesh we are no match for his evil schemes and his power.
>
> Dear Lord, we are wary of him, but we are not afraid. We know from your holy word that his power was broken at the cross. Jesus removed his ultimate tactic when, in his resurrection, he conquered death. Through the power of the Holy Spirit we have the weapons we need to defend ourselves from his attacks.
>
> Teach us to walk as children of victory, not as prisoners of war. Teach us how to wage a war whose outcome is determined, whose triumph is secure. Teach us, above all, to guard our walk with you, for you are our victory. You are our prize and our reward. You are our peace. Thank you Lord.

13
THE TRIBULATION

If you ask any uninformed person about the content of the book of Revelation, they will likely know one thing about it. They will know that it is about a time of great tribulation. It is true. Of its 22 chapters, 6 through 19 deal primarily with the period of time we call the Tribulation, according to a futurist interpretation.

There is not universal agreement as to the meaning of these events. Remember in chapter 3 of this book we discussed the various interpretive approaches. We said that some see those chapters as symbolic of the turbulent history of the church age, and they don't look for a literal tribulation period at the end of this age. This is the historical approach to interpretation. Those of the Preterest school of interpretation believe they represent the persecutions of the first century church. Spiritualists allegorize everything in the book. They say that wars and famines really represent spiritual struggles in the individual life of a believer. However, many see the events of the book as future and, to some degree, literal. That is, they see in them symbolic warnings of literal events and movements yet to come. As I have already explained and defended, this futurist position is my understanding. Therefore, remember that this book is written from the Futurist point of view. The interpreter's view of Revelation is shaped by his interpretive position on the Tribulation.

At the time the Revelation vision was written down, the fulfillment was obviously in the future, so of course the sense is Futurist. But the events seem beyond our now-known historical experience, either first century or church-age in general. Therefore, unless you allegorize them and dilute their enormity, they best fit a future timetable. Furthermore, we are not left to our own speculation about the book of Revelation. Teaching about the Tribulation is prevalent in both Old and New Testament prophetic writings.

This topic cannot be whisked away as an obscurity. There are scores of prominent Old Testament references to a great end-of-the-age turmoil on the earth. Now there have been many times of tribulation for Israel during her turbulent history. In Old Testament prophecy there are many references to exiles, wars, enemy invasions, and famines that have later became historical occasions. However even those which speak of near-term fulfillments often also contain a component with an eschatological view, that is, with a view toward end-time fulfillment. In fact all of the literature formally classified as prophecy in the Old Testament was written during the time preceding or during the exile of the Northern and Southern Kingdoms to Assyria and Babylon. Much of that prophecy found fulfillment in those events. Yet it is here, in this same context, that the rich cache of end-time prophecy is found.

No special interpretive ability is needed to identify the following passages as relating to an end-of-the-age tribulation:

Isaiah 13:6-9 (RSV)
[6] Wail, for the day of the LORD is near; as destruction from the Almighty it will come! [7] Therefore all hands will be feeble, and every man's heart will melt, [8] and they will be dismayed. Pangs and agony will seize them; they will be in anguish like a woman in travail. They will look aghast at one another; their faces will be aflame. [9] Behold, the day of the LORD comes, cruel, with wrath and fierce anger, to make the earth a desolation and to destroy its sinners from it.

Ezekiel 30:2-3 (NASB)
[2] "Son of man, prophesy and say, 'Thus says the Lord GOD, "Wail, 'Alas for the day!' [3] "For the day is near, Even the day of the LORD is near; It will be a day of clouds, A time of doom for the nations.

Joel 2:31-32 (NASB)
[31] "The sun will be turned into darkness And the moon into blood Before the great and awesome day of the LORD comes. [32] "And it will come about that whoever calls on the name of the LORD Will be delivered; For on Mount Zion and in Jerusalem There will be those who escape, As the LORD has said, Even among the survivors whom the LORD calls.

Jeremiah 30:7 (NASB)
[7] 'Alas! for that day is great, There is none like it; And it is the time of Jacob's distress, But he will be saved from it.

Isaiah 28:21-22 (RSV)
[21] For the LORD will rise up as on Mount Pera'zim, he will be wroth as in the valley of Gibeon; to do his deed -- strange is his deed! and to work his work -- alien is his work! [22] Now therefore do not scoff, lest your bonds be made strong; for I have heard a decree of destruction from the Lord GOD of hosts upon the whole land.

Many New Testament scriptures also point to a coming tribulation.

Matthew 24:21 (NASB)
[21] "For then there will be a great tribulation, such as has not occurred since the beginning of the world until now, nor ever will.

Mark 13:24-26 (ESV)
[24] "But in those days, after that tribulation, the sun will be darkened, and the moon will not give its light, [25] and the stars will be falling from heaven, and the powers in the heavens will be shaken. [26] And then they will see the Son of Man coming in clouds with great power and glory.

Revelation 3:10 (ESV)
[10] Because you have kept my word about patient endurance, I will keep you from the hour of trial that is coming on the whole world, to try those who dwell on the earth.

What is the Tribulation?

The Tribulation will be a time of unprecedented anguish and agony on earth, occurring at the end of the church age, and signaling the final countdown toward the return of Jesus. The distress experienced during this time will be caused by political upheaval, military campaigns, convulsions of nature, and 'plagues' sent directly from the hand of God. For Christians it will be a time of widespread persecution by world governments.

There are several themes that run together through the Tribulation. Together they make up this phenomenon of distress. We will discuss these themes briefly, then attempt to put together a chronological agenda of it. The tribulation is…

<u>The Initiation of God's Fulfilled Purpose</u>
When things start to happen in the end-time sequence, they begin with the Tribulation.

Revelation 5:1-14 (ESV)
[1] Then I saw in the right hand of him who was seated on the throne a scroll written within and on the back, sealed with seven seals. [2] And I saw a mighty angel proclaiming with a loud voice, "Who is worthy to open the scroll and break its seals?" [3] And no one in heaven or on earth or under the earth was able to open the scroll or to look into it, [4] and I began to weep loudly because no one was found worthy to open the scroll or to look into it. [5] And one of the elders said to me, "Weep no more; behold, the Lion of the tribe of Judah, the Root of David, has conquered, so that he can open the scroll and its seven seals." [6] And between the throne and the four living creatures and among the elders I saw a Lamb standing, as though it had been slain,

> *with seven horns and with seven eyes, which are the seven spirits of God sent out into all the earth. [7] And he went and took the scroll from the right hand of him who was seated on the throne. [8] And when he had taken the scroll, the four living creatures and the twenty-four elders fell down before the Lamb, each holding a harp, and golden bowls full of incense, which are the prayers of the saints. [9] And they sang a new song, saying, "Worthy are you to take the scroll and to open its seals, for you were slain, and by your blood you ransomed people for God from every tribe and language and people and nation, [10] and you have made them a kingdom and priests to our God, and they shall reign on the earth." [11] Then I looked, and I heard around the throne and the living creatures and the elders the voice of many angels, numbering myriads of myriads and thousands of thousands, [12] saying with a loud voice, "Worthy is the Lamb who was slain, to receive power and wealth and wisdom and might and honor and glory and blessing!" [13] And I heard every creature in heaven and on earth and under the earth and in the sea, and all that is in them, saying, "To him who sits on the throne and to the Lamb be blessing and honor and glory and might forever and ever!" [14] And the four living creatures said, "Amen!" and the elders fell down and worshiped.*

This passage is followed by the Lamb opening the seven seals one-by-one, which commences the Tribulation. This scene immediately presents us with a dilemma. We have, on the one hand, all the hosts of heaven joined in worshipful anticipation of what is about to happen. Because of its immediacy, they worship God and the lamb--Jesus. On the other hand, ahead lies the most dreadful series of events ever known on earth. People will be in terror, agony and mourning. What are we to do? Do we rejoice with the hosts of heaven? Do we panic with the inhabitants of the earth?

The Tribulation is a fulfillment of prophecy. For that reason alone, we can see in it a working out of God's purpose. If we understand nothing else in this passage of Revelation, we understand the unfolding of a plan, God's plan. We see that it was God, not some out-of-control earthly problem, who initiated its beginning. His purposes in judgment and in redemption often go hand-in-hand, and nowhere is that more evident than in prophecies about the Tribulation period.

> *Daniel 11:36 (NASB)*
> *[36] "Then the king will do as he pleases, and he will exalt and magnify himself above every god and will speak monstrous things against the God of gods; and he will prosper until the indignation is finished, for that which is decreed will be done.*

It is early in our study of the Tribulation, but as we progress, it will become increasingly evident that behind it is the ultimate purpose of the Creator.

The Climax of the Satanic World Kingdom

Again, what is the Tribulation? As we have said, in the book of Revelation there seem to be several themes running parallel. One of those themes is the proliferation of evil. The Tribulation is a period of time that will see the culmination of every evil intent and agenda into a global conspiracy against God and those who call on His name. As Satan marshals his followers into a cohesive political kingdom, worldwide turmoil will occur and persecution will swell, first against Christians, and later against the Jews.

> *2 Thessalonians 2:7-10 (NASB)*
> *[7] For the mystery of lawlessness is already at work; only he who now restrains will do so until he is taken out of the way. [8] Then that lawless one will be revealed whom the Lord will slay with the breath of His mouth and bring to an end by the appearance of His coming; [9] that is, the one whose coming is in accord with the activity of Satan, with all power and signs and false wonders, [10] and with all the deception of wickedness for those who perish, because they did not receive the love of the truth so as to be saved.*

> *Matthew 24:9 (NASB)*
> *[9] "Then they will deliver you to tribulation, and will kill you, and you will be hated by all nations because of My name.*

> *Revelation 13:7-8 (ESV)*
> *[7] Also it [antichrist] was allowed to make war on the saints and to conquer them. And authority was given it over every tribe and people and language and nation, [8] and all who dwell on earth will worship it, everyone whose name has not been written before the foundation of the world in the book of life of the Lamb who was slain.*

As we see the Tribulation unfold, one aspect will be the rallying solidarity of the kingdom of Satan. It will be unchallengeable for a time. Its authority will span the globe.

The Wrath of God Against the World System

The return of Christ will climax the tribulation period. It will be an outpouring of God's anger against Satan's world kingdom. He will come as a conqueror.

> *Psalm 110:5-6 (NASB)*
> *⁵ The Lord is at Your right hand; He will shatter kings in the day of His wrath. ⁶ He will judge among the nations, He will fill them with corpses, He will shatter the chief men over a broad country.*

At the time of Christ's appearing, we read

> *Revelation 19:15 (ESV)*
> *¹⁵ From his mouth comes a sharp sword with which to strike down the nations, and he will rule them with a rod of iron. He will tread the winepress of the fury of the wrath of God the Almighty.*

A Perfecting of the Saints

The Tribulation is a time of perfecting of the company of the saints. This perfecting is seen in two ways. First, the Tribulation will be a time of culling. It will drive those alive at the time to one side or the other. There will be no neutrality, and the cost of believing in Christ will be very high. It will serve to eliminate those without commitment, and to strengthen those in weakness. Those who have compromised their faith while playing church, will be brought either to repentance or to separation.

> *Revelation 2:5 (ESV)*
> *⁵ Remember therefore from where you have fallen; repent, and do the works you did at first. If not, I will come to you and remove your lampstand from its place, unless you repent.*

> *Revelation 3:19-20 (ESV)*
> *¹⁹ Those whom I love, I reprove and discipline, so be zealous and repent. ²⁰ Behold, I stand at the door and knock. If anyone hears my voice and opens the door, I will come in to him and eat with him, and he with me.*

The second means of perfecting is through the suffering itself. Those who hold a commitment to Jesus will suffer for it. Suffering is a curious thing. No one wants to suffer. Yet it is through suffering that growth occurs. In much the same way that physical exhaustion yields a stronger body (no pain—no gain), suffering for our faith grows spiritual strength. Furthermore, suffering for our faith identifies us with the Savior who also suffered. A fellowship of suffering is created.

> *Philippians 3:10 (ESV)*
> *¹⁰ that I may know him and the power of his resurrection, and may share his sufferings, becoming like him in his death,*

Revelation 7:9-10,13-17 (ESV)
⁹ After this I looked, and behold, a great multitude that no one could number, from every nation, from all tribes and peoples and languages, standing before the throne and before the Lamb, clothed in white robes, with palm branches in their hands, ¹⁰ and crying out with a loud voice, "Salvation belongs to our God who sits on the throne, and to the Lamb!" . . . ¹³ Then one of the elders addressed me, saying, "Who are these, clothed in white robes, and from where have they come?" ¹⁴ I said to him, "Sir, you know." And he said to me, "These are the ones coming out of the great tribulation. They have washed their robes and made them white in the blood of the Lamb. ¹⁵ "Therefore they are before the throne of God, and serve him day and night in his temple; and he who sits on the throne will shelter them with his presence. ¹⁶ They shall hunger no more, neither thirst anymore; the sun shall not strike them, nor any scorching heat. ¹⁷ For the Lamb in the midst of the throne will be their shepherd, and he will guide them to springs of living water, and God will wipe away every tear from their eyes."

1 Peter 4:12-13 (ESV)
¹² Beloved, do not be surprised at the fiery trial when it comes upon you to test you, as though something strange were happening to you. ¹³ But rejoice insofar as you share Christ's sufferings, that you may also rejoice and be glad when his glory is revealed.

<u>The Restoration of Israel</u>
Finally, we see in the Tribulation the running theme of Israel. It is a time when Israel will finally confront her error, and turn to God, embracing Jesus as Lord.

Romans 11:26-27 (RSV)
²⁶ and so all Israel will be saved; as it is written, "The Deliverer will come from Zion, he will banish ungodliness from Jacob"; ²⁷ "and this will be my covenant with them when I take away their sins."

Keep these last two topics in mind throughout the next few chapters, for they represent God's expressed purpose for humanity: 1) redeem Gentile believers from all nations, and 2) redeem Israel.

Romans 11:30-33 (RSV)
³⁰ Just as you were once disobedient to God but now have received mercy because of their disobedience, ³¹ so they have now been disobedient in order that by the mercy shown to you they also may receive mercy. ³² For God has consigned all men to disobedience, that he may have mercy upon all. ³³ O the depth of the riches and

wisdom and knowledge of God! How unsearchable are his judgments and how inscrutable his ways!

When Will the Tribulation Begin?

We cannot resist wanting to learn as much as possible about the timing associated with end-time events such as the Tribulation. Jesus did give us some signals. Let us examine what has been revealed, and see what we can learn.

If Israel is the focal point for knowing what is happening in God's plan, then what specifically are we watching for? The most important end-time prophecy chronology in the Bible is Jesus' narrative just before his death. This speech is often called the Olivet Discourse because it was delivered on the Mount of Olives just outside Jerusalem. It is found in all three synoptic Gospels; in Matthew 24 and 25, Mark 13, and Luke 21. There are some differences between these three accounts. These differences, though small, contribute mightily to our difficulties in understanding. One thing is clear from all three, seen in light of subsequent history. The discourse begins with prophecy that seemingly was fulfilled just about forty years later with the destruction of the Jerusalem temple by the Roman army, and ends with the yet-future second coming of Jesus. What lies in between is not so obvious in its timing. Here it is highly recommended that the reader lay aside this book momentarily, and read the Olivet Discourse in its entirety from all three gospels. Then return to the following discussion.

<u>The Olivet Discourse</u>
To begin, let's examine the question that prompted this teaching. We need to back up to the events leading up to the question to understand the question itself. Jesus had just been openly rejected by the Jewish leaders, and had rebuked them sharply. Then he departed from the temple for the last time. His final exit was foreseen by the prophet Ezekiel.

> *Ezekiel 11:23 (NASB)*
> [23] *The glory of the LORD went up from the midst of the city and stood over the mountain which is east of the city.*

Here now, having left through the Eastern Gate, He climbed the Mount of Olives. As he left, he cried...

> *Matthew 23:37-39 (NASB)*
> [37] *"Jerusalem, Jerusalem, who kills the prophets and stones those who are sent to her! How often I wanted to gather your children together, the way a hen gathers her chicks under her wings, and you were unwilling.* [38] *"Behold, your house is being left to you desolate!*

39 *"For I say to you, from now on you will not see Me until you say, 'BLESSED IS HE WHO COMES IN THE NAME OF THE LORD!'"*

Your house is a reference to the temple. It was now desolate because Jesus had vacated it. From the building of the original tabernacle in the time of Moses, the glory of God had dwelt in the Holy Place. Now as Jesus left, rejected by the Jewish leaders, God's Spirit left with him.

Matthew 24:1-2 (NASB)
1 *Jesus came out from the temple and was going away when His disciples came up to point out the temple buildings to Him.* *2* *And He said to them, "Do you not see all these things? Truly I say to you, not one stone here will be left upon another, which will not be torn down."*

About forty years later, the desolation became final in 70 AD when the Roman army, under General Titus, destroyed the city and the temple. Jewish zealots had forced the hand of the Roman military. The temple was built of white limestone. To destroy it, the soldiers stacked wood around it and burned it. The limestone exploded and crumbled. The gold that had lined the ceiling was melted in the fire, and ran down into the cracks between the floor stones. In order to get at the gold, the soldiers pried up the huge floor stones. Thus Jesus' words were fulfilled to the letter. Literally every stone was thrown down or dug up. Its destruction took a year and a half; it was that massive. What is remarkable is that Herod had built that temple with Roman support. Now that same Rome destroyed the temple it had helped to build. Who could have predicted that? Jesus did!

The Question Asked
Matthew 24:3 (NASB)
3 *As He was sitting on the Mount of Olives, the disciples came to Him privately, saying, "Tell us, when will these things happen, and what will be the sign of Your coming, and of the end of the age?"*

To understand this question requires some insight into the prevailing Jewish beliefs of that time. First, the leaders of Israel believed that the coming of God's Messiah was imminent. This expectation was also held by the common people, among whom it fanned a fire of hope. By the time of Jesus, the messianic hope was at a fever pitch. However their understanding of the Messiah was not as a spiritual savior, but primarily as a political and military savior--someone who could throw off the yoke of Roman occupation.

Second, while a Messiah was expected, there was no understanding of him coming, then leaving and coming a second time. Granted, the rabbis were baffled by the two very different characteristics that were presented of him in prophecy: victorious king, and suffering servant. Some proposed two different messiahs. But two comings of the same person were apparently not even contemplated. The prevailing messianic concept was of a heroic leader/warrior because that was what the people thought was their greatest need. Now Jesus had told his followers many times that he would go away and come again later. However, this teaching never sank in until after his death and resurrection.

With this background, we can see that the disciples thought they were asking only one question. *When will this happen, and what will be the sign of your coming and of the end of the age?* In their thinking, the fall of Jerusalem, the return of Jesus to establish his own kingdom, and the end of the age were all contemporaneous events that comprised *the Day of the Lord.* From our perspective we can separate the fall of Jerusalem from the return of Jesus, and so we can see that there are actually two separate questions: 1) When would Jerusalem fall? and 2) When would Jesus return and bring the current age to a conclusion? Jesus did not correct their presumption, but rather gave a twofold answer, addressing both questions.

He did this masterfully. His answers addressed both questions, yet he avoided clearly telling them the end of the age was far into the future. He did not want to take away the ever-present hope of his near return. If he had laid out a time line for them, this motivating hope would have been lost from saints throughout the church age. This would have been contrary to his command to *"Watch."* The timing of Jesus' return is clearly something God wishes to keep a mystery. This is not a random decision of His, but is for a purpose. If we would be obedient to Jesus' instructions as taught in the Olivet discourse, then we would concentrate less on knowing *when,* and more on 'watching' as we discussed in Chapter 2.

The Olivet Discourse – Depth, Not Confusion

As you read this discourse in all three gospels, you see different perspectives on the prophecies, based on what each included. This is not a violation of the fact of the Holy Spirit's leading these gospel writers. Rather it shows how the Spirit spoke through each individual a unique and true message, giving us a multifaceted answer, while concealing His sovereign timing from us. If the timing seems confusing, maybe it is because we hold a skewed perspective of what he is telling us.

> *1 Corinthians 14:33 (KJV)*
> *33 For God is not the author of confusion, but of peace . . .*

Perhaps the following explanation will help remove some of that confusion. The beginning of the discourse clearly was fulfilled in the events that shortly followed in 70 AD. The Luke version especially makes this clear.

> *Luke 21:20-24 (ESV)*
> [20] *"But when you see Jerusalem surrounded by armies, then know that its desolation has come near.* [21] *Then let those who are in Judea flee to the mountains, and let those who are inside the city depart, and let not those who are out in the country enter it,* [22] *for these are days of vengeance, to fulfill all that is written.* [23] *Alas for women who are pregnant and for those who are nursing infants in those days! For there will be great distress upon the earth and wrath against this people.* [24] *They will fall by the edge of the sword and be led captive among all nations, and Jerusalem will be trampled underfoot by the Gentiles, until the times of the Gentiles are fulfilled.*

Here we see an unmistakable reference to the fall of Jerusalem and the Jewish diaspora and campaign of anti-Semitism that has existed since that time. The attempted eradication of the Jews by many down through the ages is history. Such attempts were made by Hitler in Nazi Germany, and are being made by Islamic Middle East neighbors today. The very next verse, however, clearly speaks of things yet future.

> *Luke 21:25-27 (ESV)*
> [25] *"And there will be signs in sun and moon and stars, and on the earth distress of nations in perplexity because of the roaring of the sea and the waves,* [26] *people fainting with fear and with foreboding of what is coming on the world. For the powers of the heavens will be shaken.* [27] *And then they will see the Son of Man coming in a cloud with power and great glory.*

These verses are no longer about Israel and Jerusalem, as the previous verses were, but about the *nations* and *the world*. These events occur during this *time of the Gentiles*, are global in scope, and lead up to the end of the age. So what we see about this discourse is that it addresses two different times. This is consistent with the two different questions the disciples had asked. The first part seems to address the question about the destruction of Jerusalem. The later part has to do with the question about Jesus' return and the end of the age.

Here we need to try to think like a Jewish rabbi. Our natural tendency is to try to find a line of demarcation for this passage. We would like to neatly divide it so that the statements concerning 70 AD can be segregated from those referring to the future. Reading in one passage, say from Luke, this can be done quite simply. But when you try to correlate this division with the passages from Matthew and Mark, the line seems to move, and the demarcation becomes blurred.

If we look at Matthew's passage parallel to Luke 21:20-24 we see a reference that is not so clearly focused on the 70 AD fall of Jerusalem. It seems to have more of an end-of-the-age perspective, although the wording is very similar.

> *Matthew 24:15-22 (NASB)*
> [15] *"Therefore when you see the ABOMINATION OF DESOLATION which was spoken of through Daniel the prophet, standing in the holy place (let the reader understand),* [16] *then those who are in Judea must flee to the mountains.* [17] *"Whoever is on the housetop must not go down to get the things out that are in his house.* [18] *"Whoever is in the field must not turn back to get his cloak.* [19] *"But woe to those who are pregnant and to those who are nursing babies in those days!* [20] *"But pray that your flight will not be in the winter, or on a Sabbath.* [21] *"For then there will be a great tribulation, such as has not occurred since the beginning of the world until now, nor ever will.* [22] *"Unless those days had been cut short, no life would have been saved; but for the sake of the elect those days will be cut short.*

There are three things about this passage that do not fit the situation of 70 AD. First there is the one *standing in the holy place 'the abomination of desolation,' spoken of through the prophet Daniel--let the reader understand.* This phrase, *abomination that causes desolation,* occurs three places in Daniel, and refers to a specific event in history. We discussed this in Chapter 12 and will investigate further in this chapter. The character of the antichrist does not seem fulfilled in Titus, the Roman general. History seems to indicate he actually restrained the destruction from what it could have been. Furthermore he never set himself up as an object of worship. It is historical fact that a pagan temple was built on the site, but that did not occur until more than 60 years after the destruction of the temple, and it was not orchestrated by Titus.

Second, there is the degree of trial the inhabitants of Jerusalem would experience. *For then there will be great distress, unequaled from the beginning of the world until now--and never to be equaled again.* This is qualified by the statement that *If those days had not been cut short, no one would survive, but for the sake of the elect those days will be shortened.* In AD 70 there was no evident supernatural intervention, the time was not cut short, and the desolation that occurred ran its course. Still, as bad as things were in Palestine, there were many survivors. That statement seems to best fit a future situation. The end-time tribulation will be even worse in Israel than situations of the past. It will be such that her only chance for survival will be a miraculous rescue by God Himself.

Thirdly, we are told that at the very end of that time of tribulation, Jesus will return.

Matthew 24:29-30 (NASB)
²⁹ "But immediately after the tribulation of those days THE SUN WILL BE DARKENED, AND THE MOON WILL NOT GIVE ITS LIGHT, AND THE STARS WILL FALL from the sky, and the powers of the heavens will be shaken. ³⁰ "And then the sign of the Son of Man will appear in the sky, and then all the tribes of the earth will mourn, and they will see the SON OF MAN COMING ON THE CLOUDS OF THE SKY with power and great glory.

That did not happen in 70 AD. We are still waiting for it to happen. This fulfillment is clearly anchored in some future time.

The controversy is whether these passages refer to AD 70 or to a future event. The Matthew account fits a future event better, but the Luke account seems to fit 70 AD nicely. Yet there is so much similarity that the two accounts are obviously the same discourse. The best answer is that collectively and individually they refer to both. Historically the two events are separate isolated happenstances. However, seen in the plan of God, and in light of many other prophecies, they are tied together. The tribulation of AD 70 is a foreshadow, a type, of that great tribulation in the last days. The similarities are not coincidental. They are part of God's intentional communication to us. He wants us to see them as a duplex of events. The first was a wakeup call to Israel to warn of the second if she did not turn in faith to her Messiah.

The Greatest Sign

If the Matthew 24 events immediately preceding the Lord's return are still future, then where are we in the scheme of things? We are not seeking to know precisely *when* (we have conceded that God has told us 'when' is not for us to know). Rather we are looking for 'approaching nearness.' This we are called to do--to read the signs and become motivated to live in preparedness for that Day. This nearness is not so much about time as it is about focus and purpose and motivation.

So where are we? This is a very exciting thing because we are actually watching amazing prophecies unfolding in our day. We have already discussed how the prophecies predicted that in the last days Israel would somehow again be in the land of Palestine, and that a temple would exist, along with regular temple sacrificial worship. A hundred years ago the idea of Israel literally inhabiting her homeland would have seemed preposterous to most people. Even though the scripture had said that God would gather the children again to Israel from their far flung dispersion, still most did not believe it. The idea defied human logic. Yet today she is there, inhabiting the land against great opposition.

Yet not all of the things predicted for Israel in the last days have come to pass. The Jews are residing in their land, but they do not currently practice temple worship. This is because there is no temple. The Jewish people don't have administrative control of the one spot where that temple can be built, according to scripture and tradition, that is, Mount Moriah. Instead, on that spot currently sits the mosque commonly called the Dome of the Rock. This is a very important Islamic center. Israel and Jerusalem itself have a large Muslim population, and to seize that site would bring instant and furious attack from all her neighbors as well as from within. Nevertheless, fundamental Jews, under the auspices of several organizations such as The Temple Institute, and many others, are at this time gathering materials and making preparation for the eventual building of a temple. How the political scene will change to allow the rebuilding of the temple remains to be seen. So it appears the stage is in the very process of being set for fulfillment of that aspect of biblical end-time prophecy.

If the Olivet Discourse teaches us how to *watch* for Jesus' return, and if it tells us to keep our eyes on Israel as a sort of indicator of where we are in the scheme of things, it also teaches us something about the chronology of end-time events. Surprisingly there are very few chronological certainties found in prophetic scripture. Although there are many scriptures that prophesy of end-of-the-age happenings, few of them provide clear information about the sequence of events. For this reason and others, I think the Olivet Discourse is the most important end-time prophecy in the Bible.

Signs of the Times
We just discussed signs of the nearness of Christ's coming. The signs were from the Olivet Discourse, and were mainly about Tribulation phenomena. Let's revisit Jesus' initial statements. They were in reply to the question by his disciples:

Matthew 24:4-8 (NASB)
⁴ And Jesus answered and said to them, "See to it that no one misleads you. ⁵ "For many will come in My name, saying, 'I am the Christ,' and will mislead many. ⁶ "You will be hearing of wars and rumors of wars. See that you are not frightened, for those things must take place, but that is not yet the end. ⁷ "For nation will rise against nation, and kingdom against kingdom, and in various places there will be famines and earthquakes. ⁸ "But all these things are merely the beginning of birth pangs.

This segment of the passage ends with an important bit of information from the Lord. It tells us how to interpret the signs he is giving us. He said, *"All these are the beginning of birth pains."* We cannot understand what he is telling us unless we first understand what this phrase means. We all understand that once birth pains begin for a pregnant woman, it is only a matter of time until the birth. It may be quite a while or not long. There may be false labor, maybe several episodes of it. Nevertheless, the pains signal that birth is in sight.

The *beginning of birth pains* indicates that there is some time yet to go when we see these events occurring. Indeed Jesus said, *". . . see to it that you are not alarmed. Such things must happen, but the end is still to come."* What do you know when labor pains first occur? You know the irreversible process has begun. You don't know the precise time it will occur, but you know it will be relatively soon. The progress of the labor toward its climax is like a crescendo. As contractions become more frequent and more intense, you know the end is approaching.

What is represented by this labor process? Most premillennialists believe it corresponds with the specific period of time we call the Tribulation. It may also include the escalating buildup toward it. If the latter be true, we could consider ourselves to be in the *beginning of birth pains* right now. If not, we are certainly in the late stages of pregnancy.

How Long Will the Tribulation Last?

We discussed in Chapter 8 of this book the interpretation of the passage:

Matthew 24:34 (NASB)
[34] "Truly I say to you, this generation will not pass away until all these things take place.

It is taken from the Olivet Discourse, following a description of the Tribulation. It is taken by many to mean that those who see the tribulation events will also see the return of Christ. From this we can predict that it will be short enough to be contained within one generation. That is still quite vague.

We have something a little more precise. In the Old Testament prophecies of Daniel there are several predictions that lead up to the end-time. The Jews were in captivity in Babylon, having been exiled there by King Nebuchadnezzar's army. Subsequently the Babylonians were conquered by the Medo-Persians, who then became sovereign over the Jews as they still resided in exile in Babylon. Let's revisit an earlier passage from this context in which the angelic messenger Gabriel tells Daniel of future events as they relate to his own people, the Jews.

Daniel 9:20-27 (NASB)
[20] Now while I was speaking and praying, and confessing my sin and the sin of my people Israel, and presenting my supplication before

the LORD my God in behalf of the holy mountain of my God, ^{21} *while I was still speaking in prayer, then the man Gabriel, whom I had seen in the vision previously, came to me in my extreme weariness about the time of the evening offering.* ^{22} *He gave me instruction and talked with me and said, "O Daniel, I have now come forth to give you insight with understanding.* ^{23} *"At the beginning of your supplications the command was issued, and I have come to tell you, for you are highly esteemed; so give heed to the message and gain understanding of the vision.* ^{24} *"Seventy weeks have been decreed for your people and your holy city, to finish the transgression, to make an end of sin, to make atonement for iniquity, to bring in everlasting righteousness, to seal up vision and prophecy and to anoint the most holy place.* ^{25} *"So you are to know and discern that from the issuing of a decree to restore and rebuild Jerusalem until Messiah the Prince there will be seven weeks and sixty-two weeks; it will be built again, with plaza and moat, even in times of distress.* ^{26} *"Then after the sixty-two weeks the Messiah will be cut off and have nothing, and the people of the prince who is to come will destroy the city and the sanctuary. And its end will come with a flood; even to the end there will be war; desolations are determined.* ^{27} *"And he will make a firm covenant with the many for one week, but in the middle of the week he will put a stop to sacrifice and grain offering; and on the wing of abominations will come one who makes desolate, even until a complete destruction, one that is decreed, is poured out on the one who makes desolate."*

Many different interpretations of this passage have been put forth. Some see only non-messianic historical events. Some take an allegorical interpretation. Some reckon in lunar years as Jews did, rather than solar years which would be more consistent with the Greek language in which it was written. The one that best fits the events of history, starting from the time of its being given, and best fits a messianic fulfillment, goes like this.

The word *"week"* or *"weeks,"* literally means a week of seven days. However, as we discussed in Chapter 3, sometimes in prophecy a day is symbolic of a year, and this is one of those times, according to the interpretation here stated. A total time of seventy-sevens represents a time period of 70 x 7 = 490 years. Look closely at the phrase . . .

Daniel 9:24-25 (NASB)
^{24} *"Seventy weeks have been decreed for your people and your holy city, to finish the transgression, to make an end of sin, to make atonement for iniquity, to bring in everlasting righteousness, to seal up vision and prophecy and to anoint the most holy place.* ^{25} *"So you are to know and discern that from the issuing of a decree to restore and rebuild Jerusalem until Messiah the Prince there will be seven*

weeks and sixty-two weeks; it will be built again, with plaza and moat, even in times of distress.

First we see that the 490 year time period being discussed had to do with *"your people,"* Daniel's people--the Jews. Again, they are the key to interpreting this passage. More specifically, it is about national Israel. It is about times when she was in her homeland, carrying on temple worship in traditional Jewish custom. The terms, *"to finish transgression, to put an end to sin, to atone for wickedness, to bring in everlasting righteousness,"* look to the redemptive work of Christ, accomplished at his first coming. The last terms, *"to seal up vision and prophecy and to anoint the most holy"* seem to have an end-time view. The phrase finds its fulfillment partially in the first advent of Christ, partly in his return.

Scholars believe that the return of Jews from exile in Babylon, under the leadership of Nehemiah took place in 445 BC, about 93 years after the giving of this prophecy. It was one of the later of several pilgrimages back to the homeland. The first, led by Ezra under authority from the Median King Darius, was for the rebuilding of a temple. This return was for the rebuilding of the walls of Jerusalem, and is described in the first two chapters of Nehemiah. King Artaxerxes showed favor to Nehemiah and the captive Jews, allowing them to return from their captivity to rebuild the walls. The phrase, *"It will be rebuilt with streets and a trench, but in times of trouble"* well describes the hostility from local enemies that the Jews experienced in this endeavor. The sixty-nine sevens in this prophecy (seven plus sixty-two) represents $69 \times 7 = 483$ years. Using the Roman solar calendar, 483 years from 445 BC would be 28 AD, the year it is thought that Jesus was baptized, and began his public ministry. According to another interpretation, using the lunar calendar of the Jews, allowing for all the conversions, leap years, etc, the year is 30 AD, the year of Christ's crucifixion. The latter seems more feasible. Either way, the timing clearly identifies the time of Jesus' first advent and earthly ministry.

"After the sixty-two 'sevens,' the Anointed One will be cut off and will have nothing" prophesied of the crucifixion of Jesus which came to pass in 30 AD. Then we read of the destruction of Jerusalem. *The people of the ruler who will come will destroy the city and the sanctuary.* Who were the people? The Romans destroyed the holy city in 70 AD. These Romans are called *the people of the ruler who is to come.* Who is this coming Roman ruler? At this point, many futurist interpreters leap to the timeframe of the second coming. They see in this ruler the antichrist. A patrimonial connection between the Roman Empire and the eventual antichrist is understood.

Before we continue, you might ask, "Why would this prophecy arbitrarily make such a time leap?" The answer lies in the earlier statement, *Seventy 'sevens' are decreed for your people and your holy city.* The 70 weeks was a countdown in elapsed time of Jerusalem's and national Israel's history. When the city was destroyed and the nation scattered by the Romans at the end of the 69 weeks, there was a pause in the countdown. We are currently in that pause. The last week represents the seven-year covenant period between Israel and the antichrist at the end of the age. "Why," you might ask, "is the countdown not resuming, since Israel is once again in her own country, and in Jerusalem?" Many believe it is because Israel is currently not able to practice temple worship, as we discussed in Chapter 21. When she is eventually able to do so, that last prophetic week (seven years) will begin to tick off toward fulfillment.

And its end will come with a flood; even to the end there will be war; desolations are determined. The beginning of the Tribulation is forecast. *"And he will make a firm covenant with the many for one week,* The antichrist will make a seven-year peace treaty with Israel. This will permit Israel to rebuild a temple and reestablish sacrificial worship. The prophetic countdown of the final week will begin. *In the middle of the week he will put a stop to sacrifice and grain offering.* After three and a half years of the treaty have elapsed, the antichrist will break the covenant, forcing a halt to temple worship. *On the wing of abominations will come one who makes desolate, even until a complete destruction, one that is decreed, is poured out on the one who makes desolate.* Instead of the worship of God, antichrist will establish an abomination in the temple. This detestable practice will be the turning point in Israel. The Jews will not acquiesce to such idolatry, causing great persecution among the Jewish people.

On the basis of this prophecy, if a literal interpretation be taken, the duration of the treaty period is determined to be seven years. This seven year period is understood to be the time of tribulation spoken of by Jesus in his Olivet discourse, and that described through much of the book of Revelation.

The seven years consists of two roughly three-and-a-half-year periods, segregated by the breaking of the treaty.

Daniel 12:10-12 (NASB)
[10] "Many will be purged, purified and refined, but the wicked will act wickedly; and none of the wicked will understand, but those who have insight will understand. [11] "From the time that the regular sacrifice is abolished and the abomination of desolation is set up, there will be 1,290 days. [12] "How blessed is he who keeps waiting and attains to the 1,335 days!

It is interesting how many times this time span of three-and-a-half-years is mentioned in this portion of Revelation. In addition to those already mentioned, here are more.

Revelation 11:2-3 (ESV)
² but do not measure the court outside the temple; leave that out, for it is given over to the nations, and they will trample the holy city for forty-two months. ³ And I will grant authority to my two witnesses, and they will prophesy for 1,260 days, clothed in sackcloth."

Revelation 12:6 (ESV)
⁶ and the woman fled into the wilderness, where she has a place prepared by God, in which she is to be nourished for 1,260 days.

Daniel 12:7 (NASB)
⁷ I heard the man dressed in linen, who was above the waters of the river, as he raised his right hand and his left toward heaven, and swore by Him who lives forever that it would be for a time, times, and half a time; and as soon as they finish shattering the power of the holy people, all these events will be completed.

Revelation 12:14 (ESV)
¹⁴ But the woman was given the two wings of the great eagle so that she might fly from the serpent into the wilderness, to the place where she is to be nourished for a time, and times, and half a time.

The time period 1260 days represents 42 months of 30 days each, as reckoned by the Jewish lunar calendar.

> Oh God, our God, our mighty God! It is surely true—you know the beginning and the end of all things. Who are we that you have seen fit to reveal to us the secrets of your plans? We are slow to believe all that you reveal, but with such evidence before us, let us resist your spirit no longer. Make us as loyal servants who seek to honor their master. Make us as blessed children who rest confidently in the arms of their father. Make us like a betrothed bride-to-be, eagerly awaiting her wedding. We see all things as ingredients in your unfolding purpose. Help us to trust your purpose. Give us the grace to persevere in trials. Burn into our souls the fervent priority to remain faithful. Amen

14
THE RISE OF AN EVIL WORLD EMPIRE

Revelation Chapters 6 through 20 cover that period of time generally understood by Futurists as the "Tribulation." Within those chapters we are confronted with three sequential series of seven events. The first of the sequences is initiated by the one-by-one opening of seven seals on a scroll, to which we have already referred. The second begins with the blowing of seven trumpets, in order. The third consists of seven bowls being poured out one at a time.

Empire Agenda

There are two different ways of understanding the sequence of these Revelation series: the seals, trumpets and bowls. One is called the chronological approach. This understanding is that all the events of Revelation chapters 6 through 19 pertain to the tribulation, and are in consecutive order, just as written. The seven seals, the seven trumpets and the seven bowls follow each other in that order. If you study the language of the interconnecting phrases, this seems to be the sense of it.

> *Revelation 8:1-2,6 (ESV)*
> *[1] When the Lamb opened the seventh seal, there was silence in heaven for about half an hour. [2] Then I saw the seven angels who stand before God, and seven trumpets were given to them. . . [6] Now the seven angels who had the seven trumpets prepared to blow them.*

It seems as the seventh seal is opened, within it are contained the seven trumpets according to the chronological interpretation. This view is further supported by the introduction of the bowls. These plagues are clearly seen as coming last.

> *Revelation 15:1, 16:1 (ESV)*
> *[1] Then I saw another sign in heaven, great and amazing, seven angels with seven plagues, which are the last, for with them the wrath of God is finished . . . [1] Then I heard a loud voice from the temple telling the seven angels, "Go and pour out on the earth the seven bowls of the wrath of God."*

The second way of understanding Revelation is called the synchronous approach, and envisions the seals, trumpets and bowls as repeating the same sequences from three different views. Looking at the content of these events leads to this kind of thinking. For example,

> *Revelation 6:12,15-17 (ESV)*
> *[12] When he opened the sixth seal, I looked, and behold, there was a great earthquake, and the sun became black as sackcloth, the full moon became like blood, . . . [15] Then the kings of the earth and the great ones and the generals and the rich and the powerful, and everyone, slave and free, hid themselves in the caves and among the rocks of the mountains, [16] calling to the mountains and rocks, "Fall on us and hide us from the face of him who is seated on the throne, and from the wrath of the Lamb, [17] for the great day of their wrath has come, and who can stand?"*

In the sixth seal the people on earth saw the face of the one who sits on the throne, and were terrified. *Hide us*, they cried, *from the wrath of the lamb*. This is clearly their response to the appearing of Christ at his second coming. Yet the more lengthy account of this coming is not given until Chapter 18. It also makes reference to a great earthquake. A great earthquake is also found in the last of the trumpet and bowl judgments. Furthermore, some of the events portrayed in the trumpet sequence are strikingly similar to parallel events in the bowl sequence (though clearly different in particulars.) Based on content and wording, the seals, trumpets and bowls are taken by some as three parallel renditions of the tribulation era. The fact that this creates repetition is not inconsistent with the style of Old Testament prophecy, as we have previously discussed.

I don't think either view fully describes the chronology of end-time events. We will look at a third way to understand these event sequences, a systematic chart of a possible harmony of these various 'judgments' in the next chapter. It is based entirely on content, not on the interconnecting language. First let's work our way through these sequences.

The breaking of the seals seem to represent the time span of the entire Tribulation period. They speak of natural disasters and political upheavals. They focus on the antichrist's rise to power, and the first five seals concentrate on the early and middle portions of the tribulation period. While the events of the first five seals are unprecedented in their severity, they could be understood to be the natural consequences of a world out of control. We believers may know they originate at the hand of God, but the majority of the inhabitants of earth will view these events as unrelated to God, until it is too late. This sequence might be subtitled, 'The Brutal Rise and Impending Demise of Antichrist's Kingdom.' The sixth seal reveals the return of Christ in judgment to a world who has rejected him.

In the trumpets we begin to see the response of God to this evil kingdom, and the conflict of kingdoms heats up. They demonstrate His direct hand in the Tribulation events. They too describe earthly plagues and traumas, but they seem to demonstrate a more direct spiritual implication to the conflict than was seen in the seals. They seem to fit best into the latter part of the Tribulation.

Thirdly, we see seven bowls being poured out. With this progression, we are told that God is revealing his wrath. Up to this point, God seems to be in control, but His vengeance is restrained, as He allows evil to run its course. At the end of the tribulation we are told of His wrath. The sixth seal, the seventh trumpet and the entire series of the bowls are said to represent God's wrath. In the bowls, we seem to see a series of events that occur rapidly near the very end of the tribulation.

Woven between and around the seals, trumpets and bowls in Revelation are a number of seemingly parenthetical visions. At strategic points the vision departs from the 'chronological' storyline to introduce and develop critical background for the narrative. These 'side bars' present us with significant information. We will address these parenthetical issues later, after first viewing the three major sequences.

The Seven Seals

In John's vision of the heavenly throne room, he saw the *lamb who was worthy* take the scroll from the hand of Him seated on the throne. The scroll was sealed with seven seals. We understood that the lamb was *the Lamb of God, who takes away the sin of the world*, that is, Jesus the crucified and risen one. (John 1:29). It was the lamb that prepared to break open the seals, and unroll the scroll. We understood that what is about to take place is not a product of natural dissipation, but rather is in the script of God's purposeful plan. It is the beginning of fulfillment of His objective.

Another question arises in this Revelation passage. What is the scroll? No one can say what is written in it. Scripture does not say. All we know is that when the seals are broken, the tribulation begins. Many say the scroll is the 'title deed to the earth.' This seems to accurately describe its effect. It seems to represent Christ's right to reign on the earth. For example, later on as the tribulation crescendos toward its climax, heavenly voices are heard.

Revelation 11:16-17 (ESV)
¹⁶ And the twenty-four elders who sit on their thrones before God fell on their faces and worshiped God, ¹⁷ saying, "We give thanks to you, Lord God Almighty, who is and who was, for you have taken your great power and begun to reign.

After the tremendous worship scene in Revelation 4 and 5, we can delay no longer. The seven seals are broken one at a time. The Tribulation begins. In the following discussion of the seals I have paralleled the opening of the seals in Revelation 6 with the corresponding passages in the Olivet Discourse to show the consistency of the two passages.

Conquest

The tribulation begins with an ambitious conqueror. Through deceitful promises, he will acquire international influence, leading into political power. This false "messiah" will make his debut by appeal and intrigue.

<u>The Opening of the First Seal</u>
The opening of the first four seals introduces the infamous 'four horsemen of the apocalypse.'

Revelation 6:1-2 (ESV)
¹ Now I watched when the Lamb opened one of the seven seals, and I heard one of the four living creatures say with a voice like thunder, "Come!" ² And I looked, and behold, a white horse! And its rider had a bow, and a crown was given to him, and he came out conquering, and to conquer.

We are not yet introduced to this rider in Revelation, but we have already met him in our study. He is none other than the antichrist, or more abstractly, he represents antichrist's campaign to power. This is the view of many futurist interpreters. Other interpreters disagree. Spiritualist interpreters believe this rider to be Christ himself. They point out the likeness of this rider to another rider in Revelation 19 who is clearly Christ:

Revelation 19:11-12,15-16 (ESV)
¹¹ Then I saw heaven opened, and behold, a white horse! The one sitting on it is called Faithful and True, and in righteousness he judges and makes war. ¹² . . . on his head are many diadems . . . ¹⁵ From his mouth comes a sharp sword with which to strike down the nations, and he will rule them with a rod of iron. He will tread the winepress of the fury of the wrath of God the Almighty. ¹⁶ On his robe and on his thigh he has a name written, King of kings and Lord of lords.

They say that in Revelation Chapter 6 the rider is Christ conquering the spiritual strongholds of this world through the spread of the Gospel, while the one in Chapter 19 is the same Christ at his bodily return.

The most widely-held futurist understanding is that the Chapter 6 person, when considered in the context of other scriptures, is the antichrist. He is portrayed much like Christ is portrayed in Chapter 19 because he will be a counterfeit of the real Christ. On his white horse, he will appear as a savior of mankind.

The Olivet Discourse—Deceit
Then this statement Jesus used to begin his Olivet Discourse will come to ultimate fulfillment:

> *Matthew 24:4-5 (NASB)*
> *^{4} And Jesus answered and said to them, "See to it that no one misleads you. ^{5} "For many will come in My name, saying, 'I am the Christ,' and will mislead many.*

Thus begins the Olivet Discourse, and thus begins the Tribulation. The rider on the horse carries a bow, but no arrows. This, and his white horse, have been interpreted by many that his early conquests will be made by bluff, or through political means. This may be in view in Daniel's prophecy about the then-yet-to-come Syrian-Greek ruler Antiochus IV Epiphanies. We said in chapter 12 of this book that this man of the second century BC was clearly in view in Daniel 11, but we also saw that he was a foreshadowing type of the end-time antichrist. This description of Antiochus might also describe antichrist.

> *Daniel 11:23 (NASB)*
> *^{23} "After an alliance is made with him he will practice deception, and he will go up and gain power with a small force of people.*

Deceit! This word describes the political intrigue with which Antiochus came to power. It is also used in several passages to characterize the campaign of the antichrist. His ability to deceive will exceed mere silver-tongue rhetoric or blustery campaign promises. He will display miraculous power.

> *2 Thessalonians 2:9-12 (ESV)*
> *^{9} The coming of the lawless one is by the activity of Satan with all power and false signs and wonders, ^{10} and with all wicked deception for those who are perishing, because they refused to love the truth and so be saved. ^{11} Therefore God sends them a strong delusion, so that they may believe what is false, ^{12} in order that all may be*

condemned who did not believe the truth but had pleasure in unrighteousness.

The very power of Satan will be displayed through him, in full view of all people. By this, he will astound and control the world, that is, those who do not believe in Jesus, and call on him as Lord.

Even now, the stage is being set for the antichrist's arrival. The first incidents signaling the progression toward Jesus' return will be the emergence of deceitful teacher-leaders. They will come from within the ranks of those looking for a modern day messiah. Their deceit will involve false claims of messianic identity. Now, I know what you are thinking at this point. "There have always been false teachers and imposters." That is true, but there have never been more cults than there are today. Some have made prominent headlines. Many of us more mature readers vividly remember reading with amazed horror the outcome of the followers of Jim Jones' so called Doomsday Cult in 1978 in Jonestown, Guyana, and later of David Koresh's Branch Davidians in 1993 outside Waco, Texas. In 1997 the Heaven's Gate cult likewise followed their leader, Marshal Applewhite, in a spiritual pilgrimage of mass suicide. Their followers were not the down-and-out of society. They were the educated and well-to-do. Spiritual deception is seen with increasing frequency at all levels of our culture. Cult religions will deceive many, leading them away from the true doctrine of God. Read the papers. Browse the bookshelves at your local secular bookstore. Cult websites abound. Have you ever seen so many religions? Apparently this practice, which has always existed, will become more frequent in the last days. This is just a forerunner of the ultimate deceit, and is setting the stage by creating spiritual confusion and desperation.

Outside of Christianity, the prevailing global culture is promoting variety in religious thinking in an effort to destroy true religion. Secular bookstores are filled with every imaginable kind of religious thinking (except biblical Christianity). In the United States today, religious diversity is not simply accommodated, it is applauded as politically correct. This speaks for itself. Religious diversity equals religious confusion. The evasive quest for interpersonal harmony and acceptance has been elevated above biblical truth. This new definition of tolerance undermines real faith. It is hostile to dogmatic truth. All of this is setting the stage for the greatest imposter of all – the antichrist.

World War

<u>The Opening of the Second Seal</u>
Revelation 6:3-4 (ESV)
³ When he opened the second seal, I heard the second living creature say, "Come!" ⁴ And out came another horse, bright red. Its

rider was permitted to take peace from the earth, so that people should slay one another, and he was given a great sword.

These commands to *come* are spoken from heaven, and directed to the horsemen. After each command, we read, . . . *another horse came.* This horse and its rider signal in war. The deceit works only so long. Then the newly-acquired military power takes up the cause. Peace will be taken from the earth. It will seem like everyone is at war.

<u>The Olivet Discourse—World War</u>
We also see this next development in the parallel passage of the Olivet Discourse:

Matthew 24:6-7a (NASB)
⁶ "You will be hearing of wars and rumors of wars. See that you are not frightened, for those things must take place, but that is not yet the end. ⁷ "For nation will rise against nation, and kingdom against kingdom, . . .

Nation against nation, kingdom against kingdom—the original Greek wording gives the connotation of both political and ethnic rivalries proliferating.

Again we can see in today's current events a posturing for such a reality. "There have been wars as far back as history records, so what kind of sign is this?" you might be asking. Yes, but there has never been the proliferation of war as there has been in the last few decades. The twentieth century introduced us to 'world war'--twice. Nations are now so politically and economically interdependent that any skirmish becomes a potentially global affair. At any given time, now, there are a dozen significant international struggles going on, any one of which could escalate. War dominates our headlines much of the time. All of this takes place within a global agenda for world peace. Could the words of the Old Testament prophet Jeremiah regarding Israel also find fulfillment for us today?

Jeremiah 6:13-14 (NASB)
¹³ "For from the least of them even to the greatest of them, Everyone is greedy for gain, And from the prophet even to the priest Everyone deals falsely. ¹⁴ "They have healed the brokenness of My people superficially, Saying, 'Peace, peace,' But there is no peace.

This statement seems very close to home. Our prayers following the horrific terrorist attacks of September 11, 2001 were open and frequent for a short time. For a brief season, expressions of true faith were tolerated. But soon we returned to our politically correct agenda. Some suggested that the proper response for our country was repentance--repentance from the national sins of wholesale abortion, homosexuality, drug and alcohol abuse, violence, hate, racism, and a myriad of other crimes against God. These suggestions drew such ridicule from liberal profiteers that the voices were drowned out by the uproar. Again, the stage-setting progresses.

Emerging from the chaos of war, antichrist appears victorious. But what often follows war?

Famine

The Opening of the Third Seal
Revelation 6:5-6 (ESV)
⁵ When he opened the third seal, I heard the third living creature say, "Come!" And I looked, and behold, a black horse! And its rider had a pair of scales in his hand. ⁶ And I heard what seemed to be a voice in the midst of the four living creatures, saying, "A quart of wheat for a denarius, and three quarts of barley for a denarius, and do not harm the oil and wine!"

Widespread war brings widespread famine and illness. The price of wheat and barley indicates that a day's wages would buy only enough of the basest food to feed a person for one day. Do not even think of buying oil or wine, the provisions for finer dining. Even false religion promotes famine. For example, India is prime among the starving of the world. Yet it is not because of lack of good farmland or a shortage of crops, but rather because the Hindu religion prevents the eating of animals, believing them to be people, reincarnated. These sacred animals, rather than being a food source, are added to the population of mouths that must be fed. One internet world-hunger website states that every 23 seconds a child dies of hunger. It will be much worse during this end-of-age episode.

The Olivet Discourse—Famine
Likewise the Olivet Discourse states:

Matthew 24:7 (NASB)
⁷ ". . . and in various places there will be famines and earthquakes.

Death

The Opening of the Fourth Seal
Revelation 6:7-8 (ESV)
⁷ When he opened the fourth seal, I heard the voice of the fourth living creature say, "Come!" ⁸ And I looked, and behold, a pale horse! And its rider's name was Death, and Hades followed him.

> *And they were given authority over a fourth of the earth, to kill with sword and with famine and with pestilence and by wild beasts of the earth.*

Death will come over a fourth part of the earth, which seems to mean that a fourth of earth's population will die. That is a horrific series of events. There is some disagreement whether the number is to be taken literally. This is a problem with the synchronous view. In the seal judgments one fourth of the earth's resources and people are affected. In the trumpets, one-third is affected, and in the bowl series, all are affected.

There has actually been a decrease in the percent of the world's people that are underfed in the last twenty years or so, but not in the actual numbers of persons. Looking at a longer time frame, this century has faced unparalleled world famine due to population increase, ethnic persecution, and war.

The Olivet Discourse—Death

While there is no specific verse about death in the Olivet Discourse, it is implied in the *nation against nation, famines and earthquakes* of Matt 24:6-7. Let's not overlook that little phrase *and earthquakes*. This last century has seen a barrage of major earthquakes. The US Geological Society reports that since the recording of earthquakes, the number of quakes claiming at least 50,000 lives stands at twenty-two worldwide, the earliest in 856 AD. Eleven of those have occurred since the beginning of the 20th century. This last century recorded 109 earthquakes of a magnitude that claimed at least 1000 lives. I, myself, can recall a number of major earthquakes within the last twenty five years: China, Mexico City, Iran, Japan, India, Turkey, Indonesia, and Italy to mention a few. As I was writing the first draft of this book, a major offshore earthquake produced a massive tsunami, a series of huge waves, that devastated portions of the Southeast Asian and African shoreline, with a death toll estimated at 180,000. Its carnage was splashed on the television screen nightly for weeks. In March of 2011, a 9.0 offshore earthquake sent a huge tsunami crashing into Tohoku, Japan, killing nearly 16,000 people. It also resulted in several nuclear power plant meltdowns. This hit home with me because I had worked in Tohoku for a shot time.

Martyrdom

The Opening of the Fifth Seal

> *Revelation 6:9-11 (ESV)*
> *^{9} When he opened the fifth seal, I saw under the altar the souls of those who had been slain for the word of God and for the witness they had borne. ^{10} They cried out with a loud voice, "O Sovereign Lord, holy and true, how long before you will judge and avenge our*

blood on those who dwell on the earth?" ¹¹ Then they were each given a white robe and told to rest a little longer, until the number of their fellow servants and their brothers should be complete, who were to be killed as they themselves had been.

Martyrdom of believers is the next facet of the tribulation mentioned. In case there is any doubt that this refers to Christians rather than Jews, we parallel this passage with the next passage from the Mount of Olives teaching.

The Olivet Discourse--Martyrdom
Matthew 24:9-10 (NASB)
⁹ "Then they will deliver you to tribulation, and will kill you, and you will be hated by all nations because of My name. ¹⁰ "At that time many will fall away and will betray one another and hate one another.

This persecution will cause even many so-called believers to be deceived and to lose their love for one another, and for Jesus. This will effect a purging of the church. Those not truly led and empowered by the Holy Spirit will be deceived, or will lose heart and turn away.

He who stands firm to the end will be saved. This statement has brought much confusion. Those who do not believe that embracing the lordship of Christ is essential for salvation say that this '*saving*' is the promise of saving from physical death; that somehow standing firm in the faith will protect against the threat of death. This cannot be its meaning since verse 9 just told us that some would be *put to death*. No, this saving is not about saving from death, but about saving through death. The power to stand firm in the faith in the face of persecution will be given by the Spirit of God, invoked by the grace of God. It will not depend on our bravery--this will surely fail. We should, therefore, resolve that we will throw ourselves wholly into the arms of God. He will not abandon us, even if we die. Note that a warning for perseverance in the faith occurs repeatedly in end-time scriptures:

Matthew 24:12-13 (NASB)
¹² "Because lawlessness is increased, most people's love will grow cold. ¹³ "But the one who endures to the end, he will be saved.

Revelation 2:10 (ESV)
¹⁰ Do not fear what you are about to suffer. Behold, the devil is about to throw some of you into prison, that you may be tested, and for ten days you will have tribulation. Be faithful unto death, and I will give you the crown of life.

And look at this one, spoken by Jesus as he sent his disciples out two-by-two to preach the kingdom. Although the immediate context was the persecution they might encounter as they went, it is clear that a greater persecution is in view, since the scripture speaks of persecution at the hand of Gentiles, while they were sent only to the *house of Israel*. Jesus sees the greater persecution they would experience later in their lives, which would be a preview of that which his end-time disciples also would face.

> *Matthew 10:18-22 (NASB)*
> *[18] and you will even be brought before governors and kings for My sake, as a testimony to them and to the Gentiles. [19] "But when they hand you over, do not worry about how or what you are to say; for it will be given you in that hour what you are to say. [20] "For it is not you who speak, but it is the Spirit of your Father who speaks in you. [21] "Brother will betray brother to death, and a father his child; and children will rise up against parents and cause them to be put to death. [22] "You will be hated by all because of My name, but it is the one who has endured to the end who will be saved.*

When you think of Christian persecution, what comes to mind? I'll bet the first thought of many is that of first century saints being persecuted by the Roman emperor Nero. Persecution of Christians has continued since the time of the early church, boiling up at various times, in diverse places. Did you know that more Christians have been martyred in the last one hundred years than in all the previous centuries combined since the beginning of the faith? That's right! Most of that persecution has taken place in Africa and Asia at the hands of Islamic militants, or extremists of other world religions, and has been largely and deliberately ignored by the liberal major news media in this country.

Here in the United States, the defamation of Christianity has progressed systematically to the present situation. The name of God mentioned openly will often bring public whiplash. In the name of religious 'tolerance,' Christianity is chained into a corner while all other religions are encouraged to exercise their religious freedom. Where will our freedom of faith go next? We have not yet, for the most part, been physically persecuted for our faith in this country. However that prospect, which at one time in my younger years seemed implausible, now appears a realistic possibility. Christian persecution has increased exponentially in the last century. Could this be a *birth pain*? Many Bible students believe so. It seems to set the stage.

This campaign of Christian persecution will take place concurrently with the Jews enjoying a restoration to their temple worship, and that through a treaty with the world ruler who will come. If not instrumentally involved in the persecution of Christians, they at least enjoy an amicable relationship with those who perpetrate it. Thus, throughout the first part of the tribulation, the Jews continue their hostile rejection of their Messiah, the same rejection that has continued since the crucifixion of Jesus.

Turning Point

The remainder of the seal openings, and of the corresponding passages in the Olivet Discourse, seem to best fit into the last half of the Tribulation. Their agenda will be resumed in chapters 17, 18, and 19. Likewise, the trumpets and bowls will be addressed as we look at the latter three-and-a-half years.

In summary, it appears that the opening of the seals covers the entire period of time we call the tribulation. Following is a chart that summarizes what I have been saying by paralleling the events of the Olivet discourse and the opening of the seven seals.

Parallelism of the Olivet Discourse and the Seven Seals of Revelation	
Olivet Discourse (Matthew 24)	Seven Seals (Revelation 6)
v 4-5 many will deceive	1st seal - conqueror on white horse
v 6-7a wars and rumors of wars	2nd seal - war on a red horse
v 7b famines and earthquakes	3rd seal - famine on a black horse
	4th seal - death on a pale horse
v 9-13 persecution of Christians	5th seal - Souls of martyrs in heaven
v 15-22 Abomination of Desolation, persecution of Israel	
v 29 celestials fall	6th seal - great earthquake, celestials fall, men hide from face of Lamb of God
v 30-32 Son of Man coming on the clouds	
	7th seal - silence in heaven, prepare for trumpets to sound

> How patient you are with Your wayward and hostile creation, oh God. You who created us, and then redeemed us deserve praise and worship without end. Yet what do men bring to You? The evil of this world bring You defiance. They shake their fists in Your face and exalt themselves. Even Your chosen people—the Jews—have turned on you. We long for a restoration of

appropriate praise and adoration of Your holiness. We long for a turn of heart especially in those who most ought to love You. Have mercy we pray, and bring us all to the place of devotion and security. Amen

15
GOD'S WRATH AGAINST THE EMPIRE

We discovered in the last chapter that the first half of the tribulation will see an unprecedented rise of evil and hardship in the world. Although we were not introduced to the engineer of that conspiracy in the Olivet Discourse, nor personally in the seal openings, we understood from the prophecies of Daniel that he will be on the scene and in control. We identified him with many New Testament passages as the antichrist. Under his ambitious campaigns we saw deceit, war, famine, death and persecution of Christians. These are not isolated one-time events. They continue throughout the Tribulation.

> *Daniel 9:26 (NASB)*
> *[26] . . . And its end will come with a flood; even to the end there will be war; desolations are determined.*

These, among many other scriptures that might be cited, demonstrate that war and persecution of Christians, once begun, will be ongoing throughout the Tribulation.

The Benchmark Treachery

At this point, Matthew's version of the Olivet Discourse introduces the breaking of the seven-year covenant by the antichrist. As we have discussed, this pivotal event marks the midpoint of the Tribulation.

> *Matthew 24:15-22 (NASB)*
> *[15] "Therefore when you see the ABOMINATION OF DESOLATION which was spoken of through Daniel the prophet, standing in the holy place (let the reader understand), [16] then those who are in Judea must flee to the mountains. [17] "Whoever is on the housetop must not go down to get the things out that are in his house. [18] "Whoever is in the field must not turn back to get his cloak. [19] "But woe to those who are pregnant and to those who are nursing babies in those days! [20] "But pray that your flight will not be in the winter, or on a Sabbath. [21] "For then there will be a great tribulation, such as has not occurred since the beginning of the world until now, nor ever will. [22]*

> *"Unless those days had been cut short, no life would have been saved; but for the sake of the elect those days will be cut short.*

The antichrist shall have begun his campaign at or before the beginning of the Tribulation, and he shall have carried out persecution against Christians from early on in that period. He shall have, early on, befriended the Jews and made a covenant with them. It is apparently this covenant that shall have allowed the rebuilding of the temple and the reestablishment of temple worship. But this particular rebellious act against God is the benchmark event that divides the Tribulation in half, and that divides all mankind clearly into two camps. Nothing more is said of this antichrist in the Olivet Discourse. However the whole of Revelation 13 is reserved for him, as we discussed in some detail in Chapter 12 of this book.

Convulsions in the Creation

The Opening of the Sixth Seal

It seems that the next opened seal takes us to a time late in the Tribulation, just before the return of Christ. Here our early birth pains turn to hard labor.

> *Revelation 6:12-14 (ESV)*
> *[12] When he opened the sixth seal, I looked, and behold, there was a great earthquake, and the sun became black as sackcloth, the full moon became like blood, [13] and the stars of the sky fell to the earth as the fig tree sheds its winter fruit when shaken by a gale. [14] The sky vanished like a scroll that is being rolled up, and every mountain and island was removed from its place.*

The Olivet Discourse—Celestial Upheaval

The reason for placing the sixth seal at or near the end of the seven-year period is because of the parallel verse in Matthew:

> *Matthew 24:29 (NASB)*
> *[29] "But immediately after the tribulation of those days THE SUN WILL BE DARKENED, AND THE MOON WILL NOT GIVE ITS LIGHT, AND THE STARS WILL FALL from the sky, and the powers of the heavens will be shaken.*

Luke's version states:

> *Luke 21:25-26 (ESV)*
> *[25] "And there will be signs in sun and moon and stars, and on the earth distress of nations in perplexity because of the roaring of the sea and the waves, [26] people fainting with fear and with foreboding*

of what is coming on the world. For the powers of the heavens will be shaken.

Christ's Glorious Return

<u>The Olivet Discourse—Christ in the Clouds</u>
The traumatic shaking of the heavenly bodies is portrayed as an immediate predecessor of the return of Christ.

Matthew 24:29-30 (NASB)
[29] ... the powers of the heavens will be shaken. [30] "And then the sign of the Son of Man will appear in the sky, and then all the tribes of the earth will mourn, and they will see the SON OF MAN COMING ON THE CLOUDS OF THE SKY with power and great glory.

Keep this earthquake and the shaking of the heavenly bodies in mind because they serve as a benchmark in time. The great earthquake is the only event that occurs in all three sequences—seals, trumpets and bowls. These events occur immediately before, and perhaps continuing to, the return of Christ.

This is a central event in prophetic history, finally unfolding. In this, God initiates the ultimate fulfillment of His redemptive purpose.

<u>The Opening of the Sixth Seal, Continued</u>
In the seal sequence, we are still in the sixth seal. The Revelation text records:

Revelation 6:15-17 (ESV)
[15] Then the kings of the earth and the great ones and the generals and the rich and the powerful, and everyone, slave and free, hid themselves in the caves and among the rocks of the mountains, [16] calling to the mountains and rocks, "Fall on us and hide us from the face of him who is seated on the throne, and from the wrath of the Lamb, [17] for the great day of their wrath has come, and who can stand?"

What about you and me, if we are alive at that time? What about believers? Will we mourn, or will we be like the rejoicing angles? The Olivet discourse is clear.

Matthew 24:30-31, 39-41 (NASB)
[30] "And then the sign of the Son of Man will appear in the sky, and then all the tribes of the earth will mourn, and they will see the SON OF MAN COMING ON THE CLOUDS OF THE SKY with power and great glory. [31] "And He will send forth His angels with A GREAT

TRUMPET and THEY WILL GATHER TOGETHER His elect from the four winds, from one end of the sky to the other...[39] *... so will the coming of the Son of Man be.* [40] *"Then there will be two men in the field; one will be taken and one will be left.* [41] *"Two women will be grinding at the mill; one will be taken and one will be left.*

Let me offer an analogy I think describes this traumatic situation for us. Imagine yourself a prisoner of war in an enemy concentration camp. Imagine the most terrible conditions. The camp itself has been under heavy attack for some time. Suddenly, out of nowhere comes a surprise invasion rescue force. With lightening-quick speed they overtake the camp. The guards are in terror, for they are the victims of the attack. What about you? Do you fear the attack? No, you are being rescued. You would welcome the invaders. So it will be when Jesus and his heavenly army rescue us from the doomed world kingdom.

> Dear Lord God almighty, how consumed we are just to read these passages and imagine ourselves caught in the middle of it. Thank you, that you have promised us a certain and sure rescue. Whether from the midst of strife, or from the grave, we put our hope in this rescue. Without it we realize we are helpless before the great traumas of that day. Without your rescuing grace, we can neither stand in times of tribulation, nor stand before you in glory. We pray for your grace to empower us to keep our faith strong through all that life brings our way, including tribulation. Help us know that your wrath is not against us, but against an evil, unbelieving world. Thank you for the redemption of our souls. Thank you that Jesus' death and resurrection make eternity sure for those of us who have made you Lord. Amen

The Opening of the Seventh Seal
Revelation 8:1-6 (ESV)

[1] When the Lamb opened the seventh seal, there was silence in heaven for about half an hour. [2] Then I saw the seven angels who stand before God, and seven trumpets were given to them. [3] And another angel came and stood at the altar with a golden censer, and he was given much incense to offer with the prayers of all the saints on the golden altar before the throne, [4] and the smoke of the incense, with the prayers of the saints, rose before God from the hand of the angel. [5] Then the angel took the censer and filled it with fire from the altar and threw it on the earth, and there were peals of thunder, rumblings, flashes of lightning, and an earthquake. [6] Now the seven angels who had the seven trumpets prepared to blow them.

Preparing for Christ's Cleansing Conquest
The last of the seals was opened, and after a pause of silence, the trumpets prepared to be sounded. What is the half-hour of silence? Much speculation has been made. Perhaps it is a sort of reverential pause to emphasize the seriousness and finality of what is about to take place. Perhaps it is intended to portray God like a father who takes a deep breath before reluctantly administering a punishment to his young son. Perhaps in this silence we feel the pain in God's heart. Perhaps God was pausing to savor the sweet aroma of the prayers of his people.

The censer from the altar normally burned incense in a Jewish worship ceremony. Here the incense represents the prayers of the saints, just as then. After the prayers go up, a strange thing happens. An angel filled the censer with fire which was then thrown down to the earth. If the seals initiated the movement of end-time events, this casting down of the censer and the subsequent sounding of the trumpets usher in the direct intervention of God as He sets about to bring judgment upon the world kingdom. Finally the silence is broken.

The Blowing of Seven Trumpets

The First Four Trumpets are Sounded
Revelation 8:7-12 (ESV)
⁷ The first angel blew his trumpet, and there followed hail and fire, mixed with blood, and these were thrown upon the earth. And a third of the earth was burned up, and a third of the trees were burned up, and all green grass was burned up. ⁸ The second angel blew his trumpet, and something like a great mountain, burning with fire, was thrown into the sea, and a third of the sea became blood. ⁹ A third of the living creatures in the sea died, and a third of the ships were destroyed. ¹⁰ The third angel blew his trumpet, and a great star fell from heaven, blazing like a torch, and it fell on a third of the rivers and on the springs of water. ¹¹ The name of the star is Wormwood. A third of the waters became wormwood, and many people died from the water, because it had been made bitter. ¹² The fourth angel blew his trumpet, and a third of the sun was struck, and a third of the moon, and a third of the stars, so that a third of their light might be darkened, and a third of the day might be kept from shining, and likewise a third of the night.

So much speculation has been made about these events that one might think they were history. There is not consensus as to whether these are literal descriptions of the plagues God sends, or whether they are figurative. While the most common Premillennial position is that they are at least somewhat literal, the events are so foreign to anything ever experienced that it is difficult to imagine them. Could they be describing a meteor shower, a collision with a comet, or some such natural phenomena? Why does it have to be explainable in terms of experiential events? After all, this is from the hand of Him who created heaven and earth. I am inclined to let them speak for themselves, and leave them in mystery until their occurrence reveals their meaning.

Three Woes—God's Assault on the Kingdom of Antichrist
After the first four trumpets have sounded and their events occurred, a bone chilling thing happens.

> *Revelation 8:13 (ESV)*
> *[13] Then I looked, and I heard an eagle crying with a loud voice as it flew directly overhead, "Woe, woe, woe to those who dwell on the earth, at the blasts of the other trumpets that the three angels are about to blow!"*

What?! How can it get worse? The natural world appears to have collapsed, killing huge numbers of people. The basic necessities of life, solar energy, crops and water are severely crippled, and now we are told *Woe* because of what is yet to come.

The First Woe
As the last three trumpets sound, the earth is assaulted by the 'three woes.' With these three plagues, intense spiritual warfare breaks forth into the physical realm.

> *Revelation 9:1-12 (ESV)*
> *[1] And the fifth angel blew his trumpet, and I saw a star fallen from heaven to earth, and he was given the key to the shaft of the bottomless pit. [2] He opened the shaft of the bottomless pit, and from the shaft rose smoke like the smoke of a great furnace, and the sun and the air were darkened with the smoke from the shaft. [3] Then from the smoke came locusts on the earth, and they were given power like the power of scorpions of the earth. [4] They were told not to harm the grass of the earth or any green plant or any tree, but only those people who do not have the seal of God on their foreheads. [5] They were allowed to torment them for five months, but not to kill them, and their torment was like the torment of a scorpion when it stings someone. [6] And in those days people will seek death and will not find it. They will long to die, but death will flee from them. [7] In appearance the locusts were like horses prepared for battle: on their heads were what looked like crowns of gold; their faces were like human faces, [8] their hair like women's hair, and their teeth like lions' teeth; [9] they had breastplates like breastplates of iron, and the noise of their wings was like the noise of many chariots with horses*

rushing into battle. ⁱ⁰ They have tails and stings like scorpions, and their power to hurt people for five months is in their tails. ¹¹ They have as king over them the angel of the bottomless pit. His name in Hebrew is Abaddon, and in Greek he is called Apollyon. ¹² The first woe has passed; behold, two woes are still to come.

Speculations about these locusts are never-ending. For example, one persistent interpretation is that John was seeing, in his vision, a picture of modern helicopter warfare. The sting is its weaponry. However this does not satisfy the statements about them torturing men for five months, but not being allowed to kill them.

In the ancient world, locust swarms brought famine and starvation as crops were totally stripped. But these locusts were told not to touch the crops as a normal locust would. They were to attack men—those men who do not have the seal of God. For the first time we see a selective plague. It is reminiscent of the plague of locusts in Egypt when God punished Pharaoh for his oppression of the Hebrew people. The locusts had gone everywhere except into the land of Goshen where the Hebrews lived. From here forward, a distinction is made between God's people and the followers of antichrist. The Woes only fell upon the enemies of God.

The Second Woe
Revelation 9:13-21 (ESV)
¹³ Then the sixth angel blew his trumpet, and I heard a voice from the four horns of the golden altar before God, ¹⁴ saying to the sixth angel who had the trumpet, "Release the four angels who are bound at the great river Euphrates." ¹⁵ So the four angels, who had been prepared for the hour, the day, the month, and the year, were released to kill a third of mankind. ¹⁶ The number of mounted troops was twice ten thousand times ten thousand; I heard their number. ¹⁷ And this is how I saw the horses in my vision and those who rode them: they wore breastplates the color of fire and of sapphire and of sulfur, and the heads of the horses were like lions' heads, and fire and smoke and sulfur came out of their mouths. ¹⁸ By these three plagues a third of mankind was killed, by the fire and smoke and sulfur coming out of their mouths. ¹⁹ For the power of the horses is in their mouths and in their tails, for their tails are like serpents with heads, and by means of them they wound. ²⁰ The rest of mankind, who were not killed by these plagues, did not repent of the works of their hands nor give up worshiping demons and idols of gold and silver and bronze and stone and wood, which cannot see or hear or walk, ²¹ nor did they repent of their murders or their sorceries or their sexual immorality or their thefts.

If these mounted troupes are literal military combatants, it is speculated that the only conceivable source of such a large number of warriors is the Far East, perhaps India, China, Indonesia or several such countries in alliance. From the fact that they crossed the Euphrates River, we know they came from at least that far east. Many equate this with the armies of the Battle of Armageddon because of its magnitude. But the Armageddon conflict is local to Israel, while the devastation here is apparently much wider than that. Maybe it is the Armageddon army on its way to Armageddon, leaving a wide path of destruction wherever it goes. The devastating, polluting effects of heavy widespread modern warfare might be in view in the fire, smoke and sulfur. Then it ends with this:

> *Revelation 11:13-14 (ESV)*
> *[13] And at that hour there was a great earthquake, and a tenth of the city fell. Seven thousand people were killed in the earthquake, and the rest were terrified and gave glory to the God of heaven. [14] The second woe has passed; behold, the third woe is soon to come.*

Here we come again to our benchmark earthquake. This great earthquake may play a major role in the conversion of Israel, since *the survivors were terrified and gave glory to the God of heaven.*

The Third Woe

> *Revelation 11:15-19 (ESV)*
> *[15] Then the seventh angel blew his trumpet, and there were loud voices in heaven, saying, "The kingdom of the world has become the kingdom of our Lord and of his Christ, and he shall reign forever and ever." [16] And the twenty-four elders who sit on their thrones before God fell on their faces and worshiped God, [17] saying, "We give thanks to you, Lord God Almighty, who is and who was, for you have taken your great power and begun to reign. [18] The nations raged, but your wrath came, and the time for the dead to be judged, and for rewarding your servants, the prophets and saints, and those who fear your name, both small and great, and for destroying the destroyers of the earth." [19] Then God's temple in heaven was opened, and the ark of his covenant was seen within his temple. There were flashes of lightning, rumblings, peals of thunder, an earthquake, and heavy hail.*

The Seven Bowls of God's Wrath

Four chapters of parenthetical visions separate the seventh trumpet in Revelation and the pouring out of the bowls of God's wrath. We will jump ahead to the bowl judgments, pausing only at one verse in Revelation 15.

Revelation 15:1 (ESV)
¹ Then I saw another sign in heaven, great and amazing, seven angels with seven plagues, which are the last, for with them the wrath of God is finished.

These judgments seem to come in rapid succession as the wrath of God climaxes toward its full fury. The first plague reminds us that their target is the kingdom of antichrist.

Revelation 16:1-21 (ESV)
¹ Then I heard a loud voice from the temple telling the seven angels, "Go and pour out on the earth the seven bowls of the wrath of God." ² So the first angel went and poured out his bowl on the earth, and harmful and painful sores came upon the people who bore the mark of the beast and worshiped its image. ³ The second angel poured out his bowl into the sea, and it became like the blood of a corpse, and every living thing died that was in the sea. ⁴ The third angel poured out his bowl into the rivers and the springs of water, and they became blood. ⁵ And I heard the angel in charge of the waters say, "Just are you, O Holy One, who is and who was, for you brought these judgments. ⁶ For they have shed the blood of saints and prophets, and you have given them blood to drink. It is what they deserve!" ⁷ And I heard the altar saying, "Yes, Lord God the Almighty, true and just are your judgments!" ⁸ The fourth angel poured out his bowl on the sun, and it was allowed to scorch people with fire. ⁹ They were scorched by the fierce heat, and they cursed the name of God who had power over these plagues. They did not repent and give him glory. ¹⁰ The fifth angel poured out his bowl on the throne of the beast, and its kingdom was plunged into darkness. People gnawed their tongues in anguish ¹¹ and cursed the God of heaven for their pain and sores. They did not repent of their deeds. ¹² The sixth angel poured out his bowl on the great river Euphrates, and its water was dried up, to prepare the way for the kings from the east. ¹³ And I saw, coming out of the mouth of the dragon and out of the mouth of the beast and out of the mouth of the false prophet, three unclean spirits like frogs. ¹⁴ For they are demonic spirits, performing signs, who go abroad to the kings of the whole world, to assemble them for battle on the great day of God the Almighty. ¹⁵ ("Behold, I am coming like a thief! Blessed is the one who stays awake, keeping his garments on, that he may not go about naked and be seen exposed!") ¹⁶ And they assembled them at the place that in Hebrew is called Armageddon. ¹⁷ The seventh angel poured out his bowl into the air, and a loud voice came out of the temple, from the throne, saying, "It is done!" ¹⁸ And there were flashes of lightning, rumblings, peals of thunder, and a great earthquake such as there had never been since man was on the earth, so great was that

earthquake. [19] The great city was split into three parts, and the cities of the nations fell, and God remembered Babylon the great, to make her drain the cup of the wine of the fury of his wrath. [20] And every island fled away, and no mountains were to be found. [21] And great hailstones, about one hundred pounds each, fell from heaven on people; and they cursed God for the plague of the hail, because the plague was so severe.

Both the trumpet sequence and the bowl sequence present a vast army ready for battle. I believe they both speak of the same battle. Only here is its destination told. It is from this verse that we name the greatest battle of all the ages. Armageddon! The battle itself does not seem to be included as part of this plague, just the gathering for it. Both trumpets and bowls end with a huge hailstorm following close on the heels of history's worst earthquake. These phenomena, together with the shaking of heavenly bodies revealed in the Olivet Discourse, and mentioned as contemporaneous with the earthquake at the end of the seals, seem to be climactic events that signal in the return of Jesus.

Following is a chart showing a possible alignment of the seal, trumpet and bowl judgments. Time is progressing as you move down the chart, although there is no time-line proportionality intended.

In this proposed tribulation agenda, I suggest a common ending point for the three sequences—the sign of the return of Jesus. The starting points are, however, all different. The breaking of the seals begins at the onset of the seven-year tribulation, and spans the entire tribulation period. The sounding of the trumpets begins later. How much later is not intended to be reflected proportionally in the table. However one of the woes lasts five months, so perhaps that sets a minimum boundary on the duration. Finally, the pouring out of the seven bowls begins, presumably very late in the tribulation period.

All three sequences have the great earthquake in common at, or near, their culmination. Paralleling these three sequences with the Olivet Discourse, we can identify the two immediate precursors to Christ's return: the great earthquake, and the *shaking* or *fall* of the celestial bodies.

A PROPOSED SEQUENCE OF THE SEALS, TRUMPETS AND BOWLS

OPENING OF SEALS	BLOWING OF TRUMPETS	POURING OUT OF BOWLS
1ST Seal – Conqueror on white horse	1ST Trumpet – Hail and fire destroy 1/3 of vegetation	1ST Bowl – Painful sores on those of antichrist's kingdom
2nd Seal – War on red horse	2nd Trumpet – Blazing mountain into sea, 1/3 turns to blood	2nd Bowl – All seas turn to blood
3rd Seal – Famine on black horse	3rd Trumpet – Blazing torch poisons 1/3 of fresh water	3rd Bowl – All fresh water turns to blood
4th Seal – Death on pale horse	4th Trumpet – 1/3 of celestials dark	4th Bowl - Sun scorches men with intense heat
5th Seal – Souls of martyrs in heaven	5th Trumpet (1st Woe) – smoke from abyss, stinging locusts torment God's enemies	5th Bowl - Kingdom of antichrist plunged into darkness
6th Seal – Great earthquake, celestials fall, men hide from face of Christ	6th Trumpet (2nd Woe) –Euphrates dries up, 200,000,000 mounted troupes kill 1/3 of mankind, Great earthquake	6th Bowl - Euphrates river dries up for kings from the East to pass
7th Seal – Silence in heaven	7th Trumpet (3rd Woe) –Kingdoms of world become kingdoms of Christ	7th Bowl – Great earthquake and huge hailstones

16
THE FIRST RESURRECTION AND RAPTURE

The Rapture

Paul's first letter to the Thessalonians describes an event commonly referred to today as the 'rapture' of the church. The Greek word for it is *harpazo*, meaning to 'snatch up.' It refers to the catching up of the saints at the Lord's return.

> *1 Thessalonians 4:13-17 (NASB)*
> *[13] But we do not want you to be uninformed, brethren, about those who are asleep, so that you will not grieve as do the rest who have no hope. [14] For if we believe that Jesus died and rose again, even so God will bring with Him those who have fallen asleep in Jesus. [15] For this we say to you by the word of the Lord, that we who are alive and remain until the coming of the Lord, will not precede those who have fallen asleep. [16] For the Lord Himself will descend from heaven with a shout, with the voice of the archangel and with the trumpet of God, and the dead in Christ will rise first. [17] Then we who are alive and remain will be caught up together with them in the clouds to meet the Lord in the air, and so we shall always be with the Lord.*

Note that *God will bring with him* [Jesus] *those who have fallen asleep in Jesus,* while at the same time *the dead in Christ will rise first.* How can they both *come with him,* and *rise from the dead* at that time? Actually, this is consistent with our understanding of the two components of resurrection, the perpetual life of the person's spirit, and the eventual resurrection of a new, immortal body. The spirits of deceased saints will have been in heaven with Christ since death, and now come with him. The resurrection body is given them at this time as it is *raised incorruptible.* This passage supports that understanding.

In this passage we are also told about the change that occurs in those believers still living at the time of its occurrence. They will be *caught up* along with the resurrected dead. From Chapter 8 we saw in I Corinthians 15 that at the time of this catching up, the living are changed and given their immortal bodies. Let's read it once again.

1 Corinthians 15:51-53 (NKJV)
⁵¹ Behold, I tell you a mystery: We shall not all sleep, but we shall all be changed-- ⁵² in a moment, in the twinkling of an eye, at the last trumpet. For the trumpet will sound, and the dead will be raised incorruptible, and we shall be changed. ⁵³ For this corruptible must put on incorruption, and this mortal must put on immortality.

In the 1 Thessalonians 4 passage, there is no chronology of preceding or following events, just the description of the rapture itself. About the application of this scripture, there is no controversy. All agree, it pertains to the rapture of the saints. That is where the agreement ends. Now we address a question that divides premillennial students into one of several groups. Therefore, it is controversial. The question is, 'When will the church be raptured?' Among certain church groups, it is such a powder-keg issue that they withhold fellowship from those of competing views.

When Will the First Resurrection and Rapture Occur?

Within the context of premillennialism, there are several views. The reference point is the 'tribulation.' Does the rapture occur before, during, or after the tribulation? I confess, I struggled with this question for many years. I read everything about it I could find. I had taken a pre-tribulation position, more out of default than out of conviction. I felt I had to adopt some view, so I tried to accept this most popular view, but was troubled by inconsistencies of it. After praying intensely for insight, my revelation came one morning about 2:00 AM after laying sleepless thinking about it. It is unusual for me to have trouble sleeping, but this had become a torturous subject. I got up from my restless bed, went into my office, prayed, and turned in my Bible to Matthew 24 where I re-read, for the umpteenth time, the most clearly comprehensive chronology for the event found anywhere in scripture. There it was, as evident to me as day and night. Since that experience, the validity of the understanding I discovered has become increasingly clear and solid in my conviction.

From the description of the rapture in this passage, make careful note of the following phrases: the loud shout, the voice of the archangel, the trumpet blast, the meeting in the clouds, in the air. Keep these descriptive phrases in mind as you read the following, for they are clear signs that will lead us in this matter.

In his Olivet Discourse Jesus gave this description of his return:

Matthew 24:29-31, 40-41 (NASB)
²⁹ "But immediately after the tribulation of those days THE SUN WILL BE DARKENED, AND THE MOON WILL NOT GIVE ITS LIGHT, AND THE STARS WILL FALL from the sky, and the powers

of the heavens will be shaken. [30] "And then the sign of the Son of Man will appear in the sky, and then all the tribes of the earth will mourn, and they will see the SON OF MAN COMING ON THE CLOUDS OF THE SKY with power and great glory. [31] "And He will send forth His angels with A GREAT TRUMPET and THEY WILL GATHER TOGETHER His elect from the four winds, from one end of the sky to the other. . . . [40] "Then there will be two men in the field; one will be taken and one will be left. [41] "Two women will be grinding at the mill; one will be taken and one will be left.

Here again we have the *clouds of the sky, power and great glory*, angels attending, a *loud trumpet call*, and a gathering together of the elect. The parallel description is unmistakable. This is clearly describing the same event as our passages from I Corinthians 15 and from I Thessalonians 4. If that is true, we learn that this will occur *immediately after the tribulation of those days*. This tribulation refers to events described in the preceding verses, and speaks of a time of severe hardship on the earth. So according to this literal interpretation of these passages, there will be a time of severe tribulation and persecution on earth, followed by the return of Christ and the simultaneous 'catching away' of the saints, both living and dead.

In a previous chapter, we considered several purposes being fulfilled in the return of Christ. One of those purposes was to usher in salvation to those who trust in Jesus as Savior and Lord. We never discussed the means by which this would occur, however. Now, we see that it happens through resurrection. Resurrection culminates the salvation process. It begins with a faith-response to the gospel. It is sealed with the Holy Spirit's indwelling. The believer lives his life by faith, not by sight. Finally, all faith and hope is fulfilled in reality at the resurrection.

Now, I have just made some rather matter-of-fact claims about some very disputed issues. As I have said, scholars are not in agreement about the timing of the rapture. This is the most significant difference in interpretation of end-of-age sequences among premillennialists.

I uphold a post-tribulation rapture viewpoint. Nearly every preacher or teacher on prime time radio and television supports a pre-tribulation rapture viewpoint. That view gets much more exposure than other views. I have felt somewhat alone with this perspective at times. However, since expressing it, I have encountered many who agree with me, including a couple of ministers. Unfortunately, they are not on radio or television; their view is not getting wide exposure. So, you might be asking, "How can you (meaning me, an unknown in Christian circles of influence) be right, while all of those many well-educated preachers and teachers on radio and TV, along with many, many pastors filling pulpits every Sunday, be mistaken?

Why should your view have any legitimacy worth even my slightest consideration?"

Besides the issue of legitimacy, the pre-trib rapture is very popular. Who wouldn't like a free bypass around the great tribulation, should it come in our lifetime? So, am I being presumptuous to embrace such a view? If you are entertaining this thought, just know that I have asked myself the same question. Yet my understanding from the scriptures compels me to proceed with confidence.

Why are supporters of a pre-tribulation rapture so unified in their teaching on this issue? That is easy to answer. Influential supporters of this view have created a paradigm of mammoth proportions. Whole denominations and church affiliations have bought into it and established it to the extent that anyone in their ranks who disagrees is censored and ostracized. To adopt an alternative view on this would be professional suicide. It has been made a core doctrinal issue in many church organizations. Many pastors and theologians have spent a lifetime promoting it and are in no position to entertain any other view. They are fettered and blinded by tradition. I am not constrained by any such professional dogmas. In this chapter I will present systematic arguments in favor of a post-tribulation rapture. Using scripture alone, I will address, head-on, the most common reasons given for a pre-trib rapture, and render them either incorrect, or non-compelling.

The Reference Point—the Tribulation
To understand the various chronologies, we must first grasp the tribulation concept which was discussed in chapter 15. The general premillennial view is that there will be a specific period of unprecedented hardship including persecution of Christians and Jews at the end of the church age. During this tribulation, Satan will attempt to set up an evil worldwide kingdom. He will do this through his agent, referred to in prophecy by many names, but best known as antichrist. During a seven-year period, the antichrist will elevate himself and his kingdom, all the while persecuting the people of God. Finally, God's judgments begin to fall on the antichrist and his kingdom. The very creation is shaken as God destroys the powers of evil. The Tribulation is understood by most premillennialists to last for seven years, divided into two three-and-a-half year halves. The *great tribulation* is understood by some to be the entire seven-year period. Others say only the last half of the seven years is the *great Tribulation*. The timing issue of the rapture and resurrection of the church hinges on when it occurs in relation to this tribulation period.

Because controversy has troubled so many, and because I have been specifically asked for clarity on this issue, I will present a systematic summary of the major views, followed by supporting and contradictory arguments for each, based on significant points of difference.

Pre-Tribulation Rapture View Summarized

This very popular view professes that the rapture of the church occurs before the tribulation. It is simply called the 'pre-tribulation rapture' view. This pre-trib view is supported by many dispensationalists, although not all; some dispensationalists hold to a different rapture view.

According to this pre-trib view, the rapture will remove believers (Christians living at the time, and those who have previously died) from the earth before the tribulation begins in order to rescue them from the coming judgments of God. The rapture is seen as a secret, silent disappearance. The saints will simply disappear from earth and meet the Lord bodily in the sky, unseen by those left behind. Nonbelievers will remain to experience the tribulation and many will die. Many others will come to salvation during the tribulation, and face much persecution. Among those converting during the tribulation will be the Jews. Israel as a whole will come to acknowledge Jesus as her Messiah. According to this view, the *marriage supper of the lamb* and the *judgment seat of Christ* will take place in heaven during this period of earthly tribulation.

To overcome chronological problems such as the obvious contradiction to Matt 24:29-31 that this scenario creates, proponents construct a two-tiered *first resurrection*. That is, they propose that there are two occasions of the first resurrection of saints. The resurrection prior to the tribulation is the first tier. The tribulation saints, those who come to faith during the tribulation period, are later resurrected at Christ's return, after the tribulation, along with the Old Testament saints, as the second tier.

Upon the return of Christ at the end of the tribulation, the already-raptured church will return with him. The actual return of Christ to earth will be visible to all, and will be with great glory and power, unlike the rapture which had occurred quietly, secretly. The deceased tribulation converts will be resurrected and the still living converts will be changed into their 'resurrection bodies' at his coming. This finalizes the *first resurrection* consisting of both the raptured saints and the raised tribulation saints, occurring in two stages seven years apart. The 1970's best-seller <u>The Late Great Planet Earth</u> by Hal Lindsey, and the more recent popular <u>Left Behind</u> book series by Tim LaHaye and Jerry Jenkins are based on this interpretation. A time line of this view looks like this:

	↑ RAPTURE		↓ RETURN OF CHRIST
CHURCH AGE	TRIBULATION		DISCUSSED LATER

There are some influential men and institutions that have aggressively promoted the pre-tribulation view, much in the manner of a commercial sales campaign, imposing ecclesiastical sanctions on defectors. An increasing number of students have read scripture, and questioned.

Post-Tribulation Rapture View Summarized
This view holds that there is only one occasion of the *first resurrection* of the saints. The resurrection of dead saints and the rapture of all saints occurs at the return of Christ at the end of the tribulation. At his coming, Christ will destroy the evil empire of Satan.

In this view, the saints still alive at that time must go through the tribulation. Many will be martyred for their faith. They will be 'kept' primarily in the sense that they will be given God's grace to endure, and not lose their faith. The marriage supper of the Lamb will occur following this holy union of saints with their Savior. This is the view I accept, and strongly support as being the most biblically consistent. This chronology can be summarized like this:

```
                    RETURN OF CHRIST |
                                     ▼
                                     ▲ RAPTURE
                                     |
----------------------------------------------------------------
   CHURCH AGE     |    TRIBULATION    |   DISCUSSED LATER
```

Mid-Tribulation Rapture View Summarized
This view holds that the church will endure the first half of the tribulation, but will be raptured at its midpoint. Believers are thus spared the most intense part of the tribulation. Variations of this belief place the rapture at various intermediate points during the tribulation time line. This view is relatively obscure. Robert Van Kampen proposes what he calls a 'pre-wrath rapture' that has gained some interest. It places the rapture during the last half of the tribulation, probably close to the end. It occurs after the persecution of Christianity by antichrist, but before the wrath of God, which he differentiates. He claims that this view satisfies all the scriptural problems associated with the pre- and post- views.

The Underlying Foundation of Each View
The motivating principles behind the various views, the driving forces for their perspectives, are different.

> 1) For the Pre-tribulation view, the essential foundational belief is that the church is not appointed to suffer wrath. The tribulation is seen as God's wrath. Therefore a sequence is constructed in which New Testament saints are removed from the earth in the rapture prior to the tribulation.

2) For the Post-tribulation rapture view, the basis for its placement of the rapture is the apparent chronologies given in pertinent scripture passages. There are only a few passages that contribute to this sequential arrangement of events, but they are consistent and clear.

3) Mid-tribulation and Pre-wrath views are founded primarily as an attempt to overcome apparent difficulties of the pre- and post- views.

Here are the major questions and arguments that weigh in on the determination of when the rapture will occur.

Are Two Different Events Described in Scripture?
In order to accommodate their problem with the chronology passages, those holding to a pre-tribulation rapture have fabricated a scenario in which the first resurrection occurs in two installments—one before the tribulation, one at the time of the second coming of Christ at the end of the tribulation.

This view is relatively new; it was first proposed by English minister Edward Irving in about 1830. It was developed and promoted by John Nelson Darby of the Brethren Church in Ireland and Scotland, a Pentecostal revival movement of that period. It later spread to the United States where it gained widespread institutional support. Prior to that time, the idea of two stages of the first resurrection had apparently never been considered. This construction is extra-biblical. Nowhere in scripture is such a two-stage first resurrection directly mentioned. But how about indirectly? Are there two different events described, a secret rapture and, later, a glorious ingathering?

Pre-trib proponents believe in two separate episodes of the first resurrection that are very different in description. The resurrection of tribulation saints at the time of the second coming of Jesus is understood by all views to occur with great power and glory. On the other hand, the pre-trib rapture is said to come as a mystery, secretly, quietly. The following verses are usually quoted in support of this belief:

> *1 Corinthians 15:51-52a (NKJV)*
> *[51] Behold, I tell you a mystery: We shall not all sleep, but we shall all be changed--* [52] *in a moment, in the twinkling of an eye, . . .*
>
> *2 Peter 3:10a (ESV)*
> *[10] But the day of the Lord will come like a thief,*

What about this *mystery* concept? Neither of these verses, or any other, describe a silent, secret rapture. The word 'mystery' does not mean 'secret and undetected,' but is a technical term referring to something previously unknown. Every prophecy student understands that. It does not support the secret rapture concept.

The thief analogy has been widely used as a metaphor for a silent rapture. In the pre-trib view, you are led to imagine a burglar who sneaks into your house quietly while you sleep and robs you. You never knew a thing about it until morning. However, the imagery in these scriptures does not describe 'stealth,' but 'surprise.' The thief in Jesus' narratives is not a burglar who comes in and out undetected, but a bandit who attacks when least expected, and the attack is overt and violent. We see this in the following:

Mark 3:27 (ESV)
[27] But no one can enter a strong man's house and plunder his goods, unless he first binds the strong man. Then indeed he may plunder his house.

Neither of these scriptures supports a secret rapture. Jesus strongly warns against looking for a secret meeting with him at his return:

Matthew 24:26-27 (KJV)
[26] Wherefore if they shall say unto you, Behold, he is in the desert; go not forth: behold, he is in the secret chambers; believe it not. [27] For as the lightning cometh out of the east, and shineth even unto the west; so shall also the coming of the Son of man be.

His return will be like lightning that lights the whole sky, that is, visible to all. We all know that lightning is accompanied by thunder, so the picture is one of a very visible (and likely audible) event. There is not a single description in scripture of a silent, secret rapture. References are always about surprise.

Let's look at the descriptions and compare them, to see how different they are. We will begin with the passage that everyone agrees is speaking of the rapture, regardless of when it occurs:

1 Thessalonians 4:16-17 (NASB)
[16] For the Lord Himself will descend from heaven with a shout, with the voice of the archangel and with the trumpet of God, and the dead in Christ will rise first. [17] Then we who are alive and remain will be caught up together with them in the clouds to meet the Lord in the air, and so we shall always be with the Lord.

We started with this passage because it is the most generally descriptive of all the biblical accounts. Note that 1) Christ comes down from heaven, 2) there is a loud command, 3) and a voice of the archangel, 4) there is a trumpet blast, 5) the dead in Christ are raised to life, 6) those still living, together with the raised deceased saints, are caught up to meet the Lord, 7) the meeting is in the clouds, and 8) in the air (or sky). Does this sound secret and silent? Keep these descriptive characteristics in mind.

Now let's look at a scripture that clearly pertains to the resurrection at the time of Christ's coming at the end of the tribulation.

> *Matthew 24:30-31 (NASB)*
> *[30] "And then the sign of the Son of Man will appear in the sky, and then all the tribes of the earth will mourn, and they will see the SON OF MAN COMING ON THE CLOUDS OF THE SKY with power and great glory. [31] "And He will send forth His angels with A GREAT TRUMPET and THEY WILL GATHER TOGETHER His elect from the four winds, from one end of the sky to the other.*

Let's compare these two passages. a) First, we have the appearing *in the sky* and *coming on the clouds* in Matthew. In I Thessalonians we see the Lord will *come down from heaven . . . in the clouds*, and *in the air*. b) Second, we find in Matthew that at his coming he *will gather his elect,* and in I Thessalonians *the dead in Christ will rise first. After that, we who are still alive and are left will be caught up together with them . . . to meet the Lord . . .* c) Third, we see his coming will be with his angels, and that their function is in the gathering of the saints. In Matthew we read he will *send his angels* who will *gather his elect.* In I Thessalonians we see that his coming will be accompanied by *the voice of the archangel,* upon which *the dead in Christ will rise...* d) Fourth, in Matthew we see that the coming is accompanied *with a loud trumpet call,* and in I Thessalonians it is *with the trumpet call of God.* We have already seen this trumpet speaking of the resurrection in I Corinthians:

> *1 Corinthians 15:51-52 (NKJV)*
> *[51] Behold, I tell you a mystery: We shall not all sleep, but we shall all be changed-- [52] in a moment, in the twinkling of an eye, at the last trump . . .*

Are these passages describing two very different events or are they two descriptions of the same event? The pre-tribulation rapture view, by necessity, insists that these are two different events. But when you put the passages side-by-side, the answer is obvious. They are the same. The concept of two very different episodes of the resurrection beginning with a secret rapture is not supported in scripture.

The parallel content indicates that these passages speak of the same event. The phrase in I Thessalonians, *the dead in Christ will rise first. After that, we who are still alive and are left will be caught up together with them* clearly ties the first resurrection and the rapture together as approximately concurrent events. Therefore, both must occur at the time of Christ's return.

What Do the Biblical Chronologies Teach?
If the rapture and the gathering of the saints at the return of Christ are one and the same thing, how do we know that the return of Christ described in the Matthew 24:30-31 passage we just studied occurs after the tribulation? We are clearly told in scripture. The whole section of scripture preceding this scripture describes this tribulation in some detail. Then the transitional verse just prior to it reads:

> *Matthew 24:29-30 (NASB)*
> *²⁹ "But immediately after the tribulation of those days THE SUN WILL BE DARKENED, AND THE MOON WILL NOT GIVE ITS LIGHT, AND THE STARS WILL FALL from the sky, and the powers of the heavens will be shaken. ³⁰ "And then the sign of the Son of Man will appear in the sky, and then all the tribes of the earth will mourn, and they will see the SON OF MAN COMING ON THE CLOUDS OF THE SKY with power and great glory.*

The events of Matthew 24:29 and following clearly take place *after the tribulation of those days*. If the event described in I Thessalonians 4 (which everyone takes as referring to the rapture) is the same as that described in Matthew 24 and in 1 Corinthians 15, then the rapture must occur at that time, that is, *after the tribulation*.

Another passage that may be taken as a chronology of events is found in Revelation. In chapters 4 through 18 the period of the tribulation is described. Chapter 19 describes the return of Jesus. On the heels of that description we are introduced to the first resurrection:

> *Revelation 20:4-5 (ESV)*
> *⁴ Then I saw thrones, and seated on them were those to whom the authority to judge was committed. Also I saw the souls of those who had been beheaded for the testimony of Jesus and for the word of God, and those who had not worshiped the beast or its image and had not received its mark on their foreheads or their hands. They came to life and reigned with Christ for a thousand years. ⁵ The rest of the dead did not come to life until the thousand years were ended. This is the first resurrection.*

If we believe the order of presentation has any relationship to the chronological sequence of events, then this passage places the first resurrection at about the time of Christ's victorious coming, and after the tribulation.

Another strong contribution to the chronology of the rapture is found in Paul's second letter to the Thessalonians. In the Thessalonian church, Paul had to correct and pacify some of the saints. Someone had been spreading a disturbing false doctrine that a secret *day of the Lord* had already come, leaving the Thessalonians behind. This false teaching had been falsely attributed to the apostles. In this passage, he sets the record straight.

> *2 Thessalonians 2:1-3 (NASB)*
> *¹ Now we request you, brethren, with regard to the coming of our Lord Jesus Christ and our gathering together to Him, ² that you not be quickly shaken from your composure or be disturbed either by a spirit or a message or a letter as if from us, to the effect that the day of the Lord has come. ³ Let no one in any way deceive you, for it will not come unless the apostasy comes first, and the man of lawlessness is revealed, the son of destruction,*

Paul assures them that their *gathering together to him* [Christ] (referring to the rapture) has not already come. He tells them the way they can know this is because the *man of lawlessness* (antichrist) must be revealed to them before the rapture will occur. From this passage we learn two important chronological facts. First, it places the coming of Christ and the ingathering of the saints together as roughly contemporaneous events. Second, this passage says that neither of these events will occur until after the antichrist has been revealed. The revealing of antichrist will occur during the tribulation. The rapture and coming of the Lord cannot occur prior to the beginning of the tribulation period. Both of these points are consistent with Matt 24:29-31.

So far we have only looked at chronology-related passages supporting the Post-trib view. There is a reason why we haven't looked at any of the chronological scriptures supporting the pre-trib view. There aren't any. If the rapture occurs prior to the tribulation, it would seem to be a pivotal event. Why is there not a single reference to a pre-tribulation rapture in the chronological sequences of Matthew 24 or in Revelation? Talk about a secret, silent event, it is so secret that it is not even mentioned in the prophetic chronologies. This silence speaks loudly and clearly.

<u>Was John's Call to *Come Up Here* Symbolizing the Rapture?</u>
At this point, the Pre-trib supporters might disagree that scripture is silent. They might remind us that at the beginning of the portion of Revelation which discusses the tribulation we find this passage:

> *Revelation 4:1-2 (ESV)*
> *¹ After this I looked, and behold, a door standing open in heaven! And the first voice, which I had heard speaking to me like a trumpet,*

said, "Come up here, and I will show you what must take place after this." ² At once I was in the Spirit, and behold, a throne stood in heaven, with one seated on the throne.

According to the pre-trib proponents this call to John in his vision to *come up here* symbolizes the rapture of the church, of which John is a representative. This popular argument is lame, pathetically lame. The fact that this point of view would rely on such a flimsy foundation makes this particular argument a liability to the pre-trib view, not an asset. The fact is, John was told to *come* and to *go* several times during the visions of Revelation.

Revelation 10:8a (ESV)
⁸ Then the voice that I had heard from heaven spoke to me again, saying, "Go, take the scroll . . ."

Revelation 11:1a (ESV)
¹ Then I was given a measuring rod like a staff, and I was told, "Rise and measure the temple . . .

Revelation 17:1-3 (ESV)
¹ Then one of the seven angels who had the seven bowls came and said to me, "Come, I will show you . . . ³ And he carried me away in the Spirit into a wilderness . . .

Revelation 21:9-10 (ESV)
⁹ Then came one of the seven angels who had the seven bowls full of the seven last plagues and spoke to me, saying, "Come, I will show you the Bride, the wife of the Lamb." ¹⁰ And he carried me away in the Spirit to a great, high mountain, and showed me the holy city Jerusalem coming down out of heaven from God,

The few chronologies about the rapture available to us in scripture powerfully and clearly place it at or near the end of the tribulation time span. No scriptural chronology supports a pre-trib rapture.

<u>Is the Church Destined for Wrath?</u>
The impelling argument for the pre-tribulation rapture is this concept. All other arguments are just supporting arguments. This is foundational. Supporters of this view believe that the tribulation is God's wrath, or righteous anger, against a wicked and unbelieving world. They relate it to the *Day of the Lord,* which culminates in his return and ultimately in final judgment. They believe that God's wrath is not aimed at the church, as made clear in the following verses:

> *1 Thessalonians 5:9 (NASB)*
> ⁹ *For God has not destined us for wrath, but for obtaining salvation through our Lord Jesus Christ,*
>
> *1 Thessalonians 1:10 (NASB)*
> ¹⁰ *and to wait for His Son from heaven, whom He raised from the dead, that is Jesus, who rescues us from the wrath to come.*
>
> *Romans 5:9 (RSV)*
> ⁹ *Since, therefore, we are now justified by his blood, much more shall we be saved by him from the wrath of God.*
>
> *John 5:24 (NKJV)*
> ²⁴ *"Most assuredly, I say to you, he who hears My word and believes in Him who sent Me has everlasting life, and shall not come into judgment, but has passed from death into life.*
>
> *Revelation 3:10 (ESV)*
> ¹⁰ *Because you have kept my word about patient endurance, I will keep you from the hour of trial that is coming on the whole world, to try those who dwell on the earth.*

They hold that whenever 'God's wrath' is in view, it includes and begins with, the tribulation, and that the tribulation is God's wrath against sinful men. It is not intended for the true church. The saints are not destined for God's wrath. Therefore, according to this pre-trib view, He will rapture them out of this world before the tribulation begins.

The destruction of Sodom, and flood of Noah were given as examples by Jesus of how people would be surprised by the coming wrath.

> *Luke 17:26-29 (ESV)*
> ²⁶ *Just as it was in the days of Noah, so will it be in the days of the Son of Man.* ²⁷ *They were eating and drinking and marrying and being given in marriage, until the day when Noah entered the ark, and the flood came and destroyed them all.* ²⁸ *Likewise, just as it was in the days of Lot—they were eating and drinking, buying and selling, planting and building,* ²⁹ *but on the day when Lot went out from Sodom, fire and sulfur rained from heaven and destroyed them all—*

Peter later referred to these two same events, but expanded on them to include the idea of God's rescue of Noah and of Lot.

2 Peter 2:4-9 (ESV)
⁴ For if God did not spare angels when they sinned, but cast them into hell and committed them to chains of gloomy darkness to be kept until the judgment; ⁵ if he did not spare the ancient world, but preserved Noah, a herald of righteousness, with seven others, when he brought a flood upon the world of the ungodly; ⁶ if by turning the cities of Sodom and Gomorrah to ashes he condemned them to extinction, making them an example of what is going to happen to the ungodly; ⁷ and if he rescued righteous Lot, greatly distressed by the sensual conduct of the wicked ⁸ (for as that righteous man lived among them day after day, he was tormenting his righteous soul over their lawless deeds that he saw and heard); ⁹ then the Lord knows how to rescue the godly from trials, and to keep the unrighteous under punishment until the day of judgment,

Paul repeatedly spoke of this idea that God's wrath was only for the ungodly, not for the righteous.

Romans 2:6-10 (RSV)
⁶ For he will render to every man according to his works: ⁷ to those who by patience in well-doing seek for glory and honor and immortality, he will give eternal life; ⁸ but for those who are factious and do not obey the truth, but obey wickedness, there will be wrath and fury. ⁹ There will be tribulation and distress for every human being who does evil, the Jew first and also the Greek, ¹⁰ but glory and honor and peace for every one who does good, the Jew first and also the Greek.

Romans 5:9 (RSV)
⁹ Since, therefore, we are now justified by his blood, much more shall we be saved by him from the wrath of God.

Romans 9:22-23 (RSV)
²² What if God, desiring to show his wrath and to make known his power, has endured with much patience the vessels of wrath made for destruction, ²³ in order to make known the riches of his glory for the vessels of mercy, which he has prepared beforehand for glory,

1 Thessalonians 1:9-10 (NASB)
⁹ For they themselves report about us what kind of a reception we had with you, and how you turned to God from idols to serve a living and true God, ¹⁰ and to wait for His Son from heaven, whom He raised from the dead, that is Jesus, who rescues us from the wrath to come.

So how can we reconcile this apparent dilemma? In the book of Revelation, the tribulation is portrayed primarily in three series of events. There is the breaking of seven seals one-by-one. That is followed by the blowing of seven trumpets. Finally, seven bowls are poured out. With each seal, trumpet and bowl, something cataclysmic happens on the earth. In John's vision, these symbols are opened, blown and poured in heaven. In fact, Christ begins it all by personally opening the seven seals. Therefore, all these events are seen as God's direct wrath against a sinful world. Thus we have the foundational premise for the doctrine of a pre-tribulation rapture.

In holding to a post-tribulation rapture, I agree that Christians are not destined for the wrath of God. The supporting scriptures are clear on that. No argument against it can be made without contradicting scripture.

My objection to the rationale leading to a pre-trib rapture lies in our understanding of the word *wrath*. Those holding to a pre-trib rapture are making a significant assumption. They are assuming that the entire seven year tribulation time frame is a display of God's wrath. In holding to a post-trib rapture, I challenge that assumption. I suggest that when we consult scripture, it shows the word wrath does not refer to the entire tribulation, as is commonly supposed, but refers very specifically to the pouring out of the bowls near the end of the tribulation, including the judgment that will occur at the coming of Jesus.

The three series of apocalyptic events--opening the seals, blowing the trumpets, and pouring out the bowls--seem to cover three different time-spans during the Tribulation period, but each series climaxes with the same common event, the return of Jesus. The three series of events are nested together so that the seals seem to cover the entire tribulation period. The trumpets appear to cover a much shorter time at the end of the tribulation. The bowls cover an even shorter time at the very end. This parallelism is shown in the chart at the end of the previous chapter.

When Does God's Wrath Appear?

We earlier referred to the many occurrences of the word *wrath* in the book of Revelation, referring specifically to God's wrath. If we look at the location of that word's usage in those passages, we find that it does not occur until near the end of the first two series at a point near to when Jesus returns. Note the following scriptures:

Revelation 6:12a,16-17 (ESV)
*[12] When he opened the sixth seal, . . . [16] calling to the mountains and rocks, "Fall on us and hide us from the face of him who is seated on the throne, and from the **wrath** of the Lamb, [17] for the great day of their **wrath** has come, and who can stand?"*

Revelation 11:15,18 (ESV)
*¹⁵ Then the seventh angel blew his trumpet, and there were loud voices in heaven, saying, "The kingdom of the world has become the kingdom of our Lord and of his Christ, and he shall reign forever and ever." . . . ¹⁸ The nations raged, but your **wrath** came, and the time for the dead to be judged, and for rewarding your servants, the prophets and saints, and those who fear your name, both small and great, and for destroying the destroyers of the earth."*

Revelation 14:19-20 (ESV) [referring to the pouring out of the bowls]
*¹⁹ So the angel swung his sickle across the earth and gathered the grape harvest of the earth and threw it into the great winepress of the **wrath** of God. ²⁰ And the winepress was trodden outside the city, and blood flowed from the winepress, as high as a horse's bridle, for 1,600 stadia.*

Revelation 19:11,15 (ESV)
*¹¹ Then I saw heaven opened, and behold, a white horse! The one sitting on it is called Faithful and True, and in righteousness he judges and makes war. . . . ¹⁵ From his mouth comes a sharp sword with which to strike down the nations, and he will rule them with a rod of iron. He will tread the winepress of the fury of the **wrath** of God the Almighty.*

These scriptures refer to *wrath* demonstrated in judgment that appears to take place just before, and at, Christ's return, not throughout the tribulation period. It shows up in the sixth seal, at the seventh trumpet and in all the bowls, all of which overlap timewise in my proposed chart in chapter 15. Each of the three series ends with the return of Jesus. The last of the bowls also includes the great battle that ensues at his return. All of this is part of God's wrath. In the pouring out of the bowls, we see the great wrath of the Creator.

Maybe your initial objection to this scenario is this. "What about the fact that all these tribulation events occur as seals are opened by Christ himself, and as trumpets are blown in heaven at God's command? Doesn't that show that they are all judgments from the wrath of God?" It's true that all of this is to be done according to God's plan and timing. However, the events of the first part of the tribulation are not necessarily extraterrestrial, supernatural events. God allows and uses evil armies and natural disasters to accomplish His purpose in the events of the tribulation. In this He shows his sovereignty in all things.

The fact that these first events are initiated at the hand of God reminds us that these events are not outside His control or plan. In the early and middle tribulation period the sovereignty of God is being primarily exercised indirectly, just as it is right now in the church age. God works within the framework of his natural laws most of the time. Even now, when disaster strikes us, we often ask "Why?" In the same way the wars, famines, illnesses, temperature extremes, and poison water of the first part of the tribulation make us ask, "What is this, if not a direct judgment?" Then, as now, we might see the apparent randomness of such events, the indiscriminant injustice, the hatred and anger, and ask, "Where is God in all this?" God is allowing the enemy to exercise control for a little longer.

The fallout of a church living in a cursed world, which hates its people and its message, is persecution. This too is part of God's plan, but it is not the wrath of God being poured out. Rather in these early and middle tribulation events, those of the seals and the trumpets, the ungodly are storing up His wrath against themselves for the future, a future that is very near for them.

The pouring out of the bowls is a different matter. Many scholars, including those of pre-trib disposition, believe the pouring out of the bowls will be a very rapid, intense salvo of events immediately prior to, and just after Jesus' return. Understanding that, we see again that the wrath of God is not referred to until the very end of the tribulation. These events immediately precede or immediately follow Christ's return. In them we do see the direct hand of God in wrathful judgment. In them we do see the pouring out of God's wrath.

> *Revelation 15:1 (ESV)*
> [1] *Then I saw another sign in heaven, great and amazing, seven angels with seven plagues, which are the last, for with them the* **wrath** *of God is finished.*

> *Revelation 15:7, 16:1 (ESV)*
> [7] *And one of the four living creatures gave to the seven angels seven golden bowls full of the* **wrath** *of God who lives forever and ever . . .* [1] *Then I heard a loud voice from the temple telling the seven angels, "Go and pour out on the earth the seven bowls of the* **wrath** *of God."*

> *Revelation 16:17a,19-20 (ESV)*
> [17] *The seventh angel poured out his bowl into the air . . .* [19] *The great city was split into three parts, and the cities of the nations fell, and God remembered Babylon the great, to make her drain the cup of the wine of the fury of his* **wrath**. [20] *And every island fled away, and no mountains were to be found.*

God's Wrath Makes a Distinction

In the pouring out of God's wrath from the seven bowls, we also see the onset of something else peculiar and significant. At the same time that God's wrath is revealed, we see for the first time during the tribulation, a distinction being made by God. The plagues are specifically directed at the enemies of God, not at the saints.

Revelation 16:2 (ESV)
² So the first angel went and poured out his bowl on the earth, and harmful and painful sores came upon the people who bore the mark of the beast and worshiped its image.

The wrath of God poured out in the first of the bowl-plagues only affects those who have pledged their loyalty to the kingdom of darkness.

Revelation 16:3-6 (ESV)
³ The second angel poured out his bowl into the sea, and it became like the blood of a corpse, and every living thing died that was in the sea. ⁴ The third angel poured out his bowl into the rivers and the springs of water, and they became blood. ⁵ And I heard the angel in charge of the waters say, "Just are you, O Holy One, who is and who was, for you brought these judgments. ⁶ For they have shed the blood of saints and prophets, and you have given them blood to drink. It is what they deserve!"

As the plagues of God's wrath continue, we see that the enemies of God, those who have persecuted the saints and spilled their blood, are the ones made to drink blood.

Revelation 16:10 (ESV)
¹⁰ The fifth angel poured out his bowl on the throne of the beast, and its kingdom was plunged into darkness. People gnawed their tongues in anguish

We see these plagues directed only at the kingdom of evil, the kingdom of the beast, those having the mark of the beast. They are the kingdom of unbelieving, unrighteous people living during the tribulation. They warn unbelievers of all ages of a coming judgment.

How God will cause these plagues to fall only on the wicked is not immediately clear. We are reminded of the plagues God brought upon the Egyptians by the hand of Moses, but in that case, the Hebrews were separated geographically a short distance from the Egyptians. There were ten plagues brought against the Egyptians. The first three plagues, the Nile turned to blood, throngs of frogs and swarms of gnats, came upon the whole of Egypt including the Hebrews living in Goshen. Beginning with the fourth plague and thereafter a distinction was made.

> *Exodus 8:22-23 (NKJV)*
> *[22] And in that day I will set apart the land of Goshen, in which My people dwell, that no swarms of flies shall be there, in order that you may know that I am the LORD in the midst of the land. [23] I will make a difference between My people and your people. Tomorrow this sign shall be.*

The Lord predicted and executed a swarm of flies. But the flies did not invade Goshen. Likewise, the remaining plagues all made a distinction between the Egyptians and the Hebrews; death of livestock, boils, hail and fire, locusts, darkness and death of the firstborn. The children of Israel living in Egypt in the region of Goshen were spared them. It is significant that the Exodus narrative emphasizes this distinction.

God's Wrath Appears
In parallel manner, it appears that in the book of Revelation the last three trumpet judgments, called *the three woes*, and the seven bowl judgments, all make a distinction between the kingdom of Christ and the kingdom of antichrist. Only those bearing the mark of the beast will experience them firsthand. And note that this occurs precisely when the word *wrath* first appears, referring to God's wrath and vengeance against the unbelieving world. These plagues initiate God's wrath. Thus, believers will not be the target of God's wrath, not because they have been raptured away ahead of time, but because God will make a distinction. The saints will not be spared from the first part of the tribulation, that which occurs prior to the wrath of God. The former part is indicative of the wrath of the antichrist and Christians will very much be subject to his persecution. There will be many martyrs.

'Rescuing' and 'keeping from trial' do not necessarily imply removing the saints out of the world. Pre-trib rapture proponents refer to the Old Testament accounts of Noah and of Lot as examples of God removing His people before bringing destruction. But there are also accounts where saints were not rescued out of a situation, but saved through it. Examples of this type of rescue can be found in the protection of the Israelites from the plague of death in Egypt, the saving of Daniel from the lions, and the rescue of Shadrach, Meshech and Abednego from the fiery furnace, all of whom were rescued 'in the midst of' the trial, not 'out of' it. So if believers are to suffer persecution at the hands of antichrist, what precisely are they being rescued from? They are being protected from loss of faith. Their faith and salvation are protected. In fact, their persecution is credited to them for a greater weight of glory.

Aren't Christians Predicted to be Persecuted During the Tribulation?
One powerful argument in favor of Christians and God-fearing people being present during the tribulation is in Jesus' warnings to his followers that they will be persecuted during this time.

Matthew 24:7-13 (NASB)
[7] "For nation will rise against nation, and kingdom against kingdom, and in various places there will be famines and earthquakes. [8] "But all these things are merely the beginning of birth pangs. [9] "Then they will deliver you to tribulation, and will kill you, and you will be hated by all nations because of My name. [10] "At that time many will fall away and will betray one another and hate one another. [11] "Many false prophets will arise and will mislead many. [12] "Because lawlessness is increased, most people's love will grow cold. [13] "But the one who endures to the end, he will be saved.

Revelation 6:9 (ESV)
[9] When he opened the fifth seal, I saw under the altar the souls of those who had been slain for the word of God and for the witness they had borne.

Revelation 20:4 (ESV)
[4] Then I saw thrones, and seated on them were those to whom the authority to judge was committed. Also I saw the souls of those who had been beheaded for the testimony of Jesus and for the word of God, and those who had not worshiped the beast or its image and had not received its mark on their foreheads or their hands. They came to life and reigned with Christ for a thousand years.

Believers in Jesus are clearly the target of persecution during this tribulation period. Pre-trib believers say that these are not a continuation of the church into the tribulation, but will be those who convert after the tribulation begins. They claim that their conversion will come after the rapture has removed the church. However, when Jesus warned his disciples about coming tribulation, he said *you will be handed over. . . you will be hated . . . 'You'*, not 'they', were the recipients of this message. *You* the church. He directs these warnings to the church. The persecution of Christians during the tribulation strongly supports a post-tribulation resurrection scenario.

The Issue of the Missing Word
In the book of Revelation the angel tells John . . .

Revelation 1:19 (ESV)
[19] Write therefore the things that you have seen, those that are and those that are to take place after this.

Revelation chapters 1-3 comprise *what you have seen* and *what is now* (at the time of the writing of the book). Chapters 4-22 are about *what will take place later*, the future, and of these, chapters 4-20 are about the tribulation period. Now in Revelation chapters 1-3 the words *church* or *churches* occur eighteen times. During the tribulation in chapters 4-20, these words do not occur again. Supporters of a pre-tribulation rapture believe this is because the church will not be present at that time, but will be in heaven already, taken in the pre-tribulation rapture.

The fact is, a major portion of the passages in Revelation chapters 4-20 depict heavenly scenes, so if the use of the word *church* is an indicator of the church's presence, why is the word *church* not used in those heavenly passages either?

A better explanation for the word *church* not occurring in chapters 4-20 is that in chapters 1-3 when the word *church* is used, John is recording word-for-word what he is being told to write, while in chapters 4-22 he is recording his own description of the visions he sees. In the latter, he was careful not to add his own interpretive commentary. He stopped short of specific identification in many passages that are obvious to us. In this, he is the perfect eye-witness. I don't believe the missing word *church*, is evidence of the rapture having occurred before the tribulation.

The Same Words
While we are on the subject of words, here is evidence favoring only one first resurrection event. It is not a proof text on the issue, in my opinion, but it certainly lends weight to the post-trib rapture scenario. The post-trib view says that the rapture and the second coming resurrection of saints is one-and-the-same event occurring at the end of the tribulation. Pre-trib advocates say the rapture and the second-coming are two separate events, separated by the seven-year tribulation.

Here is that word evidence. New Testament Greek language uses identical words in discussing both events—the rapture and the second coming resurrection of saints. Identical use of these words can be taken as evidence that they are, in fact, one, single event. We will look at three such words. Some of the references quoted may be redundant from previous or following passages in this chapter, but are repeated here for clarity.

The first Greek word is **Parousia** which is translated as *coming* (22 times) and *presence* (twice) in the King James Version and signals an arrival. Some of those uses have nothing to do with the coming of Christ. Here are some that do, along with their assignment of application, whether pre-trib or post trib:

Matthew 24:24 (NIV2011)
²⁴ For false messiahs and false prophets will appear (Parousia) and perform great signs and wonders to deceive, if possible, even the elect. [this verse considered second-coming by all]

1 Thessalonians 3:13 (NIV2011)
¹³ May he strengthen your hearts so that you will be blameless and holy in the presence (Parousia) *of our God and Father when our Lord Jesus comes with all his holy ones.* [second coming by all]

1 Thessalonians 4:15 (NIV2011)
¹⁵ According to the Lord's word, we tell you that we who are still alive, who are left until the coming (Parousia) of the Lord, will certainly not precede those who have fallen asleep. [Considered as applying to rapture by pre-trib doctrine]

James 5:8 (NIV2011)
⁸ You too, be patient and stand firm, because the Lord's coming (Parousia) is near. [rapture by pre-tribers]

A second Greek word used in scripture for both events is ***Apokalupis***. It is translated in the KJV as *appearing, coming, revelation* and *be revealed.* Here are some scriptures using that word:

2 Thessalonians 1:7 (NIV2011)
⁷ and give relief to you who are troubled, and to us as well. This will happen when the Lord Jesus is revealed (apokalupis) *from heaven in blazing fire with his powerful angels.* [post-trib resurrection by all]

1 Corinthians 1:7 (NIV2011)
⁷ Therefore you do not lack any spiritual gift as you eagerly wait for our Lord Jesus Christ to be revealed. (apokalupis) [rapture by pre-tribers]

Epiphaneia is a third Greek word used to speak of the second coming and also of the catching away of the saints. It is translated *appearing* (5 times) and *brightness* (once) in the KJV and *coming* by other translations. Here are a couple of examples:

> *2 Timothy 4:8 (NIV2011)*
> *⁸ Now there is in store for me the crown of righteousness, which the Lord, the righteous Judge, will award to me on that day—and not only to me, but also to all who have longed for his appearing.* (epiphancia) [rapture by pre-tribers]

> *2 Thessalonians 2:8 (NIV2011)*
> *⁸ And then the lawless one will be revealed, whom the Lord Jesus will overthrow with the breath of his mouth and destroy by the splendor of his coming.* (epiphancia) [second coming by all]

The identical use of these words in scripture to refer to both the rapture and the second coming strongly suggests that they are the same event. If they are the same event, then they occur at the end of the tribulation period. Thus, in that agenda, the church age extends through the tribulation. This is contrary to the popular pre-tribulation rapture view which ends the church age with the rapture before the tribulation begins.

<u>The Removal of the Holy Spirit</u>
One supporting claim for the pre-trib rapture has to do with the Holy Spirit. In this view, the Spirit of God is a righteous force in the world. His presence limits evil from having total reign. The antichrist cannot establish his satanic kingdom until the Holy Spirit is removed from restraining him. Since the Holy Spirit indwells the hearts of Christians, this occurs when the rapture of the church takes place. They believe that is what is being discussed in the following letter of Paul to the Thessalonians:

> *2 Thessalonians 2:3,6-9 (ESV)*
> *³ Let no one deceive you in any way. For that day will not come, unless the rebellion comes first, and the man of lawlessness is revealed, the son of destruction, ··· ⁶ And you know what is restraining him now so that he may be revealed in his time. ⁷ For the mystery of lawlessness is already at work. Only he who now restrains it will do so until he is out of the way. ⁸ And then the lawless one will be revealed, whom the Lord Jesus will kill with the breath of his mouth and bring to nothing by the appearance of his coming. ⁹ The coming of the lawless one is by the activity of Satan with all power and false signs and wonders,*

The pre-trib view says that the one who holds back the power of lawlessness is the Holy Spirit, and his being taken out of the way occurs at the time of the rapture.

While it is true the Holy Spirit inhabits all true followers of Jesus, it may be presumptuous to think that the Holy Spirit can only be present and operate on earth through Christians. Scripture tells us He was here in the beginning:

Genesis 1:2 (RSV)
² . . . and the Spirit of God was moving over the face of the waters.

He was also active in the Old Testament times, prior to the indwelling of the Spirit under the new covenant. No, removal of the saints with the rapture does not necessitate the vacating from earth of God's Spirit. So what, then, is meant by this scripture? It may well be that the restrainer is the Holy Spirit. That does not necessarily equate his *being taken out of the way* with the rapture of the church. It may be that someone besides the Holy Spirit is meant here. It has been suggested this might be the archangel Michael. This verse remains mysterious, and for me, is inconclusive.

The Unknowable Time
Another argument often put forth in support of a pre-tribulation rapture is based on this statement by Jesus:

Matthew 24:36-39 (NASB)
³⁶ "But of that day and hour no one knows, not even the angels of heaven, nor the Son, but the Father alone. ³⁷ "For the coming of the Son of Man will be just like the days of Noah. ³⁸ "For as in those days before the flood they were eating and drinking, marrying and giving in marriage, until the day that Noah entered the ark, ³⁹ and they did not understand until the flood came and took them all away; so will the coming of the Son of Man be.

This quotation is repeated in Mark 13:32. Proponents of the pre-trib view reason that the period of time immediately preceding Christ's return is well defined in duration--the seven year tribulation period. Furthermore, the midpoint of those seven years is marked by a significant event, namely the breaking of a peace treaty between the antichrist and the Jewish nation. Therefore, the rapture could not occur at the end of the tribulation as a surprising event. It doesn't seem consistent with this proclamation of Jesus. The predicted durations of both the tribulation and the last half of the tribulation would seem to be an accurate predictor of a post-trib rapture, contrary to Jesus statement. The pre-trib view, however, seems totally consistent with His words.

This argument is viable, but not compelling in supporting a pre-trib view. It is based on several assumptions. The first assumption is that the beginning point of the seven-year tribulation will be precisely known to earth's inhabitants. It is a very pivotal event in God's agenda, but its exact time may not be clear to those experiencing life on earth at the time. To them, there may be a long series of events, any one of which might be considered the *beginning of sorrows*.

A second assumption is that the broken peace treaty will be clearly and widely known. Again, the precise point of the breaking of the treaty may be clear in heaven, but on earth, it may be marked by a progression of events: increasing hostility, some specific breach of faith unknown to us, a proclamation by antichrist, desecration of the temple, persecution of Jews. What seems clear on the pages of scripture may be unclear to people living through it.

Another assumption on which this is based is a generalizing of Jesus words, *No one knows about that day or hour. . .* to mean 'no one has any idea at all. However it is possible that he worded it the way he did on purpose. He may not be saying. "No one has a clue what is coming," but rather literally "No one can predict the precise day and hour."

When Jesus made his proclamation about no one knowing the day or hour, he could have meant that no one living at that time would know. Perhaps he was not saying no one could know right up until it happens. He did claim that even *the son* did not know the *hour or day*, and we readily concede that this referred only to Jesus in his incarnation, and after his reinstatement in glory, he no doubt knows. Maybe Jesus' statement does not apply to wise believers living during the tribulation. Be careful of common assumptions.

I'm not offering these last arguments as evidence for a post-tribulation view, but just to show that the pre-trib argument about the unknowable time is not a compelling one. If I can imagine several things that might blur our understanding of Jesus' meaning in this passage, I am sure God could come up with many more to overcome our most obvious first-glance objections.

In Conclusion
I believe the arguments in favor of the rapture occurring before the tribulation are essentially circumstantial. There is no passage of scripture that directly, clearly places the rapture before the tribulation. This view requires the fabrication of a two-stage *first resurrection*, a concept nowhere identifiable in scripture. I insist that I Thessalonians 4:14-17 and Matthew 24:30-41 describe the same event, the one further described in I Corinthians 15:51-54 and Revelation 20:4-6.

The arguments in favor of a post-tribulation rapture are well founded and supported by the biblical record. With both views there are questions that are difficult to answer, but the post-trib view is far more consistent with scripture, in my opinion. Therefore, I believe that scripture places the time of the rapture at the end of the tribulation period, virtually simultaneous with the resurrection of the righteous and the second coming of Jesus. These three events are inseparable.

Having said that, I join with my brothers who hold other views regarding timing of the rapture, as together we share our common hope of glory. I would not hold the same regard for a belief that denied the literal return of Christ. But differences related to timing are not fundamental to the faith. A correct understanding of these matters aids in an accurate expectation of things to come, but does not separate sheep from goats. This issue must not be a source of division. Our beliefs should be filtered through the reality-check that we are discussing things that are beyond us all. We will all be in for some surprises, I'm sure.

So What?
Now having said that, the question you may be asking, if you have waded through these arguments and are still on board, is this: "Why does it make any difference when the rapture occurs? Isn't that just something for prophecy students to debate?" While it may not be an essential of the faith, there is a very important reason to correctly understand what the Bible says about it. We have already discussed how being faithful does not exempt us from the persecution of an antichristian world. Jesus told his followers that those who endure until the end will be saved. We need to prepare ourselves to endure, for living a lifestyle that is out of step with the world. This is not end-of-the-world hysteria. It is a call to bedrock allegiance, an allegiance that every generation of Christians has been called to. Why should we expect Christians living at the time of the tribulation be spared persecution when millions through the ages have not. It will become especially essential when tribulation comes, whether it be soon, or a ways into the future.

If you are like me, then you have probably imagined yourself in the tribulation, being persecuted for your faith. It is not something pleasant to think about, but it could happen. Who knows? When I think about it, I have one main anxiety. It is not fear of being persecuted. It is the fear that I will cave in and not remain faithful. Jesus has some words of reassurance for us in this matter:

> *Luke 21:12-15 (ESV)*
> *[12] But before all this they will lay their hands on you and persecute you, delivering you up to the synagogues and prisons, and you will be brought before kings and governors for my name's sake. [13] This*

will be your opportunity to bear witness. [14] Settle it therefore in your minds not to meditate beforehand how to answer, [15] for I will give you a mouth and wisdom, which none of your adversaries will be able to withstand or contradict.

In the flesh, all of us have limitations to what we can endure before selling out. But God promises us divine power to be able to endure. The grace of God will meet our need. Don't expect Him to give you today the grace you might need tomorrow. Trust Him to come to your rescue in that hour. This is why Paul wrote . . .

> 2 Corinthians 12:9-10 (NASB)
> [9] And He has said to me, "My grace is sufficient for you, for power is perfected in weakness." Most gladly, therefore, I will rather boast about my weaknesses, so that the power of Christ may dwell in me. [10] Therefore I am well content with weaknesses, with insults, with distresses, with persecutions, with difficulties, for Christ's sake; for when I am weak, then I am strong.

And why Peter wrote . . .

> 1 Peter 5:6-7 (ESV)
> [6] Humble yourselves, therefore, under the mighty hand of God so that at the proper time he may exalt you, [7] casting all your anxieties on him, because he cares for you.

That is why Jesus said, [14] Settle it therefore in your minds not to meditate beforehand how to answer, Our endurance lies in His strength. We are simply told to remain faithful, seeking Him.

Who Will Be Taken in the First Resurrection

Who will be resurrected in the first resurrection? So far we have called them saints. Those who hold to a pre-trib rapture say that only the New Testament saints will be taken in the rapture and that Old Testament saints will be resurrected at Christ's return. A post-trib rapture must necessarily include both Old and New Testament saints. What does the Bible say?

> 1 Corinthians 15:22-23 (NKJV)
> [22] For as in Adam all die, even so in Christ all shall be made alive.
> [23] But each one in his own order: Christ the firstfruits, afterward those who are Christ's at His coming.

1 Thessalonians 4:16 (NASB)
16 For the Lord Himself will descend from heaven with a shout, with the voice of the archangel and with the trumpet of God, and the dead in Christ will rise first.

Matthew 24:31 (NASB)
31 "And He will send forth His angels with A GREAT TRUMPET and THEY WILL GATHER TOGETHER His elect from the four winds, from one end of the sky to the other.

It is not clear from these verses alone what is meant by *his elect, his saints, those who belong to him*. It is clear that they are the ones who *belong to Christ*, those who are *in Christ*. But this does not restrict it to New Testament Christians. In the larger sense, it could also include the Old Testament faithful. That these who never knew Jesus by name still embraced him in faith is made clear in passages such as the following.

Hebrews 11:24-26 (ESV)
24 By faith Moses, when he was grown up, refused to be called the son of Pharaoh's daughter, 25 choosing rather to be mistreated with the people of God than to enjoy the fleeting pleasures of sin. 26 He considered the reproach of Christ greater wealth than the treasures of Egypt, for he was looking to the reward.

Moses lived 1000 years before Jesus, and died, still in Old Testament times. Yet it says he did what he did *for the sake of Christ*. About Abraham, who lived 1500 years before him, Jesus said:

John 8:56 (NKJV)
56 Your father Abraham rejoiced to see My day, and he saw it and was glad."

In the 'faith chapter,' Hebrews 11, we read of Old Testament saints who made sacrificial demonstrations of faith. We are told that they did not see God's promises, but looked for a future fulfillment. Then we read an interesting statement:

Hebrews 11:39-40 (NKJV)
39 And all these, having obtained a good testimony through faith, did not receive the promise, 40 God having provided something better for us, that they should not be made perfect apart from us.

The perfection of the Old Testament saints will be together *with us*, that is with the New Testament church. It may mean they will be included in the first resurrection and rapture of saints. This is not the traditional view, but I think it is plausible, based on this scripture passage, and on the basis of a post-tribulation rapture.

The Last Resurrection

The first resurrection will be the raising to life of the deceased elect of Christ, and (in my post-tribulation viewpoint) is quickly followed by the rapture of the saints. The Bible speaks of another resurrection occurring afterward.

> *Revelation 20:4-7,13 (ESV)*
> *⁴ Then I saw thrones, and seated on them were those to whom the authority to judge was committed. Also I saw the souls of those who had been beheaded for the testimony of Jesus and for the word of God, and those who had not worshiped the beast or its image and had not received its mark on their foreheads or their hands. They came to life and reigned with Christ for a thousand years. ⁵ The rest of the dead did not come to life until the thousand years were ended. This is the first resurrection. ⁶ Blessed and holy is the one who shares in the first resurrection! Over such the second death has no power, but they will be priests of God and of Christ, and they will reign with him for a thousand years. ⁷ And when the thousand years are ended, Satan will be released from his prison . . . ¹³ And the sea gave up the dead who were in it, Death and Hades gave up the dead who were in them, and they were judged, each one of them, according to what they had done.*

Here we have mention of the thousand-year period known in prophecy talk as the 'millennium.' This concept is not newly introduced in this passage; only the 1000 year duration is novel. Here we note that a second resurrection is mentioned that occurs after the millennium. So the first resurrection and the second, or last, resurrection are separated in time by this thousand-year span. The millennium will be looked at in more detail in Chapter 24.

<u>Why a Second Resurrection?</u>
In verse 13 of the passage just read, we see that the purpose for which the second resurrection will occur is judgment. Here is where all those other people groups will have their day of reckoning, because it is written . . .

> *Hebrews 9:27 (ESV)*
> *²⁷ And just as it is appointed for man to die once, and after that comes judgment, . . .*

The *second death* is a term for final eternal punishment. Note here that those taken in the first resurrection will not be in danger of suffering the fate of the final punishment. Their destiny is already secure. They are already justified by their faith in Jesus Christ. They are signed, sealed and delivered by him. This is glorious and comforting truth.

> *Ephesians 1:13-14 (ESV)*
> *¹³ In him you also, when you heard the word of truth, the gospel of your salvation, and believed in him, were sealed with the promised Holy Spirit, ¹⁴ who is the guarantee of our inheritance until we acquire possession of it, to the praise of his glory.*

> *Ephesians 4:30 (ESV)*
> *³⁰ And do not grieve the Holy Spirit of God, by whom you were sealed for the day of redemption.*

Those of the second resurrection must rise after the millennium, for they must face their Creator.

The Bottom Line

Resurrection is an unspeakable blessing to those who are willing to give themselves to the Lord Jesus Christ. For them it means blessing beyond any earthly experience. It means they will retain their life and their identity into eternity, in a blessed existence, freed from all bondage to sin. Most importantly, they will forever be in the loving presence of a gracious God.

For those who do not know Jesus, who will not devote their life to him, it means something very different. Resurrection guarantees they will also retain their life after death, and their identity. For them this is not a blessing. Resurrection means their life of self-will will not simply meld into a sea of souls and gently fade from the mind of God, losing their identity and the responsibility for their actions. No, they will stand alone and exposed, solely accountable for their lives.

> *Hebrews 4:13 (ESV)*
> *¹³ And no creature is hidden from his sight, but all are naked and exposed to the eyes of him to whom we must give account.*

> > Oh what a blessing you have provided for us. Lord, we know that with great grace comes great responsibility to receive it. If any one reading these words has not claimed you as their Savior and Lord, may they be stunned by the eternal gravity of this subject we have been discussing. May a holy fear draw them to you when nothing else will. Now Lord, as for those of us who have this hope of glory, we worship you with jubilant hearts.

How can we express the joyful anticipation of being changed from forgiven sinner (but still tethered to a world of dissipation) to your glorified child, transformed from all corruption into perfect unchangeable union with you. Thank you God. Thank you Jesus. Thank you Spirit of God living within us. Amen

17
MYSTERY BABYLON THE GREAT

Revelation is filled with symbolism and signs requiring careful inquiry to understand. We often may employ educated speculation in our interpretation. Many scholars will scream at the suggestion that any speculation is involved, but it is undeniable. Since the fulfillment may be in the future, we must do our best to harmonize symbolism with straightforward biblical context, trying at the same time to mesh it with current world conditions. So the speculation should not be seen as mere supposition. It is guided speculation—guided by similar scriptural language, by parallel symbolism elsewhere, and by historical or current events. Note a distinction between a history-based fulfillment (such as is embodied in futurist, historical and preterist beliefs) and a spiritualization approach to interpretation which divorces these symbols from any historical context. While spiritual principles may sometimes be imbedded in some of these passages, the evidence of already-fulfilled prophecy teaches us that while symbolic, they represent historical (past, present, or future) events.

One such topic leaps into our narrative about two-thirds of the way through Revelation. It is called, in this written vision, *Mystery Babylon* and *Babylon the Great*. Without introduction or explanation, Babylon the Great is thrust into the spotlight:

Revelation 14:8 (ESV)
⁸ Another angel, a second, followed, saying, "Fallen, fallen is Babylon the great, she who made all nations drink the wine of the passion of her sexual immorality."

What is Mystery Babylon?

With that brief sweep, Babylon is introduced. Yet from that short statement we learn several things about her. The feminine pronoun is later to be explained; she is symbolized by a prostitute. Her influence reached to *all the nations*. She *made* them *drink*, demonstrating an aggressive, irresistible seduction. Repeatedly in biblical prophecy, marital infidelity is used to characterize unfaithfulness to God, and prostitution portrays seducing false religions. On that basis, she seems to be some global idolatrous influence, enticing people away from God. Finally, two chapters later we read:

Revelation 16:18-19 (ESV)
¹⁸ And there were flashes of lightning, rumblings, peals of thunder, and a great earthquake such as there had never been since man was on the earth, so great was that earthquake. ¹⁹ The great city was split into three parts, and the cities of the nations fell, and God remembered Babylon the great, to make her drain the cup of the wine of the fury of his wrath.

Chronologically, the fall of Mystery Babylon probably falls just before the return of Christ, since it is linked with the great earthquake. However it is described here in Revelation. Babylon's fall is seen here to come from God. Just as her seduction was portrayed as an intoxicating cup, God's punishment is also pictured as a cup of destruction.

Revelation 17:1-2 (ESV)
¹ Then one of the seven angels who had the seven bowls came and said to me, "Come, I will show you the judgment of the great prostitute who is seated on many waters, ² with whom the kings of the earth have committed sexual immorality, and with the wine of whose sexual immorality the dwellers on earth have become drunk."

In the vision, the angel is taking John to see the destruction of Babylon, described as before.

Revelation 17:3-7 (ESV)
³ And he carried me away in the Spirit into a wilderness, and I saw a woman sitting on a scarlet beast that was full of blasphemous names, and it had seven heads and ten horns. ⁴ The woman was arrayed in purple and scarlet, and adorned with gold and jewels and pearls, holding in her hand a golden cup full of abominations and the impurities of her sexual immorality. ⁵ And on her forehead was written a name of mystery: "Babylon the great, mother of prostitutes and of earth's abominations." ⁶ And I saw the woman, drunk with the blood of the saints, the blood of the martyrs of Jesus. When I saw her, I marveled greatly. ⁷ But the angel said to me, "Why do you marvel? I will tell you the mystery of the woman, and of the beast with seven heads and ten horns that carries her.

A vulgar, richly clothed prostitute riding on a red beast with seven heads and ten horns! The beast was covered with blasphemous names. The blasphemy is understood to be against God. The woman was drunk with the blood of the saints, the church. This means she caused their bloodshed and relished their suffering.

Revelation 17:8-18 (ESV)
⁸ The beast that you saw was, and is not, and is about to rise from the bottomless pit and go to destruction. And the dwellers on earth whose names have not been written in the book of life from the foundation of the world will marvel to see the beast, because it was and is not and is to come. ⁹ This calls for a mind with wisdom: the seven heads are seven mountains on which the woman is seated; ¹⁰ they are also seven kings, five of whom have fallen, one is, the other has not yet come, and when he does come he must remain only a little while. ¹¹ As for the beast that was and is not, it is an eighth but it belongs to the seven, and it goes to destruction. ¹² And the ten horns that you saw are ten kings who have not yet received royal power, but they are to receive authority as kings for one hour, together with the beast. ¹³ These are of one mind, and they hand over their power and authority to the beast. ¹⁴ They will make war on the Lamb, and the Lamb will conquer them, for he is Lord of lords and King of kings, and those with him are called and chosen and faithful." ¹⁵ And the angel said to me, "The waters that you saw, where the prostitute is seated, are peoples and multitudes and nations and languages. ¹⁶ And the ten horns that you saw, they and the beast will hate the prostitute. They will make her desolate and naked, and devour her flesh and burn her up with fire, ¹⁷ for God has put it into their hearts to carry out his purpose by being of one mind and handing over their royal power to the beast, until the words of God are fulfilled. ¹⁸ And the woman that you saw is the great city that has dominion over the kings of the earth."

The woman is the city that will rule over the earth. Could it literally be a city of Babylon? No such city currently exists having that much influence. Furthermore, the region of Babylon has no hills. It is flat as a pancake. What currently existing city might fit this description? New York houses the United Nations, not to mention Wall street and untold commercial interests. NYC is the main economic gateway into the greatest materialistic economy on earth. How about Washington DC? Here the greatest military power of our day sits. One city often interpreted in this way, is Jerusalem. But it is said this city sits on *seven hills*. What city sits on seven hills? Jerusalem sits on two hills—Moriah and Zion.

Rome, of course, has been identified as 'the city built on seven hills.' This is not just some romantic tourist-catching phrase. Since ancient times it has been so called. I once sat in the penthouse restaurant of the Hotel Eden in Rome. The dining room had windows all the way around giving a 360° panoramic view of the city. On each table was a legend identifying what you were seeing. The seven hills were identified—Palatine, Aventine, Capitoline, Quarinal, Viminal, Esquiline and Caelian. Rome literally ruled over the kings of the earth at the time this vision was given. She continues to influence through the power of the Roman Catholic Church. Rome clearly fits this symbolism like no other literal city.

Why was the city called Babylon, rather than Rome? When this vision was given, remember that John, the penman, was incarcerated by Romans at hard labor. Had the Roman officials read his writings with the name of Rome splattered across its text, both he and those to whom they were being sent would have suffered greater persecution. God protected them in this way. The Babylon namesake was fitting. The historic Babylon was the site of the first empire after the great flood, as we discussed in Chapter 10. That empire was the inventor of idolatry. Rome was now (at the time of writing) what Babylon had been then. Many emblems of Roman religion originated in ancient Shinar, the kingdom of Nimrod. Furthermore, remember our development of would-be one-world empires in the prophecies of Daniel. They all had spiritual roots in ancient Babylon. The last one was represented by the fourth of a series of four beasts.

> *Daniel 7:7 (NASB)*
> *⁷ "After this I kept looking in the night visions, and behold, a fourth beast, dreadful and terrifying and extremely strong; and it had large iron teeth. It devoured and crushed and trampled down the remainder with its feet; and it was different from all the beasts that were before it, and it had ten horns.*

We clearly identified that all four beasts represented four successive world empires, the first being the Babylonian Empire and the fourth one being the Roman Empire.

> *Daniel 7:24-25 (NASB)*
> *²⁴ 'As for the ten horns, out of this kingdom ten kings will arise; and another will arise after them, and he will be different from the previous ones and will subdue three kings. ²⁵ 'He will speak out against the Most High and wear down the saints of the Highest One, and he will intend to make alterations in times and in law; and they will be given into his hand for a time, times, and half a time.*

This fourth beast, the Roman Empire seems to leap from the times of ancient Rome to the end-time period we call the tribulation, identified by its three and a half year time reference. Many believe, based on this, that the antichrist and his kingdom will arise out of the European community. The breakup of the old Roman Empire is said by some to have been into ten countries. Europe's political divisions have varied slightly through the centuries, but in the end, ten rulers, or presidents are again in view. Recall also the description of the antichrist emergence in Revelation 13.

Revelation 13:1 (NASB)
¹ And the dragon stood on the sand of the seashore. Then I saw a beast coming up out of the sea, having ten horns and seven heads, and on his horns were ten diadems, and on his heads were blasphemous names.

Not all agree with this future interpretation. By the time of Revelation's visions, persecution of Christians was already in full swing under Roman Caesar Nero and the emperors who followed, Rome was already drunk on the blood of the saints. Preterist interpreters believe this first century persecution is what was in view here. However, the number of martyrs has since swelled to many times greater than that persecution, and continues to escalate. In the end time, many Futurists believe that persecution of Christians will be wholesale and legal everywhere. This won't consist of simply isolated hate crimes, but will be promoted by governing authorities.

More seems to be in view here than just a city. Clearly there is represented here a socio-political entity. Rome is the emperial seat of the Vatican. A long-time Protestant interpretation of this identifies the woman with the Roman church. The lavishness of her riches gotten at the expense of the world, and at the expense of non-Roman Christians shows her illicit income. *The waters you saw, where the prostitute sits, are peoples, multitudes, nations and languages.* Certainly Roman Catholicism has great influence over the entire earth. 'Rome,' then, takes in huge global influence and political power. Furthermore, the Catholic system of practices and beliefs is viewed as idolatrous by many Bible-believing Christians. The most prevalent current view within protestant interpretation sees the great harlot in these passages as a future government-mandated religion. Many of the relics of Romanism will be incorporated, and will become a bridge for adherents to more-easily cross into the new religion.

The Fall of Babylon the Great

It is believed by many that the Roman church will provide an idolatrous structure from which an end-time false religion will evolve. Now note that the woman is riding on the beast. The false religion will serve the needs of the antichrist for a while, and he will use it to promote himself. Ultimately, the beast corroborates with the other ten kings to destroy the false religion. In its place, the antichrist himself will stand up as the omnipotent king of earth. He will be god to those who have not embraced Jesus as Lord.

Revelation 18:1-24 (ESV)
¹ After this I saw another angel coming down from heaven, having great authority, and the earth was made bright with his glory. ² And he called out with a mighty voice, "Fallen, fallen is Babylon the great! She has become a dwelling place for demons, a haunt for

every unclean spirit, a haunt for every unclean bird, a haunt for every unclean and detestable beast. [3] *For all nations have drunk the wine of the passion of her sexual immorality, and the kings of the earth have committed immorality with her, and the merchants of the earth have grown rich from the power of her luxurious living."* [4] *Then I heard another voice from heaven saying, "Come out of her, my people, lest you take part in her sins, lest you share in her plagues;* [5] *for her sins are heaped high as heaven, and God has remembered her iniquities.* [6] *Pay her back as she herself has paid back others, and repay her double for her deeds; mix a double portion for her in the cup she mixed.* [7] *As she glorified herself and lived in luxury, so give her a like measure of torment and mourning, since in her heart she says, 'I sit as a queen, I am no widow, and mourning I shall never see.'* [8] *For this reason her plagues will come in a single day, death and mourning and famine, and she will be burned up with fire; for mighty is the Lord God who has judged her."*

[9] *And the kings of the earth, who committed sexual immorality and lived in luxury with her, will weep and wail over her when they see the smoke of her burning.* [10] *They will stand far off, in fear of her torment, and say, "Alas! Alas! You great city, you mighty city, Babylon! For in a single hour your judgment has come."* [11] *And the merchants of the earth weep and mourn for her, since no one buys their cargo anymore,* [12] *cargo of gold, silver, jewels, pearls, fine linen, purple cloth, silk, scarlet cloth, all kinds of scented wood, all kinds of articles of ivory, all kinds of articles of costly wood, bronze, iron and marble,* [13] *cinnamon, spice, incense, myrrh, frankincense, wine, oil, fine flour, wheat, cattle and sheep, horses and chariots, and slaves, that is, human souls.* [14] *"The fruit for which your soul longed has gone from you, and all your delicacies and your splendors are lost to you, never to be found again!"* [15] *The merchants of these wares, who gained wealth from her, will stand far off, in fear of her torment, weeping and mourning aloud,* [16] *"Alas, alas, for the great city that was clothed in fine linen, in purple and scarlet, adorned with gold, with jewels, and with pearls!* [17] *For in a single hour all this wealth has been laid waste." And all shipmasters and seafaring men, sailors and all whose trade is on the sea, stood far off* [18] *and cried out as they saw the smoke of her burning, "What city was like the great city?"* [19] *And they threw dust on their heads as they wept and mourned, crying out, "Alas, alas, for the great city where all who had ships at sea grew rich by her wealth! For in a single hour she has been laid waste.* [20] *Rejoice over her, O heaven, and you saints and apostles and prophets, for God has given judgment for you against her!"* [21] *Then a mighty angel took up a stone like a great millstone and threw it into the sea, saying, "So will Babylon the great city be thrown down with violence, and will be found no more;* [22] *and the sound of harpists and musicians, of flute*

players and trumpeters, will be heard in you no more, and a craftsman of any craft will be found in you no more, and the sound of the mill will be heard in you no more, ²³ and the light of a lamp will shine in you no more, and the voice of bridegroom and bride will be heard in you no more, for your merchants were the great ones of the earth, and all nations were deceived by your sorcery. ²⁴ And in her was found the blood of prophets and of saints, and of all who have been slain on earth."

While the world is agonizing over the fall of this city with its worldwide influence and economic enticements, the saints are not mourning. *Rejoice over her, O heaven, and you saints and apostles and prophets, for God has given judgment for you against her!"* That which has fallen is the persecutor of God's people.

We have not quite brought the Tribulation to its close. That we will do in the next chapter.

> O Lord, how we long to be free from the pain and futility of this life. How we wait for righteousness to rule. Teach us to detach ourselves from the base desires of this life that lure us away from complete devotion to you. Teach us to put our hope in you rather than in the rewards of this world, a world that is destined to perish. Amen

Anticipating the Tribulation

When we see the world we know beginning to unravel, it can be unsettling. Even as Christians, we have found our place in the world, and change seems traumatic. We see these signs escalating, and this points us toward the climax. We might be uneasy about the way things are going, and we might even be apprehensive about the climax. For this reason Jesus said, ". . . but see to it that you are not alarmed. Such things must happen . . ."* This is a significant statement of comfort for us. What does a child do when he is afraid? He runs to his parents for security. He doesn't know what the parent will do about the situation, but he is confident he will be secure in his parent's arms. And so we should run to Him who has planned all these happenings, knowing they are ultimately and eternally for our benefit. As Luke narrates later in this discourse, Jesus said,

Luke 21:28 (ESV)
²⁸ Now when these things begin to take place, straighten up and raise your heads, because your redemption is drawing near."

The child trusts his parent. The sheep trust their shepherd. His instruction to not be alarmed comforts us because we know we can trust ourselves into his care. Who else would you trust in that time?

We have a type of this heavenly rescue in the coming of Moses to free the Israelites from Egyptian slavery. When he came, the Hebrews' suffering inflated for a time. Persecution increased. They asked Moses to leave. But the final outcome was a great blessing for them. They had to learn to trust in the God of Moses, the great Yahweh. They had to throw off all their acquired allegiances to Egyptian gods.

Can God save His people in the midst of tribulation?

> *Psalm 5:10-12 (NASB)*
> *[10] Hold them guilty, O God; By their own devices let them fall! In the multitude of their transgressions thrust them out, For they are rebellious against You. [11] But let all who take refuge in You be glad, Let them ever sing for joy; And may You shelter them, That those who love Your name may exult in You. [12] For it is You who blesses the righteous man, O LORD, You surround him with favor as with a shield.*

What does it mean for God to save us? It does not always mean that He will shelter us from hardship or tribulation, as any faithful believer can attest to. Refer again to Jesus' words of comfort to the saints in the church of Smyrna who were beginning to suffer persecution.

> *Revelation 2:10 (ESV)*
> *[10] Do not fear what you are about to suffer. Behold, the devil is about to throw some of you into prison, that you may be tested, and for ten days you will have tribulation. Be faithful unto death, and I will give you the crown of life.*

Jesus said the same thing in the Olivet Discourse:

> *Matthew 24:9,13 (RSV)*
> *[9] "Then they will deliver you up to tribulation, and put you to death; and you will be hated by all nations for my name's sake. , , , [13] But he who endures to the end will be saved.*

This clearly does not refer to the hedge of protection from persecution that many claim, since these verses warn that many will be put to death during that time. So what comfort do we receive from these verses? Let me ask this. In your heart, what is your greatest fear, should you face such tribulation? I don't know about you, but I know what lurks in my thoughts. Sure, I have thought about the hardship, the possible pain, the fear. But the thing that looms larger than anything else is the concern that I might not stand firm; that I might crumble under the crushing fear I would experience. I don't want to be a coward, but like most of us, it is hard to know my endurance limits in a situation like that. My greatest fear is that I might be tempted beyond what I am able to bear, and deny my Savior. Therefore these verses encourage me to stand firm, knowing that my salvation is secure, and my reward is made great by my faithfulness. After all, did God not promise . . .

1 Corinthians 10:13 (NASB)
[13] No temptation has overtaken you but such as is common to man; and God is faithful, who will not allow you to be tempted beyond what you are able, but with the temptation will provide the way of escape also, so that you will be able to endure it.

Our greatest earthly need is not to avoid tribulation, but to remain faithful in the face of it. God's greatest promise is not to shelter us from trouble, but to sustain us. You see, this verse from 1 Corinthians is not saying that God will lighten your tribulation to be less than your tolerance level. Rather that during hardship He will increase His grace to you so that you can withstand it. Furthermore, we are assured that, while we may experience persecution at the hands of the antichristian world, we are not targets of the punishment of God's wrath when He brings the evil world to its destruction.

Isaiah 26:19-21 (RSV)
[19] Thy dead shall live, their bodies shall rise. O dwellers in the dust, awake and sing for joy! For thy dew is a dew of light, and on the land of the shades thou wilt let it fall. [20] Come, my people, enter your chambers, and shut your doors behind you; hide yourselves for a little while until the wrath is past. [21] For behold, the LORD is coming forth out of his place to punish the inhabitants of the earth for their iniquity, and the earth will disclose the blood shed upon her, and will no more cover her slain.

God will keep His own, whether by protection from tribulation or through the protection of death. No one can rob the soul of the faithful, and none can snatch the soul of those who have faithfully departed this life. Therefore we joyfully repeat . . .

Luke 21:28 (ESV)
[28] Now when these things begin to take place, straighten up and raise your heads, because your redemption is drawing near."

What a great perspective to have. This is the attitude of one who knows his citizenship is in heaven, and who has completely placed his life and soul under the Lordship of Jesus. His earthly world may crumble, but he has a heavenly vision. *Be of good cheer. I have overcome the world. (John 16:33)* This pilgrim mentality is a perspective that all of us are called to; one we can reach if we so commit and dedicate our lives.

> Lord, we do not look forward to hardship. Perhaps ours will be small, but perhaps not. We understand that one day there will be great tribulation on earth, not equaled in history. We know that you did not destine us for your punishing wrath, so somehow you will keep us faithful. We do not know all your ways, but teach us to simply live in trust. May we live our lives, not focused on the tribulation, but on our redemption we have in your son. This tribulation makes us specially thankful for him. Thank you for Jesus. Thank you, Jesus. Amen

18
THE RETURN OF CHRIST

Chapter 7 of this book brought the atoning work of Jesus into focus from the Old Testament prophetic scriptures. We saw the centrality of God's plan of redemption in all of scripture. We discussed how the foundation of faith in a coming Messiah was primarily through prophetic foretelling. We discussed how prophecy was proclaimed not only by the words and pen of the prophets, but also through symbolic worship practices such as animal sacrifice and Passover, and through situational lessons such as the near-sacrifice of Isaac and in the experience of Jonah. All of this led us to the cross. Atonement was made reality by the substitutionary sacrifice of Jesus on the cross, in our stead. Atonement is the first primary step of redemption, but not the end of it. The final step will be realized at his return.

> *Hebrews 9:27-28 (ESV)*
> *^{27} And just as it is appointed for man to die once, and after that comes judgment, ^{28} so Christ, having been offered once to bear the sins of many, will appear a second time, not to deal with sin but to save those who are eagerly waiting for him.*

In Chapter 1 we made an appeal to Christians to develop a yearning for Christ's return. We who rejoice over his first coming, and the atoning work of the cross, should also joyfully anticipate his return. That frame of mind should be instinctive if we have the right relationship with him. In this section we will investigate particular aspects of his return, and of that yearning we are called to hold.

The Purpose of His Return

Why will there be a second coming of Jesus Christ? To answer we must seek to understand the intention of God. To appreciate the eternal objective we have to put on our wide-angle vision. That ultimate purpose sweeps through the biblical text, and both encompasses and transcends all of our historical experience. It is visualized in creation. It is the consistent motive that is reflected in the providence of His sustaining, benevolent oversight. That purpose literally dominates the New Testament theological landscape. Most importantly for you and me, it is the divine goal that will secure our eternal destiny. It is this intention of God that gives us our purpose and our significance.

This purpose has the greatest priority in the teachings of Jesus, as presented in the four gospel accounts. Its centrality is carried on into Acts, and the letters. It is at center stage in Revelation. We are not left to wonder what that divine intention is.

That overriding intention and purpose is embodied in the terms *Kingdom of God* and *Kingdom of heaven*. (The two terms have identical meaning. Matthew preferred the latter term. The other writers exclusively used the former one.) Kingdom terminology is familiar to most Christians, but for many, the kingdom concept remains either vague, or too restrictive in one's application. So basic is the kingdom to God's purpose in prophecy that we need to briefly discuss it in a general sense.

Jesus' Return will Lead the Kingdom of God to Fulfillment
Jesus taught extensively on the kingdom. Many of his parables are introduced by the phrase, *The kingdom of heaven is like . . .* In teaching the disciples to pray, he told them their first priority was to petition, *Thy kingdom come, Thy will be done on earth as it is in heaven.* His teaching ministry was characterized like this:

Matthew 4:23 (NASB)
23 Jesus was going throughout all Galilee, teaching in their synagogues and proclaiming the gospel of the kingdom, and healing every kind of disease and every kind of sickness among the people.

Luke 4:43 (ESV)
43 but he said to them, "I must preach the good news of the kingdom of God to the other towns as well; for I was sent for this purpose."

Luke 16:16 (ESV)
16 "The Law and the Prophets were until John; since then the good news of the kingdom of God is preached, and everyone forces his way into it.

Matthew 24:14 (NASB)
14 "This gospel of the kingdom shall be preached in the whole world as a testimony to all the nations, and then the end will come.

What is the Kingdom of God? Let's begin by asking an even more general question. What does it mean for a king to have a kingdom? He must have sovereign rule over a certain territory. In our western world experience, the rule of a dictator or king is not so vivid. In the Holy Land of early New Testament times, the concept was very well understood. The king was not subject to any one or any law. His rule was absolute. The kingdom of God is where He rules.

OK, so where does God rule? There is the general sense of His omnipotent sovereignty over the whole creation. However, in creating men in His own image, He gave them free choice. In this, He temporarily limited His sovereign oversight in the hearts of unbelieving people. Thus it is said that Satan is the *god of this age* and *the prince of this world*. This present age has been called the 'church age' because in this age the true church is the kingdom on earth. Initiation into faith includes an acceptance of the lordship of Jesus Christ in one's life. His lordship is synonymous with his being sovereign in that person's life. That sovereignty identifies that life as kingdom territory. Thus a Christian is a part of the kingdom, even as he lives in this world, about which Jesus said:

John 18:36 (NASB)
36 Jesus answered, "My kingdom is not of this world. If My kingdom were of this world, then My servants would be fighting so that I would not be handed over to the Jews; but as it is, My kingdom is not of this realm."

As Christians, we are aliens in enemy territory, journeying in this present world, but having our citizenship in heaven. The concept of *the kingdom of God* came to a climactic crescendo when Jesus was revealed at his first advent, but not to complete fulfillment. During his earthly walk, Jesus introduced the kingdom as that realm of people who would give him sovereign lordship in their hearts. He told Pontius Pilate that his kingdom was *not of this world*, else his followers would have fought for it. So from the gospels we have come to see the kingdom as spiritual, not political.

However in the last days, both Old and New Testament prophecies paint a different picture of the kingdom. In these prophetic scriptures the kingdom is spoken of as a political entity as well as spiritual and personal. In fact, as the end approaches, the distinction between spiritual and political seems to blur.

At the present time, the kingdom on earth is restricted to those who adequately embrace Christ as Sovereign Lord. They abide in faith, in hope and in love. This does not mean that He is impotent over those people who do not voluntarily call Him Lord. He simply has not chosen to enforce His rightful rule over all creation yet, but waits for a time of His own choosing. That day is coming. It is called in scripture, *the day of the Lord*. But for now, *the kingdom of heaven is within you*. Now it is spiritual and limited. A time will come when it will be political as well as spiritual, and will be all-encompassing. Therefore, the *kingdom of God* views both a present, personal God-sovereignty, and a future, universal divine sovereignty.

Some Old Testament passages reveal the promise of a kingdom in its enlarged sense.

> *Daniel 2:44 (NASB)*
> *⁴⁴ "In the days of those kings the God of heaven will set up a kingdom which will never be destroyed, and that kingdom will not be left for another people; it will crush and put an end to all these kingdoms, but it will itself endure forever.*

> *Psalm 145:13 (NASB)*
> *¹³ Your kingdom is an everlasting kingdom, And Your dominion endures throughout all generations.*

> *Daniel 7:13-14 (NASB)*
> *¹³ "I kept looking in the night visions, And behold, with the clouds of heaven One like a Son of Man was coming, And He came up to the Ancient of Days And was presented before Him. ¹⁴ "And to Him was given dominion, Glory and a kingdom, That all the peoples, nations and men of every language Might serve Him. His dominion is an everlasting dominion Which will not pass away; And His kingdom is one Which will not be destroyed.*

The New Testament continues that same theme. Mary was foretold:

> *Luke 1:31-33 (ESV)*
> *³¹ And behold, you will conceive in your womb and bear a son, and you shall call his name Jesus. ³² He will be great and will be called the Son of the Most High. And the Lord God will give to him the throne of his father David, ³³ and he will reign over the house of Jacob forever, and of his kingdom there will be no end."*

> *Revelation 11:15 (ESV)*
> *¹⁵ Then the seventh angel blew his trumpet, and there were loud voices in heaven, saying, "The kingdom of the world has become the kingdom of our Lord and of his Christ, and he shall reign forever and ever."*

Throughout all of the prophetic sequence, both the realm of personal kingdom indwelling, and the realm of the fulfilled universal kingdom, the issue is this: 'Who is sovereign? Who rules? Who is Lord?' There are those who teach that Jesus preached more than one gospel. They say that the gospel of the kingdom is one gospel, and the gospel of salvation is another gospel. This teaching is based on a very incomplete understanding of what salvation is about. Paul had strong words for those who teach such a message:

Galatians 1:6-8 (NASB)
⁶ I am amazed that you are so quickly deserting Him who called you by the grace of Christ, for a different gospel; ⁷ which is really not another; only there are some who are disturbing you and want to distort the gospel of Christ. ⁸ But even if we, or an angel from heaven, should preach to you a gospel contrary to what we have preached to you, he is to be accursed!

There is only one gospel, and no other. When Jesus preached the gospel of the kingdom, he was preaching the gospel of eternal salvation. To enter into salvation is to enter into the kingdom of God. Have you made Jesus the sovereign in your life? Salvation without acknowledging his lordship is not scriptural.

Jesus will return for the fundamental purpose of establishing the Kingdom of God as universal reality—*on earth as it is in heaven*. Prior to his return, the kingdom will have existed in the hearts of faithful people. At his second advent, the kingdom will be established as a political entity encompassing the whole earth.

Ephesians 1:9-12 (ESV)
⁹ making known to us the mystery of his will, according to his purpose, which he set forth in Christ ¹⁰ as a plan for the fullness of time, to unite all things in him, things in heaven and things on earth. ¹¹ In him we have obtained an inheritance, having been predestined according to the purpose of him who works all things according to the counsel of his will, ¹² so that we who were the first to hope in Christ might be to the praise of his glory.

1 Corinthians 15:23-28 (NASB)
²³ But each in his own order: Christ the first fruits, after that those who are Christ's at His coming, ²⁴ then comes the end, when He hands over the kingdom to the God and Father, when He has abolished all rule and all authority and power. ²⁵ For He must reign until He has put all His enemies under His feet. ²⁶ The last enemy that will be abolished is death. ²⁷ For HE HAS PUT ALL THINGS IN SUBJECTION UNDER HIS FEET. But when He says, "All things are put in subjection," it is evident that He is excepted who put all things in subjection to Him. ²⁸ When all things are subjected to Him, then the Son Himself also will be subjected to the One who subjected all things to Him, so that God may be all in all.

Colossians 1:16-20 (ESV)
¹⁶ For by him all things were created, in heaven and on earth, visible and invisible, whether thrones or dominions or rulers or

authorities—all things were created through him and for him. [17] And he is before all things, and in him all things hold together. [18] And he is the head of the body, the church. He is the beginning, the firstborn from the dead, that in everything he might be preeminent. [19] For in him all the fullness of God was pleased to dwell, [20] and through him to reconcile to himself all things, whether on earth or in heaven, making peace by the blood of his cross.

This Christ is both the beneficiary and the means of the purpose. Paul expressed it thus:

Philippians 2:9-11 (ESV)
[9] Therefore God has highly exalted him and bestowed on him the name that is above every name, [10] so that at the name of Jesus every knee should bow, in heaven and on earth and under the earth, [11] and every tongue confess that Jesus Christ is Lord, to the glory of God the Father.

It includes him receiving this very creation as his inheritance. It is about his bringing all things into unity and equity. It is about the glory of the Father and the Son being unanimously worshipped—yes--worshipped with uninhibited, pure, genuine, undistracted adoration! John's Revelation describes this worship this way.

Revelation 4:11 (ESV)
[11] "Worthy are you, our Lord and God, to receive glory and honor and power, for you created all things, and by your will they existed and were created."

And Paul concludes...

Romans 11:36 (RSV)
[36] For from him and through him and to him are all things. To him be glory for ever. Amen.

In this future time, the purpose of the Creator and the response of the creation will converge. All incongruences will disappear; all injustices will be set right. The appearance of Jesus will be the climactic step toward the accomplishment of the perfect will and desire of God. As far as end-time events, his second coming is the dominant centerpiece of the whole panorama. The most enthralling thing about that for us is that we can play a part in that ultimate euphoric experience, a victorious part. We can be significant in an eternal world.

While kingdom establishment and fulfillment is the overriding and foundational purpose to be fulfilled by Jesus at his return, the plan is multifaceted. The goal of the eternal will is to culminate in a series of events set in motion at Christ's return. There are a number of supporting objectives to be fulfilled. To grasp the many facets is to embrace the ultimate purpose as revealed from the mind of God.

That is, to understand the big picture, we must look at a number of intermediate purposes that combine to bring about the whole. Although I call them intermediate, I mean they are intermediate in scope. These intermediate purposes are all significant, not only in bringing about the ultimate objective, but also as an essential and eternal component of that final and endless goal. So what are the various facets, the intermediate purposes that are served by the second coming of Jesus? With fear and trembling, let us try to identify the major facets.

<u>Jesus' Return will Bring Judgment on Unbelievers</u>
In the Old Testament as well as the New, *the Day of the Lord* is a phrase that occurs several times in prophetic writings. It should send ominous chills upon the enemies of God. It is always associated with a day of reckoning, a day of judgment. It was understood to be a time at the ending of this present age. Here are several miscellaneous references from the Old Testament prophets.

> *Isaiah 2:12-21 (RSV)*
> *[12] For the LORD of hosts has a day against all that is proud and lofty, against all that is lifted up and high; [13] against all the cedars of Lebanon, lofty and lifted up; and against all the oaks of Bashan; [14] against all the high mountains, and against all the lofty hills; [15] against every high tower, and against every fortified wall; [16] against all the ships of Tarshish, and against all the beautiful craft. [17] And the haughtiness of man shall be humbled, and the pride of men shall be brought low; and the LORD alone will be exalted in that day. [18] And the idols shall utterly pass away. [19] And men shall enter the caves of the rocks and the holes of the ground, from before the terror of the LORD, and from the glory of his majesty, when he rises to terrify the earth. [20] In that day men will cast forth their idols of silver and their idols of gold, which they made for themselves to worship, to the moles and to the bats, [21] to enter the caverns of the rocks and the clefts of the cliffs, from before the terror of the LORD, and from the glory of his majesty, when he rises to terrify the earth.*

> *Isaiah 13:9-13 (RSV)*
> *[9] Behold, the day of the LORD comes, cruel, with wrath and fierce anger, to make the earth a desolation and to destroy its sinners from it. [10] For the stars of the heavens and their constellations will not give their light; the sun will be dark at its rising and the moon will not shed its light. [11] I will punish the world for its evil, and the*

wicked for their iniquity; I will put an end to the pride of the arrogant, and lay low the haughtiness of the ruthless. [12] I will make men more rare than fine gold, and mankind than the gold of Ophir. [13] Therefore I will make the heavens tremble, and the earth will be shaken out of its place, at the wrath of the LORD of hosts in the day of his fierce anger.

Isaiah 34:8 (RSV)
[8] For the LORD has a day of vengeance, a year of recompense for the cause of Zion.

Zephaniah 2:1-3 (RSV)
[1] Come together and hold assembly, O shameless nation, [2] before you are driven away like the drifting chaff, before there comes upon you the fierce anger of the LORD, before there comes upon you the day of the wrath of the LORD. [3] Seek the LORD, all you humble of the land, who do his commands; seek righteousness, seek humility; perhaps you may be hidden on the day of the wrath of the LORD.

This time called *the Day of the Lord* appears to refer to a specific occasion in the future when judgment would begin for those alive on earth at the time it occurs. It was thought of as ushering in the general judgment, but its emphasis was on a temporal judgment on sinful living men, cleansing earth for the events to follow. This *Day of the Lord* concept is further heralded by New Testament writers, with the added revelation that it is coupled with the return of Jesus.

Acts 2:19-21 (ESV)
[19] And I will show wonders in the heavens above and signs on the earth below, blood, and fire, and vapor of smoke; [20] the sun shall be turned to darkness and the moon to blood, before the day of the Lord comes, the great and magnificent day. [21] And it shall come to pass that everyone who calls upon the name of the Lord shall be saved.'

1 Thessalonians 4:16, 5:1-3 (NASB)
[16] For the Lord Himself will descend from heaven with a shout, with the voice of the archangel and with the trumpet of God, and the dead in Christ will rise first. . . . [1] Now as to the times and the epochs, brethren, you have no need of anything to be written to you. [2] For you yourselves know full well that the day of the Lord will come just like a thief in the night. [3] While they are saying, "Peace and safety!" then destruction will come upon them suddenly like labor pains upon a woman with child, and they will not escape.

> *2 Thessalonians 2:1-3 (ESV)*
> *[1] Now concerning the coming of our Lord Jesus Christ and our being gathered together to him, we ask you, brothers, [2] not to be quickly shaken in mind or alarmed, either by a spirit or a spoken word, or a letter seeming to be from us, to the effect that the day of the Lord has come. [3] Let no one deceive you in any way. For that day will not come, unless the rebellion comes first, and the man of lawlessness is revealed, the son of destruction,*

> *Revelation 6:12-17 (ESV)*
> *[12] When he opened the sixth seal, I looked, and behold, there was a great earthquake, and the sun became black as sackcloth, the full moon became like blood, [13] and the stars of the sky fell to the earth as the fig tree sheds its winter fruit when shaken by a gale. [14] The sky vanished like a scroll that is being rolled up, and every mountain and island was removed from its place. [15] Then the kings of the earth and the great ones and the generals and the rich and the powerful, and everyone, slave and free, hid themselves in the caves and among the rocks of the mountains, [16] calling to the mountains and rocks, "Fall on us and hide us from the face of him who is seated on the throne, and from the wrath of the Lamb, [17] for the great day of their wrath has come, and who can stand?"*

So we see in the second coming of Christ a purging, a smelting, a purifying of the earth. This cleansing will come at the expense of men's comfort and self-security. Enemies of God will be destroyed or brought into submission. Details of this are given in several scriptural prophecies, and will be discussed later. For now, it is important we understand that judgment of sin will be a facet of his return. Now before we become overcome with apprehension, let us look into the next facet or purpose for his coming.

<u>Jesus' Return will Destroy the Kingdom of Satan</u>
The following verses are given to demonstrate this purpose for his return. The work of the Devil is not only personal, but also global and political, as we will clearly learn in those later chapters.

> **Ephesians 6:12 (ESV)**
> *[12] For we do not wrestle against flesh and blood, but against the rulers, against the authorities, against the cosmic powers over this present darkness, against the spiritual forces of evil in the heavenly places.*

> *Romans 8:37-39 (KJV)*
> *[37] Nay, in all these things we are more than conquerors through him that loved us. [38] For I am persuaded, that neither death, nor life, nor angels, nor principalities, nor powers, nor things present, nor things*

to come, [39] Nor height, nor depth, nor any other creature, shall be able to separate us from the love of God, which is in Christ Jesus our Lord.

In the end, the enemies of God will not only be individuals who have lived sinful and unrepentant lives. Whole nations will be led by Satanic conspiracy to rise up against Jesus Christ and his cause. The battle is portrayed as both spiritual and political.

Revelation 18:2-6 (ESV)
[2] And he called out with a mighty voice, "Fallen, fallen is Babylon the great! She has become a dwelling place for demons, a haunt for every unclean spirit, a haunt for every unclean bird, a haunt for every unclean and detestable beast. [3] For all nations have drunk the wine of the passion of her sexual immorality, and the kings of the earth have committed immorality with her, and the merchants of the earth have grown rich from the power of her luxurious living." [4] Then I heard another voice from heaven saying, "Come out of her, my people, lest you take part in her sins, lest you share in her plagues; [5] for her sins are heaped high as heaven, and God has remembered her iniquities. [6] Pay her back as she herself has paid back others, and repay her double for her deeds; mix a double portion for her in the cup she mixed.

Revelation 19:19-21 (ESV)
[19] And I saw the beast and the kings of the earth with their armies gathered to make war against him who was sitting on the horse and against his army. [20] And the beast was captured, and with it the false prophet who in its presence had done the signs by which he deceived those who had received the mark of the beast and those who worshiped its image. These two were thrown alive into the lake of fire that burns with sulfur. [21] And the rest were slain by the sword that came from the mouth of him who was sitting on the horse, and all the birds were gorged with their flesh.

Revelation 11:16-18 (ESV)
[16] And the twenty-four elders who sit on their thrones before God fell on their faces and worshiped God, [17] saying, "We give thanks to you, Lord God Almighty, who is and who was, for you have taken your great power and begun to reign. [18] The nations raged, but your wrath came, and the time for the dead to be judged, and for rewarding your servants, the prophets and saints, and those who fear your name, both small and great, and for destroying the destroyers of the earth."

These scriptures summarize the satanic kingdom that we discussed in chapter 11. There we traced the prophetic picture of Satan's schemes in the geo-political arena.

Jesus' Return will Usher in Salvation
In the scripture from I Thessalonians that I quoted earlier, I left some verses out, as indicated, since they did not pertain to judgment. Here is the same passage expanded with a lead-in of previous verses and with intermediate and trailing verses included:

1 Thessalonians 4:13-5:11 (NASB)
[13] But we do not want you to be uninformed, brethren, about those who are asleep, so that you will not grieve as do the rest who have no hope. [14] For if we believe that Jesus died and rose again, even so God will bring with Him those who have fallen asleep in Jesus. [15] For this we say to you by the word of the Lord, that we who are alive and remain until the coming of the Lord, will not precede those who have fallen asleep. [16] For the Lord Himself will descend from heaven with a shout, with the voice of the archangel and with the trumpet of God, and the dead in Christ will rise first. [17] Then we who are alive and remain will be caught up together with them in the clouds to meet the Lord in the air, and so we shall always be with the Lord. [18] Therefore comfort one another with these words. [1] Now as to the times and the epochs, brethren, you have no need of anything to be written to you. [2] For you yourselves know full well that the day of the Lord will come just like a thief in the night. [3] While they are saying, "Peace and safety!" then destruction will come upon them suddenly like labor pains upon a woman with child, and they will not escape. [4] But you, brethren, are not in darkness, that the day would overtake you like a thief; [5] for you are all sons of light and sons of day. We are not of night nor of darkness; [6] so then let us not sleep as others do, but let us be alert and sober. [7] For those who sleep do their sleeping at night, and those who get drunk get drunk at night. [8] But since we are of the day, let us be sober, having put on the breastplate of faith and love, and as a helmet, the hope of salvation. [9] For God has not destined us for wrath, but for obtaining salvation through our Lord Jesus Christ, [10] who died for us, so that whether we are awake or asleep, we will live together with Him. [11] Therefore encourage one another and build up one another, just as you also are doing.

Now we see the other side of this *Day of the Lord*. For the enemies of God, that day will be a dreaded event, but for the children of God . . . *God did not appoint us to suffer wrath but to receive salvation through our Lord Jesus Christ.* He will come as our Savior on that day. Again we read:

Hebrews 9:27-28 (ESV)
²⁷ And just as it is appointed for man to die once, and after that comes judgment, ²⁸ so Christ, having been offered once to bear the sins of many, will appear a second time, not to deal with sin but to save those who are eagerly waiting for him.

2 Thessalonians 1:6-10 (ESV)
⁶ since indeed God considers it just to repay with affliction those who afflict you, ⁷ and to grant relief to you who are afflicted as well as to us, when the Lord Jesus is revealed from heaven with his mighty angels ⁸ in flaming fire, inflicting vengeance on those who do not know God and on those who do not obey the gospel of our Lord Jesus. ⁹ They will suffer the punishment of eternal destruction, away from the presence of the Lord and from the glory of his might, ¹⁰ when he comes on that day to be glorified in his saints, and to be marveled at among all who have believed, because our testimony to you was believed.

From our self-oriented viewpoint, this ushering in of salvation is the most important aspect of Christ's return. However we have stated that the foundational purpose is the establishment of His kingdom, and that this is primarily about Him and His will. How is the salvation aspect viewed in the Lord's perspective? The amazing fact that we discover as we look at scripture is that this is a major priority with Him too. Remember the prayer of Jesus just before his arrest and passion.

John 17:24-26 (NASB)
²⁴ "Father, I desire that they also, whom You have given Me, be with Me where I am, so that they may see My glory which You have given Me, for You loved Me before the foundation of the world. ²⁵ "O righteous Father, although the world has not known You, yet I have known You; and these have known that You sent Me; ²⁶ and I have made Your name known to them, and will make it known, so that the love with which You loved Me may be in them, and I in them."

Shortly afterwards as the disciples joined him in his last Passover meal, he laid out a pledge of fidelity and anticipation for their reuniting.

Matthew 26:29 (NASB)
²⁹ "But I say to you, I will not drink of this fruit of the vine from now on until that day when I drink it new with you in My Father's kingdom."

This is more than accomplishing a plan, or scheme. It is beyond attaining an objective or goal. Here Jesus bares his heart's longing. He shows us that he desires our companionship and love and friendship. Can you fathom that? The Creator of the universe has a deep yearning, a burning passion, to enjoy a close relationship with you and me! Can any thought be more astonishing? To express this in terms we can take in, the Bible uses the analogy of a family relationship to express this closeness.

John 1:12 (NASB)
¹² But as many as received Him, to them He gave the right to become children of God, even to those who believe in His name,

1 John 3:1 (ESV)
¹ See what kind of love the Father has given to us, that we should be called children of God; and so we are. The reason why the world does not know us is that it did not know him.

But even that does not express the extent of his passionate love for us. He uses an even more endearing, engaging metaphor to more fully reveal his heart-felt love.

John 14:2-3 (NASB)
² "In My Father's house are many dwelling places; if it were not so, I would have told you; for I go to prepare a place for you. ³ "If I go and prepare a place for you, I will come again and receive you to Myself, that where I am, there you may be also.

We have already discussed this reference to a Jewish marriage custom. Do you see it? He is, so to speak, proposing marriage to us. That is how strong his passion for us is. The day of the wedding itself is described in Revelation...

Revelation 19:7-9 (ESV)
⁷ Let us rejoice and exult and give him the glory, for the marriage of the Lamb has come, and his Bride has made herself ready; ⁸ it was granted her to clothe herself with fine linen, bright and pure"— for the fine linen is the righteous deeds of the saints. ⁹ And the angel said to me, "Write this: Blessed are those who are invited to the marriage supper of the Lamb." And he said to me, "These are the true words of God."

The salvation that is brought to us by the return of Christ describes two types of rescue. First there is the redemption of our bodies from the spiritual ravages of a sin-torn world. We will be rescued from the temptation and from the penalty of our sin. All our earthly lives we have been plagued with the realization that we were hypocrites. While we professed the newness of life, we found ourselves regularly battling the desires of the flesh. This rescue will bring precious relief and resolution to this struggle, and fit us for eternity with our holy Savior.

Romans 8:19-24 (RSV)
[19] *For the creation waits with eager longing for the revealing of the sons of God;* [20] *for the creation was subjected to futility, not of its own will but by the will of him who subjected it in hope;* [21] *because the creation itself will be set free from its bondage to decay and obtain the glorious liberty of the children of God.* [22] *We know that the whole creation has been groaning in travail together until now;* [23] *and not only the creation, but we ourselves, who have the first fruits of the Spirit, groan inwardly as we wait for adoption as sons, the redemption of our bodies.* [24] *For in this hope we were saved. Now hope that is seen is not hope. For who hopes for what he sees?*

2 Timothy 4:8 (ESV)
[8] *Henceforth there is laid up for me the crown of righteousness, which the Lord, the righteous judge, will award to me on that Day, and not only to me but also to all who have loved his appearing.*

Titus 2:11-14 (RSV)
[11] *For the grace of God has appeared for the salvation of all men,* [12] *training us to renounce irreligion and worldly passions, and to live sober, upright, and godly lives in this world,* [13] *awaiting our blessed hope, the appearing of the glory of our great God and Savior Jesus Christ,* [14] *who gave himself for us to redeem us from all iniquity and to purify for himself a people of his own who are zealous for good deeds.*

1 Corinthians 1:7-9 (NASB)
[7] *so that you are not lacking in any gift, awaiting eagerly the revelation of our Lord Jesus Christ,* [8] *who will also confirm you to the end, blameless in the day of our Lord Jesus Christ.* [9] *God is faithful, through whom you were called into fellowship with His Son, Jesus Christ our Lord.*

Second, we see in the return of Jesus the timely rescue of the living saints not only from their own sinful nature, but also from a world committed to their destruction. We are talking of a time when believers in Jesus Christ will be under severe persecution by the prevailing world leaders. The people of God will be under great, direct, physical attack.

Matthew 24:12-14, 21-22, 29-31 (NASB)
[12] *"Because lawlessness is increased, most people's love will grow cold.* [13] *"But the one who endures to the end, he will be saved.* [14] *"This gospel of the kingdom shall be preached in the whole world as a testimony to all the nations, and then the end will come. . . .* [21] *"For then there will be a great tribulation, such as has not occurred*

> *since the beginning of the world until now, nor ever will.* ²² *"Unless those days had been cut short, no life would have been saved; but for the sake of the elect those days will be cut short. . . .* ²⁹ *"But immediately after the tribulation of those days THE SUN WILL BE DARKENED, AND THE MOON WILL NOT GIVE ITS LIGHT, AND THE STARS WILL FALL from the sky, and the powers of the heavens will be shaken.* ³⁰ *"And then the sign of the Son of Man will appear in the sky, and then all the tribes of the earth will mourn, and they will see the SON OF MAN COMING ON THE CLOUDS OF THE SKY with power and great glory.* ³¹ *"And He will send forth His angels with A GREAT TRUMPET and THEY WILL GATHER TOGETHER His elect from the four winds, from one end of the sky to the other.*

Here we simply seek to understand that redemption of the saints is a key part of the reason for Christ's return. For us it is paramount. It is everything!!

<u>Jesus' Return will Confirm Israel in Messianic Belief</u>
Now the sparks begin to fly. The fate and role of Israel in the last days is one of the key issues that divides premillennial interpreters, and shapes much of the rest of their understanding of end-time events. Once more, let me postpone a more thorough analysis of scriptures about end-time Israel until Chapters 21 through 23. Rather, let us simply understand that part of the purpose in Christ's return is in the establishing of Israel in belief. Let us further understand this Israel is the political, historical, literal nation of people we call the Jews.

In the following scripture Paul has just spent considerable time lamenting the unbelief of his fellow countrymen, referred to as *their transgression*. It is unmistakable that he has been talking of the literal nation of Israel.

> *Romans 11:11-14, 26-32 (RSV)*
> ¹¹ *So I ask, have they stumbled so as to fall? By no means! But through their trespass salvation has come to the Gentiles, so as to make Israel jealous.* ¹² *Now if their trespass means riches for the world, and if their failure means riches for the Gentiles, how much more will their full inclusion mean!* ¹³ *Now I am speaking to you Gentiles. Inasmuch then as I am an apostle to the Gentiles, I magnify my ministry* ¹⁴ *in order to make my fellow Jews jealous, and thus save some of them. . . .* ²⁶ *and so all Israel will be saved; as it is written, "The Deliverer will come from Zion, he will banish ungodliness from Jacob";* ²⁷ *"and this will be my covenant with them when I take away their sins."* ²⁸ *As regards the gospel they are enemies of God, for your sake; but as regards election they are beloved for the sake of their forefathers.* ²⁹ *For the gifts and the call*

of God are irrevocable. ³⁰ Just as you were once disobedient to God but now have received mercy because of their disobedience, ³¹ so they have now been disobedient in order that by the mercy shown to you they also may receive mercy. ³² For God has consigned all men to disobedience, that he may have mercy upon all.

Paul did not invent these thoughts. They were reflective of several Old Testament scriptures literally interpreted, such as the following:

Isaiah 34:8 (RSV)
⁸ For the LORD has a day of vengeance, a year of recompense for the cause of Zion.

Zechariah 12:3, 8-10 (RSV)
³ On that day I will make Jerusalem a heavy stone for all the peoples; all who lift it shall grievously hurt themselves. And all the nations of the earth will come together against it. . . . ⁸ On that day the LORD will put a shield about the inhabitants of Jerusalem so that the feeblest among them on that day shall be like David, and the house of David shall be like God, like the angel of the LORD, at their head. ⁹ And on that day I will seek to destroy all the nations that come against Jerusalem. ¹⁰ "And I will pour out on the house of David and the inhabitants of Jerusalem a spirit of compassion and supplication, so that, when they look on him whom they have pierced, they shall mourn for him, as one mourns for an only child, and weep bitterly over him, as one weeps over a first-born.

Micah 4:6-7 (NASB)
⁶ "In that day," declares the LORD, "I will assemble the lame And gather the outcasts, Even those whom I have afflicted. ⁷ "I will make the lame a remnant And the outcasts a strong nation, And the LORD will reign over them in Mount Zion From now on and forever.

The *exiles* and those he has *brought to grief* and those under his rule in *Mount Zion* refer to the people of the nation of Israel. With regard to whether this refers to Israel, or is figuratively used for people in general today, there is little ambiguity in these and other prophecies. Those who wish to remove Israel from the scene of the last days create their own ambiguity.

To summarize, these various topics are not separate purposes, but parts of one grand purpose—fulfillment of the Kingdom of God. This list of the various aspects or facets is not exhaustive, but perhaps will engender an appreciation of the scope of that purpose. It is the purpose of God, and we are called to adopt it as our purpose too. The fulfillment of this purpose is set in motion at Christ's second coming.

A Description of Christ's Second Coming

As we read of Jesus preparing for his ascension in the opening of the book of Acts, we find:

> *Acts 1:6-11 (ESV)*
> *⁶ So when they had come together, they asked him, "Lord, will you at this time restore the kingdom to Israel?" ⁷ He said to them, "It is not for you to know times or seasons that the Father has fixed by his own authority. ⁸ But you will receive power when the Holy Spirit has come upon you, and you will be my witnesses in Jerusalem and in all Judea and Samaria, and to the end of the earth." ⁹ And when he had said these things, as they were looking on, he was lifted up, and a cloud took him out of their sight. ¹⁰ And while they were gazing into heaven as he went, behold, two men stood by them in white robes, ¹¹ and said, "Men of Galilee, why do you stand looking into heaven? This Jesus, who was taken up from you into heaven, will come in the same way as you saw him go into heaven."*

Thus, the early church had a mission and a motive. The mission-- evangelism. The impetus behind this evangelism, and indeed behind life itself, was the future hope they placed in the return of their Lord. This was their motivation. They had heard many predictions by Jesus about his return, but did not understand until he was taken from them. In his Olivet Discourse, he had said . . .

> *Matthew 24:23-30 (NASB)*
> *²³ "Then if anyone says to you, 'Behold, here is the Christ,' or 'There He is,' do not believe him. ²⁴ "For false Christs and false prophets will arise and will show great signs and wonders, so as to mislead, if possible, even the elect. ²⁵ "Behold, I have told you in advance. ²⁶ "So if they say to you, 'Behold, He is in the wilderness,' do not go out, or, 'Behold, He is in the inner rooms,' do not believe them. ²⁷ "For just as the lightning comes from the east and flashes even to the west, so will the coming of the Son of Man be. ²⁸ "Wherever the corpse is, there the vultures will gather. ²⁹ "But immediately after the tribulation of those days THE SUN WILL BE DARKENED, AND THE MOON WILL NOT GIVE ITS LIGHT, AND THE STARS WILL FALL from the sky, and the powers of the heavens will be shaken. ³⁰ "And then the sign of the Son of Man will appear in the sky, and then all the tribes of the earth will mourn, and they will see the SON OF MAN COMING ON THE CLOUDS OF THE SKY with power and great glory.*

Jesus, as he had stood before the Sanhedrin, had answered his accusers...

> *Matthew 26:64 (NASB)*
> *⁶⁴ Jesus said to him, "You have said it yourself; nevertheless I tell you, hereafter you will see THE SON OF MAN SITTING AT THE RIGHT HAND OF POWER, and COMING ON THE CLOUDS OF HEAVEN."*

Later John wrote...

> *Revelation 1:5-7 (ESV)*
> *⁵ . . . To him who loves us and has freed us from our sins by his blood ⁶ and made us a kingdom, priests to his God and Father, to him be glory and dominion forever and ever. Amen. ⁷ Behold, he is coming with the clouds, and every eye will see him, even those who pierced him, and all tribes of the earth will wail on account of him. Even so. Amen.*

This became a core part of the teaching of the early church. The apostles taught it to their audiences, and called men to come to grips with the fact that there would someday be a day of reckoning. For example, in his first sermon on the day of Pentecost, Peter spoke to the people of Jerusalem, saying . . .

> *Acts 3:19-21 (ESV)*
> *¹⁹ Repent therefore, and turn back, that your sins may be blotted out, ²⁰ that times of refreshing may come from the presence of the Lord, and that he may send the Christ appointed for you, Jesus, ²¹ whom heaven must receive until the time for restoring all the things about which God spoke by the mouth of his holy prophets long ago.*

The accounts are consistent. When Jesus comes, his arrival will be in the sky, in the clouds. It will be visible to all men. It will be sudden in occurrence and global in scale. It will be with great power and glory. Now this was significant because many false teachings apparently circulated during the days of the early church about the return of Christ. Some said he would come secretly, or that he had already come.

> *2 Thessalonians 2:1-2 (ESV)*
> *¹ Now concerning the coming of our Lord Jesus Christ and our being gathered together to him, we ask you, brothers, ² not to be quickly shaken in mind or alarmed, either by a spirit or a spoken word, or a letter seeming to be from us, to the effect that the day of the Lord has come.*

Many such teachings are now very popular and dominate the bookstores. Many people I have discussed this topic with have a fear that they will not recognize Jesus at his second coming, like many failed to recognize him at his first coming. That will not be an issue. Everyone, friend and foe will recognize him. More importantly, he will recognize us.

His Glorious Appearing

The second coming of Jesus Christ will be very different from his first coming. Instead of being born in obscurity, he will return in a way consistent with the original Jewish perception of Messiah's coming. He will come in great power and glory. He will come to redeem his cherished church from the fallen world, and to rescue the earth from the power of Satan. He will come in vengeance against his enemies. He will come in judgment. John was shown a vision of it, and he relates it to us in Revelation 19.

> *Revelation 19:11-16 (ESV)*
> *[11] Then I saw heaven opened, and behold, a white horse! The one sitting on it is called Faithful and True, and in righteousness he judges and makes war. [12] His eyes are like a flame of fire, and on his head are many diadems, and he has a name written that no one knows but himself. [13] He is clothed in a robe dipped in blood, and the name by which he is called is The Word of God. [14] And the armies of heaven, arrayed in fine linen, white and pure, were following him on white horses. [15] From his mouth comes a sharp sword with which to strike down the nations, and he will rule them with a rod of iron. He will tread the winepress of the fury of the wrath of God the Almighty. [16] On his robe and on his thigh he has a name written, King of kings and Lord of lords.*

His robe is dipped in blood, a symbol of destruction of unbelieving people. The 'armies of heaven arrayed in white linen' is a reference to this passage a few verses earlier, and refers to the saints taken up at his return.

> *Revelation 19:7-8 (ESV)*
> *[7] Let us rejoice and exult and give him the glory, for the marriage of the Lamb has come, and his Bride has made herself ready; [8] it was granted her to clothe herself with fine linen, bright and pure"— for the fine linen is the righteous deeds of the saints.*

The sharp two-edged sword of his mouth is the power of his command to separate and destroy. Just as he had created all things by the power of his command, now he will destroy every unredeemed thing by that same power.

The Unique Message of Jerusalem's East Gate

If you visit Jerusalem today, you will likely be taken to a spectacular overlook of the city on the Mount of Olives. The Mount of Olives lies immediately to the east of Jerusalem, and between them, running from north to south, is the Kidron River valley. The well-known Garden of Gethsemane is located on the Mount of Olives, near the city. Travelers to Jerusalem from the east must make a steep ascent from Jericho on the east side of the mountain which lies at 1300 feet below sea level, to the mountain crest which reaches nearly 2700 feet, a rise of about three-fourths of a mile. Then they must descend down its westward face to the Kidron valley and back up the opposite bank a short distance to the city's eastern wall. One would have to be pretty physically fit to make this journey.

Looking from the Mount of Olives, you might be intrigued by the gate in the wall in front of you—the East Gate (also called 'the Golden Gate'). It is a most intriguing sight. It is closed off by stonework. It is the only closed gate. It is a double gate, indicating heavy traffic, yet there is no road leading up to it or through it. There is what appears to be a cemetery in front of it on the Kidron's west bank. And you cannot miss the golden dome of the Mosque of Omar (the Dome of the Rock) glistening in the sunlight directly behind it. Every one of these features is significant.

Prophecy about the return of Jesus is not limited to New Testament writings. It is also found in the Old Testament, and it is found not only in sacred scripture, but also in structural and archaeological evidences which speak to us from history. The reason for this attention on the East Gate is that it figures prominently into messianic prophecy. It is the entrance associated with the coming and going of the presence of God (symbolically) or Messiah (literally) into the temple. It is the gate of Jesus' entrance on Palm Sunday in 30 AD. It is his prophesied entrance at his second coming, a prediction that is considered significant by Jews, Christians and Muslims.

In Solomon's day, in Nehemiah's day, and in Jesus' day, the Jewish temple stood on the location where presently the mosque is situated, just inside the East Gate. In those days, the gate was open, and it was a main thoroughfare. The original eastern wall was built by Solomon when he built the first temple. The walls and temple were destroyed in 587 BC by the invading Babylonians, and Jerusalem was captured and its people exiled. Nehemiah returned and rebuilt the city walls in 445 BC, and he mentions the East Gate matter-of-factly:

Nehemiah 3:29 (NASB)
[29] ... *And after him Shemaiah the son of Shecaniah, the keeper of the East Gate, carried out repairs.*

Nehemiah's walls and gates were what existed during the time of Christ. They were destroyed by the Romans in 70 AD. In about the 6th or 7th century AD the Byzantines rebuilt the city walls, and those are what we see today. Around the beginning of the sixteenth century AD, Palestine fell under the control of the Ottoman Empire. These Turkish Muslims were led by Sultan Suleiman who, in 1541, closed up the East Gate and planted a Muslim cemetery in front of it. This condition remains to this day. Although his purpose is not recorded, general assumption is that these actions were taken to prevent the Jewish Messiah from entering that gate, as prophesied. On the western slope of the Mount of Olives, opposite the small Muslim cemetery, is an enormous Jewish cemetery stretching up to the overlook point. It has tombs dating to ancient times, and includes nobility and commoners, prophets, priests and kings. Jewish hopefuls pay high prices today to be buried there so as to be resurrected near the gate of Messiah's entry.

Since Solomon's wall was first built around the temple (including the East Gate) the city has grown. New outer walls expanded its boundaries to the north, south and west. However, the eastern wall is essentially in the same location as the original. Archaeological evidence indicates the present East Gate may be built right over the ruins of the previous one.

God's Glory Departs and Enters Through the East Gate

When Judah fell into idolatry and abandoned the Lord, He brought judgment upon them as he had warned. That judgment came by their being captured and exiled by the Babylonians. About seven years before that invasion occurred, God sent a vision through his prophet Ezekiel depicting God's Glory departing from the temple.

> *Ezekiel 10:18-19 (NASB)*
> *[18] Then the glory of the LORD departed from the threshold of the temple and stood over the cherubim. [19] When the cherubim departed, they lifted their wings and rose up from the earth in my sight with the wheels beside them; and they stood still at the entrance of the east gate of the LORD'S house, and the glory of the God of Israel hovered over them.*

> *Ezekiel 11:22-23 (NASB)*
> *[22] Then the cherubim lifted up their wings with the wheels beside them, and the glory of the God of Israel hovered over them. [23] The glory of the LORD went up from the midst of the city and stood over the mountain which is east of the city.*

When God's glory departed from the temple, it was a short time until disaster came upon them. He had not utterly deserted his people. The punishment was a temporary one, according to the Prophet Jeremiah.

> *Jeremiah 25:11 (NASB)*
> *[11] 'This whole land will be a desolation and a horror, and these nations will serve the king of Babylon seventy years.*

Jeremiah 29:10 (NASB)
[10] *"For thus says the LORD, 'When seventy years have been completed for Babylon, I will visit you and fulfill My good word to you, to bring you back to this place.*

Seven years after the Babylonian invasion, Ezekiel was given another vision. It depicts the return of divine presence and glory, entering through the gate facing east.

Ezekiel 43:1-5 (NASB)
[1] *Then he led me to the gate, the gate facing toward the east;* [2] *and behold, the glory of the God of Israel was coming from the way of the east. And His voice was like the sound of many waters; and the earth shone with His glory.* [3] *And it was like the appearance of the vision which I saw, like the vision which I saw when He came to destroy the city. And the visions were like the vision which I saw by the river Chebar; and I fell on my face.* [4] *And the glory of the LORD came into the house by the way of the gate facing toward the east.* [5] *And the Spirit lifted me up and brought me into the inner court; and behold, the glory of the LORD filled the house.*

This could be predicting the return from Babylonian exile, but it may also be a long-range vision which foresees Christ entering Jerusalem on Palm Sunday, 30 AD.

<u>Jesus' East Gate Entry on Palm Sunday</u>
The prophet Zechariah wrote this prophecy that found its fulfillment when Jesus came the first time.

Zechariah 9:9 (RSV)
[9] *Rejoice greatly, O daughter of Zion! Shout aloud, O daughter of Jerusalem! Lo, your king comes to you; triumphant and victorious is he, humble and riding on an ass, on a colt the foal of an ass.*

As Jesus entered Jerusalem on that original Palm Sunday, the New Testament gospel accounts do not explicitly specify which gate he entered. However it is implicitly identified by the direction from which he came. As he and his disciples were heading toward Jerusalem, they came upon a small village called Bethpage. Bethpage is located on the Mount of Olives, and it is there that he borrowed the donkey on which he rode into Jerusalem. The road that winds down the mountain was a main road of travel, and the East Gate was the only non-military gate in the vicinity. This gate is further implied by the fact that upon entering the city, he went immediately into the temple. The East Gate opens in front of the temple mount.

Matthew 21:10-12 (NASB)
[10] When He had entered Jerusalem, all the city was stirred, saying, "Who is this?" [11] And the crowds were saying, "This is the prophet Jesus, from Nazareth in Galilee." [12] And Jesus entered the temple and drove out all those who were buying and selling in the temple, and overturned the tables of the money changers and the seats of those who were selling doves.

The people were quoting from a messianic psalm:

Psalm 118:24-26 (NASB)
[24] This is the day which the LORD has made; Let us rejoice and be glad in it. [25] O LORD, do save, we beseech You; O LORD, we beseech You, do send prosperity! [26] Blessed is the one who comes in the name of the LORD; We have blessed you from the house of the LORD.

Matthew 21:9 (NASB)
[9] The crowds going ahead of Him, and those who followed, were shouting, "Hosanna to the Son of David; BLESSED IS HE WHO COMES IN THE NAME OF THE LORD; Hosanna in the highest!"

A couple of days later, Jesus brooded over Jerusalem, saying:

Matthew 23:37-39 (NASB)
[37] "Jerusalem, Jerusalem, who kills the prophets and stones those who are sent to her! How often I wanted to gather your children together, the way a hen gathers her chicks under her wings, and you were unwilling. [38] "Behold, your house is being left to you desolate! [39] "For I say to you, from now on you will not see Me until you say, 'BLESSED IS HE WHO COMES IN THE NAME OF THE LORD!'"

Note that he made this statement *after* his triumphal entry on Palm Sunday. He was clearly anticipating his second coming.

The East Gate Sealed

Ezekiel was given another prediction regarding the East Gate. This was given after the Babylonian invasion.

Ezekiel 44:1-3 (NASB)
[1] Then He brought me back by the way of the outer gate of the sanctuary, which faces the east; and it was shut. [2] The LORD said to me, "This gate shall be shut; it shall not be opened, and no one shall enter by it, for the LORD God of Israel has entered by it; therefore it shall be shut. [3] "As for the prince, he shall sit in it as prince to eat

bread before the LORD; he shall enter by way of the porch of the gate and shall go out by the same way."

Ezekiel 46:12 (NASB)
[12] "When the prince provides a freewill offering, a burnt offering, or peace offerings as a freewill offering to the LORD, the gate facing east shall be opened for him. And he shall provide his burnt offering and his peace offerings as he does on the sabbath day. Then he shall go out, and the gate shall be shut after he goes out.

These passages are somewhat vague in their interpretation, but it makes reference to *the gate facing east* being *shut*, and then being *opened* for *the prince*. Historically the only substantial closing up of the East Gate is that which was done in the 16th century more than 2100 years after the prophecy was given, and the evidence of that remains for us today.

The East Gate of Jesus' Second Coming
When Jesus returns, he will come as a conquering warrior. He will come in judgment against his enemies, and will vanquish them in short order.

Hebrews 9:27-28 (ESV)
[27] And just as it is appointed for man to die once, and after that comes judgment, [28] so Christ, having been offered once to bear the sins of many, will appear a second time, not to deal with sin but to save those who are eagerly waiting for him.

At his first coming, Jesus was the 'suffering servant.' We saw unparalleled 'grace.' At his second coming, the 'truth' of his glorious holiness will be paramount. *Grace and truth* characterize Christ. The prophet Zechariah was given a message about this cataclysmic second coming.

Zechariah 14:1-5 (RSV)
[1] Behold, a day of the LORD is coming, when the spoil taken from you will be divided in the midst of you. [2] For I will gather all the nations against Jerusalem to battle, and the city shall be taken and the houses plundered and the women ravished; half of the city shall go into exile, but the rest of the people shall not be cut off from the city. [3] Then the LORD will go forth and fight against those nations as when he fights on a day of battle. [4] On that day his feet shall stand on the Mount of Olives which lies before Jerusalem on the east; and the Mount of Olives shall be split in two from east to west by a very wide valley; so that one half of the Mount shall withdraw northward, and the other half southward. [5] And the valley of my mountains shall be stopped up, for the valley of the mountains shall touch the side of it; and you shall flee as you fled from the

earthquake in the days of Uzzi'ah king of Judah. Then the LORD your God will come, and all the holy ones with him.

The *holy ones with him* are, no doubt, the same as those saints who came with him dressed in white linen in Revelation 19. They are not coming to fight the battle. Jesus will handle that. They are there to share in the victory procession.

Psalm 68:17-18 (NKJ)
17 The chariots of God are twenty thousand, even thousands of thousands; the Lord is among them as in Sinai, in the Holy Place. 18 You have ascended on high, you have led captivity captive; you have received gifts among men, even from the rebellious, that the LORD God might dwell there.

It was common practice in biblical times that a conquering army would return home in a victory procession, along with their captives and their possessions. Isaiah prophesied of Christ's triumphal entry into Jerusalem at his return:

Isaiah 60:11 (RSV)
11 Your gates shall be open continually; day and night they shall not be shut; that men may bring to you the wealth of the nations, with their kings led in procession.

The battle will be short, and the victory decisive in favor of heaven's king. In the New Testament, Paul projects this victory march ahead figuratively to the present times, teaching his readers to live as *more than conquerors* in a hostile world.

2 Corinthians 2:14 (ESV)
14 But thanks be to God, who in Christ always leads us in triumphal procession, and through us spreads the fragrance of the knowledge of him everywhere.

Thus, the East Gate is a visible emblem of our hope in Christ's return, and an assurance of his victory over the kingdom of Satan in the greatest war ever fought. By prophecy, it stands there closed up as stark evidence of the certainty of Christ's sovereignty in the historical affairs of this world. By prophecy it stands as a clarion reminder that 'Jesus is coming again.'

> Lord, hear our prayer. Teach us to love your appearing. Teach us to long for the sight of your glorious presence. As we contemplate this most pivotal event in history, make it our hope and our purpose, we pray. May we

learn to wait for it as a reunion of joy. Make it the hope that lifts us above life's hardship and futility, into the heavenly realm where our citizenship resides. May this reality empower us for service. Amen

19
ARMAGEDDON: CHRIST VICTORIOUS

When Jesus was a small boy growing up in Nazareth, he must have climbed the short distance up the mountainside where he lived, to its peak, many times. From there he would have had a panoramic view looking northwestward upon the Mediterranean Sea. His corridor of vision would have been bounded on the right by the Galilean mountains, and on the left by the distant Mount Carmel. Between them sprawled the wide valley of Megiddo and its Kishon River. Perhaps Joseph took him there to teach him of Israel's rich history. Perhaps he taught him of events occurring within their very view--such stories as the victory of the Israelites over the Canaanites in that valley under the judge Deborah, or the great victory of Elijah over the prophets of Baal on Mount Carmel. God had powerfully revealed His omnipotence in that place.

I cannot help but wonder at what age Jesus became aware of what would one day take place there. Could it be that even as a young man, he gazed over that valley, and his spirit envisioned the armies of the world gathered there for the greatest military campaign ever fought?

Armageddon's Flashpoint

What could induce the whole world to attack Israel? If we look for observable, political reasons, we might first ask a similar question: "How can such a small nation dominate world politics?" Yet it does. We know that the Middle East simmers in animosity against Israel, and the global need for the huge oil reserves in that part of the world has set up a sensitive co-existence between Israel and the rest of the world. As time goes on, it seems Israel is becoming increasingly offensive to her Islamic neighbors. The nations of the world are becoming increasingly dependent on oil from those countries. Those oil exporting countries of the Mid-East are losing economic influence, and out of frustration, are resorting to more aggressive relational positions toward oil importing countries such as the United States. Today's terrorist strategies are a symptom of this frustration. If Israel were eliminated from existence, it seems to her enemies that many of their problems would disappear. In short, Israel's global relationship is a political time bomb.

We see, from the verse in Isaiah we just read, that Zion (Jerusalem) is the heart of the controversy:

> *Isaiah 34:8 (RSV)*
> *⁸ For the LORD has a day of vengeance, a year of recompense for the cause of Zion.*

What is Armageddon?

The term *Armageddon* has become a by-word, even among the biblically illiterate, for any cataclysmic situation. It may have widespread application, but it originates in prophetic scripture where its meaning is very specific. At the end of the bowl judgments in Chapter 14, we saw the marshaling of a huge army from the east into the land of Israel. As they gathered, great multitudes were slaughtered in their path. The nations of the earth will be in conspiracy. This was foreseen by the Old Testament prophets and psalmists.

> *Psalm 2:1-8 (NASB)*
> *¹ Why are the nations in an uproar And the peoples devising a vain thing? ² The kings of the earth take their stand And the rulers take counsel together Against the LORD and against His Anointed, saying, ³ "Let us tear their fetters apart And cast away their cords from us!" ⁴ He who sits in the heavens laughs, The Lord scoffs at them. ⁵ Then He will speak to them in His anger And terrify them in His fury, saying, ⁶ "But as for Me, I have installed My King Upon Zion, My holy mountain." ⁷ "I will surely tell of the decree of the LORD: He said to Me, 'You are My Son, Today I have begotten You. ⁸ 'Ask of Me, and I will surely give the nations as Your inheritance, And the very ends of the earth as Your possession.*

Armageddon will be, at its root cause, a war by evil people against the *LORD and against his Anointed One*. The Anointed One is, of course, Jesus. He will be made King over the earth by the decree of the Father. God Himself will install the Son as *King on Zion*. Many kings inherit their throne by royal tradition, some are installed by the decree of men, and some seize kingship by force. Jesus is installed by God Almighty, Creator and Lord over all. Who can find a higher sanction? The enemy nations of Israel will be hostile to this coronation, but God will not be intimidated.

> *Isaiah 34:1-8 (RSV)*
> *¹ Draw near, O nations, to hear, and hearken, O peoples! Let the earth listen, and all that fills it; the world, and all that comes from it.*

² *For the LORD is enraged against all the nations, and furious against all their host, he has doomed them, has given them over for slaughter. ³ Their slain shall be cast out, and the stench of their corpses shall rise; the mountains shall flow with their blood. ⁴ All the host of heaven shall rot away, and the skies roll up like a scroll. All their host shall fall, as leaves fall from the vine, like leaves falling from the fig tree. ⁵ For my sword has drunk its fill in the heavens; behold, it descends for judgment upon Edom, upon the people I have doomed. ⁶ The LORD has a sword; it is sated with blood, it is gorged with fat, with the blood of lambs and goats, with the fat of the kidneys of rams. For the LORD has a sacrifice in Bozrah, a great slaughter in the land of Edom. ⁷ Wild oxen shall fall with them, and young steers with the mighty bulls. Their land shall be soaked with blood, and their soil made rich with fat. ⁸ For the LORD has a day of vengeance, a year of recompense for the cause of Zion.*

Revelation 16:16 (ESV)
¹⁶ And they assembled them at the place that in Hebrew is called Armageddon.

Armageddon, from *Har Megiddo*, that is, Valley of Megiddo, is named as the site of that battle in only this one scripture. In one other passage, although not called by that name, this battle is identified by a reference to Jezreel, an ancient city in the Valley of Megiddo.

Hosea 1:11 (RSV)
¹¹ And the people of Judah and the people of Israel shall be gathered together, and they shall appoint for themselves one head; and they shall go up from the land, for great shall be the day of Jezreel.

Joel 3:1-2,11-14 (NASB)
¹ "For behold, in those days and at that time, When I restore the fortunes of Judah and Jerusalem, ² I will gather all the nations And bring them down to the valley of Jehoshaphat. Then I will enter into judgment with them there On behalf of My people and My inheritance, Israel, Whom they have scattered among the nations; And they have divided up My land . . . ¹¹ Hasten and come, all you surrounding nations, And gather yourselves there. Bring down, O LORD, Your mighty ones. ¹² Let the nations be aroused And come up to the valley of Jehoshaphat, For there I will sit to judge All the surrounding nations. ¹³ Put in the sickle, for the harvest is ripe. Come, tread, for the wine press is full; The vats overflow, for their wickedness is great. ¹⁴ Multitudes, multitudes in the valley of decision! For the day of the LORD is near in the valley of decision.

This Valley of Jehoshaphat is a symbolic title. It has reference to 2 Chronicles 20:25-27 telling of a great victory from Israel's past, brought about by God, while under the reigning king by that name. It is identified geographically as the Valley of Beracah, a valley south of Jerusalem extending from Bethlehem to Hebron. Although the slaughter there sounds like that of Armageddon, they seem to actually be two different lines of battle, perhaps occurring simultaneously.

All Earthly Hope Lost

> *Zechariah 14:1-2 (RSV)*
> *¹ Behold, a day of the LORD is coming, when the spoil taken from you will be divided in the midst of you. ² For I will gather all the nations against Jerusalem to battle, and the city shall be taken and the houses plundered and the women ravished; half of the city shall go into exile, but the rest of the people shall not be cut off from the city.*

With seemingly the whole world attacking Jerusalem, the nation and the city appear to be lost. Global anti-Semitism will fan the mindless hatred of the invading armies. With heated, satanic fervor they will pour into the valleys of Israel, bloodthirsty and eager. When they attack, the conquest is quick. There is no one on earth to save them now.

Yet, note that it is God who will gather the nations to attack Jerusalem. Why is He taking credit for this horrific event? This clearly is shown to be according to His plan. What is the plan? How can this come to anything good?

Divine Rescue

> *Psalm 110:1-7 (NASB)*
> *¹ The LORD says to my Lord: "Sit at My right hand Until I make Your enemies a footstool for Your feet." ² The LORD will stretch forth Your strong scepter from Zion, saying, "Rule in the midst of Your enemies." ³ Your people will volunteer freely in the day of Your power; In holy array, from the womb of the dawn, Your youth are to You as the dew. ⁴ The LORD has sworn and will not change His mind, "You are a priest forever According to the order of Melchizedek." ⁵ The Lord is at Your right hand; He will shatter kings in the day of His wrath. ⁶ He will judge among the nations, He will fill them with corpses, He will shatter the chief men over a broad country. ⁷ He will drink from the brook by the wayside; Therefore He will lift up His head.*

The phrases *"you will receive the dew of your youth"* and *"He will drink from a brook beside the way"* are expressions symbolizing the divine energy and power that Jesus will have, in battle-warrior terminology. The lifting up of the head is symbolic of the exhilaration of receiving divine strength. This phraseology is seen in these passages:

Psalm 3:3 (NASB)
³ But You, O LORD, are a shield about me, My glory, and the One who lifts my head.

Psalm 27:6 (NASB)
⁶ And now my head will be lifted up above my enemies around me, And I will offer in His tent sacrifices with shouts of joy; I will sing, yes, I will sing praises to the LORD.

The heavenly rescue will not occur until it appears all is lost. The invasion of Jerusalem will have taken place. The city will already be devastated and defiled. The enemies of Israel will be in full control.

Sometimes God works that way in our everyday lives too. It is not that He relishes making our lives miserable. But He knows the value of eternal purposes over temporal desires, and He places a high priority on our eternal lives. When we are in desperate need of some spiritual grace, He is willing to sacrifice our comfort and temporary well-being for that which is eternal, if need be. The important message is that He will save. And so He will do for Jerusalem in that day.

Ezekiel 38:18 - 39:7 (NASB)
¹⁸ "It will come about on that day, when Gog comes against the land of Israel," declares the Lord GOD, "that My fury will mount up in My anger. ¹⁹ "In My zeal and in My blazing wrath I declare that on that day there will surely be a great earthquake in the land of Israel. ²⁰ "The fish of the sea, the birds of the heavens, the beasts of the field, all the creeping things that creep on the earth, and all the men who are on the face of the earth will shake at My presence; the mountains also will be thrown down, the steep pathways will collapse and every wall will fall to the ground. ²¹ "I will call for a sword against him on all My mountains," declares the Lord GOD. "Every man's sword will be against his brother. ²² "With pestilence and with blood I will enter into judgment with him; and I will rain on him and on his troops, and on the many peoples who are with him, a torrential rain, with hailstones, fire and brimstone. ²³ "I will magnify Myself, sanctify Myself, and make Myself known in the sight of many nations; and they will know that I am the LORD."' ¹ "And you, son of man, prophesy against Gog and say, 'Thus says the Lord GOD, "Behold, I am against you, O Gog, prince of Rosh, Meshech and

Tubal; ² *and I will turn you around, drive you on, take you up from the remotest parts of the north and bring you against the mountains of Israel.* ³ *"I will strike your bow from your left hand and dash down your arrows from your right hand.* ⁴ *"You will fall on the mountains of Israel, you and all your troops and the peoples who are with you; I will give you as food to every kind of predatory bird and beast of the field.* ⁵ *"You will fall on the open field; for it is I who have spoken," declares the Lord GOD.* ⁶ *"And I will send fire upon Magog and those who inhabit the coastlands in safety; and they will know that I am the LORD.* ⁷ *"My holy name I will make known in the midst of My people Israel; and I will not let My holy name be profaned anymore. And the nations will know that I am the LORD, the Holy One in Israel.*

The thirty-eighth and thirty-ninth chapters of Ezekiel are believed by many premillennialists to refer to a different battle than Armageddon--an earlier one. Their earlier placement of it is based on the statements about Israel dwelling in seeming security which, they say, could not apply in the second half of the Tribulation after the antichrist's switch from ally to enemy. Nevertheless, it obviously belongs in the end-time sequence, and I agree with many others who prefer to incorporate it as part of that same great war. It is difficult for me to imagine two wars of such huge magnitude, both ended by divine intervention, and after the first one—life as usual. Not only that, but the scriptures portray these battles ending with Israel and all the nations coming to a full knowledge of God as the Holy One of Israel. If this be true, and if it occurred prior to Armageddon, prior to the tribulation as some teach, then how could the tribulation even occur?

At this point, when it seems absolutely hopeless for Israel . . .

Revelation 19:11-19 (ESV)
¹¹ Then I saw heaven opened, and behold, a white horse! The one sitting on it is called Faithful and True, and in righteousness he judges and makes war. ¹² *His eyes are like a flame of fire, and on his head are many diadems, and he has a name written that no one knows but himself.* ¹³ *He is clothed in a robe dipped in blood, and the name by which he is called is The Word of God.* ¹⁴ *And the armies of heaven, arrayed in fine linen, white and pure, were following him on white horses.* ¹⁵ *From his mouth comes a sharp sword with which to strike down the nations, and he will rule them with a rod of iron. He will tread the winepress of the fury of the wrath of God the Almighty.* ¹⁶ *On his robe and on his thigh he has a name written, King of kings and Lord of lords.* ¹⁷ *Then I saw an angel standing in the sun, and with a loud voice he called to all the birds that fly directly overhead, "Come, gather for the great supper of God,* ¹⁸ *to eat the flesh of kings, the flesh of captains, the flesh of mighty men, the flesh of*

horses and their riders, and the flesh of all men, both free and slave, both small and great." ¹⁹ And I saw the beast and the kings of the earth with their armies gathered to make war against him who was sitting on the horse and against his army.

Zechariah 14:3-15 (RSV)
³ Then the LORD will go forth and fight against those nations as when he fights on a day of battle. ⁴ On that day his feet shall stand on the Mount of Olives which lies before Jerusalem on the east; and the Mount of Olives shall be split in two from east to west by a very wide valley; so that one half of the Mount shall withdraw northward, and the other half southward. ⁵ And the valley of my mountains shall be stopped up, for the valley of the mountains shall touch the side of it; and you shall flee as you fled from the earthquake in the days of Uzzi'ah king of Judah. Then the LORD your God will come, and all the holy ones with him. ⁶ On that day there shall be neither cold nor frost. ⁷ And there shall be continuous day (it is known to the LORD), not day and not night, for at evening time there shall be light. ⁸ On that day living waters shall flow out from Jerusalem, half of them to the eastern sea and half of them to the western sea; it shall continue in summer as in winter. ⁹ And the LORD will become king over all the earth; on that day the LORD will be one and his name one. ¹⁰ The whole land shall be turned into a plain from Geba to Rimmon south of Jerusalem. But Jerusalem shall remain aloft upon its site from the Gate of Benjamin to the place of the former gate, to the Corner Gate, and from the Tower of Han'anel to the king's wine presses. ¹¹ And it shall be inhabited, for there shall be no more curse; Jerusalem shall dwell in security. ¹² And this shall be the plague with which the LORD will smite all the peoples that wage war against Jerusalem: their flesh shall rot while they are still on their feet, their eyes shall rot in their sockets, and their tongues shall rot in their mouths. ¹³ And on that day a great panic from the LORD shall fall on them, so that each will lay hold on the hand of his fellow, and the hand of the one will be raised against the hand of the other; ¹⁴ even Judah will fight against Jerusalem. And the wealth of all the nations round about shall be collected, gold, silver, and garments in great abundance. ¹⁵ And a plague like this plague shall fall on the horses, the mules, the camels, the asses, and whatever beasts may be in those camps.

The Outcome

Revelation 19:20-21 (ESV)
²⁰ And the beast was captured, and with it the false prophet who in its presence had done the signs by which he deceived those who had received the mark of the beast and those who worshiped its image.

These two were thrown alive into the lake of fire that burns with sulfur. [21] And the rest were slain by the sword that came from the mouth of him who was sitting on the horse, and all the birds were gorged with their flesh.

Although the duration of the fight is not given, the sense seems to be that it will be short and decisive. The enemy's leaders, the beast and false prophet, will be captured and thrown into Hell. Note that the victory is won by the rider on the white horse, the King of kings and Lord of lords.

Ezekiel 39:11-16 (NASB)
[11] "On that day I will give Gog a burial ground there in Israel, the valley of those who pass by east of the sea, and it will block off those who would pass by. So they will bury Gog there with all his horde, and they will call it the valley of Hamon-gog. [12] "For seven months the house of Israel will be burying them in order to cleanse the land. [13] "Even all the people of the land will bury them; and it will be to their renown on the day that I glorify Myself," declares the Lord GOD. [14] "They will set apart men who will constantly pass through the land, burying those who were passing through, even those left on the surface of the ground, in order to cleanse it. At the end of seven months they will make a search. [15] "As those who pass through the land pass through and anyone sees a man's bone, then he will set up a marker by it until the buriers have buried it in the valley of Hamon-gog. [16] "And even the name of the city will be Hamonah. So they will cleanse the land."'

The cleanup from this massive slaughter, even with the help of hoards of birds, and with modern heavy mining and excavating equipment, will take seven months. The valley mentioned is not clear. It could be the Valley of Megiddo, or it could be the valley of the Jordan River. (The sentence is perhaps better translated, "the valley to the east of the [Mediterranean] sea.") At any rate, we have already seen that many valleys around Jerusalem could be burial grounds since the city will be completely surrounded by the largest military force ever assembled, and all of them will die in the battle. Again we have the number seven, indicating the completeness of the cleansing.

The Divine Two-Edged Sword

How will they die? The scripture says, *"The rest of them were killed with the sword that came out of the mouth of the rider on the horse . . ."* What is this talking about? To understand this symbolism, we must have some scriptural background. Remember that this is not the first time we have seen this sword. In the initial vision of Revelation, John, wrote . . .

Revelation 1:16 (ESV)
16 In his right hand he held seven stars, from his mouth came a sharp two-edged sword, and his face was like the sun shining in full strength.

This is not a random statement. The sword is frequently used in scripture as a synonym for war in general, or for violent death in combat. An extension of that idea is the power that authority wields, as intended in this writing from Paul, speaking about civil authorities:

Romans 13:4 (KJV)
4 For he is the minister of God to thee for good. But if thou do that which is evil, be afraid; for he beareth not the sword in vain: for he is the minister of God, a revenger to execute wrath upon him that doeth evil.

The issue in this case is power. God is all-powerful, so in that sense He could be said to brandish a sword of authority. What normally comes from the mouth? Words. But these are not just any words we are talking about. They are God's words. There are literally hundreds of passages discussing God's words to us, and several that equate them to a sword. Here are just a few.

Ephesians 6:17 (ESV)
17 and take the helmet of salvation, and the sword of the Spirit, which is the word of God,

Hebrews 4:12 (ESV)
12 For the word of God is living and active, sharper than any two-edged sword, piercing to the division of soul and of spirit, of joints and of marrow, and discerning the thoughts and intentions of the heart.

Acts 2:37 (ESV)
37 Now when they heard this [the gospel] *they were cut to the heart, and said to Peter and the rest of the apostles, "Brothers, what shall we do?"*

In these scriptures we see the power of the sword as it refers to authority and power in God's written word. We see a sword of judgment. In this life, the written word convicts the heart of a sinner. In another time the spoken word will bring down consuming judgment. In the beginning the divine word spoke, and the creation existed out of nothing. He spoke, and order came from chaos. The divine word was spoken by the One we call the Living Word.

> *John 1:1-3 (NIV2011)*
> *¹ In the beginning was the Word, and the Word was with God, and the Word was God. ² He was with God in the beginning. ³ Through him all things were made; without him nothing was made that has been made.*

Cannot the same word, the same power and authority that spoke the world into creation, can it not speak again, and bring annihilation? The point is, in this great battle, the Word will have the victory because of His limitless power. His omnipotence is so incalculable that He need only speak, and the enemy will be destroyed.

The Victory of Christ
In winning this war, the person of the antichrist will be destroyed forever. The False Prophet will be eliminated with him. These were the earthly leaders. What about God's ancient nemesis, the underlying conspirator, our real enemy—the dragon, Satan?

> *Revelation 20:1-2 (ESV)*
> *¹ Then I saw an angel coming down from heaven, holding in his hand the key to the bottomless pit and a great chain. ² And he seized the dragon, that ancient serpent, who is the devil and Satan, and bound him for a thousand years,*

With this capture, the age-old satanic conspiracy will come to a halt. Earth's inhabitants will find themselves in a world free from the devil's influence for the first time since Eden. What will happen next?

> Victory is Yours, oh God. You, oh Christ, have won the war of the ages. There was never doubt in heaven about the outcome because you are the omnipotent almighty. Still, we are so prone to lose heart and hope. Strengthen us, we pray, to keep our faith and confidence in you firm in all situations. Lord, whether through life's ongoing tribulations, or through the final test, teach us to rely on your grace. May the sword of your word make us victorious in every situation. Lead us in the ways of righteousness for your sake. Make us to make You our hope and reward. May we live for nothing more, but this only. Amen

The Call to Arms

But we cannot understand the situation fully if we look only for political causes. Consider again the following scripture from Revelation.

Revelation 16:13-14,16 (ESV)
[13] And I saw, coming out of the mouth of the dragon and out of the mouth of the beast and out of the mouth of the false prophet, three unclean spirits like frogs. [14] For they are demonic spirits, performing signs, who go abroad to the kings of the whole world, to assemble them for battle on the great day of God the Almighty . . . [16] And they assembled them at the place that in Hebrew is called Armageddon.

Armageddon will be the cataclysmic consequence of Satan's evil conspiracy. It can only be understood in light of the underlying spiritual struggle that is being waged between the kingdom of heaven and the kingdom of darkness. While the warfare is motivated in the spiritual realm, its battles are waged in the earthly theater.

The vision of three evil spirits looking like frogs is symbolic of some diabolical agenda, perhaps with a propaganda campaign of some sort. Such spiritual tactics are common in national and international politics. We experience them daily. Consider the ongoing, carefully engineered conspiracy to eliminate vestiges of religion from our common society on the basis of political correctness. Behind all such campaigns is a spiritual scheme and a spiritual enemy. The spirit of antichrist is active.

The frog, an unclean creature in Jewish thought, represents the evil essence of its purpose. We are told its mission. The satanic spirits will so manipulate the minds of the leaders of earthly nations that they will be coerced to join the conspiracy. They will heed the call to battle against Jerusalem.

The Old Testament prophet Ezekiel was given this preview of the marshaling of troops in that day.

Ezekiel 38:1-17 (NASB)
[1] And the word of the LORD came to me saying, [2] "Son of man, set your face toward Gog of the land of Magog, the prince of Rosh, Meshech and Tubal, and prophesy against him [3] and say, 'Thus says the Lord GOD, "Behold, I am against you, O Gog, prince of Rosh, Meshech and Tubal. [4] "I will turn you about and put hooks into your jaws, and I will bring you out, and all your army, horses and horsemen, all of them splendidly attired, a great company with buckler and shield, all of them wielding swords; [5] Persia, Ethiopia and Put with them, all of them with shield and helmet; [6] Gomer with all its troops; Beth-togarmah from the remote parts of the north with all its troops—many peoples with you. [7] "Be prepared, and prepare yourself, you and all your companies that are assembled about you,

and be a guard for them. ⁸ "After many days you will be summoned; in the latter years you will come into the land that is restored from the sword, whose inhabitants have been gathered from many nations to the mountains of Israel which had been a continual waste; but its people were brought out from the nations, and they are living securely, all of them. ⁹ "You will go up, you will come like a storm; you will be like a cloud covering the land, you and all your troops, and many peoples with you." ¹⁰ 'Thus says the Lord GOD, "It will come about on that day, that thoughts will come into your mind and you will devise an evil plan, ¹¹ and you will say, 'I will go up against the land of unwalled villages. I will go against those who are at rest, that live securely, all of them living without walls and having no bars or gates, ¹² to capture spoil and to seize plunder, to turn your hand against the waste places which are now inhabited, and against the people who are gathered from the nations, who have acquired cattle and goods, who live at the center of the world.' ¹³ "Sheba and Dedan and the merchants of Tarshish with all its villages will say to you, 'Have you come to capture spoil? Have you assembled your company to seize plunder, to carry away silver and gold, to take away cattle and goods, to capture great spoil?'"' ¹⁴ "Therefore prophesy, son of man, and say to Gog, 'Thus says the Lord GOD, "On that day when My people Israel are living securely, will you not know it? ¹⁵ "You will come from your place out of the remote parts of the north, you and many peoples with you, all of them riding on horses, a great assembly and a mighty army; ¹⁶ and you will come up against My people Israel like a cloud to cover the land. It shall come about in the last days that I will bring you against My land, so that the nations may know Me when I am sanctified through you before their eyes, O Gog." ¹⁷ 'Thus says the Lord GOD, "Are you the one of whom I spoke in former days through My servants the prophets of Israel, who prophesied in those days for many years that I would bring you against them?*

Who are these people? The people of Magog are said to be from an extreme northern land. Without going into detail about language origins, they are understood by most scholars to identify Russia. Meshech and Tubal are believed to be ancient names for Moscow and Tobolsk, major Russian cities today. Persia is modern day Iran. Cush and Put are identified as Ethiopia and Libya, and are so translated by the King James Version. They were the same two North African countries they are today. Gomer is thought by scholars to refer to what is today East Germany, perhaps including parts of Poland. The Armenian area of Turkey is believed to be identified here in the name Beth Togarmah. The seeds of this gathering for war can already be seen in the anti-Semitic legacy of these countries.

Notice that there is an opposition to this invasion of Israel. The nations of Sheba and Dedan may represent the present-day countries of Yemen and Oman. Joining them is Tarshish and her merchants. Tarshish has traditionally been taken to be Spain. However note the reference to her merchants. England once had the greatest merchant marine and the greatest naval force in the world. *Tarshish and her villages* is rendered *Tarshish and her young lions* in the King James, which is the more frequent meaning of the original Hebrew word kephir. If that is the meaning, and if Great Britain is Tarshish, the young lions probably refers to her offspring in the way of colonization, and could include the United States, Australia, South Africa, and many other countries still holding a predominantly English culture. In this scripture, these countries mount an objection, but it seems no more than a diplomatic protest.

20
THE IMMINENCE OF HIS COMING

Scripture teaches we cannot predict the *day* and *hour* of the coming of Christ. Rather than speculating, we are admonished to *watch*. To watch is to keep a continuous vigilance for his return. This is contrary to our inquisitive tendencies. We want to set a time. We want a schedule. We want to know how long until we have to get serious about our standing with God. Jesus specifically warned against date-setting.

The apostles and the early church had a zeal for the return of Christ, but can you imagine how they would have felt if Jesus had told them it would be 2000 years (at least) until he returned? Much of their faithfulness in the face of persecution stemmed from their anticipation of his return. He did not clarify that notion, rather they were told his coming would be like *a thief in the night* or a long-in-coming *bridegroom*. He wanted them to hold that vigilant mindset because all who do not, will be surprised. Likewise he has not told us when he will come, except to say that it will occur *at a time when you do not expect.* He wants us to also remain 'on guard' until that day.

Biblical Signs

However he also told his followers to discern the signs of the times. While we cannot predict the specific time, we can certainly see things moving in the direction he predicted. Furthermore I believe we are seeing, in our day, a proliferation of these signs signaling an acceleration toward that day. It seems plausible that that day could come in the not-too-distant future! What are the signs? What are some of the biblical predictions that are now current events?

<u>Geophysical and Political Signs</u>
In the New Testament Jesus told his disciples:

> *Matthew 24:5-7, 29-30 (NASB)*
> *⁵ "For many will come in My name, saying, 'I am the Christ,' and will mislead many. ⁶ "You will be hearing of wars and rumors of wars. See that you are not frightened, for those things must take place, but that is not yet the end. ⁷ "For nation will rise against*

nation, and kingdom against kingdom, and in various places there will be famines and earthquakes . . . ²⁹ "But immediately after the tribulation of those days THE SUN WILL BE DARKENED, AND THE MOON WILL NOT GIVE ITS LIGHT, AND THE STARS WILL FALL from the sky, and the powers of the heavens will be shaken. ³⁰ "And then the sign of the Son of Man will appear in the sky, and then all the tribes of the earth will mourn, and they will see the SON OF MAN COMING ON THE CLOUDS OF THE SKY with power and great glory.

Prior to the return of Jesus, there will be a time of tribulation on the earth. Some of the things that characterize the tribulation seem to already be in the making. While events such as wars, famines and earthquakes have always been with us, their frequency and scope seem to have proliferated over the last hundred years.

The Nation Israel
Israel as a nation appears to play heavily in end-time prophecies. The early church anticipated the return of Jesus, and because of details given in Old Testament prophecies, believed that Israel would be involved, with her temple worship. But Jerusalem was destroyed in 70 AD, including the temple, and the rest of Israel was exiled over the next several decades, to the far corners of the Roman Empire. With the passing of time, it seemed more and more difficult to see how a literal fulfillment could happen. For nearly 2,000 years Israel had no national identity, no cohesiveness, no homeland. The prospect of her being around when Jesus returned seemed impossible to Christians as well, and most thought she was extinct.

Then in the late nineteenth century a movement began to restore Israel to her ancient homeland, and on May 14, 1948 Israel declared herself a sovereign nation. Today, in spite of regular turmoil with the surrounding nations, she is a modern oasis of human dignity and well-being amidst a wilderness of fragile, afflicted neighbors.

This turn of events was without precedent. Never had a nation been exiled for a hundred years and then been restored, let alone for 1800 years. No prognosticator could have predicted it. Only by God's plan and purpose could it have been foretold, and then come to pass. This is a remarkable fulfillment of prophecy that has taken place within the memory of many reading this book. Not only does this set the stage for a literal fulfillment of further prophecy; it demonstrates God's active purpose at work in the affairs of men during this present age.

In Matthew's gospel account of Jesus' prophetic discourse on the Mount of Olives, he has told his disciples about events leading up to the second coming. Then he makes this statement...

Matthew 24:32-34 (NASB)
³² "Now learn the parable from the fig tree: when its branch has already become tender and puts forth its leaves, you know that summer is near; ³³ so, you too, when you see all these things, recognize that He is near, right at the door. ³⁴ "Truly I say to you, this generation will not pass away until all these things take place.

This generation is easily assumed by a casual reader to mean the generation of the original hearers of this discourse. This assumption has led to whole branches of interpretation. However, the most feasible interpretation of verse 34, that *this generation will certainly not pass away until all these things have happened,* is that *this generation* refers to the generation that witnesses the signs predicted in the preceding verses. In other words, when the signs begin to be evident, all of the *Day of the Lord* events will happen within the span of that generation.

Now what was the lesson of the fig tree? Three different plants are commonly given in Old Testament scripture as figurative representations of the nation Israel: the olive tree, the grapevine, and the fig tree. Therefore, many see in this fig tree a reference to Israel. Jesus had just finished telling of the impending destruction of Jerusalem, specifically of the temple. In his statement about the fig tree's twigs getting tender and its leaves coming out, we see a foreshadowing of Israel's restoration in the last days. According to this view, the generation that witnesses the events described will see the return of Jesus in their lifetime.

Demarcation of Believers
Matthew 24:12-13 (NASB)
¹² "Because lawlessness is increased, most people's love will grow cold. ¹³ "But the one who endures to the end, he will be saved.

I remember as a young man being perplexed that I could not tell the difference between Christians and non-Christians. As the end of the age approaches and oppression of believers in Jesus grows, the distinction between believers and non-believers will become increasingly evident. Nominal Christians will fall away, being spiritually unequipped to face the heat, and leaving a more holy church. Faithful believers will be purified by dependent faith, having been stripped of all other credentials. They will be refined in the fire of persecution. These are the true believes--those who will persevere.

We already see this persecution taking place in many places in the world. In Africa and Asia a majority of the countries are hostile to Christianity. In these countries Christians are imprisoned or killed. Even here in the United States, a country founded on Christian principles, there is a persecution underway. Public schools enforce gags on teachers and students who display any emblem of Christian faith, or openly pray or witness. Other religions enjoy more freedom of expression. Even at the university level, professors are told that any teaching that even hints of the reality of God will be grounds for passing over for advancement, or even for dismissal.

Christianity is now being portrayed as a "hate" cult. Meanwhile, Islam, and other religions who have openly attacked the United States through terrorism, are promoted as the victims of this hatred. The reason is because Christians believe that there is only one way into heaven—Jesus Christ. This exclusiveness does not fit with social engineers who have defined the concept of 'tolerance.' (Tolerance no longer means what it once did. Now the demand is that we all admit the equal validity of every religion, or we are being intolerant.) Intolerance can result in punishment, in some cases. Are these trends helping set the stage for the all-out persecution of believers during the tribulation?

<u>The Gospel Preached to All Nations</u>
When persecution occurs, the result is an elevated evangelistic spirit within the true church. The urgency of the quest to make disciples seems to flare up during such times. Today as the plight of believers around the world is becoming known, and even as our freedoms of the faith in this country are under attack, there is a swell in missionary activity.

> *Matthew 24:14 (NASB)*
> *^{14} "This gospel of the kingdom shall be preached in the whole world as a testimony to all the nations, and then the end will come.*

This scripture used to seem to require some supernatural fulfillment because of the enormity of the task. There is a passage in Revelation that describes just that, and is taken by many as the fulfillment of this passage.

> *Revelation 14:6-7 (ESV)*
> *^{6} Then I saw another angel flying directly overhead, with an eternal gospel to proclaim to those who dwell on earth, to every nation and tribe and language and people. ^{7} And he said with a loud voice, "Fear God and give him glory, because the hour of his judgment has come, and worship him who made heaven and earth, the sea and the springs of water."*

Therefore, the spread of missionary evangelism is not a sign that can be used to anticipate the nearness of Christ's return, they say. Perhaps so, but the accelerated global spread of the gospel in the last few decades has made fulfillment foreseeable within a few decades, based on missionary outreach. It would seem that if a supernatural fulfillment is in view in Matt 24:14, it will have to happen soon to beat an evangelistic fulfillment. This should not be taken to mean that the whole world will be converted by that effort. (That is the message of post-millennialists who believe that world-wide evangelistic success will usher in the millennium, apart from the return of Jesus.) Regarding the success rate of the gospel message, Jesus said, ". . . few there be that find it." --'it' meaning heaven. Matt 24:14 simply means that every people group will have the opportunity to hear and consider the gospel message.

Non-Biblical Indicators of Approaching Crisis

We look to the scriptures for guidance and understanding of what lies ahead. There are also non-biblical factors that cause us to expect that the earth is headed for crisis. Perhaps foremost on this list is world population. According to the US Bureau of Census, in the time of Christ the world population is estimated to have been about 170 million people. It had doubled in about 1300 years, and doubled again after another 420 years, again in another 150 years, again in 80 years, and finally again after only about 50 years, which brings us to the present population of over six billion. The following figure is a graphical representation of this growth. At the present time the worldwide average population density is approximately 90 persons per square mile. Projections based on the current rate of increase can't reach too far into the future without running out of space.

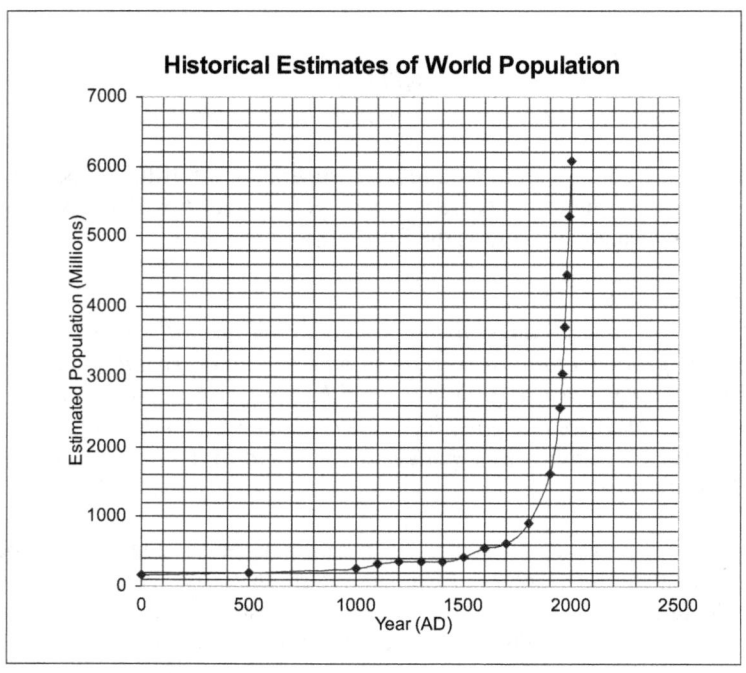

Other crisis indicators, real or perceived, include environmental pollution, increased earthquakes, food shortage, energy shortage, lowering of atmospheric oxygen due to receding tropical forests, loss of the ozone layer, global warming, health crises such as AIDS and other 'new' organic diseases.

Wait! This list sounds ominous, but before you are tempted to panic, consider this. While these various conditions may serve as signs that the earth is heading toward crisis, and while they may bring much misery to this earth, these issues will not be the cause of the end of life as we know it. If it were so, we could view them as inevitable, and dismiss ourselves of any responsibility to God. The Bible tells us that the end will come when God decides to bring judgment on this sinful world, and to redeem His own. By His direct intervention, this present age will be terminated, not by natural self-destruction. God may employ some of these natural factors as instruments of His wrath as he pours out judgment on living men and women, but if so, they will happen at His cue, not by some inevitable progression of circumstance.

It is important that we distinguish this truth. We must anticipate a judgment of God ahead. God has made it perfectly clear, underscoring it by the vast number of passages predicting it. We must communicate this to others so that they too can repent and *escape the wrath to come.*

If this is true, why bring these crisis points into the discussion? I highlight these outside indicators, not to try to extrapolate to a natural end, but to say that the end will come BEFORE any of these natural situations bring self-destruction.

> Lord God, we have come to understand that your return means something very different to us who belong to you than it does to those who do not know you. Unbelievers have reason to dread that day. But you have told us to anticipate it with great joy and excitement. Lord, we confess that our natural instincts make us apprehensive of what is to come. So now we ask two things of You. First Lord, forgive us our carnal instincts that battle against our faith. We pray Your Spirit will cause us to trust in your promises and your purposes. Second, put within us a genuine eagerness for the return of Jesus. Make us seethe with a longing to see his face. Make this longing so intrinsic to our walk with you that it shapes our relationship with you, like a romance should. Come soon Lord Jesus, we pray. Amen

21
WHAT ABOUT ISRAEL?

If you open a newspaper to the front page, it is not unlikely you'll find an article having to do with Israel. World events regularly are eclipsed by Israel's latest circumstances. The population of Israel is about 6.5 million, only 1/10th of one percent of the world's population. Yet no nation plays a more strategic role in the global community. It is not because of military might or great natural resources that Israel is so prominent. What is it that lifts her into the world's limelight so regularly?

Israel is unique among all the nations of the world. Most people today are ignorant of this uniqueness, and hold her to be just another small nation, and an overblown one at that. To appreciate her special position, we must look very briefly to her origin, her history and her destiny for it is there we will find the secret of Israel.

Israel Unique in Origin

The Calling Out of a People
In the days of repopulation after the great flood, people settled in family-groups around which a tribe or clan formed. Many clans flocculated together to form cities. A patriarch or elder of each clan served as both the religious and judicial leader. Many of these groups fell into idolatry. This lifestyle and its religious practices became increasingly contemptible, often including child sacrifice and sexual promiscuity. They were an abomination to God. As we discussed previously, the spread of idolatry was not just a happenstance. It was due to the active, aggressive influence of Satan who promoted it.

It was out of this lifestyle that God called out one man to separate himself from his native culture and journey to a distant place he did not know. He was told that he was being called to give birth to a new people group, distinct from the other peoples. They were distinct by their unique calling. From the onset they were characterized by the notion of belonging to God. Thus, Abraham and his sons and grandsons became the patriarchs of a great nation, the Hebrew nation--Israel.

Genesis 12:1-6 (RSV)
¹ Now the LORD said to Abram, "Go from your country and your kindred and your father's house to the land that I will show you. ² And I will make of you a great nation, and I will bless you, and make your name great, so that you will be a blessing. ³ I will bless those who bless you, and him who curses you I will curse; and by you all the families of the earth shall bless themselves." ⁴ So Abram went, as the LORD had told him; and Lot went with him. Abram was seventy-five years old when he departed from Haran. ⁵ And he [God] brought him [Abraham] outside and said, "Look toward heaven, and number the stars, if you are able to number them." Then he said to him, "So shall your descendants be." ⁶ And he believed the LORD; and he reckoned it to him as righteousness.

The Patriarchs of Faith

These promises made by God to Abraham are known as the Abrahamic Covenant. Abraham's faith in the promise of God was the basis and hallmark of the nation Israel.

Genesis 17:6-8 (RSV)
⁶ I will make you exceedingly fruitful; and I will make nations of you, and kings shall come forth from you. ⁷ And I will establish my covenant between me and you and your descendants after you throughout their generations for an everlasting covenant, to be God to you and to your descendants after you. ⁸ And I will give to you, and to your descendants after you, the land of your sojournings, all the land of Canaan, for an everlasting possession; and I will be their God."

Make no mistake, God's call to Abraham was more than descendants and land. Although the promise included these blessings, it was foremost a relational covenant. God promised Abraham *to be your God and the God of your descendants after you*. Abraham grasped the eternal component of this promise, and clung to it all his life. Reflecting on this account, the writer of the New Testament book of Hebrews said this:

Hebrews 11:11-16 (ESV)
¹¹ By faith Sarah herself received power to conceive, even when she was past the age, since she considered him faithful who had promised. ¹² Therefore from one man, and him as good as dead, were born descendants as many as the stars of heaven and as many as the innumerable grains of sand by the seashore. ¹³ These all died in faith, not having received the things promised, but having seen them and greeted them from afar, and having acknowledged that they were strangers and exiles on the earth. ¹⁴ For people who speak thus make it clear that they are seeking a homeland. ¹⁵ If they had been

thinking of that land from which they had gone out, they would have had opportunity to return. ⁶ But as it is, they desire a better country, that is, a heavenly one. Therefore God is not ashamed to be called their God, for he has prepared for them a city.

In essence, the call of Abraham, the call that initiated the nation Israel, was a relational covenant. However, there were also temporal blessings promised as a result of that relationship. To Abraham, whose marriage with his wife had been barren, God promised descendants beyond counting. Furthermore, He promised him the land of Canaan as a homeland for this new nation.

Israel Unique in History

<u>The Bondage and Exodus Period</u>
While the call came in Abraham's day, and the descendants began to multiply, the people did not yet have their land, but were nomadic, moving from place to place. Through a series of events precipitated by a great famine, they became enslaved by Egyptian kings, and were in bondage there for 400 years. During that time they became forced laborers. There they multiplied from a few dozen to over a million people. God raised up Moses to lead the people to freedom. Through a series of powerful miracles administered by Moses, God delivered the Hebrew people from their Egyptian bondage. It was to Moses that God gave his Ten Commandments and numerous more detailed regulations, along with promises for the Hebrews--the Mosaic Covenant. After 40 years of wandering in the wilderness, God raised up Joshua who led them into Canaan. The land was occupied by very evil and idolatrous people, and God told him that the Israelites were to take the land away from the pagan tribes. He was giving it to the Israelites as their inheritance. They were told to completely drive out their predecessors because of their evil character.

Numbers 33:50-55 (NASB)
⁵⁰ Then the LORD spoke to Moses in the plains of Moab by the Jordan opposite Jericho, saying, ⁵¹ "Speak to the sons of Israel and say to them, 'When you cross over the Jordan into the land of Canaan, ⁵² then you shall drive out all the inhabitants of the land from before you, and destroy all their figured stones, and destroy all their molten images and demolish all their high places; ⁵³ and you shall take possession of the land and live in it, for I have given the land to you to possess it. ⁵⁴ 'You shall inherit the land by lot according to your families; to the larger you shall give more inheritance, and to the smaller you shall give less inheritance. Wherever the lot falls to anyone, that shall be his. You shall inherit according to the tribes of your fathers. ⁵⁵ 'But if you do not drive out the inhabitants of the land from before you, then it shall come about

that those whom you let remain of them will become as pricks in your eyes and as thorns in your sides, and they will trouble you in the land in which you live.

The Period of the Judges

Israel grew as a nation. Through the ages she was sometimes loyal to God's call and obedient to His commands. At other times the people became self-absorbed, self-serving, and disloyal to God. They began to worship other gods or to worship God in a way inappropriate for His holy character. When this occurred, God used the surrounding pagan nations to punish Israel by attacking and subduing them for a season. It is often in the valleys of hardship and despair that we remember God and turn to Him, and it was no different for the Israelites. When they repented of their sinfulness and turned back to God, He delivered them by raising up a leader whom He would empower to be victorious over the nation's enemies. Using this anointed leader, God would intervene to deliver Israel from her captors and restore her to fellowship with Himself. This process repeated itself many times during the period of the judges.

The Kingdom Period

Later, the nation became a kingdom. Her second king was David. With David, God made a covenant--the Davidic Covenant. He promised an everlasting kingdom in which David's descendants would forever occupy the throne.

> *2 Samuel 7:12,16 (ESV)*
> *[12] When your days are fulfilled and you lie down with your fathers, I will raise up your offspring after you, who shall come from your body, and I will establish his kingdom . . . [16] And your house and your kingdom shall be made sure forever before me. Your throne shall be established forever.'*

Now we understand that the ultimate fulfillment of that promise is found in Jesus. Since Jesus is of the lineage of David, humanly speaking, and since his kingdom is an everlasting kingdom, this promise is fulfilled in him. It is what the end-time events are all about. We repeatedly see this promise repeated in prophecy throughout the Old Testament.

The Period of Spiritual Decline and Punishment

After the death of David's son, King Solomon, civil war divided the kingdom. The southern kingdom of Judah contained Jerusalem, the seat of the kingdom and the temple. The northern kingdom Israel se t up its own capitol and religious center. Their self-styled worship was not proper according to the commandment of God. Over a 200 year span, the northern kingdom slowly declined as they fell into idolatry and perversion. It was during this period that many of the prophets lived and prophesied. Through them God warned Israel of impending punishment at the hand of their enemies unless they repented and turned back to Him. They did not. Finally, they were attacked, captured and exiled by the Assyrians from the east. The exiles of the northern kingdom never returned in any comprehensive way.

Meanwhile, the kingdom of Judah was also sliding into a decline which lagged that of the northern kingdom. Miniature revivals failed to stop the general trend into idolatry. Again, God sent prophets. Again, the warnings went largely unheeded. Finally, the empire of Babylon under Nebuchadnezzar sent its armies against Judah, capturing and exiling everyone important to Babylon. As punishment for her disloyalty, God allowed Judah to be stripped bare. Her people were displaced to Babylon where they lived as unwilling inhabitants in the very idolatrous culture of Babylon.

Restoration and Occupation
But God did not leave His people in punishment. Their Babylonian captors were themselves captured by the Medes who became the new masters of Judah. After seventy years in exile, their punishment was complete. God orchestrated their return in a miraculous way, restoring them to their land under the leadership of Ezra, Nehemiah and Zerubbabel. Thus closes the historical narrative of the Old Testament.

At first the restored Judah was a vassal to the Medes and Persians. Later she gained full independence when the Medo-Persians fell to upstart Greece. Judah itself was later captured as Alexander's army spread like a blanket over the known world. The Greeks occupied Judah for 170 years, during which her people were badly mistreated. It was during this period that Antiochus Epiphanes, mentioned in chapter 12, reigned. Finally Israel revolted and threw off her Grecian overlords, gaining again her independence. After about 110 years of autonomy, the Romans invaded the land of Israel, again subjecting Judah to grievous occupation. The rise of these last two empires and their occupation of Palestine are not narrated in the biblical books of history because they occurred during the 400 year silent period between the Old and New Testaments. However, they are clearly predicted in detail in the Old Testament prophetic writings. They were chronicled in prophetic foretelling, so that God's purpose in all these affairs of men is clearly seen. In this way, he created an anticipation for a supernatural rescue.

Messiah
At the opening of the New Testament, we find Israel already under Roman occupation. The time was rife with expectations of a coming Messiah. There were several reasons for this hope.

One was the burden of the Roman occupation. Since there seemed to be no logical expectation of a revolution against powerful Rome, the hope of the people turned to God. They longed for Him to again miraculously deliver, as He had so many times before. Many looked for a Messiah who would be a military leader armed with supernatural power from God.

A second reason they were looking for a Messiah was because of a sort of spiritual awakening. For centuries the Hebrews had seen themselves as God's righteous people. Yet after repeated episodes of spiritual failure followed by punishment, repentance and restoration, and now in the middle of one more such cycle, there were stirrings of national repentance and spiritual revival. They had come to realize they were incapable of pleasing God, and needed a dominant spiritual leader to guide their return to God's favor. Their despair over past failure and disillusionment with corrupt religious leaders had evolved into a longing for that allusive holiness to which they had been called.

Perhaps the most powerful factor that produced this messianic expectation was the understanding of such a Messiah from prophecy. The circumstances of his predicted arrival seemed to correspond to their present situation. No prophecy was more potent in this regard than one particular prophecy of Daniel, today called the 'prophecy of the seventy weeks' given to Daniel late in his life while in exile in Babylon. An excerpt reads:

Daniel 9:20-26 (NASB)
[20] Now while I was speaking and praying, and confessing my sin and the sin of my people Israel, and presenting my supplication before the LORD my God in behalf of the holy mountain of my God, [21] while I was still speaking in prayer, then the man Gabriel, whom I had seen in the vision previously, came to me in my extreme weariness about the time of the evening offering. [22] He gave me instruction and talked with me and said, "O Daniel, I have now come forth to give you insight with understanding. [23] "At the beginning of your supplications the command was issued, and I have come to tell you, for you are highly esteemed; so give heed to the message and gain understanding of the vision. [24] "Seventy weeks have been decreed for your people and your holy city, to finish the transgression, to make an end of sin, to make atonement for iniquity, to bring in everlasting righteousness, to seal up vision and prophecy and to anoint the most holy place. [25] "So you are to know and discern that from the issuing of a decree to restore and rebuild Jerusalem until Messiah the Prince there will be seven weeks and sixty-two weeks; it will be built again, with plaza and moat, even in times of distress. [26] "Then after the sixty-two weeks the Messiah will be cut off and have nothing, and the people of the prince who is to come will destroy the city and the

sanctuary. And its end will come with a flood; even to the end there will be war; desolations are determined.

When written in about 538 BC, all of the predictions were yet future, and meant nothing logical to Daniel. Shortly afterward, the exiles from Judah were allowed to return to their homeland to rebuild the temple under the leadership of Ezra. Still later, under Nehemiah, another contingency was dispatched to Jerusalem to rebuild the city walls. The time frame of *seventy weeks,* is meaningless if understood to be literal weeks. However, the Hebrew term *shabuwa* has been used to refer to years in some instances. In Gen 29:27-30 Jacob is said to have worked a week for the right to marry Laban's daughter, then we are clearly told that he worked for Laban seven years. So the time frame of Daniel is widely understood to mean 70x7 = 490 years according to this day-year manner of interpretation. That period of time was to be the span between the decree to return and rebuild Jerusalem and the coming of the *anointed one.* By the time the New Testament opens, the decree was a historical reality. King Artaxerxes had given the decree to Nehemiah in about 445 BC. Using the Jewish lunar calendar, it has been calculated from that date there were precisely 490 years until Jesus' triumphal entry into Jerusalem just before his crucifixion. You can see that this prophecy set a very specific time frame for the coming of Messiah, and the people were well aware that the time was near.

The expectation of a coming Messiah conceived a more genuine and vital faith among the common people than the Jewish rituals and legalistic customs were able to produce. It is equally true that the exact nature of the Messiah was a mystery to them. Would he be a military leader, a politician, a priest, an angel? His mission was also vague, but virtually everyone's view included deliverance of national Israel from the Roman occupation.

Jesus did not turn out to be the political liberator the people were expecting. Instead, he preached about holiness and confronted the hypocrisy of the Jewish leaders. For this, they conspired to kill him. At first, Jesus was popular, but the people ultimately followed the influence of their leaders and rejected him, handing him over to the Roman authorities for crucifixion. By doing so, history was following the plan of God. It was his death that was the atoning sacrifice for the sins of the whole world. By his death, we can be forgiven of our sins, if we appropriate that forgiveness for ourselves by embracing his sacrificial death, and thus giving him the lordship of our lives.

Messianic Rejection
Although the Jews were behaving consistent with God's plan, they were nonetheless guilty of willfully rejecting their Messiah, the very Son of God. When they rejected him, the gospel was taken from them, and carried to the Gentiles.

Romans 9:30-33 (RSV)
[30] What shall we say, then? That Gentiles who did not pursue righteousness have attained it, that is, righteousness through faith; [31] but that Israel who pursued the righteousness which is based on law did not succeed in fulfilling that law. [32] Why? Because they did not pursue it through faith, but as if it were based on works. They have stumbled over the stumbling stone, [33] as it is written, "Behold, I am laying in Zion a stone that will make men stumble, a rock that will make them fall; and he who believes in him will not be put to shame."

Romans 11:7-10 (RSV)
[7] What then? Israel failed to obtain what it sought. The elect obtained it, but the rest were hardened, [8] as it is written, "God gave them a spirit of stupor, eyes that should not see and ears that should not hear, down to this very day." [9] And David says, "Let their table become a snare and a trap, a pitfall and a retribution for them; [10] let their eyes be darkened so that they cannot see, and bend their backs for ever."

Dispersion

When Israel rejected her Messiah, she was rejected by God. About thirty-five years later, Israel revolted against the occupying Romans, and was invaded and captured. Jerusalem was captured and destroyed. The temple was leveled. In about 130 AD, after another uprising, most of the Jews were exiled and dispersed to other lands throughout the Roman Empire. Their land was inhabited by nomadic peoples from surrounding regions.

Jewish communities sprung up all over the empire. Since there was no homeland attachment, they were, to a degree, absorbed into the cultures of the host countries. The 'Diaspora' seemed to effectively eliminate national Israel from existence. In many regions Jews met with anti-Semitism. This mysterious hatred of Jews is still a prevalent attitude in much of the world today. It is not due to their rejection of the Messiah, and therefore somehow justifiable, as some would say. This hatred originated in the mind of Satan. It is still the mind of Satan that promotes it today. However, God's rejection of Israel was not permanent, as we shall shortly see.

In the seventh century, Islam began building its dominion in Arabia. It has now become the dominant religion of the entire Middle East, Central Asia, Indonesia, and large portions of Africa, and has large followings in every part of the world. Its method of evangelism in many places was, and still is, forced conversion. Many of the people living in the Palestine region were engulfed by Islam, such that the sparse population of the region was essentially Muslim by the nineteenth century.

Her Re-gathering

In the later part of the 1800's the Zionist movement began. Its goal was to claim back the land of national Israel and gather into it all Jews who would go. The movement brought great opposition from the Islamic community. This movement took stair-steps toward reality after each of the World Wars of the 20th century. The protests of neighboring Islamic countries were ignored. The treaty countries of World War II recognized Israel, and the Jewish pilgrims responded in 1948 by jubilantly declaring themselves a nation. Immediately her small population was attacked by Islamic neighbors, but she was victorious in her war for autonomy and independence, gaining a solid foothold in the new homeland. There she has been since that time. Her new presence has been laced with turmoil originating from the strife with her neighbors. She has been attacked by Egypt and Syria in their effort to destroy her. The non-Jews living in Israel have congregated in the West Bank, declaring themselves "Palestinians," and the rest of the Islamic world has taken up their cause. Islam has made itself the principle enemy of Israel. The United States has been a strong ally to Israel, which marks us as an enemy in the eyes of many of the Middle East people. Recently, an anti-Semitic trend has eroded Israeli-US ties.

Israel Unique in Destiny

To grasp the uniqueness of Israel, it is necessary to understand her covenant relationship with God. There were actually several covenants, and they were of two types: 'conditional' and 'unconditional.' Conditional covenants were agreements or promises by God to bless Israel in a certain way if she would be faithful in a particular manner. The Mosaic Covenant was of this type. Unconditional covenants were simply promises with no strings attached. The Abrahamic and Davidic Covenants were of this type, and it is these that promised Israel an eternal future. About this unconditional covenant relationship, Paul wrote:

> *Romans 11:28-29 (RSV)*
> *^{28} As regards the gospel they are enemies of God, for your sake; but as regards election they are beloved for the sake of their forefathers.*
> *^{29} For the gifts and the call of God are irrevocable.*

In light of this truth, we must look at the experiences of Israel as being part of His plan and will for the Jews. The two major exiles in Judah's history are no exception, and must be seen in this same way. They were engineered by God. I suggest that we should view them in two ways. First, they are seen as punishment and discipline on her unfaithfulness, with a view to ultimate restoration. Second, these exiles are seen as part of God's comprehensive plan for bringing salvation to the whole world, not just to the Jewish people. When this has been accomplished, the Jews will be re-established in belief. Again Paul said:

Romans 11:25-27 (RSV)
²⁵ Lest you be wise in your own conceits, I want you to understand this mystery, brethren: a hardening has come upon part of Israel, until the full number of the Gentiles come in, ²⁶ and so all Israel will be saved; as it is written, "The Deliverer will come from Zion, he will banish ungodliness from Jacob"; ²⁷ "and this will be my covenant with them when I take away their sins."

The re-gathering of Jews to Israel after the first exile into Babylon was truly a unique event. At no other time in history has a people been able to reestablish itself as a nation after decades in exile. However, if that was unique, the reestablishment of Israel in Palestine in the twentieth century after more than 1800 years in exile is miraculous in a huge way. So unique was it that God demonstrated it this way to His prophet Ezekiel.

Ezekiel 37:1-14 (NASB)
¹ The hand of the LORD was upon me, and He brought me out by the Spirit of the LORD and set me down in the middle of the valley; and it was full of bones. ² He caused me to pass among them round about, and behold, there were very many on the surface of the valley; and lo, they were very dry. ³ He said to me, "Son of man, can these bones live?" And I answered, "O Lord GOD, You know." ⁴ Again He said to me, "Prophesy over these bones and say to them, 'O dry bones, hear the word of the LORD.' ⁵ "Thus says the Lord GOD to these bones, 'Behold, I will cause breath to enter you that you may come to life. ⁶ 'I will put sinews on you, make flesh grow back on you, cover you with skin and put breath in you that you may come alive; and you will know that I am the LORD.'" ⁷ So I prophesied as I was commanded; and as I prophesied, there was a noise, and behold, a rattling; and the bones came together, bone to its bone. ⁸ And I looked, and behold, sinews were on them, and flesh grew and skin covered them; but there was no breath in them. ⁹ Then He said to me, "Prophesy to the breath, prophesy, son of man, and say to the breath, 'Thus says the Lord GOD, "Come from the four winds, O breath, and breathe on these slain, that they come to life."'" ¹⁰ So I prophesied as He commanded me, and the breath came into them, and they came to life and stood on their feet, an exceedingly great army. ¹¹ Then He said to me, "Son of man, these bones are the whole house of Israel; behold, they say, 'Our bones are dried up and our hope has perished. We are completely cut off.' ¹² "Therefore prophesy and say to them, 'Thus says the Lord GOD, "Behold, I will open your graves and cause you to come up out of your graves, My people; and I will bring you into the land of Israel. ¹³ "Then you will know that I am the LORD, when I have opened your graves and caused you to come up out of your graves, My people. ¹⁴ "I will put

My Spirit within you and you will come to life, and I will place you on your own land. Then you will know that I, the LORD, have spoken and done it," declares the LORD.'"

Other Old Testament prophets clearly predicted this unfathomable event. As far back as Moses, God brought this message:

Deuteronomy 4:26-31 (NASB)
^{26} I call heaven and earth to witness against you today, that you will surely perish quickly from the land where you are going over the Jordan to possess it. You shall not live long on it, but will be utterly destroyed. ^{27} "The LORD will scatter you among the peoples, and you will be left few in number among the nations where the LORD drives you. ^{28} "There you will serve gods, the work of man's hands, wood and stone, which neither see nor hear nor eat nor smell. ^{29} "But from there you will seek the LORD your God, and you will find Him if you search for Him with all your heart and all your soul. ^{30} "When you are in distress and all these things have come upon you, in the latter days you will return to the LORD your God and listen to His voice. ^{31} "For the LORD your God is a compassionate God; He will not fail you nor destroy you nor forget the covenant with your fathers which He swore to them.

This prophecy was pronounced by Moses in his farewell address, just before the Israelites were about to enter the promised land. Way back then the plan was known to God. He saw their exile, but also note that, *When you are in distress and all these things have happened to you* is followed by, *...in later days you will return to the LORD your God and obey him.*

Jeremiah 30:10-11 (NASB)
^{10} 'Fear not, O Jacob My servant,' declares the LORD, 'And do not be dismayed, O Israel; For behold, I will save you from afar And your offspring from the land of their captivity. And Jacob will return and will be quiet and at ease, And no one will make him afraid. ^{11} 'For I am with you,' declares the LORD, 'to save you; For I will destroy completely all the nations where I have scattered you, Only I will not destroy you completely. But I will chasten you justly And will by no means leave you unpunished.'

Jeremiah prophesied in the southern kingdom of Judah during the dark days prior to and during her first exile by the Babylonians. This prophecy promised that Israel would be saved *out of* the land of her exile. Earlier prophecies in Jeremiah chapters 25 and 29 had more specifically predicted that the duration of the exile would be seventy years, and that afterwards the Babylonians would be destroyed, as is also told here. This all came to pass precisely. The great empires of Assyria and Babylon shortly disappeared into history, but Israel lives on.

But notice the statement that, *Jacob will again have peace and security, and no one will make him afraid.* Although Judah and the remnants of Israel returned from exile under Ezra and Nehemiah in a miraculous deliverance, and although they re-built their temple and re-built the walls of Jerusalem, still they never did dwell securely. They were continually under foreign domination or the threat of such from that time forward, right up through the time of the New Testament. They never had sovereignty over the old walled city of Jerusalem again until June 7, 1967. This prophecy seems to have a higher view also in sight, that of the millennial kingdom. This distant view is clear in Isaiah's prophecy.

> *Isaiah 11:11-12 (RSV)*
> *[11] In that day the Lord will extend his hand yet a second time to recover the remnant which is left of his people, from Assyria, from Egypt, from Pathros, from Ethiopia, from Elam, from Shinar, from Hamath, and from the coastlands of the sea. [12] He will raise an ensign for the nations, and will assemble the outcasts of Israel, and gather the dispersed of Judah from the four corners of the earth.*

This scripture makes it perfectly clear that there is, in God's view, a second return from exile, an exile that was not just to the countries to the East, but one that was to *the four quarters of the earth*. This clearly fits the Roman exile. The following passage, also from Isaiah, gives a glimpse of the Lord's purpose in doing this. It is a pronouncement by God the Father upon His Son, as told by the Son.

> *Isaiah 49:5-9 (RSV)*
> *[5] And now the LORD says, who formed me from the womb to be his servant, to bring Jacob back to him, and that Israel might be gathered to him, for I am honored in the eyes of the LORD, and my God has become my strength -- [6] he says: "It is too light a thing that you should be my servant to raise up the tribes of Jacob and to restore the preserved of Israel; I will give you as a light to the nations, that my salvation may reach to the end of the earth." [7] Thus says the LORD, the Redeemer of Israel and his Holy One, to one deeply despised, abhorred by the nations, the servant of rulers: "Kings shall see and arise; princes, and they shall prostrate themselves; because of the LORD, who is faithful, the Holy One of Israel, who has chosen you." [8] Thus says the LORD: "In a time of favor I have answered you, in a day of salvation I have helped you; I have kept you and given you as a covenant to the people, to establish the land, to apportion the desolate heritages; [9] saying to the*

prisoners, 'Come forth,' to those who are in darkness, 'Appear.' They shall feed along the ways, on all bare heights shall be their pasture;

Wow! Here God opens up His purpose in sending His servant. The phrases *come out,* and *be free* refer to the calling of Israel out of the land of her exile. He could have just saved and redeemed Israel; that is the plan all the Jews would expect of their Messiah. That would have been a miracle. But no! This Messiah would do something far greater. He would first bring salvation to the whole world, then also save Israel as the culmination of the whole scheme.

Jeremiah 31:15-17 (NASB)
[15] Thus says the LORD, "A voice is heard in Ramah, Lamentation and bitter weeping. Rachel is weeping for her children; She refuses to be comforted for her children, Because they are no more." [16] Thus says the LORD, "Restrain your voice from weeping And your eyes from tears; For your work will be rewarded," declares the LORD, "And they will return from the land of the enemy. [17] "There is hope for your future," declares the LORD, "And your children will return to their own territory.

The first portion of this passage is that prophecy commonly read at Christmas regarding the slaughter of infant boys by Herod in the Bethlehem area. Satan, in his attempt to destroy the Christ, used Herod as his hit man. This scripture is quoted in the nativity passage in Matthew as showing this fulfillment. But it is clear when we read the longer Jeremiah passage that more is in sight than this. The focus shifts to national Israel. God promises to bring them back, in the end.

Ezekiel 37:25-28 (NASB)
[25] "They [Israel] will live on the land that I gave to Jacob My servant, in which your fathers lived; and they will live on it, they, and their sons and their sons' sons, forever; and David My servant will be their prince forever. [26] "I will make a covenant of peace with them; it will be an everlasting covenant with them. And I will place them and multiply them, and will set My sanctuary in their midst forever. [27] "My dwelling place also will be with them; and I will be their God, and they will be My people. [28] "And the nations will know that I am the LORD who sanctifies Israel, when My sanctuary is in their midst forever."""

Many of these predictions were partially fulfilled in the first return from exile under Ezra and Nehemiah. From the time of their utterances, the first return from exile was relatively near-term. But it is obvious that a more widespread dispersion than just to Babylon is in view, pointing to the later one under the Romans when the dispersion was among *the nations, all the nations,* to *the far corners of the earth,* and this would occur *a second time.* We are seeing in our day the beginning of fulfillment of these prophecies.

Do not assume, however, that this is a sign of messianic faith on the part of national Israel. Their faith is not toward Jesus at this time, or even toward God. The fact is, the majority of Palestinian Jews today live an essentially secular life. Many have given up their hope of redemption. But these events are fulfilling prophecy and setting the stage for more prophecy to be fulfilled. A major miracle will be required to establish faith in Israel in the last days, and that miracle is prophesied. To the Roman church, Paul quoted from Isaiah 59 . . .

> *Romans 11:26 (RSV)*
> *²⁶ and so all Israel will be saved; as it is written, "The Deliverer will come from Zion, he will banish ungodliness from Jacob";*

It will take a miracle that can only come from God for Israel to be established in faith. In that sense, the times and attitudes are very much like they were just before his first coming. Discerning messianic Jews realize that human effort will not produce this return to God, but only the power of God, as displayed in His Messiah, can reach their godless souls.

Now let's rewind many centuries. The prevailing understanding of prophecy during apostolic and post-apostolic times had been that Israel would somehow be literally restored in her homeland. This was based on their knowledge of end-time prophecies. As time lapsed after the exile and dispersion of the Jews by the Romans, the prospect of their literal return seemed to grow dim. Most people in Christian circles eventually gave up on a literal fulfillment of these prophecies. Instead, a doctrine came into wide acceptance called 'transfer theology.' It proposed that since the Jews rejected their Messiah, the gospel was taken from them and given to Gentiles and many of them accepted him. Therefore, the as-yet-unfulfilled promises made to and about Israel became fulfilled in the church, not in national Israel. According to this view, the church is Israel in a covenant sense. This doctrine was supported by scriptures such as:

> *Romans 4:16 (RSV)*
> *¹⁶ That is why it depends on faith, in order that the promise may rest on grace and be guaranteed to all his descendants -- not only to the adherents of the law but also to those who share the faith of Abraham, for he is the father of us all,*

> *Romans 9:7-8 (RSV)*
> *⁷ and not all are children of Abraham because they are his descendants; but "Through Isaac shall your descendants be named."*
> *⁸ This means that it is not the children of the flesh who are the*

children of God, but the children of the promise are reckoned as descendants.

Galatians 3:7-9 (NASB)
⁷ Therefore, be sure that it is those who are of faith who are sons of Abraham. ⁸ The Scripture, foreseeing that God would justify the Gentiles by faith, preached the gospel beforehand to Abraham, saying, "ALL THE NATIONS WILL BE BLESSED IN YOU." ⁹ So then those who are of faith are blessed with Abraham, the believer.

Galatians 3:28-29 (NASB)
²⁸ There is neither Jew nor Greek, there is neither slave nor free man, there is neither male nor female; for you are all one in Christ Jesus. ²⁹ And if you belong to Christ, then you are Abraham's descendants, heirs according to promise.

Will the Real Israel Please Stand Up?

But is transfer theology valid? The early church firmly expected a national restoration of Israel in a literal sense. Transfer doctrine came much later, and did not derive from an improved understanding of God's plan as revealed in scripture. It originated out of unbelief. It was the doubting of pragmatic minds that declared in so many words, 'God can't possibly restore Israel out of her hopeless present situation.'

What about the fact that the Jews as a nation rejected their Messiah? Did not God reject them? Paul addresses this question head-on:

Romans 9:25-31 (RSV)
²⁵ As indeed he says in Hose'a, "Those who were not my people I will call `my people,' and her who was not beloved I will call `my beloved.'" ²⁶ "And in the very place where it was said to them, `You are not my people,' they will be called `sons of the living God.'" ²⁷ And Isaiah cries out concerning Israel: "Though the number of the sons of Israel be as the sand of the sea, only a remnant of them will be saved; ²⁸ for the Lord will execute his sentence upon the earth with rigor and dispatch." ²⁹ And as Isaiah predicted, "If the Lord of hosts had not left us children, we would have fared like Sodom and been made like Gomor'rah." ³⁰ What shall we say, then? That Gentiles who did not pursue righteousness have attained it, that is, righteousness through faith; ³¹ but that Israel who pursued the righteousness which is based on law did not succeed in fulfilling that law.

Here we have the concept of the *remnant*. The Lord had future plans for Israel, but only a very small number of first-century Jews believed. Most, including Israel's leaders, rejected Jesus as their Messiah. They could not accept a gospel of faith when their concept of righteousness was so rooted in the meritorious keeping of rigid laws and guidelines. Although they were devoted, their loyalty was to the ritual, not to God himself.

> *Romans 10:20-21 (RSV)*
> [20] Then Isaiah is so bold as to say, "I have been found by those who did not seek me; I have shown myself to those who did not ask for me." [21] But of Israel he says, "All day long I have held out my hands to a disobedient and contrary people."

This rejection of her Messiah by Israel became the opportunity for the gospel to be taken to Gentiles. It initiated missionary evangelism *to the uttermost parts of the earth*. But is God finished with Israel?

> *Romans 11:11-12 (RSV)*
> [11] So I ask, have they stumbled so as to fall? By no means! But through their trespass salvation has come to the Gentiles, so as to make Israel jealous. [12] Now if their trespass means riches for the world, and if their failure means riches for the Gentiles, how much more will their full inclusion mean!

> *Romans 11:25 (RSV)*
> [25] Lest you be wise in your own conceits, I want you to understand this mystery, brethren: a hardening has come upon part of Israel, until the full number of the Gentiles come in,

Israel's rejection by God is neither total nor permanent. According to God's plan, Israel will largely continue in unbelief until He determines the process complete. Then what?

> *Romans 11:26-32 (RSV)*
> [26] and so all Israel will be saved; as it is written, "The Deliverer will come from Zion, he will banish ungodliness from Jacob"; [27] "and this will be my covenant with them when I take away their sins." [28] As regards the gospel they are enemies of God, for your sake; but as regards election they are beloved for the sake of their forefathers. [29] For the gifts and the call of God are irrevocable. [30] Just as you were once disobedient to God but now have received mercy because of their disobedience, [31] so they have now been disobedient in order that by the mercy shown to you they also may receive mercy. [32] For God has consigned all men to disobedience, that he may have mercy upon all.

22
THE CONVERSION OF ISRAEL

As we have already said, there is much misunderstanding about the role of Israel in the last days. We discussed transfer doctrine whereby the Church replaces Israel under the new covenant, and Israel as a national entity is eliminated from the picture, never to be heard from again. On the other extreme, some believe that God will revert back to an Old Testament economy during the tribulation. Many have incorrectly concluded that in order for national Israel to literally fulfill the end-time prophecies, God would revert back to the Mosaic covenant in the last days. He would accept an inferior level of faith.

This is not the case at all. At no time has God regressed in His historical revelation of Himself through His covenants.

Now it is true that prophecy predicts that an Old Testament type of worship will be rejuvenated during the last days. Daniel predicted the abomination of desolation would *stand in the holy place*, that is, in the temple. He also prophesied that the *daily sacrifice* would be halted. This is confirmed in Matthew 24. So, yes, such a mode of worship with temple and sacrifice is predicted, and will take place in Israel in the last days, as prophesied. Yes, it appears from scripture that Israel will indeed re-establish its old covenant practices of worship during the early part of the last days. That does not presume that God will have reverted back to the former covenant, or that he has accepted their sacrifices. (That would violate all New Testament teaching.) It simply means Israel is still acting in unbelief at that point in time. They will be anticipating a messiah, but not THE Messiah, the Lord Jesus Christ.

According to the scripture we just read at the end of Chapter 21 of this book, *God has bound all men* [Jew and Gentile] *over to disobedience so that he may have mercy on them all*. Both Jew and Gentile must be saved by grace, through faith. The gospel of Jesus Christ is, and forevermore will be, the saving message. The prediction is not that a different mode of salvation will come, prior to Christ's second coming. Rather it is that national Israel will come to faith in Jesus according to the one-and-only gospel of salvation in Jesus Christ.

Her widespread coming to saving faith in Jesus will not occur until after the events of Daniel's temple worship vision, after the events of Matthew 24 relating to temple worship. Yes, Israel will practice their primitive worship, but no, God will not accept their sacrifices of unbelief.

> *Acts 17:30-31 (ESV)*
> *30 The times of ignorance God overlooked, but now he commands all people everywhere to repent, 31 because he has fixed a day on which he will judge the world in righteousness by a man whom he has appointed; and of this he has given assurance to all by raising him from the dead."*

When the time of the Lord's favor toward Israel comes, it will occur by a coming to faith in the sacrificial death and resurrection of Jesus. It will come when they wholeheartedly call Jesus "Lord."

> *Psalm 102:12-16 (NASB)*
> *12 But You, O LORD, abide forever, And Your name to all generations. 13 You will arise and have compassion on Zion; For it is time to be gracious to her, For the appointed time has come. 14 Surely Your servants find pleasure in her stones And feel pity for her dust. 15 So the nations will fear the name of the LORD And all the kings of the earth Your glory. 16 For the LORD has built up Zion; He has appeared in His glory.*

> *Zechariah 12:10-14 (RSV)*
> *10 "And I will pour out on the house of David and the inhabitants of Jerusalem a spirit of compassion and supplication, so that, when they look on him whom they have pierced, they shall mourn for him, as one mourns for an only child, and weep bitterly over him, as one weeps over a first-born. 11 On that day the mourning in Jerusalem will be as great as the mourning for Hadadrim'mon in the plain of Megid'do. 12 The land shall mourn, each family by itself; the family of the house of David by itself, and their wives by themselves; the family of the house of Nathan by itself, and their wives by themselves; 13 the family of the house of Levi by itself, and their wives by themselves; the family of the Shim'e-ites by itself, and their wives by themselves; 14 and all the families that are left, each by itself, and their wives by themselves.*

When the Lord is revealed in the hearts of the Jewish people, Israel will repent in bitter anguish for rejecting her Messiah. She will weep openly, every member of her. She will embrace him in faith--faith in the gospel of his atoning work on the cross. Her embrace will be wholehearted and genuine.

> *Romans 11:26 (RSV)*
> *²⁶ and so all Israel will be saved; as it is written . . .*

Who Are the Elect?
There is confusion over the use of the word "elect" in scripture. In the Old Testament it always referred to the faithful of the nation of Israel and Judah. How about in the New Testament? Does *elect* still refer to Israel? Some believe it does. In Mark 13 we see the angels being sent to *gather his elect from the four winds, from the ends of the earth to the ends of the heavens.* This is parallel to Matthew 24, and speaks of the rapture, or in-gathering of the church. A few verses earlier, Jesus spoke about false christs who would *deceive even the elect--if that were possible. If that were possible,* could surely not be said of the Jews. They will have been living under history's greatest deception for centuries--believing Jesus to have been a heretic. No, in the New Testament the word *elect* refers to the church.

God's Sovereign Plan for Israel

Things did not go ideally for Israel in her relationship with God, it would seem. Yet this rejection of her Messiah was not a failure of Gods plan.

> *Romans 9:6 (RSV)*
> *⁶ But it is not as though the word of God had failed. For not all who are descended from Israel belong to Israel,*

God's Sovereignty
Her rejection had been prophesied. We know that God is omniscient and sees and knows all things. He knows the future, too. That is the basis for prophetic validity. From that perspective alone it is easy to understand prophecy as nothing more than prediction, albeit perfect prediction. God foreknows; therefore he speaks. But the fullness of God's involvement in history is not fully described by this view. God is more than just a precise prognosticator.

Scripture teaches that God knows the future of things because He is the One who orchestrates that future. This is called the 'sovereignty' of God. It teaches us that God is providentially active in His creation to accomplish His good will. Hundreds of Old Testament passages declare this thought. Here are a couple:

> *Isaiah 46:10 (RSV)*
> *¹⁰ declaring the end from the beginning and from ancient times things not yet done, saying, `My counsel shall stand, and I will accomplish all my purpose,'*

Job 12:13-14 (NASB)
¹³ "With Him are wisdom and might; To Him belong counsel and understanding. ¹⁴ "Behold, He tears down, and it cannot be rebuilt; He imprisons a man, and there can be no release.

New Testament writers expressed this too:

Ephesians 1:11 (ESV)
¹¹ In him we have obtained an inheritance, having been predestined according to the purpose of him who works all things according to the counsel of his will,

His sovereignty is seen nowhere more clearly than in the atoning work of Jesus on the cross.

Ephesians 3:11 (ESV)
¹¹ This was according to the eternal purpose that he has realized in Christ Jesus our Lord,

Acts 2:23 (ESV)
²³ this Jesus, delivered up according to the definite plan and foreknowledge of God, you crucified and killed by the hands of lawless men.

The volume of such passages is huge, and this teaching cannot be ignored. God's sovereignty is not a passive or abstract idea. Neither is God simply reactive to what happens like a master chess player. His sovereignty is an active power that drives history.

This is a very controversial concept among students of scripture. Some believe God controls everything at all times, and that we are essentially puppets. Others of the opposite extreme believe God created, then stepped away and allowed the world to determine its own course. Most people believe God exercises sovereignty in some things, but allows us some degree of freedom at the same time. I do not intend to drown us in this issue. I only point out that God is indeed sovereign and imposes His own will whenever He wishes. An understanding of this point is essential in order to grasp what He is doing in Israel.

God's Sovereign Dealing with Israel
His sovereign intervention in the affairs of men is especially evident with respect to the nation Israel. This unique arena of His sovereignty is highlighted extensively in scripture. It was evident in the lineage of the patriarchs.

Romans 9:6-15 (RSV)
⁶ But it is not as though the word of God had failed. For not all who are descended from Israel belong to Israel, ⁷ and not all are children of Abraham because they are his descendants; but "Through Isaac shall your descendants be named." ⁸ This means that it is not the children of the flesh who are the children of God, but the children of the promise are reckoned as descendants. ⁹ For this is what the promise said, "About this time I will return and Sarah shall have a son." ¹⁰ And not only so, but also when Rebecca had conceived children by one man, our forefather Isaac, ¹¹ though they were not yet born and had done nothing either good or bad, in order that God's purpose of election might continue, not because of works but because of his call, ¹² she was told, "The elder will serve the younger." ¹³ As it is written, "Jacob I loved, but Esau I hated." ¹⁴ What shall we say then? Is there injustice on God's part? By no means! ¹⁵ For he says to Moses, "I will have mercy on whom I have mercy, and I will have compassion on whom I have compassion."

Then Jacob, father of the clans of Israel, became the chosen one, and his offspring, the favored people.

Romans 11:7-10 (RSV)
⁷ What then? Israel failed to obtain what it sought. The elect obtained it, but the rest were hardened, ⁸ as it is written, "God gave them a spirit of stupor, eyes that should not see and ears that should not hear, down to this very day." ⁹ And David says, "Let their table become a snare and a trap, a pitfall and a retribution for them; ¹⁰ let their eyes be darkened so that they cannot see, and bend their backs for ever."

God gave the Israelites a dull spirit and blinded spiritual eyes and ears. He did this in order that the gospel, first offered to the Jews, might be taken to the Gentiles. This demonstrates the depth of God's love for the world, that He would blind and deafen His firstborn (Israel) for a season in order to also reach out and make Gentiles His legitimate children. In this He shows us His mercy.

Romans 11:30-36 (RSV)
³⁰ Just as you were once disobedient to God but now have received mercy because of their disobedience, ³¹ so they have now been disobedient in order that by the mercy shown to you they also may receive mercy. ³² For God has consigned all men to disobedience, that he may have mercy upon all. ³³ O the depth of the riches and wisdom and knowledge of God! How unsearchable are his judgments and how inscrutable his ways! ³⁴ "For who has known the mind of the Lord, or who has been his counselor?" ³⁵ "Or who has given a

gift to him that he might be repaid?" ³⁶ *For from him and through him and to him are all things. To him be glory for ever. Amen.*

This sovereign strategy of God not only allowed the gospel to reach Gentiles, but it also will ultimately lead the Jews into the kind of relationship with Him that He desires. Rather than their arrogant sense of exclusive security, He wants the Jews to repent and be thankful for His mercy toward them, like the Gentiles are. *For God has bound all men over to disobedience so that he may have mercy on them all.*

Israel will eventually come to see herself as having lived an enemy of God. When she comes to the realization that she has, for centuries, rejected the true Messiah of God, she will have reached that point. Then she will be able to accept and apply what Paul wrote to the Roman Christians:

> *Romans 3:10-11,19-24 (RSV)*
> ¹⁰ *as it is written: "None is righteous, no, not one;* ¹¹ *no one understands, no one seeks for God. . . .* ¹⁹ *Now we know that whatever the law says it speaks to those who are under the law, so that every mouth may be stopped, and the whole world may be held accountable to God.* ²⁰ *For no human being will be justified in his sight by works of the law, since through the law comes knowledge of sin.* ²¹ *But now the righteousness of God has been manifested apart from law, although the law and the prophets bear witness to it,* ²² *the righteousness of God through faith in Jesus Christ for all who believe. For there is no distinction;* ²³ *since all have sinned and fall short of the glory of God,* ²⁴ *they are justified by his grace as a gift, through the redemption which is in Christ Jesus,*

This will become a reality in Israel in the last days of the present age, just before Christ returns.

> Lord God, we seek your face. Teach us to seek you on your terms. We confess our tendency to parade before you our own self-righteousness. May we not stand in shame before you in the filthy rags of our own virtue. How like the first century Jews we are. Our minds know that this is not the way to your heart, but that you seek a penitent spirit. Help us make this more than a doctrinal abstraction. Help us make it a personal principle we live by. Then we shall enjoy your fellowship. Then we will bask in your loving presence in unashamed joy. Amen

Israel--God's Sign of the Times

God has spoken to the whole of humanity about His love for us. He has spoken in many ways.

> *Hebrews 1:1-2 (ESV)*
> *¹ Long ago, at many times and in many ways, God spoke to our fathers by the prophets, ² but in these last days he has spoken to us by his Son, whom he appointed the heir of all things, through whom also he created the world.*

His message is for all, but the historical and geographical context of end time prophecy is presented relative to Israel. No major end-time passage can be sequentially understood if we extract national Israel from it. Thus, Israel is like God's clock and compass. Of course we do not know specific times, but from scripture we do know certain sequences. By watching her, we see the wheels of God's plans turning, so to speak.

The return of Jesus is the centerpiece of end-time events. Everything prior to it anticipates it. Everything after it springs forward from it. It is natural to want to know something of the sequence of events that are associated with this second coming. Whenever we speak of Jesus' coming, it rarely brings to mind only that one isolated event, as climactic as it will be. Rather our minds are spontaneously flooded with many other concepts such as tribulation, glory, judgment, and so on. Then we want to know how they all fit together. We want some word from God about when to expect what. Jesus told his disciples this parable:

> *Matthew 24:32-35 (NASB)*
> *³² "Now learn the parable from the fig tree: when its branch has already become tender and puts forth its leaves, you know that summer is near; ³³ so, you too, when you see all these things, recognize that He is near, right at the door. ³⁴ "Truly I say to you, this generation will not pass away until all these things take place. ³⁵ "Heaven and earth will pass away, but My words will not pass away.*

Here we are told to recognize certain signs that signal the approach of his coming. Many take this passage to be nothing more specific than just a general admonition to know the signs of the time. But many others see a more specific message in this parable. The sign given is that of the fig tree. The fig tree was familiar to all living in Israel at the time of Jesus. But it was more than just a tree. The fig tree, like the grape vine, was a symbol of prosperity, blessing, and security, as the following verses show.

Micah 4:4 (NASB)
⁴ Each of them will sit under his vine And under his fig tree, With no one to make them afraid, For the mouth of the LORD of hosts has spoken.

Zechariah 3:10 (RSV)
¹⁰ In that day, says the LORD of hosts, every one of you will invite his neighbor under his vine and under his fig tree."

But the fig tree and grape vine were still more than that. Since Israel saw herself as God's people, and believed herself the recipient of God's blessings, these prosperity symbols became symbols of the nation itself. God uses this symbolism a number of times in scripture. For example...

Hosea 9:10 (RSV)
¹⁰ Like grapes in the wilderness, I found Israel. Like the first fruit on the fig tree, in its first season, I saw your fathers...

Luke 13:6-9 (ESV)
⁶ And he told this parable: "A man had a fig tree planted in his vineyard, and he came seeking fruit on it and found none. ⁷ And he said to the vinedresser, 'Look, for three years now I have come seeking fruit on this fig tree, and I find none. Cut it down. Why should it use up the ground?' ⁸ And he answered him, 'Sir, let it alone this year also, until I dig around it and put on manure. ⁹ Then if it should bear fruit next year, well and good; but if not, you can cut it down.'"

These scriptures, among many others, demonstrate the symbolism of Israel by a fig tree. This latter passage is a parable about the patience of God with Israel.

Now the point of all this is that many scholars believe this reference to the fig tree is not just a general statement about reading the signs of the times, but rather is actually giving us the specific sign to watch. That sign is Israel. I agree with this understanding, because this would have been immediately recognized in this way by a first century Jew. *As soon as its twigs get tender and its leaves come out, you know that summer is near.* Israel has lain dormant for the better part of 1800 years since its destruction and the dispersion of its inhabitants among the nations. As already discussed, she became a sovereign nation again in 1948. However there is still no temple worship. So we are seeing in our day the first signs of Israel bearing fruit, but the fruit is not there yet. *Even so, when you see all these things, you know that it is near, right at the door.*

Our Attitude Toward Israel

We have discussed that in the Old Testament the word *elect* is used to speak of Israel. The Hebrew nation was specially chosen by God, and blessed according to His purpose. But Israel was a rebellious nation, and He had to punish her often. In the New Testament she committed her greatest rejection of Him; she crucified God's Son, her promised Messiah. Out of Jesus' death and following resurrection sprouted the Christian faith. Although this was all in God's perfect plan, still the Jews were guilty of treason. They continued their rebellion by persecuting those who followed Jesus as the Messiah, as it is written in the book of Acts. As punishment for this rejection, they were destroyed as a Nation and exiled into widespread dispersion.

We further discussed how in the New Testament God cast Israel aside for a period of time known as the *times of the Gentiles*. There we see the term *elect* being applied to Christians. However we also discussed how the promises and call of Israel were *irrevocable*, and that God would again reinstate His chosen people to favor in the future. They still hold a central position in His purposes.

In that original irrevocable call of Israel, a specific promise was made by God to Abraham.

Genesis 12:3 (NASB)
³ And I will bless those who bless you, And the one who curses you I will curse. And in you all the families of the earth will be blessed."

This theme is reflected throughout the scripture in passages such as these:

Psalm 122:6-9 (NASB)
⁶ Pray for the peace of Jerusalem: "May they prosper who love you. ⁷ "May peace be within your walls, And prosperity within your palaces." ⁸ For the sake of my brothers and my friends, I will now say, "May peace be within you." ⁹ For the sake of the house of the LORD our God, I will seek your good.

Deuteronomy 7:6-8 (NASB)
⁶ "For you are a holy people to the LORD your God; the LORD your God has chosen you to be a people for His own possession out of all the peoples who are on the face of the earth. ⁷ "The LORD did not set His love on you nor choose you because you were more in number than any of the peoples, for you were the fewest of all peoples, ⁸ but because the LORD loved you and kept the oath which He swore to your forefathers, the LORD brought you out by a mighty

hand and redeemed you from the house of slavery, from the hand of Pharaoh king of Egypt.

We are not called to favor Israel because of her political merit. From a worldly view of history, the Jews are no more deserving of the land than any of the many peoples who have held autonomy there. We are called to favor Israel because they were given the land by God Himself. We are to love them because of the redemptive purpose that came through the Jewish lineage and was promised to the patriarchs. Leaving aside affections, logics, philosophies and politics, let us favor the Jews for one reason and one reason only. God's word instructs us to do so.

Prophecy shows us that a grand purpose awaits Israel in the future, according to His plans. Fundamental, Bible-believing men took this concept seriously. A firm belief by certain people that these scriptures were to be understood literally has shaped the political scene, allowing Israel to be a nation once again. God was the author of both this belief, and the ability to generate much support for it. He did it by putting his prophetic word into the hearts of influential leaders. If God is still working on Israel's behalf to fulfill His purpose, it seems we must also be supportive of that purpose. Israel is to be a major player in God's purpose for the ages. We should pray for the peace of Jerusalem, and for her spiritual redemption.

Romans 11:28 (RSV)
[28] As regards the gospel they are enemies of God, for your sake; but as regards election they are beloved for the sake of their forefathers.

Deuteronomy 14:2 (NASB)
[2] "For you are a holy people to the LORD your God, and the LORD has chosen you to be a people for His own possession out of all the peoples who are on the face of the earth.

Deuteronomy 26:18-19 (NASB)
[18] "The LORD has today declared you to be His people, a treasured possession, as He promised you, and that you should keep all His commandments; [19] and that He will set you high above all nations which He has made, for praise, fame, and honor; and that you shall be a consecrated people to the LORD your God, as He has spoken."

Psalm 135:4 (NASB)
[4] For the LORD has chosen Jacob for Himself, Israel for His own possession.

Malachi 3:17-18 (ESV)
[17] "They shall be mine, says the LORD of hosts, in the day when I make up my treasured possession, and I will spare them as a man

spares his son who serves him. *¹⁸ Then once more you shall see the distinction between the righteous and the wicked, between one who serves God and one who does not serve him.*

Romans 11:25-27 (RSV)
²⁵ Lest you be wise in your own conceits, I want you to understand this mystery, brethren: a hardening has come upon part of Israel, until the full number of the Gentiles come in, ²⁶ and so all Israel will be saved; as it is written, "The Deliverer will come from Zion, he will banish ungodliness from Jacob"; ²⁷ "and this will be my covenant with them when I take away their sins."

> Oh Lord, teach us to love the Jewish people. We recognize they are not now obedient to your will, but we also realize that your purpose is to ultimately save Israel. Teach us to pray for her for the sake of your grand purpose. Amen

While this timeless principle speaks to our own hearts today, it is not primarily a personal issue. It is a national one. Throughout history, those nations who favored Israel found themselves blessed. Nations who were enemies of Israel found themselves cursed. This is a promise that can be traced through history. The kingdoms and dynasties who were enemies of Israel are now either extinct, or are reduced to relatively minor status in today's hierarchy of nations.

This pattern has held true in recent history as well. Nations that have not favored Israel, or that have backed away from favoring Israel in the last century have seen their own demise as world-dominant powers. Great Britain, for example, was once a strong supporter of the Zionist movement. At that time she enjoyed great influence over world politics. Then political compromises led to her abandoning such support, so that by the time Israel declared itself a nation in 1048, Britain abstained in voting at a UN show of support. The United States was the first nation to show support. At the beginning of the 20th century AD, Britain was one of the dominant world powers, with colonial interests worldwide. Now she is barely a voice to be heard, and has lost most of her influence in world politics. Could it be that even now in this present time God is keeping His word concerning His promise to bless those who bless Israel, and curse those who curse her?

Over the last few decades, the United States has seen its leaders begin to compromise their support of national Israel. Interests driven by energy and conciliatory posturing with oil-producing Middle East countries have begun to be motivators, drawing us to compromise out support. Unless this trend is reversed, will the US suffer the same fate as those other nations who have abandoned her, or become her enemies?

Jeremiah 31:35-37 (NASB)
[35] Thus says the LORD, Who gives the sun for light by day And the fixed order of the moon and the stars for light by night, Who stirs up the sea so that its waves roar; The LORD of hosts is His name: [36] "If this fixed order departs From before Me," declares the LORD, "Then the offspring of Israel also will cease From being a nation before Me forever." [37] Thus says the LORD, "If the heavens above can be measured And the foundations of the earth searched out below, Then I will also cast off all the offspring of Israel For all that they have done," declares the LORD.

23
ISRAEL IN THE TRIBULATION

In Chapter 13 of this book we saw the tribulation emerge and progress. In Chapter 21 we discussed that Israel figures heavily into God's plans for the end-time events. We talked about Israel's long-time rejection of her Messiah. We also looked at her end-time revival. We talked, too, about the Lord bringing nations of Gentiles to righteousness, even as he restores Israel. About this we read . . .

> *Isaiah 49:5-7 (RSV)*
> *⁵ And now the LORD says, who formed me from the womb to be his servant, to bring Jacob back to him, and that Israel might be gathered to him, for I am honored in the eyes of the LORD, and my God has become my strength -- ⁶ he says: "It is too light a thing that you should be my servant to raise up the tribes of Jacob and to restore the preserved of Israel; I will give you as a light to the nations, that my salvation may reach to the end of the earth." ⁷ Thus says the LORD, the Redeemer of Israel and his Holy One, to one deeply despised, abhorred by the nations, the servant of rulers: "Kings shall see and arise; princes, and they shall prostrate themselves; because of the LORD, who is faithful, the Holy One of Israel, who has chosen you."*

We have read about Israel's ingathering from the nations of the world, their second such rescue (the first being their restoration from Babylon in the days of Ezra and Nehemiah.)

> *Isaiah 11:11-12 (RSV)*
> *¹¹ In that day the Lord will extend his hand yet a second time to recover the remnant which is left of his people, from Assyria, from Egypt, from Pathros, from Ethiopia, from Elam, from Shinar, from Hamath, and from the coastlands of the sea. ¹² He will raise an ensign for the nations, and will assemble the outcasts of Israel, and gather the dispersed of Judah from the four corners of the earth.*

Regarding God's delay in restoring Israel, His purpose is made clear. It is for the inclusion of all the nations.

Romans 11:25-27 (RSV)
[25] Lest you be wise in your own conceits, I want you to understand this mystery, brethren: a hardening has come upon part of Israel, until the full number of the Gentiles come in, [26] and so all Israel will be saved; as it is written, "The Deliverer will come from Zion, he will banish ungodliness from Jacob"; [27] "and this will be my covenant with them when I take away their sins."

We read of Israel's lasting peace following a great battle:

Isaiah 33:17,20-24 (RSV)
[17] Your eyes will see the king in his beauty; they will behold a land that stretches afar. . . . [20] Look upon Zion, the city of our appointed feasts! Your eyes will see Jerusalem, a quiet habitation, an immovable tent, whose stakes will never be plucked up, nor will any of its cords be broken. [21] But there the LORD in majesty will be for us a place of broad rivers and streams, where no galley with oars can go, nor stately ship can pass. [22] For the LORD is our judge, the LORD is our ruler, the LORD is our king; he will save us. [23] Your tackle hangs loose; it cannot hold the mast firm in its place, or keep the sail spread out. Then prey and spoil in abundance will be divided; even the lame will take the prey. [24] And no inhabitant will say, "I am sick"; the people who dwell there will be forgiven their iniquity.

We discussed this promise of Israel's conversion, but we did not see how it would come about. Certainly the stage will be set by the antichrist's breaking of the covenant. The Jewish people, who had for three and a half years been favored, will suddenly become his enemy. The truth of prophecy may begin to awaken in their long-dead spirits. Finding themselves without allegiance, they will be vulnerable to the message they are about to receive.

In chapters 13 and 14 of this book we discussed how the tribulation was embodied in three series of seven events, pictured as the breaking of seven seals on a scroll, the blowing of seven trumpets, and the pouring out of seven bowls. We also mentioned that, woven around these sequences, were a number of parenthetical sketches. As we view those sketches by themselves, we realize that their common theme is the redemption of Israel. We now turn our attention to them, as we seek to learn more about the process of Israel's conversion from godlessness to holiness.

The Prophecy of the Two Witnesses

In the ninth chapter of Revelation the sixth trumpet was sounded (second woe), and a series of several visions was seen. It is not until Revelation 11:14 that we read *the second woe is passed*... It is unclear whether all the material presented within those endpoints is part of the sixth trumpet, or whether some of it is parenthetical, and perhaps it doesn't matter. In the middle of this series, we read:

> *Revelation 10:7 (ESV)*
> *⁷ but that in the days of the trumpet call to be sounded by the seventh angel, the mystery of God would be fulfilled, just as he announced to his servants the prophets.*

This verse indicates that these visions are not just illusory, but represent events happening in the context of chronological time, as we understand it. One of the visions of that series tells us about a divine testimony to Israel during the Tribulation.

We are introduced to a very noteworthy affair. This event will be in the headlines every night. Live satellite television coverage will, no doubt, bring it into the homes of people all over the world. *For three and a half days men from every people, tribe, language and nation will gaze.* In fact, without modern communications, it is not possible to see how this would have been fulfilled. As you read, can you imagine the difficulty past generations must have had interpreting this passage literally? But now, it is taken for granted that a worldwide audience could exist. Whether God will use our technology to make this event known worldwide, or whether He will use a supernatural means, I don't know.

> *Revelation 11:1-6 (ESV)*
> *¹ Then I was given a measuring rod like a staff, and I was told, "Rise and measure the temple of God and the altar and those who worship there, ² but do not measure the court outside the temple; leave that out, for it is given over to the nations, and they will trample the holy city for forty-two months. ³ And I will grant authority to my two witnesses, and they will prophesy for 1,260 days, clothed in sackcloth." ⁴ These are the two olive trees and the two lampstands that stand before the Lord of the earth. ⁵ And if anyone would harm them, fire pours from their mouth and consumes their foes. If anyone would harm them, this is how he is doomed to be killed. ⁶ They have the power to shut the sky, that no rain may fall during the days of their prophesying, and they have power over the waters to turn them into blood and to strike the earth with every kind of plague, as often as they desire.*

John was given a measuring rod and told to measure the temple. This appears to be the literal Jerusalem temple, built during the first portion of the Tribulation. Again, we are not told the significance for measuring. The outer courts were to be excluded from the measurement since they would be trampled on by Gentiles for forty-two months. Some have speculated the measurement is a symbol of protection during what is about to happen there.

We have here two strange characters, to say the least. They appear as men, but have superhuman powers. God Himself empowers them. These two have a special mission. They will stand in the city of Jerusalem for three and a half years and warn its inhabitants--no, actually the whole world-- about the judgment to come. They are said to *prophesy*. They will be given supernatural abilities to protect themselves, and as signs to validate their message, much like prophets of the Old Testament, but with even greater power. In keeping with their call to repentance, they are wearing sackcloth, the traditional apparel of penance and remorse.

Who are these men? Scripture does not say. As you can imagine, speculation has run wild over this issue. The most plausible estimation of these men's identity is that they are Moses and Elijah. Moses was the lawgiver, Elijah the fearless prophet; together they represent *the law and the prophets*. It is in the writings of the Old Testament law and prophets that the Jews put their hope. It is also there that early New Testament saints discovered their Christ foretold. Here the person of Jesus was validated as the long awaited Messiah. The nature of the miracles they will perform is similar to that of both Moses and Elijah.

The link to these men's identity is strengthened in the appearance of Moses and Elijah with Jesus on the Mount of Transfiguration.

> *Matthew 17:1-3 (NASB)*
> *¹ Six days later Jesus *took with Him Peter and James and John his brother, and *led them up on a high mountain by themselves. ² And He was transfigured before them; and His face shone like the sun, and His garments became as white as light. ³ And behold, Moses and Elijah appeared to them, talking with Him.*

Here Jesus was seen in his reinstated glory, and Moses and Elijah with him. Furthermore, in the Old Testament prophecy of Malachi we read the following:

> *Malachi 4:4-6 (ESV)*
> *⁴ "Remember the law of my servant Moses, the statutes and rules that I commanded him at Horeb for all Israel. ⁵ "Behold, I will send you Elijah the prophet before the great and awesome day of the*

LORD comes. ⁶ And he will turn the hearts of fathers to their children and the hearts of children to their fathers, lest I come and strike the land with a decree of utter destruction."

The two men are called *olive trees* and *lampstands* in Revelation. This is understood by many to symbolize their mission of giving out God's message (light) and their source, God's Holy Spirit (olive trees being the source of oil burned in the lamps.)

When does this occur? The duration of forty-two months and 1260 days is assuredly to be identified with one of the halves of the Tribulation, but which one? Some believe the first half, but the hostility between Israel and antichrist does not become known until the Tribulation's midpoint. It seems the second half will be the time when Gentiles in the temple outer courts will be symptomatic of the crumbling security of Jerusalem.

Revelation 11:7-14 (ESV)
⁷ And when they have finished their testimony, the beast that rises from the bottomless pit will make war on them and conquer them and kill them, ⁸ and their dead bodies will lie in the street of the great city that symbolically is called Sodom and Egypt, where their Lord was crucified. ⁹ For three and a half days some from the peoples and tribes and languages and nations will gaze at their dead bodies and refuse to let them be placed in a tomb, ¹⁰ and those who dwell on the earth will rejoice over them and make merry and exchange presents, because these two prophets had been a torment to those who dwell on the earth. ¹¹ But after the three and a half days a breath of life from God entered them, and they stood up on their feet, and great fear fell on those who saw them. ¹² Then they heard a loud voice from heaven saying to them, "Come up here!" And they went up to heaven in a cloud, and their enemies watched them. ¹³ And at that hour there was a great earthquake, and a tenth of the city fell. Seven thousand people were killed in the earthquake, and the rest were terrified and gave glory to the God of heaven. ¹⁴ The second woe has passed; behold, the third woe is soon to come.

When the prophetic ministry of the two witnesses is completed, then antichrist will kill them, leaving them in the city streets. The worldwide audience will rejoice, but not for long. After three and a half days, they will come back to life and ascend into heaven. The parallel of this event with the death, resurrection and ascension of Christ is obvious.

Those on earth will be terrified. It must surely appear evident to some at this point that they are on the wrong side of a power struggle. Then the great earthquake hits, shaking Jerusalem and killing 7000 people. The inhabitants of Jerusalem who survive are terrified, and here we see for the first time a turn of the heart of Israel. We are told that in their fear they *gave glory to the God of heaven.*

The Vision of the Woman in Splendor Giving Birth

In Revelation Chapter 12 we looked at the vision of the splendored woman giving birth, and the dragon attempting to destroy the child. We identified the dragon as the devil, the child as Christ Jesus. We left the identifying of the woman until now. Let's revisit that passage, looking at the complete portion of the text.

Revelation 12:1-6 (ESV)
¹ And a great sign appeared in heaven: a woman clothed with the sun, with the moon under her feet, and on her head a crown of twelve stars. ² She was pregnant and was crying out in birth pains and the agony of giving birth. ³ And another sign appeared in heaven: behold, a great red dragon, with seven heads and ten horns, and on his heads seven diadems. ⁴ His tail swept down a third of the stars of heaven and cast them to the earth. And the dragon stood before the woman who was about to give birth, so that when she bore her child he might devour it. ⁵ She gave birth to a male child, one who is to rule all the nations with a rod of iron, but her child was caught up to God and to his throne, ⁶ and the woman fled into the wilderness, where she has a place prepared by God, in which she is to be nourished for 1,260 days.

In this vision we see Satan gruesomely intent to destroy the redemptive plan of God. The sweeping of one third of the stars with his tail may symbolize the rebellion of those angels who defected with Satan. Stars have in other places represented angels, as in the following:

Revelation 9:1-2 (ESV)
¹ And the fifth angel blew his trumpet, and I saw a star fallen from heaven to earth, and he was given the key to the shaft of the bottomless pit. ² He opened the shaft of the bottomless pit, . . .

Job 38:4-7 (NASB)
⁴ "Where were you when I laid the foundation of the earth? Tell Me, if you have understanding, ⁵ Who set its measurements? Since you know. Or who stretched the line on it? ⁶ "On what were its bases sunk? Or who laid its cornerstone, ⁷ When the morning stars sang together And all the sons of God shouted for joy?

That the angels did rebel, is certainly attested to in several places, such as:

Jude 1:6 (NASB)
⁶ And angels who did not keep their own domain, but abandoned their proper abode, He has kept in eternal bonds under darkness for the judgment of the great day,

2 Peter 2:4 (ESV)
⁴ For if God did not spare angels when they sinned, but cast them into hell and committed them to chains of gloomy darkness to be kept until the judgment;

This understanding of the stars being angels is plausible, and I believe it is so intended. Our Revelation vision continues.

Revelation 12:5 (ESV)
⁵ She gave birth to a male child, one who is to rule all the nations with a rod of iron, but her child was caught up to God and to his throne,

Forty days after Jesus' resurrection, he was *snatched up* into heaven. We read about it in these New Testament passages:

Luke 24:50-52 (ESV)
⁵⁰ Then he led them out as far as Bethany, and lifting up his hands he blessed them. ⁵¹ While he blessed them, he parted from them and was carried up into heaven. ⁵² And they worshiped him and returned to Jerusalem with great joy,

Acts 1:9-11 (ESV)
⁹ And when he had said these things, as they were looking on, he was lifted up, and a cloud took him out of their sight. ¹⁰ And while they were gazing into heaven as he went, behold, two men stood by them in white robes, ¹¹ and said, "Men of Galilee, why do you stand looking into heaven? This Jesus, who was taken up from you into heaven, will come in the same way as you saw him go into heaven."

Thus, Jesus was *snatched up to God and to his throne.* This snatching up was foreseen by the psalmist long before, as he prophetically wrote . . .

Psalm 110:1 (NASB)
¹ The LORD says to my Lord: "Sit at My right hand Until I make Your enemies a footstool for Your feet."

This psalm was quoted by Jesus in his own defense of his messianic office:

Luke 20:41-43 (ESV)
⁴¹ But he said to them, "How can they say that the Christ is David's son? ⁴² For David himself says in the Book of Psalms, "'The Lord said to my Lord, "Sit at my right hand, ⁴³ until I make your enemies your footstool."'

On the day of Pentecost Peter quoted it in his powerful first sermon . . .

Acts 2:32-35 (ESV)
³² This Jesus God raised up, and of that we all are witnesses. ³³ Being therefore exalted at the right hand of God, and having received from the Father the promise of the Holy Spirit, he has poured out this that you yourselves are seeing and hearing. ³⁴ For David did not ascend into the heavens, but he himself says, "'The Lord said to my Lord, "Sit at my right hand, ³⁵ until I make your enemies your footstool."'

. . . and the writer of Hebrews also referred to it as he showed the superiority of Christ over the angels. (It is, in fact, the scripture verse most quoted within scripture.)

Hebrews 1:13 (ESV)
¹³ And to which of the angels has he ever said, "Sit at my right hand until I make your enemies a footstool for your feet"?

Thus, Jesus was indeed *snatched up to God and to his throne.*

Who is the Woman?
Here we come to a controversial question--who is the woman? The biblical text does not tell us directly. Roman Catholics hold that this is the Virgin Mary. Some other interpreters believe she is the church. This makes little sense because it was Christ who spawned the church, not the church who spawned Christ. The most appropriate interpretation is that the woman is national Israel. It was out of Israel that Christ came in the flesh.

Romans 9:5 (RSV)
⁵ to them [Jews] belong the patriarchs, and of their race, according to the flesh, is the Christ. God who is over all be blessed for ever. Amen.

As additional evidence supporting Israel as the one symbolized by the woman in this vision, her appearance is nearly identical to that portrayed in a more ancient prophetic dream of Joseph, son of Jacob in the Old Testament. Joseph and his eleven brothers were to become the patriarchs of the twelve tribes of Israel.

> *Genesis 37:9-10 (RSV)*
> *⁹ Then he dreamed another dream, and told it to his brothers, and said, "Behold, I have dreamed another dream; and behold, the sun, the moon, and eleven stars were bowing down to me." ¹⁰ But when he told it to his father and to his brothers, his father rebuked him, and said to him, "What is this dream that you have dreamed? Shall I and your mother and your brothers indeed come to bow ourselves to the ground before you?"*

This strange dream was a prophecy foretelling of events that would be fulfilled within the lifetime of Joseph and his father and brothers. His father Jacob correctly interpreted that the sun and moon represented himself and Joseph's mother Rachel, and that the stars were Joseph's eleven brothers. With this symbolism the patriarchs of Israel were pictured in prophetic imagery. Now notice the similar symbolism in the Revelation passage, *a woman clothed with the sun, with the moon under her feet and a crown of twelve stars on her head.* This parallel imagery seems to identify the woman in Revelation 12 with the family of Jacob (whose name was later changed to Israel, and from whom the nation of Israel originated), and thus supports the view that the woman symbolizes Israel.

What do we learn about Israel, the woman, in this vision? The woman fled to a place of refuge for 1260 days, a theme further developed a few verses later. The time frame of 1260 days, or 3-1/2 years, suggests that it corresponds with one half of the seven-year Tribulation. As we have seen, this time span occurs several times in Revelation. This is what is understood by many futurists.

When the antichrist breaks his covenant with Israel at the midpoint of its seven-year duration, Jews suddenly find themselves public enemy number one. They must find a hiding place, and throughout the last half of the tribulation, they are endangered. If this is the proper understanding, it means that there is an unannounced break of over 2000 years between the woman giving birth in verse 5 and the woman fleeing into the desert in verse 6. This may seem bothersome to us, but the fact is, this is common construction in Jewish prophecy. Many prophetic passages speak of the first and second comings of Christ without a hint of space between them.

As an aside, interpreters of the historical school of interpretation understand this passage to be a reference to Israel's being saved from national annihilation by being dispersed among the nations in 70 AD. According to this view, the Diaspora actually protected Jews during the *times of the Gentiles*.

War in Heaven

Revelation 12:7-13 (ESV)
[7] Now war arose in heaven, Michael and his angels fighting against the dragon. And the dragon and his angels fought back, [8] but he was defeated, and there was no longer any place for them in heaven. [9] And the great dragon was thrown down, that ancient serpent, who is called the devil and Satan, the deceiver of the whole world—he was thrown down to the earth, and his angels were thrown down with him. [10] And I heard a loud voice in heaven, saying, "Now the salvation and the power and the kingdom of our God and the authority of his Christ have come, for the accuser of our brothers has been thrown down, who accuses them day and night before our God. [11] And they have conquered him by the blood of the Lamb and by the word of their testimony, for they loved not their lives even unto death. [12] Therefore, rejoice, O heavens and you who dwell in them! But woe to you, O earth and sea, for the devil has come down to you in great wrath, because he knows that his time is short!" [13] And when the dragon saw that he had been thrown down to the earth, he pursued the woman who had given birth to the male child.

Some see in this passage the original fall of Satan from God's favor. That fall took place before creation of the earth, because the devil already inhabited the serpent in the garden. Yet there are several scenes throughout scripture where the devil has an audience in heaven. He is said to be accusing the faithful ones.

Zechariah 3:1 (ESV)
[1] Then he showed me Joshua the high priest standing before the angel of the LORD, and Satan standing at his right hand to accuse him.

Job 1:6-7 (NASB)
[6] Now there was a day when the sons of God came to present themselves before the LORD, and Satan also came among them. [7] The LORD said to Satan, "From where do you come?" Then Satan answered the LORD and said, "From roaming about on the earth and walking around on it."

Of those who the devil has been accusing, it is said that *They overcame him by the blood of the Lamb and by the word of their testimony; they did not love their lives so much as to shrink from death.*

Furthermore, when the dragon is cast to the earth, he is furious *because he knows that his time is short.* This does not lend itself to an event before creation.

All of this seems to place this casting out of Satan at or near the end-time. It is not identical with the fall of Satan from God's favor. One interesting suggestion is that this casting down was fulfilled when the fifth angel sounded his trumpet. Remember a 'star' fell from the sky and '*he*' was given the key to the abyss, releasing a swarm of evil locusts that torture men. Perhaps the locusts are symbolic of the satanic and demonic invasion that will occur when Satan is cast to the earth. The imprisonment of demons, from which they are released, is seen in Peter's second letter:

2 Peter 2:4 (ESV)
⁴ For if God did not spare angels when they sinned, but cast them into hell and committed them to chains of gloomy darkness to be kept until the judgment;

Pursuit of the Woman
Revelation 12:13-17 (ESV)
¹³ And when the dragon saw that he had been thrown down to the earth, he pursued the woman who had given birth to the male child. ¹⁴ But the woman was given the two wings of the great eagle so that she might fly from the serpent into the wilderness, to the place where she is to be nourished for a time, and times, and half a time. ¹⁵ The serpent poured water like a river out of his mouth after the woman, to sweep her away with a flood. ¹⁶ But the earth came to the help of the woman, and the earth opened its mouth and swallowed the river that the dragon had poured from his mouth. ¹⁷ Then the dragon became furious with the woman and went off to make war on the rest of her offspring, on those who keep the commandments of God and hold to the testimony of Jesus. And he stood on the sand of the sea.

Here we see the two storylines come together into a single plot--the dragon being cast out of heaven to the earth, and the woman fleeing from the dragon. His full-time earthly presence and fury will result in unprecedented persecution of the woman (national Israel) as well as her offspring (Christians). Here again the woman will be taken care of in the desert for three and a half years. Where does Israel go to be out of the serpent's reach? Some see the desert as symbolic of providential protection, and see in this description a reflective parallel to the Hebrews leaving Egypt. It is the belief of some that the desert is symbolic of Gentile nations, and that the fleeing Jews will disperse themselves among other peoples. Others anticipate a literal desert safe-place, and some have suggested it might be at Petra, but without direct biblical support. One fanciful speculation suggests the eagle's wings indicate a massive airlift to safety, and further, since the eagle is the symbol of the United States, it suggests to some that the US may supply the planes. I am certainly not endorsing this level of speculation, but mention it to show the great amount of imagineering that has taken place.

It seems that this break of the seven-year covenant by the antichrist will activate a process of disillusionment in Israel. This process will escalate into outright hostility. When combined, in the collective experience of the Palestinian Jews, with the witnessing of the two prophets in Jerusalem and with other signs, there will be the making for a national change of heart. This process will initiate a conversion, and will ultimately lead to her repentance and restoration to faith. It is all part of the plan of sovereign God.

The 144,000

Throughout scripture whenever the Lord God wanted to make His truth known to a larger populace, He spoke through a champion, perhaps a prophet or king. Of course his consummate spokesman was Jesus. But he was not the final one. The apostles and evangelists spread the gospel message throughout the known world. Today, preachers and teachers continue this propagation of the word.

During the Tribulation the same tactic will be used. Besides the two witnesses we have already discussed, there will be a group of designated champions among the Jews. We read of them in the following passages.

> *Revelation 7:1-5 (ESV)*
> *^{1} After this I saw four angels standing at the four corners of the earth, holding back the four winds of the earth, that no wind might blow on earth or sea or against any tree. ^{2} Then I saw another angel ascending from the rising of the sun, with the seal of the living God, and he called with a loud voice to the four angels who had been given power to harm earth and sea, ^{3} saying, "Do not harm the earth or the sea or the trees, until we have sealed the servants of our God on their foreheads." ^{4} And I heard the number of the sealed, 144,000, sealed from every tribe of the sons of Israel: ^{5} 12,000 from the tribe of Judah were sealed, 12,000 from the tribe of Reuben, 12,000 from the tribe of Gad,* [etc]

Remember how in Egypt, just before the exodus, God had told Moses for the Hebrews to mark their doorposts with the blood of the Passover lamb. They did that, and the death angel that passed over Egypt that night spared those whose doorposts were marked. It is not as if God does not know who these people are without a mark. The mark is simply a way for those marked to identify with the fact that it was God who protected them. The seal mentioned here in the Tribulation may not necessarily be a literal, visible mark, but perhaps is simply a visionary emblem of divine protection.

Great controversies have been waged over who these people are. Some have said they are the church. Jehovah's Witnesses once claimed that they were JW's until their membership swelled past that figure, and they had to redefine their stance. To create such confusion we must completely ignore the straightforward description given in the passage. They are said to be *144,000 from all the tribes of Israel.* In case that might be mistaken as figurative for something else, the vision then identifies all twelve tribes by name, and their number. God simply could not make it any clearer. Later in Revelation we read:

> *Revelation 14:1-5 (ESV)*
> *[1] Then I looked, and behold, on Mount Zion stood the Lamb, and with him 144,000 who had his name and his Father's name written on their foreheads. [2] And I heard a voice from heaven like the roar of many waters and like the sound of loud thunder. The voice I heard was like the sound of harpists playing on their harps, [3] and they were singing a new song before the throne and before the four living creatures and before the elders. No one could learn that song except the 144,000 who had been redeemed from the earth. [4] It is these who have not defiled themselves with women, for they are virgins. It is these who follow the Lamb wherever he goes. These have been redeemed from mankind as firstfruits for God and the Lamb, [5] and in their mouth no lie was found, for they are blameless.*

The scene is said to start on Mount Zion, a literal mountain inside Jerusalem, but then without transition finds itself before the throne of heaven. This serves to remind us that we need to be open about being dogmatically literal with such figurative things, things we do not fully understand. Perhaps it reminds us that heaven cannot be thought of in terms of space and distance the way we now think. Maybe the separation of heaven from earth, of God from men, is not measured in miles, but in spiritual dimensions.

These represented by the 144,000 are without doubt the same ones mentioned in the previous passage. Although they are Jews, they *follow the Lamb wherever he goes,* showing that they are believers and followers of the resurrected Jesus. That they did not defile themselves with women is understood by most Futurists to mean that they did not commit spiritual adultery by giving allegiance to a false belief, but remained faithful, even in the face of persecution, to the one true God, and to their one Messiah-- Jesus. They are said to be *firstfruits* to God. This probably means that they are the first Tribulation converts to Christianity from among the Jews, and has in view the expectation of more to follow.

The fact that these 144,000 Jews were sealed before God's Tribulation judgments began, seems to indicate that they had a ministry to perform. Without much speculation, we can assume that they will, at the least, bear a great witness to their fellow Jews, and in fact, to the whole world. Their influence will be instrumental in the restoration of Israel to faith.

An Evangel

> *Revelation 14:6-7 (ESV)*
> *⁶ Then I saw another angel flying directly overhead, with an eternal gospel to proclaim to those who dwell on earth, to every nation and tribe and language and people. ⁷ And he said with a loud voice, "Fear God and give him glory, because the hour of his judgment has come, and worship him who made heaven and earth, the sea and the springs of water."*

This angel is one of a series of three, who proclaim something. In the vision they appear in rapid succession. The following angel warns earth's inhabitants of the fall of Babylon, followed by another warning them not to take the mark of the beast. The last two seem to put these proclamations in the latter half of the Tribulation. We do not know how they will be sensed by those on the earth. Will angels actually be visible on earth, being bodily observed and heard? Or is this symbolic of worldwide messages proclaimed in earth under unseen angelic direction? There is no way to know for sure, but the inference is that all nations will hear them. While global in influence, Israel's inhabitants certainly must be included. The first of those three messages especially will add more evidence to the case for messianic acceptance.

These visions paint for us some detail about Israel's end-time path to restoration. Without knowing all the details, we still can be certain of one thing.

> *Romans 11:26-27 (RSV)*
> *²⁶ and so all Israel will be saved; as it is written, "The Deliverer will come from Zion, he will banish ungodliness from Jacob"; ²⁷ "and this will be my covenant with them when I take away their sins."*

> *Zechariah 12:10 (RSV)*
> *¹⁰ "And I will pour out on the house of David and the inhabitants of Jerusalem a spirit of compassion and supplication, so that, when they look on him whom they have pierced, they shall mourn for him, as one mourns for an only child, and weep bitterly over him, as one weeps over a first-born.*

The psalmist saw and longed for this day when God would restore His covenant people, Israel.

Psalm 14:4-7 (ESV)
⁴ Have they no knowledge, all the evildoers who eat up my people as they eat bread and do not call upon the LORD? ⁵ There they [the evildoers] *are in great terror, for God is with the generation of the righteous. ⁶ You would shame the plans of the poor, but the LORD is his refuge. ⁷ Oh, that salvation for Israel would come out of Zion! When the LORD restores the fortunes of his people, let Jacob rejoice, let Israel be glad.*

> Oh mighty God, how marvelous is Your plan. It is vast in its scope, reaching all people. It is deep in its penetration, piercing the very heart and spirit of men. It is complex in its purpose, reconciling both Jew and Gentile to Yourself. Your strategy will accomplish Your objective, while upholding Your holiness. How beyond us are Your ways, Lord God. Great is Your presence before us. How compelling is your love for us. Teach us to be devoted to You and Your agenda. You give to Your followers joy and peace from Your secure storehouse. Amen

PART 5
FULFILLMENT

24
THE MILLENNIUM

Most people have heard the term 'Millennium.' Some know that it refers to a period of time, either literally or symbolically 1000 years in length. They may even know that something about our interpretation of this concept divides prophecy students into several categories. Yet relatively few Christians are familiar with what the Bible says about it, and fewer yet have any opinion as to how they themselves believe regarding it. Perhaps it has seemed like an obscure and irrelevant topic that only prophecy enthusiasts care about.

Well, hopefully by now you are developing such an enthusiasm about God's plan for the ages that you want to understand this also. The millennium is the earthly fulfillment of many biblical promises you may have, perhaps remorsefully, concluded must be only a figurative shadow of heavenly blessings.

An Earthly Kingdom

> *Revelation 20:1-6 (ESV)*
> *[1] Then I saw an angel coming down from heaven, holding in his hand the key to the bottomless pit and a great chain. [2] And he seized the dragon, that ancient serpent, who is the devil and Satan, and bound him for a thousand years, [3] and threw him into the pit, and shut it and sealed it over him, so that he might not deceive the nations any longer, until the thousand years were ended. After that he must be released for a little while. [4] Then I saw thrones, and seated on them were those to whom the authority to judge was committed. Also I saw the souls of those who had been beheaded for the testimony of Jesus and for the word of God, and those who had not worshiped the beast or its image and had not received its mark on their foreheads or their hands. They came to life and reigned with Christ for a thousand years. [5] The rest of the dead did not come to life until the thousand years were ended. This is the first resurrection. [6] Blessed and holy is the one who shares in the first resurrection! Over such the second death has no power, but they will be priests of God and of Christ, and they will reign with him for a thousand years.*

The millennium will be a period of time on earth initiated by the return of Jesus, and characterized by the absence of satanic temptation. Therefore it is anticipated to be a blessed time distinguished by peace, joy, contentment, purpose, long life, and best of all, the bodily presence of Jesus among us once again.

There are those who do not believe in a separate period of time at the end of the age. Rather, they say, the one thousand years is symbolic, and represents the church age. The great battle preceding it was the spiritual battle that Christ waged on the cross. His redemptive act was the victory that doomed the devil. The binding of Satan represents the preeminence of the Holy Spirit in the life of true believers. This millennial kingdom exists in the hearts of Christians, but not as a political reality. In other words, they spiritualize these prophecies. This is the essence of the A-millennial view. The main objection to this line of thinking is that it is based on a non-literal understanding of scripture where a factual interpretation seems warranted.

Another view, called post-millennialism, sees in this passage a literal distinct time period at the end of the church age, but places it chronologically prior to the return of Christ. This view sees a widespread conversion of the earth's inhabitants to Christianity during this period, through an unparalleled advance of the gospel message. At the end of it, Jesus returns to a world that awaits him with open arms. There is nothing in scripture to support this post-millennial sequence. Instead prophecy portrays a world that is increasingly hostile to the Christian faith, and current global trends seem to support that portrait.

The pre-millennial view holds that the appearing of Christ in great power brings about the binding of Satan and ushers in the millennium. Thus the second coming is premillennial; that is, it precedes the millennium. This is the straightforward and plain sequence portrayed in the Revelation of John. It is the view I believe to be accurate, and the one put forth in this writing.

Furthermore, the millennium is not symbolic of heaven or of some spiritual condition at another time. In the understanding of premillennialism, this period of time is historical and geographical. It occurs right here on earth, an earth that is geophysically the same as now.

The Kingdom that Fulfills Prophecy

In Old Testament prophecy there are many scriptures that tell of a utopian Jewish kingdom in which there is peace. In some, the nations of the earth bring homage to Jerusalem in devotion to the God of Israel. This hope was embraced by most first-century Jews who impatiently awaited this glory for Israel. Yet when you look through her history since the time of these prophecies, you will not find such a kingdom. There were brief shining moments of victory and autonomy, but nothing lasting and glorious. So where is the fulfillment of these kingdom prophecies?

Some have made the prophecies apply to a heavenly kingdom, and see them as symbolic of the bliss of eternity. Others take them as figurative predictions of the church in the new covenant. Many Christian readers, in one way or another, have written off any literal earthly fulfillment for these passages. They are simply treated as poetic wish lists and largely ignored.. The majority of Jews today also have abandoned expectations of glory for their nation.

The future millennium is the arena where these fairytale-like scenes will be played out in perfect fulfillment. It will be a kingdom, complete with a king.

> *Genesis 49:10 (KJV)*
> *[10] The sceptre shall not depart from Judah, nor a lawgiver from between his feet, until Shiloh come; and unto him shall the gathering of the people be.*

He . . . to whom it belongs is, of course, Jesus. This very early prophetic blessing ascribes the kingly reign to the tribe of Judah. The other eleven tribes were given a blessing too, but only Judah would bring forth the eternal king. It foresees a time when the nations (Gentiles) will be obedient to him to whom the kingdom rightfully belongs. Jesus is the anticipated one from the next passage. Here he is identified by his earthly family lineage. Jesus is a branch in the family tree traced back many generations to David, son of Jesse, and he was often called *Son of David*.

> *Isaiah 11:1-10 (KJV)*
> *[1] And there shall come forth a rod out of the stem of Jesse, and a Branch shall grow out of his roots: [2] And the spirit of the LORD shall rest upon him, the spirit of wisdom and understanding, the spirit of counsel and might, the spirit of knowledge and of the fear of the LORD; [3] And shall make him of quick understanding in the fear of the LORD: and he shall not judge after the sight of his eyes, neither reprove after the hearing of his ears: [4] But with righteousness shall he judge the poor, and reprove with equity for the meek of the earth: and he shall smite the earth with the rod of his mouth, and with the breath of his lips shall he slay the wicked. [5] And righteousness shall be the girdle of his loins, and faithfulness the girdle of his reins. [6] The wolf also shall dwell with the lamb, and the leopard shall lie down with the kid; and the calf and the young lion and the fatling together; and a little child shall lead them. [7] And the cow and the bear shall feed; their young ones shall lie down together: and the lion shall eat straw like the ox. [8] And the sucking*

child shall play on the hole of the asp, and the weaned child shall put his hand on the cockatrice' den. ⁹ They shall not hurt nor destroy in all my holy mountain: for the earth shall be full of the knowledge of the LORD, as the waters cover the sea. ¹⁰ And in that day there shall be a root of Jesse, which shall stand for an ensign of the people; to it shall the Gentiles seek: and his rest shall be glorious.

If all the nations will be blessed under Jesus' earthly reign, why do we see in the millennium a fulfillment of promises made long ago to Israel? It is because Jerusalem will be the capitol city of this kingdom. It is from there that Jesus will administer perfect justice and righteousness.

2 Kings 19:34 (NASB)
³⁴ 'For I will defend this city to save it for My own sake and for My servant David's sake.'"

Even in ancient times God had a purpose for His holy city. It was to be the place of redemption, for there Jesus gave himself in sacrificial payment for our sins. It will, in the millennium, also become the place of fulfillment. Then the celebration will be completed, the celebration briefly begun on the occasion of his triumphal entry, just prior to his crucifixion. Yes, Jerusalem is God's special city. He has preserved her through the ages for this day. When glory comes to Jesus, he will also bring glory to Jerusalem and to Israel, God's chosen nation.

Isaiah 65:18-25 (KJV)
¹⁸ But be ye glad and rejoice for ever in that which I create: for, behold, I create Jerusalem a rejoicing, and her people a joy. ¹⁹ And I will rejoice in Jerusalem, and joy in my people: and the voice of weeping shall be no more heard in her, nor the voice of crying. ²⁰ There shall be no more thence an infant of days, nor an old man that hath not filled his days: for the child shall die an hundred years old; but the sinner being an hundred years old shall be accursed. ²¹ And they shall build houses, and inhabit them; and they shall plant vineyards, and eat the fruit of them. ²² They shall not build, and another inhabit; they shall not plant, and another eat: for as the days of a tree are the days of my people, and mine elect shall long enjoy the work of their hands. ²³ They shall not labour in vain, nor bring forth for trouble; for they are the seed of the blessed of the LORD, and their offspring with them. ²⁴ And it shall come to pass, that before they call, I will answer; and while they are yet speaking, I will hear. ²⁵ The wolf and the lamb shall feed together, and the lion shall eat straw like the bullock: and dust shall be the serpent's meat. They shall not hurt nor destroy in all my holy mountain, saith the LORD.

Ezekiel 34:22-31 (NASB)
²² therefore, I will deliver My flock, and they will no longer be a prey; and I will judge between one sheep and another. ²³ "Then I will set over them one shepherd, My servant David, and he will feed them; he will feed them himself and be their shepherd. ²⁴ "And I, the LORD, will be their God, and My servant David will be prince among them; I the LORD have spoken. ²⁵ "I will make a covenant of peace with them and eliminate harmful beasts from the land so that they may live securely in the wilderness and sleep in the woods. ²⁶ "I will make them and the places around My hill a blessing. And I will cause showers to come down in their season; they will be showers of blessing. ²⁷ "Also the tree of the field will yield its fruit and the earth will yield its increase, and they will be secure on their land. Then they will know that I am the LORD, when I have broken the bars of their yoke and have delivered them from the hand of those who enslaved them. ²⁸ "They will no longer be a prey to the nations, and the beasts of the earth will not devour them; but they will live securely, and no one will make them afraid. ²⁹ "I will establish for them a renowned planting place, and they will not again be victims of famine in the land, and they will not endure the insults of the nations anymore. ³⁰ "Then they will know that I, the LORD their God, am with them, and that they, the house of Israel, are My people," declares the Lord GOD. ³¹ "As for you, My sheep, the sheep of My pasture, you are men, and I am your God," declares the Lord GOD.

When we pray the model prayer, the Lord's Prayer, we pray:

Matthew 6:9-10 (NASB)
⁹ "Pray, then, in this way: 'Our Father who is in heaven, Hallowed be Your name. ¹⁰ 'Your kingdom come. Your will be done, On earth as it is in heaven.

Of course we are praying for the kingdom to come within our own hearts and in the hearts of others during the church age. But there is this ultimate goal always in sight when we pray it, the goal of Christ literally receiving the devotion and adoration here on earth that he deserves from his creation. We who love him should desire for his glorification on earth as it is in heaven. That is how it will be during the millennium. Speaking of the Old Testament people of faith, the writer of Hebrews said:

Hebrews 11:13, 39-40 (ESV)
¹³ These all died in faith, not having received the things promised, but having seen them and greeted them from afar, and having acknowledged that they were strangers and exiles on the earth. . . ³⁹ And all these, though commended through their faith, did not

receive what was promised, [40] since God had provided something better for us, that apart from us they should not be made perfect.

Life in the Millennium

From the scriptures already quoted, we learn some of what life in the millennium will be like. First we see that Christ's leadership will be characterized by wisdom, compassion, power, righteousness, faithfulness, and a reverence for God the Father. We see that there will be peace on earth. Not abstract peace, but literal, political peace. No war. That has not happened since the nations were born. The bodily presence of Jesus and of God's Spirit will bring about a spirit of peace in the hearts of people. That spirit will actually permeate the whole creation, including the animal kingdom.

From our last chapter we saw that the cleansing of the Land of Israel of dead bodies after the great battle will take seven months and a large number of workers. That is how the millennium will commence.

Followers of Jesus during the church age, presumably those of the first resurrection, and those taken alive in the catching up of the saints at his appearing, will be given dominion over the nations. They are said to reign with Christ during the 1000 years.

It appears there will continue to be natural death during the millennium, but not tragic untimely death. No child will die. Life will be much longer than at present. A person at age one hundred years will still be in his youth. Death will not be violent.

People will continue to work for their living. However, their work will not be in vain. Their labor will be fruitful and each worker will be prosperous. Their efforts will be blessed by the Lord. Freed from the threat and burden of aggression, people will be released to turn their whole efforts toward constructive endeavors, and their whole hearts toward Jesus.

25
JUDGMENT

We have discussed the second coming of Jesus Christ, resurrection, the tribulation, and the Millennium. Even if these things were not true, they certainly make for adventurous reading. When we do hold them to be literal and true, 'adventurous' does not begin to describe the feelings we develop as we read and learn of things to come. Maybe 'ominous' more closely describes our inner response to them. Nevertheless, our greatest apprehensions are not about upcoming temporary periods in the divine plan, as momentous as they may be. There lurks a more pervasive and overriding question that has not been asked and answered yet. We may or may not survive these other events, but what about eternity? "What about eternity as it relates to me?" We have all heard of a pending Judgment Day. Of all prior events, this will be the most critical of all days. Do we need fear that day? Will Christians face judgment?

The End of the Millennium

Some believe the figure of 1000 years is figurative, others that it is literal. We have no reason to assume it is figurative. At any rate, the important thing to understand here is that the millennium does come to an end. It is not eternal. Three times in Chapter 20 of Revelation we read of the time *until the thousand years were ended* or *when the thousand years are over*. A distinct and limited duration of 1000 years in length will eventually be completed. About the binding of Satan, John wrote:

> *Revelation 20:3 (ESV)*
> *³ and threw him* [Satan] *into the pit, and shut it and sealed it over him, so that he might not deceive the nations any longer, until the thousand years were ended. After that he must be released for a little while.*

We see here the original divine intention to eventually bring the millennium to an end, and to briefly unbind Satan. The millennium will not be heaven, nor will it be perfect. It will simply be a time in which people are totally free to live under the lordship of Jesus Christ on earth, and free from the temptations of the evil one.

Even with the devil absent, the sinful tendency in mankind will still be present. There will be many who will not give heartfelt devotion to the

Lord. Outwardly they are under his *rod of iron*, that is, his powerful rule of righteousness and love, but inwardly they are rebelling in their spirit. Their rebellious potential simply lacks expression. We are here characterizing those who are still living in the natural state. This will not be true of those who have already been resurrected, those who were raised to meet Christ at his coming. They will have already been glorified.

> *Revelation 20:7-10 (ESV)*
> [7] *And when the thousand years are ended, Satan will be released from his prison* [8] *and will come out to deceive the nations that are at the four corners of the earth, Gog and Magog, to gather them for battle; their number is like the sand of the sea.* [9] *And they marched up over the broad plain of the earth and surrounded the camp of the saints and the beloved city, but fire came down from heaven and consumed them,* [10] *and the devil who had deceived them was thrown into the lake of fire and sulfur where the beast and the false prophet were, and they will be tormented day and night forever and ever.*

Those already glorified will not be threatened by this war, it would seem. They will be living in their heavenly bodies, immune to physical destruction. They will undoubtedly know what is going on. Still, it surely will be a traumatic event to see the people of the world over which we had shepherded for 1000 years being destroyed. This final rebellion must take place to expose those hearts not devoted to Jesus, the eternal king. Not much space is given to this great event, but it will mark the beginning of the end of life on earth as we know it today.

Ultimately, this will be a climactic, but joyous event from heaven's point of view. The millennium will give way to something better. With the millennium over, eternity will be just a judgment away.

> Lord, we read with bewilderment that even in your bodily presence some will harbor a spirit of dissention. When the opportunity arises, we are told that there will be widespread rebellion once again. Father, we cannot help reflecting on our own devotion to you. As we look deep inside, is there still a self-centered agenda to be satisfied? Is there a self-serving ego that is capable of putting self ahead of you? Are there tendencies that war against our commitment to be holy before you? Yes, Lord, I know we must say yes, there are. Forgive us for your name's sake, cleanse us and cause us to grow toward that eventual perfection that will suddenly be reality when we meet you in the air. Lord, by the power of your grace, fit us for eternity, we pray. Amen

Who Will Participate in the Millennium?

There are two main groups of people who will enter the millennium. The first consists of those inhabitants of earth who have survived the Tribulation and great battle, and are alive at the outset of the millennium. They are from every nationality and land. The second group is made up of those already having received their eternal body at Christ's return--those who *came to life and reigned with Christ a thousand years*--those of the first resurrection.

> *Revelation 20:6 (ESV)*
> *⁶ Blessed and holy is the one who shares in the first resurrection! Over such the second death has no power, but they will be priests of God and of Christ, and they will reign with him for a thousand years.*

This second group will serve as ambassadors of God to the first group. They will make His holy name known to the world during that period. This second group will be those of every nation who have embraced Jesus as Lord.

A third group will soon appear. Those living during the millennium will bear children, and new generations will come.

Some people have objected to the coexistence of people in their natural bodies (first and third groups) with those having resurrected bodies— spiritual bodies of another sort (second group). They object, saying that these bodies belong to two different realms of created order. There is no scriptural basis for this objection. To them, I simply point out that for forty days following his resurrection Jesus coexisted with his disciples, prior to his ascension. Some of that time was spent in close fellowship and teaching, just as before his death. During that time he talked with them, ate with them, and studied the scriptures with them.

The World's View of Judgment

Our modern world has embraced the humanist view that man is his own god, and is accountable to no one else. This embrace is encouraged from high-profile platforms--from Wall Street to Hollywood, from the Smithsonian to the Supreme Court, and of course, is neither unique to, nor originates within the United States. Humanism lacks authoritative foundation. In practice it ranges from a personal indifference toward God or things of a religious nature, to more organized philosophies.

The real motivation behind humanism is an alternative response to guilt. Since ancient times, such alternatives have been promoted by those seeking to rid themselves of ultimate accountability and moral responsibility. Because it's apparent foundation is emotionally and philosophically self-seeking rather than rationally and analytically truth-seeking, its disciples cannot trace roots back to any authoritative foundational source. It shows itself in a variety of belief systems, including such common ones as Atheism, Marxism, Hinduism, Buddhism, New Age, and most prevalent today, personal religious confusion, leading to apathy. The permeation of this belief confusion into our society is very advanced. Our culture's position against Christianity today is not simply apathy, but opposition. To suggest to our emancipated society that we are accountable to a divine sovereign is to invite ridicule, or worse. Judgment in any kind of ultimate sense is a politically antagonistic concept.

We Christians also find ourselves being seduced by these prominent ideologies. We too may question the literal reality of judgment. Will there really be a judgment? Would a loving God cast out anyone whom he had created? Might we be in danger of being surprised and finding ourselves condemned? These are questions every thinking person has asked himself at some time. These concerns still persist, and, aided by the social pressure of today's Godless culture, vex many believers.

Is There Any Security?

There is only one source for answers to these questions. God alone knows the beginning and end of all things, and therefore is the only one able to supply valid answers. Anyone else's answers, unless speaking from the authority of scripture, are simple guesses. There is quite a lot said about judgment in both the Old and New Testaments. As we look at these passages, we can piece together a good idea of what is expected of us, and what we can expect, on the Day of Judgment. There may be details still not conclusively understood, but there will be enough. There will be enough understanding to prepare us. There will be enough to settle our apprehensions.

<u>No Fear</u>
Modern culture has promoted a 'No Fear' mentality that is a kind of in-your-face self-sufficiency. That is a humanistic attitude. It is a false courage and it is audacity, for all of us have fears. Only someone far greater than ourselves can give assurance against the unknown. God does not want his chosen ones to be tormented by fear. I believe before we think 'judgment' we should arm ourselves to think 'sufficient.' Sufficient is the work of redemption that Jesus did. If you have believed and followed him as your Lord and Savior, then you have reason to feel secure. Judgment is a part of God's plan. If we know He is on our side, what can we fear?

1 Thessalonians 4:13,18 (NASB)
[13] But we do not want you to be uninformed, brethren, about those who are asleep, so that you will not grieve as do the rest who have no hope . . . [18] Therefore comfort one another with these words.

Ephesians 2:19-20 (ESV)
[19] So then you are no longer strangers and aliens, but you are fellow citizens with the saints and members of the household of God, [20] built on the foundation of the apostles and prophets, Christ Jesus himself being the cornerstone,

Hebrews 6:18-20 (ESV)
[18] so that by two unchangeable things, in which it is impossible for God to lie, we who have fled for refuge might have strong encouragement to hold fast to the hope set before us. [19] We have this as a sure and steadfast anchor of the soul, a hope that enters into the inner place behind the curtain, [20] where Jesus has gone as a forerunner on our behalf, having become a high priest forever . . .

Ephesians 1:13-14 (ESV)
[13] In him you also, when you heard the word of truth, the gospel of your salvation, and believed in him, were sealed with the promised Holy Spirit, [14] who is the guarantee of our inheritance until we acquire possession of it, to the praise of his glory.

Revelation 20:6 (ESV)
[6] Blessed and holy is the one who shares in the first resurrection! Over such the second death has no power, but they will be priests of God and of Christ, and they will reign with him for a thousand years.

If you belong to Jesus, you can claim to be *citizens, members of God's household*, to have *an anchor for the soul*, and to stand *firm and secure, marked in him with a seal, guaranteeing . . . redemption of those who are God's possession*. If you do belong to Jesus, read on with a hunger to know God's plans, and with the assurance that you are secure in his Son if you continue in that faith.

<u>Yes Fear</u>
If you do not belong to Jesus, this may be a troubling chapter. However, it is God's supreme appeal to you. In other places he has invited you with compassion and love. If that did not work, He now calls you from a different perspective. He warns you of where you stand with Him, and of the consequences of not belonging to Jesus Christ, and He does it while there is still time for you to make a change from being an enemy of God to a member of His family. This negative call may be different, but it is

motivated by the same love for you with which all the other appeals were made. This is His grace spread out like a welcoming canopy over you. If you reject this gracious invitation, how will you stand on that day? Note God's offer of grace and mercy. Read on with a receiving mind, and live!

> *Revelation 22:17 (ESV)*
> *[17] The Spirit and the Bride say, "Come." And let the one who hears say, "Come." And let the one who is thirsty come; let the one who desires take the water of life without price.*

Now hear this solemn warning:

> *Hebrews 10:28-29 (ESV)*
> *[28] Anyone who has set aside the law of Moses dies without mercy on the evidence of two or three witnesses. [29] How much worse punishment, do you think, will be deserved by the one who has trampled underfoot the Son of God, and has profaned the blood of the covenant by which he was sanctified, and has outraged the Spirit of grace?*

If you are a fringe believer, a 'sort-of' Christian, a fence straddler, then this chapter should push you toward one side or the other. Jesus taught that you cannot serve two masters. Neutrality makes God 'sick to His stomach' to use the imagery portrayed in Revelation 3:15-16. You may be thinking you are able to straddle, but in God's eyes you are on one side or the other. If you have come to God on your own terms rather than on His, then you may not have reason for security. The time to make things right is NOW. Go back to basics. Never mind that you may have been going to church for years. Never mind that you may know the Bible pretty well, or are involved in church activities. Going to basics means that you must humble yourself before Him and His will. It means making a decision to belong to the world no longer, but to belong to Jesus. If you are in that frame of mind, then may I suggest you jump over and read chapter 27.

A number of intermediate and temporary judgments are mentioned in scripture. There will come a time when God will carry out His final judgment. As soon as end-time events begin to unfold, there is hardly an instance where judgment is not in view. At Christ's coming he will display the wrath of God on the world. This is the initiation of the process that ultimately will end in the final judgment. *The Day of the Lord* is a concept pregnant with encompassing judgment.

Final Judgment

John was shown a vision of that final judgment, which he describes for us:

Revelation 20:11-15 (ESV)
[11] Then I saw a great white throne and him who was seated on it. From his presence earth and sky fled away, and no place was found for them. [12] And I saw the dead, great and small, standing before the throne, and books were opened. Then another book was opened, which is the book of life. And the dead were judged by what was written in the books, according to what they had done. [13] And the sea gave up the dead who were in it, Death and Hades gave up the dead who were in them, and they were judged, each one of them, according to what they had done. [14] Then Death and Hades were thrown into the lake of fire. This is the second death, the lake of fire. [15] And if anyone's name was not found written in the book of life, he was thrown into the lake of fire.

This is the most detailed description of final judgment found in the Bible. Let's examine the specific aspects that are revealed.

The Judge

The first thing John saw in this scene was the Lord sitting on the throne. When the Lord sits on His throne in judgment on that day, his holy countenance will be so devastating that every unredeemed element of creation will try to flee from his gaze, but will find nowhere to hide. His glory will sweep over everything, every heart, exposing them to scrutiny.

Hebrews 4:13 (ESV)
[13] And no creature is hidden from his sight, but all are naked and exposed to the eyes of him to whom we must give account.

Job saw a vision of God on His throne and wrote:

Job 34:21-22 (NIV2011)
[21] "His eyes are on the ways of mortals; he sees their every step. [22] There is no deep shadow, no utter darkness, where evildoers can hide.

And Solomon wrote:

Proverbs 15:11 (KJV)
[11] Hell and destruction are before the LORD: how much more then the hearts of the children of men?

Ecclesiastes 12:13-14 (NIV2011)
[3] Now all has been heard; here is the conclusion of the matter: Fear God and keep his commandments, for this is the duty of all mankind.

14 For God will bring every deed into judgment, including every hidden thing, whether it is good or evil.

In the New Testament Paul writes:

Romans 2:16 (KJV)
16 In the day when God shall judge the secrets of men by Jesus Christ according to my gospel.

1 Corinthians 4:5 (NIV2011)
5 Therefore judge nothing before the appointed time; wait until the Lord comes. He will bring to light what is hidden in darkness and will expose the motives of the heart. At that time each will receive their praise from God.

Never will God's countenance appear more awesome than on the day when He sits in ultimate judgment. Never will men be more terrified, for now eternity stretches out before them and they cannot escape its fate. Perhaps many of them will have waved away any thought of eternal destiny all their lives, and now face it for the first time. Many sneer when anyone suggests they should think beyond today, but on that day there will be no sneering, and no way to sidestep it again. The holiness of the One on the throne will totally devastate any contrary attitude.

<u>The Last Resurrection</u>
Next he sees *the dead great and small*. In our previous passage from Revelation we read that during the millennium . . .

Revelation 20:5 (ESV)
5 The rest of the dead did not come to life until the thousand years were ended. This is the first resurrection.

So now we have described for us that second resurrection, that raising of all whom were not part of the first resurrection, *great and small*--everyone else. No one will be absent on that day. People from earliest creation down to the present will stand before their judge.

Revelation 20:13 (ESV)
13 And the sea gave up the dead who were in it, Death and Hades gave up the dead who were in them . . .

All who have died, and who were not part of the first resurrection will be raised in the second resurrection.

The Books – Heavenly Record-Keeping

The age of grace is past. No longer will mercy be shown. The judgment will be completely just. Every man's life will be replayed, complete with all its good deeds and its sins. The standard for judgment will not be in question at that time, for everyone there will instinctively realize that the standard is God Himself. His righteousness will dominate the scene and permeate every corner of the farthest outskirts of the crowd. It is His holiness against which they must be starkly contrasted. Many will painfully remember the scripture they had snubbed as being prudish:

> *Romans 3:10-18, 23 (KJV)*
> *[10] As it is written, There is none righteous, no, not one: [11] There is none that understandeth, there is none that seeketh after God. [12] They are all gone out of the way, they are together become unprofitable; there is none that doeth good, no, not one. [13] Their throat is an open sepulchre; with their tongues they have used deceit; the poison of asps is under their lips: [14] Whose mouth is full of cursing and bitterness: [15] Their feet are swift to shed blood: [16] Destruction and misery are in their ways: [17] And the way of peace have they not known: [18] There is no fear of God before their eyes. . .*
> *[23] For all have sinned, and come short of the glory of God;*

In the days of the apostles, financial records were kept in ledger books-- scrolls written on parchment. *Books were opened.* The picture is that of a credit and debt accounting system. After thousands of years of man's earthly existence during which justice was not always executed and life was frequently unfair, suddenly all the inconsistencies, the unfairness, the injustice will melt away. All accounts are called in. Suddenly perfect justice will be the modus operendi of the day, and it will be a terrifying prospect for many.

The Book of Life

> *Revelation 20:12,15 (ESV)*
> *[12] . . . Then another book was opened, which is the book of life. . .[15] And if anyone's name was not found written in the book of life, he was thrown into the lake of fire.*

The *books* that were opened will bring condemnation. We already know what they will tell because no one, in-and-of himself, is righteous. All will fall short of the glory of God. None will measure up to the standard of judgment by their life's good deeds. If these books were the only books, all men and women would be condemned.

But then we read of another book. This is the Book of Life. It stands in sharp contrast to the other books. They are books of death. This book lists those whose lives have been redeemed. You might ask, "If perfect justice is done here, and if all have sinned and fallen short, how is it that any can be written in the Book of Life?" There is only one way. One way only! Jesus, who was God in the flesh, became the sacrificial payment for the sins of the world. That is why he is called the *Lamb of God*. His death on the cross is appropriated as payment of the penalty we each deserve. Therefore the penalty is paid and justice is satisfied, even while God's grace is brilliantly applied and displayed.

Without this sacrifice, there is an apparent dilemma. God is love, and wishes to have a relationship with us. That is why we were created in the first place. However to overlook our sin that separates us from Him would be to violate His perfect holiness. Along with His love, that holiness is the very essence of God's character. Because of Jesus' sacrifice, God's gracious love is displayed in forgiveness, and His holiness is preserved in perfect justice.

The righteous of all the ages are written in the Book of Life by God's command. But who are those righteous, if all have fallen short of the mark? They are the people of all ages who lived in faith. They had an awareness of the presence of God in their lives, and lived according to it in the belief that He would reward them. Through the ages God has revealed Himself and His will to us in progressively greater degree. Early on, He spoke through a few patriarchs. Later He spoke through prophets. Finally he has spoken through His Son. In every age, men and women were accountable to what had been revealed. God never required anyone to respond to that which he had not had the opportunity to know. But with each unfolding truth about God, man's responsibility became more specific. Now we have seen the Son. Now we know quite a lot of what the Father is like because of what the Son is like. We are accountable for that knowledge. We are called to faith in the God who is like Jesus in personal traits and in holiness. Those who have been privileged to live since the first advent of Jesus, and to know him as he is presented in Scripture, comprise the church. The church of Jesus Christ is the collective body of true believers in Him.

Before the time of Jesus, men were saved by obedient faith, just as they are today. Although they did not know the incarnate Christ, they believed in the Father, and even had glimpses of the Son, though vaguely. It was the same blood of Jesus on the cross that cleansed and atoned for their sins as for ours today, even though historically he was not yet revealed. God knew how the sins were removed. He saw their faith, and as Paul said of Abraham:

Romans 4:3 (KJV)
[3] For what saith the scripture? Abraham believed God, and it was counted unto him for righteousness.

And the writer of Hebrews said:

> *Hebrews 9:15 (ESV)*
> *[15] Therefore he is the mediator of a new covenant, so that those who are called may receive the promised eternal inheritance, since a death has occurred that redeems them from the transgressions committed under the first covenant.* [[the sins of the Old Testament faithful]

These are the faithful people that are found written in the Book of Life. The death of Jesus atoned for the sins of the whole world, past, present and future, and is appropriated for a person upon that person's appropriate acceptance and embrace of that essential truth. (See Chapter 27 for a more thorough road map of the journey into the saving presence of God, through Jesus Christ.)

Will Christians Face Judgment?

I have heard it said by well-intentioned, but misinformed, people that Christians will not face judgment since our sin is already forgiven. The forgiveness theology is true, but the escaping of judgment is not correct. The scriptures make it clear there is a judgment awaiting believers.

> *Romans 14:10-12 (KJV)*
> *[10] But why dost thou judge thy brother? or why dost thou set at nought thy brother? for we shall all stand before the judgment seat of Christ. [11] For it is written, As I live, saith the Lord, every knee shall bow to me, and every tongue shall confess to God. [12] So then every one of us shall give account of himself to God.*

> *2 Corinthians 5:9-10 (NASB)*
> *[9] Therefore we also have as our ambition, whether at home or absent, to be pleasing to Him. [10] For we must all appear before the judgment seat of Christ, so that each one may be recompensed for his deeds in the body, according to what he has done, whether good or bad.*

> *Matthew 7:1-2 (NASB)*
> *[1] "Do not judge so that you will not be judged. [2] "For in the way you judge, you will be judged; and by your standard of measure, it will be measured to you.*

<u>The Judgment Seat of Christ</u>
The best description of this unique judgment is given to us in a letter from Paul to the Corinthians.

1 Corinthians 3:10-15 (NIV2011)
¹⁰ By the grace God has given me, I laid a foundation as a wise builder, and someone else is building on it. But each one should build with care. ¹¹ For no one can lay any foundation other than the one already laid, which is Jesus Christ. ¹² If anyone builds on this foundation using gold, silver, costly stones, wood, hay or straw, ¹³ their work will be shown for what it is, because the Day will bring it to light. It will be revealed with fire, and the fire will test the quality of each person's work. ¹⁴ If what has been built survives, the builder will receive a reward. ¹⁵ If it is burned up, the builder will suffer loss but yet will be saved—even though only as one escaping through the flames.

How do we know this describes a judgment of Christians? First, we see that those being tried have built their lives on the foundation of Jesus Christ. Second, the last line tells us that these people *will be saved*, albeit some barely *escaping through the flames*.

In this passage we see the ministry of each believer being tested. The analogy is that of a smelting furnace in which impurities were burned out of precious metals such as gold and silver. What a person builds with is represented by two clearly distinguishable groups of materials. Gold, silver and precious stones have durable value. That is, they are precious in their essential worth, and they will survive the heat of the furnace. They represent those deeds done in this life with pure motives, and with the intent of glorifying God. They are precious in God's eyes. Who said, "You can't take it with you?"

Revelation 14:13 (ESV)
¹³ And I heard a voice from heaven saying, "Write this: Blessed are the dead who die in the Lord from now on." "Blessed indeed," says the Spirit, "that they may rest from their labors, for their deeds follow them!"

What is meant by the phrase, *their deeds will follow them?* This is talking about heavenly rewards beyond salvation. Salvation is a gift from God, based on faith. If it is a gift, then it cannot be a reward, for a reward is something deserved or earned. These rewards are also from the same gracious hand of the Creator that brought us to salvation. However they are above and beyond the gift of salvation, and are consistently connected to *what he has done* [the believer].

Matthew 5:11-12 (NASB)
¹¹ "Blessed are you when people insult you and persecute you, and falsely say all kinds of evil against you because of Me. ¹² "Rejoice

and be glad, for your reward in heaven is great; for in the same way they persecuted the prophets who were before you.

Matthew 6:19-20 (NASB)
[19] "Do not store up for yourselves treasures on earth, where moth and rust destroy, and where thieves break in and steal. [20] "But store up for yourselves treasures in heaven, where neither moth nor rust destroys, and where thieves do not break in or steal;

Matthew 10:41-42 (NASB)
[41] "He who receives a prophet in the name of a prophet shall receive a prophet's reward; and he who receives a righteous man in the name of a righteous man shall receive a righteous man's reward. [42] "And whoever in the name of a disciple gives to one of these little ones even a cup of cold water to drink, truly I say to you, he shall not lose his reward."

Matthew 16:27 (NASB)
[27] "For the Son of Man is going to come in the glory of His Father with His angels, and WILL THEN REPAY EVERY MAN ACCORDING TO HIS DEEDS.

Ephesians 6:7-8 (ESV)
[7] rendering service with a good will as to the Lord and not to man, [8] knowing that whatever good anyone does, this he will receive back from the Lord, whether he is a bondservant or is free.

Revelation 22:12 (ESV)
[12] "Behold, I am coming soon, bringing my recompense with me, to repay each one for what he has done.

Thus, one reason the believer must pass through the judgment of Christ is to receive his God-given rewards. I do not know what these will be. I am quite certain they will not be gold, silver and precious stones. God is so wonderful, so creative, so full of giving, that I think we will receive blessings that we cannot even fathom in this life. Our natural imagination does not—cannot—comprehend the rewards we will get from the Lord of glory.

1 Corinthians 2:9 (NIV2011)
[9] However, as it is written: "What no eye has seen, what no ear has heard, and what no human mind has conceived"— the things God has prepared for those who love him—

The second purpose for the judgment of Christians is to purge from them the relics of any unworthy characteristic that might be a blemish in heaven.

The other group of materials in this smelting parable is wood, hay, and straw. If you opened a birthday present and found in it nothing but some straw, what would you think of the person giving it? I imagine that is how the creator of the universe feels when we give him such a gift. These materials represent those things in our lives unworthy to be presented to God. Perhaps there are sinful habits, repented of, but never conquered. Maybe they represent good deeds done from false motives. These are things that need to be stripped from the person in the glorification process. I imagine this will be a very painful time for many of us, in some regards. Yes, Christians will have been already forgiven and glorified. However, some issues are not outright sins, but still unworthy to enter heaven. Perhaps you grudgingly agreed to serve in a certain ministry, after pressure from a leader looking for helpers. Is that a worthy attitude to bring into the throne room of heaven?

Matthew 6:1 (NASB)
[1] "Beware of practicing your righteousness before men to be noticed by them; otherwise you have no reward with your Father who is in heaven.

When Will the Judgment Seat of Christ Take Place?
There is no compelling chronology of events that places the time of this judgment seat of Christ. Dispensationalists often place it in the time frame of the first resurrection and rapture of the church. Indeed the purging aspect of this judgment seems to fit with the rapture, with being changed in the *twinkling of an eye* and made *imperishable*.

On the other hand, in the Revelation 20 description of judgment, we read of the *Book of Life* also being opened on that day. Certainly this book includes Christians. Believers seem to be among those being tried that day. Furthermore, the bestowing of eternal rewards, which occurs at the Judgment Seat of Christ, seems to better fit into this view. Until after we actually go to heaven, would those rewards be fitting? Would they be appropriate here on earth? We do not know. I lean toward placing the time and setting of the Judgment Seat of Christ identical with the great final judgment.

One more very important note needs to be said about this. We should not suppose that those of us who have been caught up in the air with Jesus at his appearing, who have become the Bride of Christ, who have become like him, and have shared his glory—we should not think it possible to still be in doubt about our eternal destiny. Don't suppose that we shall live throughout the millennium in doubt. If our faith should waver in its confidence, we will have the security of having been in the first resurrection to assure us.

Revelation 20:6 (ESV)
⁶ Blessed and holy is the one who shares in the first resurrection! Over such the second death has no power . . .

If we Christians are present before God and Christ that final judgment day, it will be to hear them say,

Matthew 25:21 (NASB)
²¹ . . . 'Well done, good and faithful slave. You were faithful with a few things, I will put you in charge of many things; enter into the joy of your master.'

Consequences of Judgment

We have already looked at the destiny of those whose names are written in the book of life. They will forever be with the Lord. What about those who are not found there?

Revelation 20:14-15 (ESV)
¹⁴ . . . This is the second death, the lake of fire. ¹⁵ And if anyone's name was not found written in the book of life, he was thrown into the lake of fire.

The lake of fire is hell. Many words in the original languages refer to death-related places. This can cause confusion, as they are often equated with heaven or hell. Here is a synopsis of the more common such words and their meanings.

Hades – Greek (New Testament) word meaning place of departed souls of the unrighteous. While it is associated with the final hell, it is also to be differentiated. Here souls were sent to await final resurrection and judgment. It was a place of torment, perhaps a precursor of the ultimate punishment.

2 Peter 2:9 (ESV)
⁹ then the Lord knows how to rescue the godly from trials, and to keep the unrighteous under punishment until the day of judgment,

Paradise – Greek for a place of extreme blessedness; a place or state in heaven where departed righteous souls go while they await their final redemption. It is the antithesis of Hades.

Luke 23:43 (ESV)
⁴³ And he said to him, "Truly, I say to you, today you will be with me in Paradise."

Abraham's Bosom – another name for Paradise based upon the Hebrew understanding of a deceased person 'returning to his fathers.'

Sheol – Hebrew (Old Testament) general word for the abode of departed souls, righteous or wicked. Beyond the grave.

Gehenna – Hebrew for Valley of Hinnom, a deep ravine south of Jerusalem and just outside its old walls. There pagans and idolatrous Israelites used to sacrifice their children to the god

Molech. By Jesus' day it had become the city dump where all garbage, sewage and dead animals were thrown to be burned. It was used as a synonym for hell, as for example:

> *Mark 9:47-48 (ESV)*
> *[47] ... thrown into hell, [Gehenna] [48] 'where their worm does not die and the fire is not quenched.'*

In our text, the lake of fire is generally understood to be the same hell in its full fury that is embodied in the word Gehenna. It is hell in its finality, for it is eternal.

> *Romans 2:5-11 (KJV)*
> *[5] But after thy hardness and impenitent heart treasurest up unto thyself wrath against the day of wrath and revelation of the righteous judgment of God; [6] Who will render to every man according to his deeds: [7] To them who by patient continuance in well doing seek for glory and honour and immortality, eternal life: [8] But unto them that are contentious, and do not obey the truth, but obey unrighteousness, indignation and wrath, [9] Tribulation and anguish, upon every soul of man that doeth evil, of the Jew first, and also of the Gentile; [10] But glory, honour, and peace, to every man that worketh good, to the Jew first, and also to the Gentile: [11] For there is no respect of persons with God.*

<u>What about Purgatory?</u>
The Roman Catholic concept of purgatory is simply not scriptural. It is said to be a time of temporary punishment so that a soul could somehow be cleansed through chastisement, and through the prayers of saints still alive. Then that soul could enter heaven. The justification that is sought through this suffering has already been procured for the Christian through the substitutionary sacrifice of Jesus, in our place. We have nothing worthy to sacrifice in our own behalf, but Jesus was worthy. The doctrine of purgatory, although it seems to share some characteristics of biblical temporary after-death places, diminishes the atoning work of Christ, making it less sufficient, and unnecessary.

In Summary

Hebrews 9:27-28 (ESV)
[27] *And just as it is appointed for man to die once, and after that comes judgment,* [28] *so Christ, having been offered once to bear the sins of many, will appear a second time, not to deal with sin but to save those who are eagerly waiting for him.*

You will one day stand before the eternal, holy God. Whether you believe it or not is immaterial to whether it will happen. It will happen. The good news is that those who have already given their lives to the lordship of Jesus Christ will have no fear on that day. They will stand victorious before a condemned world, and hear the creator say...

Matthew 25:23 (NKJV)
[23] *. . . 'Well done, good and faithful servant; you have been faithful over a few things, I will make you ruler over many things. Enter into the joy of your lord.'*

> Dear God of heaven and earth, fill us with Yourself, I pray. Fill us with the assurance of Your love and abiding presence. Fill us with promises of Your favor so that we need not fear your wrath. Fill us with a vision of Your holiness so that we may live a life of penitence. Fill us with Your holiness so that we are not stripped bare of even what we have, before Your judgment seat. Teach us to abandon self-righteousness and to lean completely on Your grace. Marvelous is Your plan, and great is Your holiness. So be it.

26
GLORY

'Pie in the sky'--a common term mocking the belief in a final reward. We hear jokes about it occasionally. One strategy of assault on the Christian faith is to mock its belief in heaven. Paul, the missionary apostle to the Gentiles, met this ridicule in Athens.

Acts 17:32 (ESV)
[32] Now when they heard of the resurrection of the dead, some mocked
. . .

Nevertheless, the concept of heaven is well founded in scripture, both Old and New Testaments. Here are just a few of the several hundred 'heaven' scriptures:

Genesis 22:11 (KJV)
[11] And the angel of the LORD called unto him out of heaven, and said, Abraham, Abraham: and he said, Here am I.

1 Kings 8:30 (ESV)
[30] And listen to the plea of your servant and of your people Israel, when they pray toward this place. And listen in heaven your dwelling place, and when you hear, forgive.

Mark 16:19 (ESV)
[9] So then the Lord Jesus, after he had spoken to them, was taken up into heaven and sat down at the right hand of God.

Philippians 3:20 (ESV)
[20] But our citizenship is in heaven, and from it we await a Savior, the Lord Jesus Christ,

What is Heaven?

The word heaven was used in the original Bible languages much like it is used in modern English, that is, it had several meanings. It could refer to the terrestrial sky, the clouds, the atmosphere, the domain of the birds.

Isaiah 55:10 (KJV)
[10] For as the rain cometh down, and the snow from heaven, and returneth not thither, but watereth the earth, and maketh it bring forth and bud, that it may give seed to the sower, and bread to the eater:

In other biblical passages it refers to the celestial sky.

Acts 2:19-20 (ESV)
[19] And I will show wonders in the heavens above and signs on the earth below, blood, and fire, and vapor of smoke; [20] the sun shall be turned to darkness and the moon to blood, before the day of the Lord comes, the great and magnificent day.

But in the large majority of biblical occurrences, heaven means that place beyond creation where God is said to dwell, and where angels abide. It is in this heaven that the throne of God stands, and Jesus is portrayed as sitting at the Father's right hand.

What is this heaven? The Bible speaks of it as a place. The ancients perceived of heaven as existing beyond the celestial sky, and being a tangible realm. Thus, heaven was 'up.' Many of its uses speak from this idea of an overhead location.

2 Kings 2:1 (NASB)
[1] And it came about when the LORD was about to take up Elijah by a whirlwind to heaven, that Elijah went with Elisha from Gilgal.

It is not unusual to find the terrestrial or celestial and spiritual blended so that they are clearly connected in imagery, if not in reality, in the language of the biblical author.

Job 22:12 (NIV2011)
[12] "Is not God in the heights of heaven? And see how lofty are the highest stars!

Acts 1:11 (ESV)
[11] and said, "Men of Galilee, why do you stand looking into heaven? This Jesus, who was taken up from you into heaven, will come in the same way as you saw him go into heaven."

While heaven is a 'place,' we do not understand it to be a physical place. It seems to be a place not found by following a chart or map. It is not a place that can be located using distance and time. It must have a very different fundamental nature from what we are familiar with. On the one hand, God is said to dwell there, seated on a throne. On the other, He is said to be spirit, invisible, and omnipresent. When we seek to rectify these concepts in terms of this world's dimensions, we fall into confusion. Heaven remains a mystery, to some extent. We see this kind of otherworldly concept in some New Testament scriptures, like this one:

Ephesians 1:3 (ESV)
³ Blessed be the God and Father of our Lord Jesus Christ, who has blessed us in Christ with every spiritual blessing in the heavenly places,

Ephesians 2:6 (ESV)
⁶ and raised us up with him and seated us with him in the heavenly places in Christ Jesus,

How can we be seated already in the heavenly realms while we are still dwelling here in this world? Is God simply identifying the seat of our citizenship? Is he stating the future as though it were already fact--a common prophetic device? Or is the language only figurative? You see, we can grasp the concept that in God's eyes, our presence in heaven is a done deal, without having a complete understanding of how it can be so. Let's not be concerned about that.

While the visions and heavenly imagery given to us in prophecy may be understood to be a figurative representation of otherwise unexplainable realities, we are no closer to grasping those realities apart from the biblical description. Therefore, acknowledging that much may be figurative, nonetheless we accept it as the explanation given us by God Himself, and so we learn from it what we believe He would have us learn, leaving subjective speculation aside. So how does the Bible describe heaven?

Windows into Heaven

A number of glimpses into heaven's inner sanctuary are given to us in Old Testament prophecies. We have quoted most of the major ones in this book already. We have read of Isaiah's vision of God seated on His throne *high and lifted up,* in Isaiah 6, attended by seraphs. In Ezekiel 1 we saw four angelic creatures with their flaming wheels, and above them the Lord himself in fiery glory. Daniel saw the Ancient of Days take his seat of judgment and one like the son of man approaching Him, and being given everlasting authority, glory and power. Then in Revelation 4 and 5 we saw unfolding the initiation of end time judgment, played out in heaven's glory, a glory remarkably similar to that revealed in the Old Testament. We have seen vivid descriptions of light, fire, hovering angels, innumerable souls and angels bowing in worship, gold, a sea of glass, precious, beautiful stones, and most glorious of all, God on His throne in indescribable splendor and awesomeness. Throughout Revelation we saw unrestrained worship and celebration from God's redeemed.

> *Revelation 5:9-14 (ESV)*
> [9] *And they sang a new song, saying, "Worthy are you to take the scroll and to open its seals, for you were slain, and by your blood you ransomed people for God from every tribe and language and people and nation,* [10] *and you have made them a kingdom and priests to our God, and they shall reign on the earth."* [11] *Then I looked, and I heard around the throne and the living creatures and the elders the voice of many angels, numbering myriads of myriads and thousands of thousands,* [12] *saying with a loud voice, "Worthy is the Lamb who was slain, to receive power and wealth and wisdom and might and honor and glory and blessing!"* [13] *And I heard every creature in heaven and on earth and under the earth and in the sea, and all that is in them, saying, "To him who sits on the throne and to the Lamb be blessing and honor and glory and might forever and ever!"* [14] *And the four living creatures said, "Amen!" and the elders fell down and worshiped.*

In all these visions the focus is on God, and Jesus with Him. We are drawn there by our need of mercy, but the emphasis is His holiness and glory; and the mood is reverent, awesome and intimidating. God is portrayed as ominous and glorious.

In the gospels, heaven is the place Jesus left to visit men on earth. Its glory was left behind for awhile as he became a man. In the book of Hebrews, heaven is the place where Jesus sits at the Father's right hand and makes intercession for us. It is the place where atonement is offered and accepted. In the Acts and the letters of the New Testament, the emphasis broadens to take in our promised part in heaven.

Besides worship, what else takes place in heaven? We will not attempt to catalog a comprehensive list of heavenly activities, although that might be quite interesting. Let's just mention a couple of specific things.

God is said to watch over and keep track of the affairs of men. He especially notes our efforts to serve Him. For example:

> *Matthew 5:11-12 (NASB)*
> [11] *"Blessed are you when people insult you and persecute you, and falsely say all kinds of evil against you because of Me.* [12] *"Rejoice and be glad, for your reward in heaven is great; for in the same way they persecuted the prophets who were before you.*

Matthew 10:29-31 (NASB)
²⁹ "Are not two sparrows sold for a cent? And yet not one of them will fall to the ground apart from your Father. ³⁰ "But the very hairs of your head are all numbered. ³¹ "So do not fear; you are more valuable than many sparrows.

Not only does God Himself take note and plan rewards for us, but apparently all of heaven is in on what is going on. They share in the Lord's feelings about it.

Luke 15:7 (ESV)
⁷ Just so, I tell you, there will be more joy in heaven over one sinner who repents than over ninety-nine righteous persons who need no repentance.

Luke 15:32 (ESV)
³² It was fitting to celebrate and be glad, for this your brother was dead, and is alive; he was lost, and is found.'"

The implied message is that the Father is joined by the heavenly hosts in His rejoicing over a saved person. We can only imagine millions of angels shouting and singing for joy before God over the salvation of a woman or man, boy or girl.

We could go on. We could talk about God's loving providential benevolence toward His creation, constantly being poured over us. We could speak of Christ's sustaining work, of his constant disciplining of his own, of his judging work. Heaven is a bustling place.

The Down-to-Earth Truth About Pie-in-the-Sky

Revelation 21:1 (ESV)
¹ Then I saw a new heaven and a new earth, for the first heaven and the first earth had passed away, and the sea was no more.

In this verse we are introduced to a startling truth. The present created order is terminal. In this and other such passages, the term *heaven* refers to the terrestrial and celestial heavens. It tells us that the created order we now know will cease to exist, according to God's great purpose. It will be replaced by another order, also of His making. In fact, Peter wrote about the destruction of the present order:

2 Peter 3:7,10-13 (ESV)
⁷ But by the same word the heavens and earth that now exist are stored up for fire, being kept until the day of judgment and destruction of the ungodly. . . . ¹⁰ But the day of the Lord will come

> *like a thief, and then the heavens will pass away with a roar, and the heavenly bodies will be burned up and dissolved, and the earth and the works that are done on it will be exposed.* ^{11} *Since all these things are thus to be dissolved, what sort of people ought you to be in lives of holiness and godliness,* ^{12} *waiting for and hastening the coming of the day of God, because of which the heavens will be set on fire and dissolved, and the heavenly bodies will melt as they burn!* ^{13} *But according to his promise we are waiting for new heavens and a new earth in which righteousness dwells.*

Isaiah in the Old Testament had been shown these things, and wrote . . .

> *Isaiah 65:17 (KJV)*
> ^{17} *For, behold, I create new heavens and a new earth: and the former shall not be remembered, nor come into mind.*

When will this destruction of the present order take place? The passage from 2 Peter said that this would occur *on the day of judgment*. We see this supported in John's apocalyptic description of the great judgment:

> *Revelation 20:11 (ESV)*
> ^{11} *Then I saw a great white throne and him who was seated on it. From his presence earth and sky fled away, and no place was found for them.*

If that is true, where is our security? We want a secure eternity. Our hope is for a heaven where we know we will be safe forever and forever. If the current creation will not last, then what will? God's word tells us precisely what will last:

> *Isaiah 66:22 (KJV)*
> ^{22} *For as the new heavens and the new earth, which I will make, shall remain before me, saith the LORD, so shall your seed and your name remain.*

> *Hebrews 12:28-29 (ESV)*
> ^{28} *Therefore let us be grateful for receiving a kingdom that cannot be shaken, and thus let us offer to God acceptable worship, with reverence and awe,* ^{29} *for our God is a consuming fire.*

We become qualified for this new order by becoming a follower of Jesus Christ. Just as the old heaven and earth will one day pass away, so our old way of rebellion against God must also pass away, and be replaced by an allegiance to Jesus and to the Father.

2 Corinthians 5:17 (NASB)
[17] Therefore if anyone is in Christ, he is a new creature; the old things passed away; behold, new things have come.

John 11:25-26 (NIV2011)
[25] Jesus said to her, "I am the resurrection and the life. The one who believes in me will live, even though they die; [26] and whoever lives by believing in me will never die. Do you believe this?"

Yes, resurrection is yet future, but our new life is already implanted in our souls. According to Paul's letter to the Ephesians, we are already *seated in the heavenly realms*, and our citizenship is there. We are just visitors, or passers-by, in this earthly life. *Aliens*, we are called. So, if our eternal home is to be heaven, what will it be like?

<u>Its Impression</u>
Up until now, the visions of heaven that have been given have focused on God's glory. In Revelation chapters 21 and 22, we are shown a very different side of heaven. In these visions the focus is on heaven, the blessed place for righteous people. Both views are glorious, but, whereas the prior images of heaven emphasize God's holiness and awesome glory, the images given to us in these two last chapters in the Bible are images of comfort and security. In the old, we revel in His majesty, but are left with a holy fear. In the new, we bask in intimate relationship with Him. Let's see what it tells us.

Revelation 21:1-4 (ESV)
[1] Then I saw a new heaven and a new earth, for the first heaven and the first earth had passed away, and the sea was no more. [2] And I saw the holy city, new Jerusalem, coming down out of heaven from God, prepared as a bride adorned for her husband. [3] And I heard a loud voice from the throne saying, "Behold, the dwelling place of God is with man. He will dwell with them, and they will be his people, and God himself will be with them as their God. [4] He will wipe away every tear from their eyes, and death shall be no more, neither shall there be mourning, nor crying, nor pain anymore, for the former things have passed away."

In this beautiful vision, heaven and earth become as one. So it will be in that day. Prior to this, God has remained separate from men. God has appeared in certain forms at certain times to certain people. He had sent His Holy Spirit to indwell New Testament believers. Yet He was not generally, visibly, bodily present with them in a way that they could literally behold Him. Now, in the new heaven, He will dwell in our very midst. Furthermore He will bring to us freedom from those things that make life sad. Only happy things will happen in heaven. This is only possible because the old order of things will be obsolete. Next we are told . . .

> *Revelation 21:5-7 (ESV)*
> *⁵ And he who was seated on the throne said, "Behold, I am making all things new." Also he said, "Write this down, for these words are trustworthy and true." ⁶ And he said to me, "It is done! I am the Alpha and the Omega, the beginning and the end. To the thirsty I will give from the spring of the water of life without payment. ⁷ The one who conquers will have this heritage, and I will be his God and he will be my son.*

The One who created all things in the beginning, will again create. It is God Himself who will make everything new. This new view is a stark contrast to the old order of things. In the old, we are connected to God through faith. In the new, we will dwell with Him. In the old, we behold His holiness always with an element of holy dread because we always saw ourselves in His presence, and we realized our unworthiness. In the new, we will have been glorified, and there will no longer be fear of the Holy. In the new, the demeanor is one of welcoming hospitality and benevolence towards us. It will assuredly be novel to us.

> *1 Corinthians 2:9 (NIV2011)*
> *⁹ However, as it is written: "What no eye has seen, what no ear has heard, and what no human mind has conceived"— the things God has prepared for those who love him—*

Our natural minds struggle to understand where God has been. How much more we must reach to imagine where He is going. All we can do is absorb these earthly images and allow them to speak to us.

We know that if God says something, it is true. Yet, to emphasize the veracity of these statements, He confirms for us again that these promises are *trustworthy and true*. How full of grace, God is. How tender toward us! Believe it, for it is true as nothing else is true.

It is done. What does this mean? Throughout the book of Revelation as we see certain events unfold, there is always something else to follow, something close at hand. It is almost wearisome to read, for there is no plateau where one can catch his breath, but must continually encounter yet another episode. Now, it is done. Now there is rest for our souls. The Alpha and Omega, the One who inhabits the vanishing points on the horizons of eternity, past and future, says *It is done.*

All of this leads up to the simple, gracious invitation. We are invited to drink of the water of life. This is a metaphor for salvation. He invites us to accept the salvation that He has provided. Note that God, Himself, is the One who gives us to drink without cost.

While the salvation is freely given, one must *overcome* in order to inherit it. It is our faith in cooperation with God's grace that brings us to salvation. And what is this overcoming?

> *1 John 2:14 (ESV)*
> *14 I write to you, fathers, because you know him who is from the beginning. I write to you, young men, because you are strong, and the word of God abides in you, and you have overcome the evil one.*
>
> *1 John 4:4 (ESV)*
> *4 Little children, you are from God and have overcome them, for he who is in you is greater than he who is in the world.*
>
> *Revelation 3:21 (ESV)*
> *21 The one who conquers, I will grant him to sit with me on my throne, as I also conquered and sat down with my Father on his throne.*

To *conquer* or *overcome*, in the sense it is used in New Testament language, means to overcome by the power of Jesus' redemptive work of atonement. In other words, it means to possess a saving relationship with God through Jesus Christ. Yet it is not void of our responsibility to be obedient to that grace given us, to overcome by living out that grace in real situations, through trials, through tribulations.

> *Revelation 12:10-11 (ESV)*
> *10 And I heard a loud voice in heaven, saying, "Now the salvation and the power and the kingdom of our God and the authority of his Christ have come, for the accuser of our brothers has been thrown down, who accuses them day and night before our God. 11 And they have conquered him by the blood of the Lamb and by the word of their testimony, for they loved not their lives even unto death.*

In this last scripture, note the little word '*and*' between the clauses. They overcome the devil *by the blood of the Lamb <u>and</u> by the word of their testimony*. Saving faith, together with God's grace, overcomes by enabling us to triumph over the circumstances of life.

<u>It's Not for Everyone</u>
> *Revelation 21:8 (ESV)*
> *8 But as for the cowardly, the faithless, the detestable, as for murderers, the sexually immoral, sorcerers, idolaters, and all liars,*

their portion will be in the lake that burns with fire and sulfur, which is the second death."

We are briefly, but forcefully, reminded of the alternative to heaven. The unredeemed will have no part in heaven, but have the *fiery lake of burning sulfur* to look forward to. The unredeemed life is typified in those sinful practices.

The New Jerusalem

As we continue in our Revelation 21 passage describing heaven, we are told of John's next vision, the vision of the New Jerusalem.

Revelation 21:1-2, 9-27 (ESV)
[1] Then I saw a new heaven and a new earth, for the first heaven and the first earth had passed away, and the sea was no more. [2] And I saw the holy city, new Jerusalem, coming down out of heaven from God, prepared as a bride adorned for her husband. . . . [9] Then came one of the seven angels who had the seven bowls full of the seven last plagues and spoke to me, saying, "Come, I will show you the Bride, the wife of the Lamb." [10] And he carried me away in the Spirit to a great, high mountain, and showed me the holy city Jerusalem coming down out of heaven from God, [11] having the glory of God, its radiance like a most rare jewel, like a jasper, clear as crystal. [12] It had a great, high wall, with twelve gates, and at the gates twelve angels, and on the gates the names of the twelve tribes of the sons of Israel were inscribed— [13] on the east three gates, on the north three gates, on the south three gates, and on the west three gates. [14] And the wall of the city had twelve foundations, and on them were the twelve names of the twelve apostles of the Lamb. [15] And the one who spoke with me had a measuring rod of gold to measure the city and its gates and walls. [16] The city lies foursquare, its length the same as its width. And he measured the city with his rod, 12,000 stadia. Its length and width and height are equal. [17] He also measured its wall, 144 cubits by human measurement, which is also an angel's measurement. [18] The wall was built of jasper, while the city was pure gold, like clear glass. [19] The foundations of the wall of the city were adorned with every kind of jewel. The first was jasper, the second sapphire, the third agate, the fourth emerald, [20] the fifth onyx, the sixth carnelian, the seventh chrysolite, the eighth beryl, the ninth topaz, the tenth chrysoprase, the eleventh jacinth, the twelfth amethyst. [21] And the twelve gates were twelve pearls, each of the gates made of a single pearl, and the street of the city was pure gold, like transparent glass. [22] And I saw no temple in the city, for its temple is the Lord God the Almighty and the Lamb. [23] And the city has no need of sun or moon to shine on it, for the glory of God gives it light, and its lamp is the Lamb. [24] By its light will the nations walk,

and the kings of the earth will bring their glory into it, [25] *and its gates will never be shut by day—and there will be no night there.* [26] *They will bring into it the glory and the honor of the nations.* [27] *But nothing unclean will ever enter it, nor anyone who does what is detestable or false, but only those who are written in the Lamb's book of life.*

John was carried *in the Spirit* to a high mountain. He realizes he was not bodily removed from his Island prison, but in the Spirit he was transported into the future. In the Spirit, God showed him what would happen after the present order was gone. Jerusalem, the gem of heaven, is seen coming into view from heaven. Note that it does not appear in and of itself, but comes *from God*. What a fabulous and tremendous city it was that John saw.

Notice how much space is given in this passage to the walls and gates of the New Jerusalem. This suggests that in them there is a significant message for us. Indeed, we shall see that this message dates back to ancient times, and peers into eternity. Let's investigate further.

The angel had told John that he would show him *the bride, the wife of the Lamb*, but then what he showed him was the heavenly city New Jerusalem. Is the wife of the lamb a city? What is meant by this? Back in Revelation chapter 19 we read:

Revelation 19:7-9 (ESV)
[7] *Let us rejoice and exult and give him the glory, for the marriage of the Lamb has come, and his Bride has made herself ready;* [8] *it was granted her to clothe herself with fine linen, bright and pure"— for the fine linen is the righteous deeds of the saints.* [9] *And the angel said to me, "Write this: Blessed are those who are invited to the marriage supper of the Lamb." And he said to me, "These are the true words of God."*

Back in the first chapter of this book we discussed that there is a symbolism running through the New Testament for the eternal relationship between Christ and his church. Let's revisit a couple of those passages. Paul wrote:

Ephesians 5:31-32 (ESV)
[31] *"Therefore a man shall leave his father and mother and hold fast to his wife, and the two shall become one flesh."* [32] *This mystery is profound, and I am saying that it refers to Christ and the church.*

He was using the metaphor of marriage to describe this relationship. Jesus made, as it were, a marriage proposal when he told his followers:

> *John 14:2-3 (NIV2011)*
> *² My Father's house has many rooms; if that were not so, would I have told you that I am going there to prepare a place for you? ³ And if I go and prepare a place for you, I will come back and take you to be with me that you also may be where I am.*

The envisioned city seems to represent the 'mansion of many rooms' where Christ promised to dwell with his people. In this passage, the main idea is not the structure, but the intimate relationship it provides with our Savior and God. Furthermore, it stands parallel to the kingdom-family structure comprised of Christ's people themselves, portrayed by Paul. Even the Old Testament/New Testament foundations are portrayed in those of the heavenly city.

> *Ephesians 2:19-22 (ESV)*
> *¹⁹ So then you are no longer strangers and aliens, but you are fellow citizens with the saints and members of the household of God, ²⁰ built on the foundation of the apostles and prophets, Christ Jesus himself being the cornerstone, ²¹ in whom the whole structure, being joined together, grows into a holy temple in the Lord. ²² In him you also are being built together into a dwelling place for God by the Spirit.*

During the present time, the kingdom structure is a temple made up of individuals who themselves are indwelt by the Spirit of God. We are *living stones*. In the new order, we will not need the Spirit to guide us. We will *be like him* (Jesus) in our devotion to God, and we will dwell in His very presence. Thus, the historical city, and the present day church both point to an intimate relational eternity in heaven, symbolized by the New Jerusalem.

This vision is by far the most comprehensive description of New Jerusalem in scripture, but it is not the first mention of it. According to the writer of the book of Hebrews, Abraham and the other patriarchs envisioned in some way that their goal and reward was a heavenly city.

> *Hebrews 11:9-16 (ESV)*
> *⁹ By faith he went to live in the land of promise, as in a foreign land, living in tents with Isaac and Jacob, heirs with him of the same promise. ¹⁰ For he was looking forward to the city that has foundations, whose designer and builder is God. . . . ¹³ These all died in faith, not having received the things promised, but having seen them and greeted them from afar, and having acknowledged that they were strangers and exiles on the earth. ¹⁴ For people who speak thus make it clear that they are seeking a homeland. ¹⁵ If they had been thinking of that land from which they had gone out, they would have had opportunity to return. ¹⁶ But as it is, they desire a better country,*

that is, a heavenly one. Therefore God is not ashamed to be called their God, for he has prepared for them a city.

Visions by the prophet Isaiah seamlessly link together the historical Jerusalem with this eternal Jerusalem, showing historical Jerusalem is a "type" of the heavenly:

Isaiah 54:11-12 (KJV)
[11] O thou afflicted, tossed with tempest, and not comforted, behold, I will lay thy stones with fair colours, and lay thy foundations with sapphires. [12] And I will make thy windows of agates, and thy gates of carbuncles, and all thy borders of pleasant stones.

Isaiah 60:18-19 (KJV)
[18] Violence shall no more be heard in thy land, wasting nor destruction within thy borders; but thou shalt call thy walls Salvation, and thy gates Praise. [19] The sun shall be no more thy light by day; neither for brightness shall the moon give light unto thee: but the LORD shall be unto thee an everlasting light, and thy God thy glory.

The historical city didn't just come to represent heaven by happenstance. God put that imagery into the minds of his chosen leaders from ancient times. He has put his stamp on the city, as expressed by the psalmist:

Psalm 87:1-3 (NIV2011)
[1] He has founded his city on the holy mountain. [2] The LORD loves the gates of Zion more than all the other dwellings of Jacob. [3] Glorious things are said of you, city of God:

Glorious things are said because the historical Jerusalem is a pre-cursor, an earnest down-payment by God to reserve our places in heaven. This heavenly Jerusalem is spiritually contrasted with the historical Jerusalem by Paul:

Galatians 4:24-26 (ESV)
[24] Now this may be interpreted allegorically: these women are two covenants. One is from Mount Sinai, bearing children for slavery; she is Hagar. [25] Now Hagar is Mount Sinai in Arabia; she corresponds to the present Jerusalem, for she is in slavery with her children. [26] But the Jerusalem above is free, and she is our mother.

John wrote of it in the early part of his Revelation visions.

Revelation 3:12 (ESV)
[12] The one who conquers, I will make him a pillar in the temple of my God. Never shall he go out of it, and I will write on him the name of my God, and the name of the city of my God, the new Jerusalem, which comes down from my God out of heaven, and my own new name.

Its Glory
The glory of God, while too holy for us to behold, has nevertheless always been the longing of the heart of the righteous. The new city will possess God's glory in full measure, shown here as brilliant radiance, and it will not frighten us. The imagery reaches to capture in a humanly understandable reference the greatness of the city's glory. Jasper is today's diamond. It was like a huge diamond, perfect in clarity and without any flaws or inclusions, reflecting pure rays of light. The source of the glory is revealed in verses 23-24. The Lord God Almighty and the Lamb are the source of the majesty, the splendor, the glory.

If you have visited the Grand Canyon, your first look upon it was undoubtedly one of awe. Perhaps you have had a close view of a mighty mountain, or some other breathtaking encounters. All these will pale compared with the glory that awaits us in heaven.

Its Symmetry and Size
We like symmetry. Even when we intentionally avoid symmetry so as to create an air of randomness or a casual appearance, there is still a tendency to compensate by maintaining balance. There is something about symmetry that completes our perception of how things should be. It relieves a certain tension when things are made symmetrical. It demonstrates intelligence of design and purpose, as opposed to accidental happenstance. The city John saw coming down from heaven was a perfectly symmetrical city.

The text seems to describe a cube with sides facing north, south east and west. A stadia is believed to be about 200 meters, so 12,000 stadia would equal roughly 1500 miles, or about the distance from New York City to Dallas. This monstrous city was envisioned to be that long, that wide and that high. Obviously construction constraints that would limit such a tall city in the present realm are not even a reality there. It doesn't seem very private. It is constructed of diamond-like material.

Its Structure
Walls and gates of ancient cities were built for protection. However, these gates were often somewhat elaborate, and the walls quite formidable, a characteristic that transcended just security. They exuded a distinct civic identity. They were emblems of a treasured uniqueness within. For the Jews, that distinctive was the temple of the Living God, just inside the wall.

Thus the walls and gates were more than protection; they also were symbolic.

The description of the New Jerusalem is rich with symbolism. The names of Jesus' twelve apostles on the foundations and of the twelve tribes of Israel on the gates show the foundational nature of the Old and New Testament historical periods to the habitation of this city. It reminds us how carefully and beautifully history was orchestrated by God to bring about this victorious moment. These names remind us that our faith—the Christian faith—is not a philosophy, a mere human plot. Neither is it founded on a single person's unsubstantiated claim of spiritual revelation. The doctrines of the Christian faith are revelations from God, given to multiple spokesmen over many centuries, all having consistent agreement. The evidence of that revelation is provided in stones and mortar, in geographical places and historical people. History and archaeology bear witness to this evidence. The architectural scope of God's redemptive plan is gloriously portrayed here. Isaiah, in Old Testament times, saw the focus of its initiation.

> *Isaiah 28:16-17 (KJV)*
> *[16] Therefore thus saith the Lord GOD, Behold, I lay in Zion for a foundation a stone, a tried stone, a precious corner stone, a sure foundation: he that believeth shall not make haste. [17] Judgment also will I lay to the line, and righteousness to the plummet: and the hail shall sweep away the refuge of lies, and the waters shall overflow the hiding place.*

Isaiah uses imagery of building stones in Jerusalem to portray Christ, the *precious cornerstone* of the new heavenly kingdom's city. Ezekiel was shown a prophetic vision for the reallocation of the land, and the rebuilding of Jerusalem under Nehemiah, following the yet-future return from Babylonian captivity. At one point, his vision seems to look past Nehemiah's city in its symbolism, but does not seem to be envisioning the New Jerusalem. Perhaps it envisions Nehemiah's city as it had expanded at the time of Jesus' ministry.

> *Ezekiel 48:29-35 (NASB)*
> *[29] "This is the land which you shall divide by lot to the tribes of Israel for an inheritance, and these are their several portions," declares the Lord GOD. [30] "These are the exits of the city: on the north side, 4,500 cubits by measurement, [31] shall be the gates of the city, named for the tribes of Israel, three gates toward the north: the gate of Reuben, one; the gate of Judah, one; the gate of Levi, one. [32] "On the east side, 4,500 cubits, shall be three gates: the gate of Joseph, one; the gate of Benjamin, one; the gate of Dan, one. [33] "On the south side, 4,500 cubits by measurement, shall be three gates: the*

gate of Simeon, one; the gate of Issachar, one; the gate of Zebulun, one. [34] *"On the west side, 4,500 cubits, shall be three gates: the gate of Gad, one; the gate of Asher, one; the gate of Naphtali, one.* [35] *"The city shall be 18,000 cubits round about; and the name of the city from that day shall be, 'The LORD is there.'"*

This passage is revealing because in it we see God's symbolic assignment made to the earthly historical Jerusalem. This is the earliest attachment of the patriarch's names to Jerusalem's gates, even telling which tribal gate faced which direction. In this prophecy, the symbolism is not relegated to a visionary heavenly Jerusalem, but is placed squarely on the historical city. Yet at no time since that prophecy do we see in scripture, or otherwise, the gates of the historical city called by those names. In this parallelism we see Jerusalem the earthly city put forth as a type of the New Jerusalem.

Furthermore, in this Ezekiel passage we see a symbolic name: *YHWH Shammah—the Lord is There.* It might seem that at the time of Jesus' triumphal entry into Jerusalem in 30 AD, this prophecy was fulfilled in his person, except for one small detail. The passage says that name shall be *from that day*. We know from history that the city has been under gentile ownership much of the time since the Romans destroyed Jerusalem in 70 AD. It has to envision either the millennial Jerusalem or the New Jerusalem. Again, the historic city can be seen as emblematic of that great city where God will dwell with his people in eternity.

The New Testament likens the church's being built up in maturity during this present age to the building of this symbolic city.

> *Ephesians 4:11-13 (ESV)*
> [11] *And he gave the apostles, the prophets, the evangelists, the shepherds and teachers,* [12] *to equip the saints for the work of ministry, for building up the body of Christ,* [13] *until we all attain to the unity of the faith and of the knowledge of the Son of God, to mature manhood, to the measure of the stature of the fullness of Christ,*

> *1 Peter 2:4-5 (ESV)*
> [4] *As you come to him, a living stone rejected by men but in the sight of God chosen and precious,* [5] *you yourselves like living stones are being built up as a spiritual house, to be a holy priesthood, to offer spiritual sacrifices acceptable to God through Jesus Christ.*

>> God, dear God how wonderful are your plans. They were in your mind before time began. You laid this foundation and made us like building stones, built together with Christ to construct your dream city. We praise you for

your new creation. Lord, how overwhelming your intentions are. The greatest achievements of man are as leaves blown away in the wind. Your works are everlasting. To think that you purposed in your heart to make a people for your good pleasure, and it was us. Your love is beyond that known to men. It is past our comprehension. Help us to learn this love, we pray. Teach us to love so that we may reciprocate with a love that is worthy of you. Amen

The Symbolic Walls and Gates
As splendid as the walls and gates of New Jerusalem are, we understand that they are not the prize. They are not the objective; not the reward. They are fitting emblems of what lies beyond themselves. Thus, we approach these descriptions as being highly symbolic. They send a message to us. What are they saying?

Its Security
One of our most fundamental needs in life is to feel secure. The fact is, we often spend much of our lives insecure, and seeking for a remedy. If we do not have enough life insurance, our future seems insecure. If stock prices drop, we worry about our future. When the terrorist attack of September 11, 2001 occurred, people the world over suddenly felt less secure. This has been the case since the earliest days of man. In biblical days people often flocked to walled cities for security from invading marauders. If the walls were high enough and thick enough, they felt a security there. For example the ancient city of Nineveh had a wall forty to fifty feet high running 2-1/2 miles along the Tigris River, then 8 miles around the city. It is said the walls were so thick that four chariots could be driven abreast along its top. It was considered one of the most impenetrable cities of its day. It is to this mental perspective that John wrote:

Revelation 21:17 (ESV)
[17] He also measured its wall, 144 cubits by human measurement, which is also an angel's measurement.

A cubit was about 18 inches long, making these walls about 216 feet thick. To the people of the first century this was a picture of security. I don't know if heaven will really have such a wall. To us, walls don't seem to picture security as they did in that day. Today, we could shoot a missile from above, but to them it was very secure. Heaven may not have a literal wall--I don't know, but it will be a place of perfect, absolute security.

Its Beauty

Within each of us there is a sense of what is beautiful. It is quite subjective, varying with different people, and with our own experiences, culture and training. Nevertheless, the concept that there is such a thing as beauty is universal. It is not our highest level need. We need survival and security before we will even stop to admire beauty. Thus, beauty is like icing on the cake. It is a luxury.

Beauty has many dimensions. At one time we admire a sunset. At another, we may enjoy the beauty in a classic musical presentation, or a lovely young girl dressed elegantly. A well designed and crafted piece of jewelry may be beautiful. These kinds of beauty appeal to the senses. Where do you suppose that sense of beauty came from? God Himself is the creator of beauty. It is not surprising, then, that the psalmist recognized and sought the beauty of the Lord.

> *Psalm 27:4 (NIV2011)*
> *4 One thing I ask from the LORD, this only do I seek: that I may dwell in the house of the LORD all the days of my life, to gaze on the beauty of the LORD and to seek him in his temple.*

> *Psalm 50:1-2 (NIV2011)*
> *1 The Mighty One, God, the LORD, speaks and summons the earth from the rising of the sun to where it sets. 2 From Zion, perfect in beauty, God shines forth.*

As John continues his description of the heavenly city, he next describes its beauty. He is still looking at its walls and gates. Every visual aspect of the city in Revelation 21 and 22 portrays beauty of the highest order. Its walls of precious stones reflect and refract the "light" like a diamond, and like glistening transparent gold. Its beauty is seen from both outside and inside as being transmitted beauty.

The Source of its Radiance

The beauty of the city is only a first glance at its glory. Glory is the radiance of God's holiness and majesty. It is the awesome display of his limitless power and infinite love in a single portrait. As John gazes at the city, he is staggered at its lavish brilliance. As he enters it, he sees the source of its radiance.

> *Revelation 21:22-23 (ESV)*
> *22 And I saw no temple in the city, for its temple is the Lord God the Almighty and the Lamb. 23 And the city has no need of sun or moon to shine on it, for the glory of God gives it light, and its lamp is the Lamb.*

This new kind of light didn't come from the sun or moon, or from a lamp. It was seen to originate from God Almighty and from the Lamb. This glory glow demonstrates the superior nature of its essence to created light. Its illumination will not be limited to natural visibility, but will be a spiritually revealing radiation, allowing us to 'see' spiritual things.

Revelation 21:24-27 (ESV)
^{24} By its light will the nations walk, and the kings of the earth will bring their glory into it, ^{25} and its gates will never be shut by day—and there will be no night there. ^{26} They will bring into it the glory and the honor of the nations. ^{27} But nothing unclean will ever enter it, nor anyone who does what is detestable or false, but only those who are written in the Lamb's book of life.

The language of verse 26 describes a victorious warrior king returning home after a campaign, parading behind him all the captives and spoils of war. The *splendor of the kings of the earth* and the *glory and honor of the nations* being brought into the heavenly city does not mean that the treasures of earthly nations will be brought into heaven to embellish it. Material elements will have been destroyed in the transition to the new heaven and new earth. Besides, what honor and glory could earthly kings add to that of heaven's throne with God seated there? The spoils of war and the honor brought into the city refers to the salvation of souls from every nation, snatched from the enemy's destructive hands, and brought victoriously into the city of eternal light, as revealed in verse 27. Their everlasting praise of Him will be the spoils of war.

Accessibility
In that same passage we see that the gates of the New Jerusalem are always open. Here is yet another symbolic lesson for us. In that city, we will have perpetual access to the Father and to Jesus, our Savior and Lord. Our presence before Him will be, at the same time, awesome and glorious, yet intimate and personal. The One who created marriage in this life will be in joyful communion with His redeemed bride. This honeymoon will never end. We will truly be home at last. This is a reminder to live as strangers and aliens in this present world, for our citizenship is in heaven.

1 Peter 2:11 (ESV)
^{11} Beloved, I urge you as sojourners and exiles . . .

Colossians 3:1-4 (ESV)
^{1} If then you have been raised with Christ, seek the things that are above, where Christ is, seated at the right hand of God. Set your minds on things that are above, not on things that are on earth. ^{3} For

you have died, and your life is hidden with Christ in God. [4] When Christ who is your life appears, then you also will appear with him in glory.

Ephesians 2:19-20 (ESV)
[19] So then you are no longer strangers and aliens, but you are fellow citizens with the saints and members of the household of God, [20] built on the foundation of the apostles and prophets, Christ Jesus himself being the cornerstone,

We are called to be outsiders in this world. We are called to be family with God Almighty. Even today, in our historical setting, we are given a foretaste of this accessibility in the gift of prayer. The writer of Hebrews said:

Hebrews 4:16 (NIV2011)
[16] Let us then approach God's throne of grace with confidence, so that we may receive mercy and find grace to help us in our time of need.

The open gates are a reminder to us to go often into the presence of God in prayer. There is where we approach intimacy with the Lord in this life.

<u>Its Immortality</u>
It is a universal hope in men and women everywhere that longs for an eternal home. This hope does not originate from the contemplations or imaginations of the natural mind. It is planted there by our Creator. Solomon stated it like this:

Ecclesiastes 3:11 (NIV2011)
[11] He has made everything beautiful in its time. He has also set eternity in the human heart; yet no one can fathom what God has done from beginning to end.

And Paul said this about the inability of the natural mind to conceive these rewards:

1 Corinthians 2:8-10 (NIV2011)
[8] None of the rulers of this age understood it, for if they had, they would not have crucified the Lord of glory. [9] However, as it is written: "What no eye has seen, what no ear has heard, and what no human mind has conceived"— the things God has prepared for those who love him— [10] these are the things God has revealed to us by his Spirit. The Spirit searches all things, even the deep things of God.

The concept and the desire of immortality is from God. Without eternity, heaven is not very heavenly. Apart from personal immortality, our hope is shallow and anemic. It is that way by God's purpose, to pull us toward Himself. It is to this deep, heartfelt need that God appeals with the next portion of the vision.

> *Revelation 22:1-5 (ESV)*
> *¹ Then the angel showed me the river of the water of life, bright as crystal, flowing from the throne of God and of the Lamb ² through the middle of the street of the city; also, on either side of the river, the tree of life with its twelve kinds of fruit, yielding its fruit each month. The leaves of the tree were for the healing of the nations. ³ No longer will there be anything accursed, but the throne of God and of the Lamb will be in it, and his servants will worship him. ⁴ They will see his face, and his name will be on their foreheads. ⁵ And night will be no more. They will need no light of lamp or sun, for the Lord God will be their light, and they will reign forever and ever.*

A whole book could be written about this passage, albeit, it is describing something which supersedes our experience. The scene described is of a beautiful garden-like park within the city. We have already talked about the security afforded the city, in John's day, by its powerful walls. In the same perspective, they now add to that security an unlimited water and food source. This is not just any stream or just any tree. The stream is called *the river of the water of life*, and it flows from the throne of the Father and of His Son, the lamb. Eternal life originates with God, and lovingly flows to those who will come.

The tree of life grows on both sides of the river. It gives fruit appropriate for each season, sufficient for every need and desire. Its leaves are for the *healing of the nations*. There is a lot to heal from. There are the ravages of sin with its alienations from God and from other people. There is tragedy to be translated into glory. There is unfairness and inequity to be rewarded with eternal blessing. We need healing from the battle scars of this life. The scene transports us back to the beginning, back to pristine Eden, before life was a battle.

> *Genesis 2:9-10 (KJV)*
> *⁹ And out of the ground made the LORD God to grow every tree that is pleasant to the sight, and good for food; the tree of life also in the midst of the garden, and the tree of knowledge of good and evil. ¹⁰ And a river went out of Eden to water the garden; and from thence it was parted, and became into four heads.*

Remember how in Eden, Adam and Eve walked with God. Now, again, we see God's throne in the midst of the city. We will look on His face. His name will be on our foreheads, signifying ownership and identity. Look again at the words of John as the new heaven was introduced:

> Revelation 21:3 (ESV)
> ³ And I heard a loud voice from the throne saying, "Behold, the dwelling place of God is with man. He will dwell with them, and they will be his people, and God himself will be with them as their God.

The consummate blessing is revealed last. All the other benefits of heaven, incomprehensible as they may be, pale in comparison with the privilege of living in intimate fellowship with our Creator and Savior. This is the thrill, the hope, the passion of the Christian.

His glory is like a light that illuminates the whole city so that there is no night, and no need of any other light. This light of His will be beyond our sensory experience. In the new heaven, we will not need sunlight to light our world; or electromagnetic waves to signal our cell phones. The laws of physics will be obsolete. Their need will be superseded by the new order.

What Will We Do in Heaven?

There have been many speculations about what we will do in heaven. Often there is an attempt to extrapolate the activities of this life into our life to come. If we are an avid gardener, then you will have a glorious garden in heaven. If you are an artist, perhaps heaven will provide divine opportunities for subjects of glory to be painted. That may or may not be an appropriate way to arrive at an answer to this question.

Obviously we will worship. But will we worship continually, perpetually? For us, that sounds like something that would get tiring after awhile. It is not my intent to speculate on heavenly activity not specifically mentioned in scripture. I will just emphasize two realities that will affect our worship.

<u>We Will Be Different</u>
We cannot gauge our desires in our new, resurrected persons by our current likes or dislikes, or by our present limitations. In our present state, we may love to worship in a congregation of believers. It may lift our spirits and elevate our souls. But after awhile, we are tired and ready for something else. It is a challenge to think about doing corporate worship continually from now on. However, when we are changed at our resurrection, we will have a completely new thirst and capacity for life and for worship. We will not have our physical natures to deal with, our old sin nature, our attention span limitations, distractions, loss of memory, competing thoughts, conflicting responsibilities, and weak hearing or eyesight. When we are

resurrected, we will have our new nature completely--the nature which God had in mind when he created us in His own image. It will be a nature that will have an insatiable appetite for God, and for His worship. Every moment spent in worship will be euphoric joy, with no limitations such as we are now plagued with. I'm not saying that we will be in congregational worship all the time. We may also worship by exploring the heavenly kingdom, or by exercising some gift, or fulfilling some duty. I don't know. Whatever we do, it will not be limited as our activities are now. Instead, we will be driven by an undiluted passion for God. We will be motivated by a hunger to know Him more fully, and which will be delightfully satisfied moment-by-moment as our relationship with Him soars for all eternity. Imagine trying to explain romantic passion to a five-year-old child. We have the same lack of conception for our new divine thirst. We trust in it anyway.

God Is Infinite
The second reality to consider is that God is much larger than our wildest imaginations can make Him out to be. Our best shot is to consider the created universe. The vast stars and galaxies show up as pinpoints of light to us. We are staggered by the vastness and grandeur of images captured by the Hubbell telescope. Effortlessly God created it all. Think of the amazing internal complexity of a single organic cell. Contemplate the cell's ability to repair itself and reproduce itself. Yet the cell is enormous compared with the size of atomic particles. Consider the size and complexity of created things, especially of human beings. Time does not permit us to attempt to catalog the wonders of the world around us, but they are obvious to all people. Yet as great as His creation is, God is far greater. He is infinite. He is infinitely larger than His created universe. He is everywhere, all the time, unlimited by time and space, or by the speed of light, or any other created thing.

God is infinitely wiser than we can imagine, as well. He knows all things for all time. He knows the location of every star, and the location of every electron in its atomic orbit at any moment in time. He designed all of the intermingled systems of nature. He designed every cell and every creature. He not only knows what is, but he knows every consequence of everything that might have happened. The unmistakable, awesome design of created complexity in nature is testimony to his creative capacities.

We will live on into eternity, and during that time, I suppose we will be perpetually exploring God's glory throughout all eternity, and never finding its limits. It will not just be exploring like one would explore the Grand Canyon. It will be plunging into an ever-increasing relational involvement with our Creator. Whatever we do and wherever we explore will be the most exciting adventure we could imagine, because of the enormously wonderful nature of God Himself.

Because of God's infinite glory and wonder, and our eager new and unlimited capacity for divine enjoyment, I expect that whatever we do will be the most exhilarating and meaningful experience we could ever imagine. Because of Jesus' unsearchable majesty and grace, our greatest experiences in this life will pale compared to being in his glorified presence. Our most important accomplishments and contributions in this life will shrink in contrast to the sense of eternal purpose and fulfillment we will know in heaven. I don't know what we will do there, but whatever it is, it will be beyond explanation in satisfaction, pleasure, gratification, and joy for us who belong to Jesus. We will be his bride forever. The honeymoon will never end.

Who Will be in the New Heaven?

The writer of the book of Hebrews describes our heavenly destination. In doing so, he tells not of the place itself, but of the identity and demeanor of its inhabitants. The tense of it speaks as of something which has already occurred. We are reminded of the *great cloud of witnesses* that have gone before us in faith. We are being reminded of the significance of the fellowship of the faithful. It is written to encourage our continued walk in faith. In doing so, it transports us figuratively to the occasion of our future entry into heaven, and of our awestruck gaping at the sight of it.

> *Hebrews 12:22-24 (ESV)*
> *²² But you have come to Mount Zion and to the city of the living God, the heavenly Jerusalem, and to innumerable angels in festal gathering, ²³ and to the assembly of the firstborn who are enrolled in heaven, and to God, the judge of all, and to the spirits of the righteous made perfect, ²⁴ and to Jesus, the mediator of a new covenant, and to the sprinkled blood that speaks a better word than the blood of Abel.*

You have come . . . to the heavenly Jerusalem! We are not arriving at the historical city of Jerusalem, built on geographical Mount Zion. This takes us to the very gates of heaven. This is the spiritual Zion. We are reminded of the *New Jerusalem* of Revelation 3:12 and 21:2, *which is coming down out of heaven from my God.* Here we find ourselves in the company of all the inhabitants of heaven, the holy and the faithful. What a company it is!

First, we are surrounded by *thousands upon thousands of angels in joyful assembly.* It is interesting that the angels are rejoicing along with the redeemed. They are happy because the joy of the Lord is reflected in their submissive countenances. When He is happy, they are happy. Their joy is genuine, for their submission is eagerly willing. This collective, reflective angelic joy was spoken about by Jesus.

Luke 15:7 (ESV)
⁷ . . . there will be more joy in heaven over one sinner who repents than over ninety-nine righteous persons who need no repentance.

Next, we have come *to the church of the firstborn*. This is the New Testament church, the true church. All the redeemed of all the ages since Jesus' first advent will be in this group. *Firstborn* refers to Jesus, since he was the preeminent one to be raised from the dead, implying others would follow. To emphasize this, mention is made of their names having been already written in heaven. We became citizens of heaven long before we arrive there, as Paul refers to in his Ephesian letter or John in his Revelation vision.

Ephesians 2:6-7 (ESV)
⁶ and raised us up with him and seated us with him in the heavenly places in Christ Jesus, ⁷ so that in the coming ages he might show the immeasurable riches of his grace in kindness toward us in Christ Jesus.

Revelation 3:12 (ESV)
¹² The one who conquers, I will make him a pillar in the temple of my God. Never shall he go out of it, and I will write on him the name of my God, and the name of the city of my God, the new Jerusalem, which comes down from my God out of heaven, and my own new name.

Yes, others would follow Paul, the apostles, and the first-generation church, and in this Hebrews passage all of these saints are joined in celebration.

Next, we have come to *God, the judge of all men*. He is the focus and purpose of heaven. He is the object of adoration and identification of every being there. All of heaven's glory, all of heaven's joy, all of heaven's security, all of heaven's peace originates from Him. He is what makes heaven heavenly. He, Himself is the ultimate reward!

Next we find we have come *to the spirits of righteous men made perfect*. This probably refers to the Old Testament faithful. This will include heroes of the faith and ordinary unknown (to us) people who believed God.

Finally we come *to Jesus, the mediator of a new covenant, and to the sprinkled blood that speaks a better word than the blood of Abel*. Jesus is right alongside the Father, his glory shining over his bride. Again, he is our redeemer and our reward. He will be joy to us unspeakable. What an affinity we will have for the one who gave his own life so that we could be with him at this very moment. We will truly dwell with him forever.

When righteous Abel died, his blood brought condemnation to his murderer, Cain. When Jesus died, his blood brought reconciliation to those responsible, that is, to all of us. It was because of all our sins that he died. And so we will remember the blood of Jesus with unrestrained appreciation for what we are experiencing in heaven. This reveals the essence of the joy in everyone in this scene. Joy unbridled! Victory celebration! Ultimate intimate relationships! Fulfillment beyond understanding!

With regard to who will be in heaven, there is one person whose presence is not specifically identified in scripture. Will that person be there? That person is you! If you know Jesus Christ as your Lord, you will indeed be one of these joyful people. If not, you can become one. Please read the next chapter.

> Dear God of heaven, although we cannot wrap our minds around the experience of heaven, we seek it with our whole heart just now. Teach us to eagerly await our eternal home with you. Teach us to love the promise of Christ's appearing. Make our thoughts dwell on you. Be our ambition, our passion, our obsession, our delight, our purpose, our fulfillment. Inhabit our every thought, oh lord, I pray.

27
PROPHECY, THE FINAL EVANGEL

What is the purpose of Bible prophecy? Why was the book of Revelation written? Why are we warned about a coming judgment and about eternal destiny? Revelation (and the Bible) proclaims this in its closing with the very words of Jesus:

> *Revelation 22:16-17 (ESV)*
> *[16] "I, Jesus, have sent my angel to testify to you about these things for the churches. I am the root and the descendant of David, the bright morning star." [17] The Spirit and the Bride say, "Come." And let the one who hears say, "Come." And let the one who is thirsty come; let the one who desires take the water of life without price.*

No more gracious an invitation is given anywhere in scripture. The entrance fee has been paid. We need, simply, to come. As I have repeatedly alleged, prophecy has an evangelical message.

In the opening chapter of Revelation, we read of Christ glorified, walking among the seven lampstands.

> *Revelation 1:20 (ESV)*
> *[20] As for the mystery of the seven stars that you saw in my right hand, and the seven golden lampstands, the seven stars are the angels of the seven churches, and the seven lampstands are the seven churches.*

The symbolism of lamps representing the churches portrays her primary mission with a frequently used evangelistic metaphor--light. For example, Jesus taught:

> *John 9:5 (NIV2011)*
> *[5] While I am in the world, I am the light of the world."*

> *Matthew 5:14-16 (NASB)*
> *[14] "You are the light of the world. A city set on a hill cannot be hidden; [15] nor does anyone light a lamp and put it under a basket, but on the lampstand, and it gives light to all who are in the house. [16]*

"Let your light shine before men in such a way that they may see your good works, and glorify your Father who is in heaven.

Paul used the light metaphor for the evangelistic mission:

Philippians 2:14-16 (ESV)
[14] Do all things without grumbling or disputing, [15] that you may be blameless and innocent, children of God without blemish in the midst of a crooked and twisted generation, among whom you shine as lights in the world, [16] holding fast to the word of life . . .

The evangelistic message, that God is calling you and me to Himself, is thus portrayed by light shining in darkness.

That message is presented in many ways. The gospels and letters of the New Testament present the *good news* of the good-will of God toward mankind. We see this good-will message in the announcement of Christ's birth, in his teaching, and in the doctrine of the New Testament letters. Unfortunately many will not receive this message. They want nothing to do with a God to whom they must be accountable. Others come, but presume to meet Him on their own terms, defining their own conditions of reconciliation.

In prophecy we are given an ultimatum. This is the sternest appeal of all. Think about it. God loves you so much that He not only gives you opportunities to follow His way, but in prophecy He warns you of the consequences of not embracing His appeal. This is like a parent training a wayward child.

In scripture, the more graciously God's grace is offered, the more intense is His anger at its rebuff. In prophecy we get a sneak preview of God's end-time wrath against those who have rejected the gift of eternal life. He has purchased that gift at the cost of His one-and-only Son. To reject such extreme grace is to treat the sacrificial death of Jesus as trivial, and to incite the Father's severest anger. This is the evangelistic appeal of prophecy. It is not popular today, because it speaks of absolute truth, contrary to today's relativistic perspective. It speaks of accountability, contrary to our culture's claims that you are the center of your own universe. It brings a discomforting challenge to our status quo. It speaks of a day or reckoning, with eternal consequences, not popular now. No one enjoys disciplinary punishment. However, if the comforting message of grace has not turned your head, He brings this disturbing and compelling warning. He wants your soul for His possession.

If the message of God's eternal plans has caused you to want to know about this salvation, then it is appropriate to set forth the biblical path of conversion from 'unbelief' to 'saving faith.' The end result is a relationship between the obedient believer and God that cannot be described by a cookbook recipe, any more than the love between a newlywed couple can be described by re-reading their wedding vows. However scripture does set out some specifics for initiation into true faith. Jesus told his disciples to *teach* a would-be follower. To presume to approach God by any self-styled method is to reject His way. We come as He said we must come, obeying His instructions. Following is a systematic presentation of the scriptural path for coming to salvation.

While prophecy warns us to seek God's salvation, it does not always provide a roadmap to get us there. We must rely on the pathway laid out in other New Testament teachings as the guide.

It starts with an Awareness of God

The gospel (good news) begins with the realization that there is indeed a God who has revealed Himself to us in His written word. In our study of prophecy as it relates to redemption, we have presented many evidences of the existence of such a God through past prophecies that are now fulfilled in history. But in the Bible, especially in prophecy, we learned of much more than the existence of God, as powerful as that is. We also have learned of his immanence. We learned that he is near, and that He works sovereignly and purposefully within His creation. Furthermore, in prophecy we see His loving kindness toward His children. This shows up repeatedly, but in prophecy, it shows up most prominently in His planned redemption.

We must Recognize Our Helplessness before God

How can we respond to God's gift of salvation if we do not recognize our need of it? A prospective believer must first come to this realization before going any further. What is important is not how we see ourselves, or even how we think others see us, but how God sees us. He does see us, and here is how He describes what he sees:

> *Romans 3:10-18 (KJV)*
> *[10] As it is written, There is none righteous, no, not one: [11] There is none that understandeth, there is none that seeketh after God. [12] They are all gone out of the way, they are together become unprofitable; there is none that doeth good, no, not one. [13] Their throat is an open sepulchre; with their tongues they have used deceit; the poison of asps is under their lips: [14] Whose mouth is full of cursing and bitterness: [15] Their feet are swift to shed blood: [16] Destruction and misery are in their ways: [17] And the way of peace have they not known: [18] There is no fear of God before their eyes.*

Not even one! That excludes all of us. That excludes you, as well. None of us is righteous before God by the merit of our own lives.

> *Romans 3:23 (KJV)*
> *²³ For all have sinned, and come short of the glory of God; . . .*

We all fall short of the glory of holiness that God requires. No one, except Jesus, ever has, nor ever will meet the requirements. This is the hopeless dilemma we face. This realization should literally scare the hell out to you if you are not yet a follower of Christ. Why are we so far from the mark God has set?

> *Isaiah 53:6 (KJV)*
> *⁶ All we like sheep have gone astray; we have turned every one to his own way; and the LORD hath laid on him the iniquity of us all.*

We are self-absorbed. Since the beginning, our greatest hindrance to godliness is our rebellious nature. Instead of desiring to please God, our first desire is to please ourselves. We are essentially and hopelessly self-centered.

There is Good News

How good God is. How loving. He did not leave us in our hopeless condition. "Gospel" means 'good news'.

> *John 3:16-17 (NIV2011)*
> *¹⁶ For God so loved the world that he gave his one and only Son, that whoever believes in him shall not perish but have eternal life. ¹⁷ For God did not send his Son into the world to condemn the world, but to save the world through him.*

We were all headed for judgment because we were hopelessly drowning in a treacherous, destructive practice—sin. Our sin showed our complete rebellion toward God. He had every right to let us go. Good riddance! But that is not God's thought.

> *Romans 6:23 (KJV)*
> *²³ For the wages of sin is death; but the gift of God is eternal life through Jesus Christ our Lord.*

This is God's grace. He is full of grace. He loved us, even in our lost condition. And so we read:

Romans 5:6-8 (KJV)
⁶ For when we were yet without strength, in due time Christ died for the ungodly. ⁷ For scarcely for a righteous man will one die: yet peradventure for a good man some would even dare to die. ⁸ But God commendeth his love toward us, in that, while we were yet sinners, Christ died for us.

Why did Christ die? Long before it happened, the prophet Isaiah was given this prophecy by God. Perhaps better than any other passage, it points us to the divine purpose.

Isaiah 53:4-6 (KJV)
⁴ Surely he hath borne our griefs, and carried our sorrows: yet we did esteem him stricken, smitten of God, and afflicted. ⁵ But he was wounded for our transgressions, he was bruised for our iniquities: the chastisement of our peace was upon him; and with his stripes we are healed. ⁶ All we like sheep have gone astray; we have turned every one to his own way; and the LORD hath laid on him the iniquity of us all.

Each of us turned to his own way. That pretty well sums up the human condition. We live to please ourselves. How serious sin is that it should cost God the life of His only Son! But oh! How loving God is that He was willing to pay that price. He laid our sins on Jesus. "That is not fair", you say. What kind of God would do such an unfair thing? The answer is: 'The One who *so loved the world that He gave His only son.*' This act does not demonstrate equity and fairness. Instead it shouts loud and clear, "God loves you to the extreme. What will you do with that?"

John 20:31 (NIV2011)
³¹ But these are written that you may believe that Jesus is the Messiah, the Son of God, and that by believing you may have life in his name.

John 11:25-26 (NIV2011)
²⁵ Jesus said to her, "I am the resurrection and the life. The one who believes in me will live, even though they die; ²⁶ and whoever lives by believing in me will never die. Do you believe this?"

Before anything can happen in you, you must first hear that good news. God has ordained that this life-saving message be spread to everyone through the instruction and testimony of His people. Why leave it to such stumbling, hesitant people to deliver so precious a cargo? Only God knows, but he has.

> *Matthew 18:18-20 (NASB)*
> [18] *"Truly I say to you, whatever you bind on earth shall have been bound in heaven; and whatever you loose on earth shall have been loosed in heaven.* [19] *"Again I say to you, that if two of you agree on earth about anything that they may ask, it shall be done for them by My Father who is in heaven.* [20] *"For where two or three have gathered together in My name, I am there in their midst."*

> *Romans 10:14-15 (KJV)*
> [14] *How then shall they call on him in whom they have not believed? and how shall they believe in him of whom they have not heard? and how shall they hear without a preacher?* [15] *And how shall they preach, except they be sent? as it is written, How beautiful are the feet of them that preach the gospel of peace, and bring glad tidings of good things!*

If you have read this far, it is too late for you. It is too late to claim ignorance about the truth of God's extravagant gesture of love to you. If you are not already a follower of the Lord Jesus Christ, you can't turn and walk away without accepting responsibility for your own unbelief. It would be willful denial. It is a personal rejection of God's gracious offer of salvation. Friend, don't be guilty of spurning the passionate expression of God's loving intentions toward you. Today is the day of salvation. Today is the acceptable day of the Lord.

Believe

Faith is our appropriate and acceptable response to the good news of God's grace. *Without faith it is impossible to please God.* Faith is believing. The belief that leads to salvation is often referred to as 'saving faith.' It is much more than just acknowledging that there is a God. James ridiculed that shallow idea.

> *James 2:19 (NIV2011)*
> [19] *You believe that there is one God. Good! Even the demons believe that—and shudder.*

Saving faith is even more than acknowledging that Jesus is the Christ. In Matthew 8:29 the demons confessed that Jesus is the Son of God. It is more than this. It is an embracing of the truth of what he has done. It is claiming it as your own promise, and being willing to reorder your life in the light of that truth. There are several aspects of saving faith that are both appropriate and essential, according to scripture.

Accurate Belief About Jesus

There are many myths about religion. There are even many about Jesus. It does matter that you believe rightly about him. Some people think all that is needed is sincerity, but sincerity is not enough. Would you want to be the first to cross a footbridge designed by someone with no engineering knowledge, simply because he was sincere? No, to be saved, you must receive and believe the correct message about Jesus. There are so many gospels being preached today that it can be confusing. The way to know the truth is to search the scriptures. The essential belief about Jesus is summed up by Paul in his letter to the Corinthians.

1 Corinthians 15:1-4 (NIV2011)
[1] Now, brothers and sisters, I want to remind you of the gospel I preached to you, which you received and on which you have taken your stand. [2] By this gospel you are saved, if you hold firmly to the word I preached to you. Otherwise, you have believed in vain. [3] For what I received I passed on to you as of first importance: that Christ died for our sins according to the Scriptures, [4] that he was buried, that he was raised on the third day according to the Scriptures,

Christ died as a sacrificial payment for your sins, was buried, and was raised back to life by the power of God. Any belief that eliminates the atoning work of Christ on the cross, or his bodily resurrection, is not saving faith. There is much, much more to be learned about Jesus, but this is the foundational and essential belief of the gospel, summarized.

Repent

Genuine faith leads to repentance. Repentance means to come face-to-face with a holy God in your unholiness, and to be overwhelmed and genuinely sorry for your condition. It is to mourn your past rebellious life. It means to take responsibility for your own sinful condition. It means to desire and commit to turn from a life characterized by sin and self-centeredness, and to turn toward a life consecrated to God. Jesus preached repentance, as had John, his forerunner.

Matthew 4:17 (NASB)
[17] From that time Jesus began to preach and say, "Repent, for the kingdom of heaven is at hand."

The apostles also taught a gospel of repentance, as in Peter's first message.

Acts 3:18-19 (ESV)
[18] But what God foretold by the mouth of all the prophets, that his Christ would suffer, he thus fulfilled. [19] Repent therefore, and turn back, that your sins may be blotted out,

One cannot come in self confidence before God and expect to be saved. An attitude of repentance is not only appropriate, but is essential to approach His grace. Jesus taught this truth with a parable:

> Luke 18:10-14 (ESV)
> [10] "Two men went up into the temple to pray, one a Pharisee and the other a tax collector. [11] The Pharisee, standing by himself, prayed thus: 'God, I thank you that I am not like other men, extortioners, unjust, adulterers, or even like this tax collector. [12] I fast twice a week; I give tithes of all that I get.' [13] But the tax collector, standing far off, would not even lift up his eyes to heaven, but beat his breast, saying, 'God, be merciful to me, a sinner!' [14] I tell you, this man went down to his house justified, rather than the other. For everyone who exalts himself will be humbled, but the one who humbles himself will be exalted."

Confess Jesus as Lord

The person possessing saving faith will gladly identify with the Lord Jesus.

> Romans 10:8-10 (KJV)
> [8] But what saith it? The word is nigh thee, even in thy mouth, and in thy heart: that is, the word of faith, which we preach; [9] That if thou shalt confess with thy mouth the Lord Jesus, and shalt believe in thine heart that God hath raised him from the dead, thou shalt be saved. [10] For with the heart man believeth unto righteousness; and with the mouth confession is made unto salvation.

A confession of faith is practiced in most Christian churches as part of the initiation into the Christian life. Beyond that inaugural confession, however, a believer is to stand ready to honor God's Son by identifying with him at every opportunity.

Now let's look more closely at what we are to confess. The scripture says we are to confess *Jesus is Lord*. Jesus is indeed Lord. That means he is sovereign. He is king. If you have confessed 'Jesus is Lord,' then you have expressed allegiance to his lordship and loyalty to his kingdom. To come to Jesus for salvation means to come to him as your king. This truth cannot remain abstract, as though his sovereignty was just a philosophical concept. It must become personal. It is to make him sovereign in your own life. It means to turn over the leadership of your life to him, and to say, "I am no longer king of my life. I now serve another king." It is the setting of that objective that marks a new believer.

Many desire to come to Jesus as Savior, but want to maintain their lives unchanged from before. The Bible knows nothing of such superficiality.

The 'easy belief' that is so prevalent today is neither scriptural nor genuine. If you look through the pages of New Testament scripture you will not find a single time where anyone, when asked how to be saved, responded by saying, "Believe in the Savior Jesus Christ." Rather, in every case, the response is always, "Believe in the Lord Jesus Christ." The emphasis is on your acceptance of his sovereignty in your life.

> *Acts 16:31 (KJV)*
> *[31] And they said, Believe on the Lord Jesus Christ, and thou shalt be saved, and thy house.*

Follow Jesus as Lord

To confess that 'Jesus is Lord' is not too difficult. After you do this, the actual carrying out of this allegiance will be a life-long pursuit. Yet the command is clear.

> *Luke 9:23-24 (ESV)*
> *[23] And he said to all, "If anyone would come after me, let him deny himself and take up his cross daily and follow me. [24] For whoever would save his life will lose it, but whoever loses his life for my sake will save it.*

The confession is only the beginning. The living of a life fully pleasing to the Lord must become the dominating quest in your life. Failure at this will come regularly, and in those times, a penitent heart evidences the grace of God in your growing life. To live any other way is to violate the confession you have made. Jesus said:

> *Matthew 7:21 (NASB)*
> *[21] "Not everyone who says to Me, 'Lord, Lord,' will enter the kingdom of heaven, but he who does the will of My Father who is in heaven will enter.*

> *1 John 2:3-6 (ESV)*
> *[3] And by this we know that we have come to know him, if we keep his commandments. [4] Whoever says "I know him" but does not keep his commandments is a liar, and the truth is not in him, [5] but whoever keeps his word, in him truly the love of God is perfected. By this we may know that we are in him: [6] whoever says he abides in him ought to walk in the same way in which he walked.*

Be Baptized

Jesus ordained that his followers be brought into the faith through a submissive act we call baptism. When he began his earthly ministry, Jesus himself was baptized by John the Baptist

Matthew 3:13-16 (NASB)
[13] Then Jesus *arrived from Galilee at the Jordan coming to John, to be baptized by him. [14] But John tried to prevent Him, saying, "I have need to be baptized by You, and do You come to me?" [15] But Jesus answering said to him, "Permit it at this time; for in this way it is fitting for us to fulfill all righteousness." Then he *permitted Him. [16] After being baptized, Jesus came up immediately from the water; and behold, the heavens were opened, and he saw the Spirit of God descending as a dove and lighting on Him,

Jesus set the example. He led the way. By his act, he consecrated the practice and the water of baptism. As his ministry moved from place to place, we see that his disciples baptized those who believed in him. It was a regular part of his message.

John 4:1-2 (NIV2011)
[1] Now Jesus learned that the Pharisees had heard that he was gaining and baptizing more disciples than John— [2] although in fact it was not Jesus who baptized, but his disciples.

After his death and resurrection, just before leaving this earth at his heavenly ascension, Jesus handed the disciples their mission marching orders in what has become known as the Great Commission. In that discourse . . .

Mark 16:15-16 (ESV)
[15] And he said to them, "Go into all the world and proclaim the gospel to the whole creation. [16] Whoever believes and is baptized will be saved, but whoever does not believe will be condemned.

The order was clear. They were to make disciples by baptizing those who believed. Shortly thereafter, when the disciples stood before the crowd on the day of Pentecost, Peter preached this same message to them.

Acts 2:37-38,41 (ESV)
[37] Now when they heard this [the gospel] *they were cut to the heart, and said to Peter and the rest of the apostles, "Brothers, what shall we do?" [38] And Peter said to them, "Repent and be baptized every one of you in the name of Jesus Christ for the forgiveness of your sins, and you will receive the gift of the Holy Spirit . . . [41] So those who received his word were baptized, and there were added that day about three thousand souls.*

As the writers of the New Testament wrote their doctrinal statements, baptism was an integral part of them. For instance Peter, discussing ancient

Noah and his family who were saved in the ark, in the flood, saved by the water, so to speak, made this analogy:

1 Peter 3:20-21 (ESV)
[20] because they formerly did not obey, when God's patience waited in the days of Noah, while the ark was being prepared, in which a few, that is, eight persons, were brought safely through water. [21] Baptism, which corresponds to this, now saves you, not as a removal of dirt from the body but as an appeal to God for a good conscience, through the resurrection of Jesus Christ,

Paul wrote of the parallel symbolism of baptism with the death, burial and resurrection of Jesus. Going under the water in symbolic death, and coming out of the water as in resurrection, we identify with his redemptive work.

Romans 6:4-5 (NASB)
[4] Therefore we have been buried with Him through baptism into death, so that as Christ was raised from the dead through the glory of the Father, so we too might walk in newness of life. [5] For if we have become united with Him in the likeness of His death, certainly we shall also be in the likeness of His resurrection,

Thus, in our confession of belief, we are called to identify with Christ's death and resurrection through baptism. The symbolism of baptism is twofold. First, it connects us with the death, burial and raising of Christ. Secondly it portrays in our mortal person the death of the old nature, and the emergence of a new life of godliness.

What is this thing we call baptism? In its original practice, a person was taken into a body of water by another believer. Then after confirming his confession of faith, the baptizer would dunk the candidate under the water momentarily, then lift him out.

You might be led to commit your life to God at some time. Later, feelings and intentions can be easily forgotten. When you are under attack from the enemy, tempting you to abandon your faith, and when difficulties of life press on you, the undeniable act of baptism is like a stake driven into the timeline of your life to mark the point of your conversion. It is the benchmark that reminds you of your eternal covenant with God. And so, as we have seen, baptism is not optional. It was commanded by Jesus himself. Baptism is practiced in different ways. Some sprinkle or pour water over the head. Others immerse the whole person in water. Does it matter? In its original language form, the word translated into English simply meant to dip, immerse or submerge. The Greek verb *baptizo* along with its noun forms had secular as well as spiritual meaning, just like our English word 'immerse' does. The original form of Christian baptism was to fully immerse a person in a body of water. This is clear not only from the Greek language construction, but from the doctrinal parallels to Jesus' death and resurrection. Furthermore, extra-biblical historical descriptions of early baptism clearly describe immersion of the whole person in water. Archaeological excavations of early churches have found that early baptismal pools were built large enough for complete immersion of the person. It is clear, in light of this, why John the apostle wrote of John the Baptist . . .

> *John 3:23 (NIV2011)*
> *[23] Now John also was baptizing at Aenon near Salim, because there was plenty of water, and people were coming and being baptized.*

Sprinkling or pouring would not have required *plenty of water*. It should be evident that scriptural baptism is by immersion. All other forms are man-ordained. There is no indication in scripture whether alternate forms will be acceptable to God, since they are not mentioned. Why not simply obey scripture in this matter?

These steps of faith, as set forth in the New Testament, apply to the initiation of a life of faith. The redeemed life continues from its birth into eternity. This is only the starting point. There is much more of salvation ahead. The life of salvation is an adventurous pilgrimage of discovery of Jesus and of the Father. It is a quest for deeper relationship, for greater godliness, for stronger hope and for a secure love.

Recognize Our Need of a Savior

"I am not that bad" you may protest. "I am a decent person. I do my best. I am honest. I don't steal. I don't cheat on my taxes. I don't hurt people."

> *Isaiah 64:6-7 (KJV)*
> *[6] But we are all as an unclean thing, and all our righteousnesses are as filthy rags; and we all do fade as a leaf; and our iniquities, like the wind, have taken us away. [7] And there is none that calleth upon thy name, that stirreth up himself to take hold of thee: for thou hast hid thy face from us, and hast consumed us, because of our iniquities.*

> *1 John 1:8-10 (ESV)*
> *[8] If we say we have no sin, we deceive ourselves, and the truth is not in us. [9] If we confess our sins, he is faithful and just to forgive us our sins and to cleanse us from all unrighteousness. [10] If we say we have not sinned, we make him a liar, and his word is not in us.*

His requirement for righteousness is so much higher than any of us can achieve that our situation is hopeless, so far as it depends on us. This is the bad news that must precede the good news of salvation—to understand our utter helplessness before God. That is why Jesus began his Sermon on the Mount with . . .

> Matthew 5:3-6 (NASB)
> [3] "Blessed are the poor in spirit, for theirs is the kingdom of heaven.
> [4] "Blessed are those who mourn, for they shall be comforted. [5] "Blessed are the gentle, for they shall inherit the earth. [6] "Blessed are those who hunger and thirst for righteousness, for they shall be satisfied.

The person who is crushed with his or her hopeless condition may not feel happy, but Jesus calls him *blessed* because he is now prepared to receive God's grace. Grace is the only avenue by which salvation comes. What a blessing it is to arrive at this awareness of our deepest need.

In Summary

The entire Bible from Genesis through Revelation is about one purpose—REDEMPTION. The long history of God's continual providence and oversight, as given in scripture, attests to the priority of that purpose in God's mind. The 'steps' for coming to salvation, as presented in the New Testament, are briefly summed up in the following:

- Realize you are unworthy of heaven because of your sins; by yourself, you will never see God's loving welcome, but will face eternal punishment
- Hear the truth of the good news that God so loved you that He gave His son to die in your behalf, then raised him from death to be your King and guarantee of eternal life
- Believe the good news with all your mind and heart
- Repent of your sinful life
- Confess Jesus as your Lord and Savior, and come to him on his terms, not yours
- Commit to submit, to the best of your ability, to Jesus as your Lord, in keeping with your profession
- Be baptized by immersion

These steps are not a platform for condemning the standing of others. It is neither our calling, nor our right, to do so. Our calling is simply to present the biblical way of salvation before the conscience of any who will listen. It is then the work of the Holy Spirit to bring a spirit of conviction into someone's heart. This leads us to our calling in the great commission. We have a responsibility to promote the agenda, the way of redemption to an unbelieving world. The urgency imposed by the pending return of Jesus should compel us to be his ambassadors in the world.

> *2 Corinthians 5:18-20 (NIV2011)*
> [18] *All this is from God, who reconciled us to himself through Christ and gave us the ministry of reconciliation:* [19] *that God was reconciling the world to himself in Christ, not counting people's sins against them. And he has committed to us the message of reconciliation.* [20] *We are therefore Christ's ambassadors, as though God were making his appeal through us. We implore you on Christ's behalf: Be reconciled to God.*

Regardless of people's hearts, the heart of God is clear in this final call. He has gone the last mile to provide a way of salvation that is within everyone's reach. He has poured His grace lavishly before us. He sacrificed His Son for our redemption. Finally, through prophecy, He has warned us of judgment. And so as the Bible ends, we read:

> *Revelation 22:10-12 (ESV)*
> [10] *And he said to me, "Do not seal up the words of the prophecy of this book, for the time is near.* [11] *Let the evildoer still do evil, and the filthy still be filthy, and the righteous still do right, and the holy still be holy."* [12] *"Behold, I am coming soon, bringing my recompense with me, to repay each one for what he has done.*

If a person is not moved from his complacency, from his vileness, from his greed, or from his egotism by the prophecies of this ending book of the Bible, there is nothing left to say. There is no stronger appeal that can be made. As the Hebrews writer says . . .

> *Hebrews 10:29 (NIV2011)*
> [29] *How much more severely do you think someone deserves to be punished who has trampled the Son of God underfoot, who has treated as an unholy thing the blood of the covenant that sanctified them, and who has insulted the Spirit of grace?*

John was told not to seal up the words of prophecy, not to conceal or ignore them, because *the time is near.* So urgency is added to warning. To embrace Christ should not be a difficult decision. In light of these prophecies, it is, to put it in street terms, a 'no-brainer.' Yet still some resist believing. Again the Hebrews writer speaks to us:

Hebrews 4:7 (ESV)
⁷ again he appoints a certain day, "Today," saying through David so long afterward, in the words already quoted, "Today, if you hear his voice, do not harden your hearts."

A time is coming when *every knee will bow, and every tongue will confess that "Jesus Christ is Lord."* You will confess this, along with everyone else. The question is, will it be from exuberant devotion as you prepare to inherit his kingdom, or from trembling terror as you anticipate a Godless eternity? Which will it be in your case? One more time we again read:

"I, Jesus, have sent my angel to give you this testimony for the churches. I am the Root and the Offspring of David, and the bright Morning Star." The Spirit and the bride say, "Come!" And let him who hears say, "Come!" Whoever is thirsty, let him come; and whoever wishes, let him take the free gift of the water of life. (Rev 22:16-17)

Revelation 22:16-17 (ESV)
¹⁶ "I, Jesus, have sent my angel to testify to you about these things for the churches. I am the root and the descendant of David, the bright morning star." ¹⁷ The Spirit and the Bride say, "Come." And let the one who hears say, "Come." And let the one who is thirsty come; let the one who desires take the water of life without price.

> Lord God Almighty, hear my prayer, I beg. May your Spirit open the heart and mind of this reader. If he or she is a follower of your way, then bless him or her for having studied this book. Bless with an inflated awareness of who You are, and who Jesus is. Bless with an insatiable appetite to know You in Your glory. Father, this reader has dared to tremble through the mighty visions of Jesus in Glory, in order to secure a deeper familiarity with you. Reward him or her with a strong assurance of Your abiding presence and grace.
>
> If this reader is not a believer, bring a spirit of submission and faith. Cause him or her to desire the truth, hope and love that can only come from you. May he or she no longer be an alien in your kingdom, but a citizen. May he find peace for his soul. May she find that eternal security. Amen

Revelation 22:20 (ESV)
[20] He who testifies to these things says, "Surely I am coming soon." Amen. Come, Lord Jesus!

Bibliography

1. Mal Couch, *Dictionary of Premillennial Theology* [1996] (Kregel Publications, Grand Rapids MI)
2. Steve Gregg, *Revelation Four Views, A Parallel Commentary* [1997] (Thomas Nelson Publishers, Nashville, TN)
3. William E. Biederwolf, *The Second Coming Bible* [1972] (Baker House, Grand Rapids, MI)
4. William Hendrikson, *More Than Conquerors: An Interpretation of the Book of Revelation* [1998 reprint of older book] (Baker Book House, Grand Rapids, MI)
5. John MacArthur, Audio Tape Series: *The Second Coming of Jesus Christ* (Grace to You Ministries, Panorama City, CA)
6. James D. Strauss, *Bible Study Textbook Series – Revelation* [1972] (College Press, Joplin, MO)
7. Mona Johnian, *Life in the Millennium* [1992] (Bridge Publishing, Inc., South Plainfield, NJ)
8. J. Vernon McGee, *Revelation Chapters 1-5* [1991] (Thomas Nelson Publishers, Nashville, Atlanta, London, Vancouver)
9. Dave MacPherson, *The Incredible Cover-Up* [1975] 5th printing [1995] (Omega Publications, Inc., Medford, OR)
10. Robert Van Kampen, *The Rapture Question Answered* [[1997] 3rd Printing [1998] (Fleming H. Revell, Grand Rapids, MI)
11. Dan O'Neill/Don Wagner, *Peace or Armageddon?* [1993] (Zondervan Publishing House, Grand Rapids, MI)
12. Tim LaHaye, *Understanding Bible Prophecy for Yourself* [1998,2001] (Harvest Publishing House Publishers, Eugene OR)
13. Tim LaHaye, *Are We Living in the End Times?* [1999] (Tyndale House Publishers, Inc., Wheaton, IL)
14. J. G. Hall, *God's Dispensational and Prophetic Plan* [1972] (Printed in USA)
15. Clarence Larkin, *Dispensational Truths* [1918] (Philadelphia, PA)
16. Louis Talbot, *An Exposition on the Book of Revelation* [1937] (William B. Eerdman, Grand Rapids, MI)
17. Series of pamphlets by Adventist Association
    The Second Coming of Christ & Rapture
    The Antichrist Beast of Revelation 13
    The Antichrist Beast, Dragon, Woman & 666
    Revelation's Judgment Hour
18. Timothy Keller, *Encounters with Jesus*, (chapter 7) [2013] (The Penguin Group, New York, NY)
19. Ray Vander Laan, *That the World May Know* video series, Sub-set *The True Easter Story,* Lesson: *The Promise Kept* (Focus on the Family, Distributed by Zondervan)

www.ingramcontent.com/pod-product-compliance
Lightning Source LLC
Chambersburg PA
CBHW071644090426
42738CB00009B/1422